DATE DUE

DE - 3 '08			

DEMCO 38-296

Handbook for Assessing and Treating Addictive Disorders

HANDBOOK FOR

ASSESSING AND TREATING ADDICTIVE DISORDERS

Edited by
CHRIS E. STOUT,
JOHN L. LEVITT,
and
DOUGLAS H. RUBEN

Greenwood Press

New York · Westport, Connecticut · London

Library of Congress Cataloging-in-Publication Data

Handbook for assessing and treating addictive disorders / edited by
    Chris E. Stout, John L. Levitt, and Douglas H. Ruben.
        p.   cm.
    Includes bibliographical references (p.   ) and index.
    ISBN 0-313-27634-X (alk. paper)
    1. Substance abuse—Treatment.   2. Substance abuse—Diagnosis.
I. Stout, Chris E.   II. Levitt, John L., 1951–   .   III. Ruben,
Douglas H.
    RC564.H355   1992
    616.86—dc20   91-35117

British Library Cataloguing in Publication Data is available.

Library of Congress Catalog Card Number: 91-35117
ISBN: 0-313-27634-X

First published in 1992

Greenwood Press, 88 Post Road West, Westport, CT 06881
An imprint of Greenwood Publishing Group, Inc.

Printed in the United States of America

The paper used in this book complies with the
Permanent Paper Standard issued by the National
Information Standards Organization (Z39.48-1984).

10 9 8 7 6 5 4 3 2 1

To our ever-tolerant and supportive wives,
Karen Beckstrand Stout and
Marilyn Jean Ruben

Contents

Contributors

Jeffrey T. Barth, Ph.D., Departments of Neuropsychology and Psychiatry, University of Virginia Medical School, Charlottesville, Virginia.

Anthony W. Heath, Ph.D., Department of Human & Family Resources, Northern Illinois University, DeKalb, Illinois.

Norman Hymowitz, Ph.D., Department of Psychiatry, University of Medicine & Dentistry of New Jersey, Newark, New Jersey.

Margo M. Jacquot, C.A.C., Forest Hospital and Foundation, Des Plaines, Illinois.

Alan M. Jaffe, Psy.D., private practice, Chicago, Illinois.

Karen L. Jaffe, Psy.D., private practice, Chicago, Illinois.

David Lansky, Ph.D., private practice, Des Plaines, Illinois.

Amy Lauderback Lee, M.A., Department of Psychology, Case Western Reserve University, Cleveland, Ohio.

John L. Levitt, Ph.D., Forest Hospital and Foundation, Des Plaines, Illinois.

James C. Overholser, Ph.D., Department of Psychology, Case Western Reserve University, Cleveland, Ohio.

A. Michael Ricciardi, Ph.D., Department of Psychology, Laurelwood Hospital, Willowbee, Ohio.

Douglas H. Ruben, Ph.D., Best Impressions International, Inc., Okemos, Michigan.

Rhonda Sheared, M.A., private practice, Des Plaines, Illinois.

Frank R. Sparadeo, Ph.D., Departments of Neuropsychology and Psychiatry, University of Virginia Medical School, Charlottesville, Virginia.

Chris E. Stout, Psy.D., Forest Hospital and Foundation, Des Plaines, Illinois.

Thomas C. Todd, Ph.D., Forest Hospital and Foundation, Des Plaines, Illinois.

Thomas J. Young, Ph.D., Department of Criminal Justice, Washburn University of Topeka, Kansas.

Preface

This book is the first compendium in ten years of major addictive disorders under a single cover. Eclectic reviews of etiology and treatment range from psychodynamic to behavioral perspectives on chemical dependency and eating disorders. The presentation of applied concepts, principles, and valid methods distills and simplifies the advanced research in clinical and experimental procedure. State-of-the-art interventions are provided against a backdrop of controversies and problems arising from treatment failure. Perspectives on current themes emphasize the interdisciplinary movement and direction toward a systems or integrative network of clinical and social services. By contrast, most other clinical guidebooks on addictive disorders neglect or only sparingly cover the comprehensive service delivery system.

As a reference book, this handbook combines sourcebook with training manual. Chapters summarize recent research findings regarding etiology, methodology, and therapist-client issues emergent from the infusion of ethical and legal regulations regarding confidentiality, onset and termination of treatment, and impartiality of therapist-client relationship. New developments also touch on the *zeitgeist* for short-term therapies focused more measurably on operational goals and objectives. Achievement of treatment outcomes in three to five months, rather than from three to five years, responds to insurance mandates for cost containment and quality assurance. Even entry into preferred provider organizations (PPOs), health maintenance organizations, and other psychiatric care management systems requires the practitioner's willingness to follow short-term therapy guidelines. Making this conversion from a traditional training approach to a short-term approach at first appears to compromise the integrity of client changes and undermine effective dynamics guiding the therapy process. But this book shows that the dynamics are not short-changed; shorter periods of therapy actually can increase utilization of training tools and thereby speed the process without the interference of many long-term therapy roadblocks (e.g., transference and countertransference, attrition, decay of motivation).

This handbook is divided into five parts. Part One, "Theories and Approaches," surveys prevalent models of analysis from which etiology and treatment issues of addiction derive. Schools of clinical thought such as the behavioral systems approach, family systems approach, and psychoanalytic systems approach are considered in terms of their benefits and shortcomings and whether the model is better served in convergence with other models.

Part Two covers the assessment of addictive disorders. Readers will find intriguing chapters on drug abuse, alcoholism, and eating disorders. Instruments for diagnosis and evaluation of alcoholism are examined in chapters 4 and 5. Chapter 6, on eating disorders, thoroughly integrates evaluative and etiological analyses. All three chapters attempt to broaden the uses of demographic analysis, ecoanalysis, and the place of traditional diagnosis in short-term outpatient and inpatient programs. Closely scrutinized are personal, marital, familial, sociocultural, and developmental factors, which become entangled in onset and maintenance of addiction.

Part Three, "Treatment of Addictive Disorders," supplies critical and practical guidelines for immediate intervention. Chapters cover cigarette smoking, alcohol and drug abuse, and eating disorders. Needed attention is paid to the social context or system of the addict around which different methods are applied. The authors repeatedly question whether a single model offers limited treatment solutions for the labyrinth of developmental dysfunctions in client addiction histories beyond the goals of sobriety, abstinence, or controlled substance use.

Part Four covers the rising concerns regarding special groups and minorities. At-risk populations under greatest scrutiny include native Americans, the elderly, closed-head injury patients, adult children of alcoholics, and teenagers. Most other handbooks assume that interventions generalize across all groups. However, despite much homogeneity, distinctions among the groups necessitate new methods on case finding, keeping clients in treatment, and aftercare plans. Additionally, there are multilevel interactions with network systems for, say, elderly and handicapped clients, compared to relatively fewer interagency contacts for adult and teenage clients.

Part Five pays needed attention to clinical issues that arise in the administration of clinical services. Problems concerning therapist-patient relationships are considered in the light of training and supervision. Confidentiality, accountability, and ethical restrictions are reviewed within the science and art of supervising substance abuse therapists. Appendixes further enjoin clinician and researcher. The appendixes contain a treatment resource guide listing key contacts, groups, and affiliations for client referral and a table on states' credentialing requirements for substance abuse counselors.

Together these chapters offer solutions to issues facing busy practitioners. The book avoids the polemics of larger compendia covering the same topic. Instead, it seeks a communication outlet for mainstream professionals and can be training preparation for graduate students.

Introduction

CHRIS E. STOUT

Addictive disorders hold a unique and controversial place in psychodiagnostic nosology and psychotherapy. Some individuals show symptoms that suggest relationships to their personality structure, others to their genetic structure. "Victim blaming" is offset by the pendulum swing to "enabling." To say the least, the field is rife with opinion. It is the goal of this book to reflect the various points of view that exist among practitioners and theorists.

This introduction broadly reviews the global areas of addiction. It highlights controversy and divergence more so than predictable, scientific fact. While mental disorders are intimately woven within our social fabric, addictive disorders seem to amplify more political and social perspectives. The biases of those treating, of those authoring policy, to those living with an addicted individual tend to influence our perceptions more so than other psychopathologies. And thus, our ideas about change and "cure" tend to follow a similar prejudice. Let us consider the *zeitgeist* of addictive disorders in several areas.

LEGALIZATION

The role of addictions in society is evident in the current debate concerning legalization and regulation of illicit drugs. This position holds that current drug laws and policies parallel prohibition of the 1930s. One of the curious phenomena of this orientation is who supports it. William F. Buckley, Jr., the articulate conservative's conservative, is allied (on the legalization issue) with Congressman James Schever (D, New York), Mayor Kurt Schomoke (Baltimore), Congressman Steny Hoyer (D, Maryland), and Congressman Fortney Stark (D,

California). But not all of the political elite support such a policy reversal. Congressman Charles Rengel (D, New York) chairs the Select Committee on Narcotics Abuse and Control and refused even to examine such an option. He wrote, "I strongly object to even the mention of legalization as an option." Assistant professor Ethan Nadelmann of Princeton University's Woodrow Wilson School of Public and International Affairs, economist Milton Friedman, and the editors of the *Economist* magazine support legalization as a means to decrease the crime rate, aid in relief of overburdened criminal and penal systems, and cut drug enforcement costs (which Nadelmann estimated at $8 billion annually).

Yale University psychiatrist and historian David Musto notes in his book *The American Disease* that society's viewpoint of drug use follows a pattern of "experimentation, and promotion of new drugs by enthusiasts, followed by widespread use and tolerance of abuse, disillusionment, and finally prohibition and sharp intolerance of abusers" (Marshall, 1988, p. 1159). The problem is that no one knows or can predict with any realistic certainty that any societal or economic benefits would indeed be realized; moreover, substance use could increase with a perceived governmental sanction. Although prohibition was generally seen to have failed due to difficulty in enforcement, public health specialists note that during prohibition, liver cirrhosis rates dropped and psychiatric commitment for alcohol-related problems diminished. Currently with alcohol's legalization, there are an estimated 110 million drinkers. Concern for marijuana and cocaine users' numbers to rise to such a level is marked.

Yet a balance of personal liberty with public health must be weighed. As Vance (1988, p. 1102) notes, continued criminalization has resulted in

people losing their cars, homes, and even their children without due process; casual drug users are jailed; people suspected of absolutely nothing are subject to random drug tests; colleges and other institutions are threatened with financial penalties unless they capitulate to federal demands that they burden their bureaucracies with anti-drug programs; government is seeking ever greater access to personal financial records; grade school children are encouraged to turn in drug users to authorities; and the society in general is inundated with alarmist propaganda which grossly exaggerates the inherent dangers of drugs.

ETIOLOGY

Etiology is a fundamental issue in scientific inquiry. Multiple causes underlying addiction disorders complicate studies further. Emphasis on genetic predisposition perhaps raises eyebrows the most. Research by Kenneth Blum and associates at the University of Texas Health Sciences Center examined brain samples from severe alcoholic and nonalcoholic control subjects. They found that the dopamine D2 receptor gene may play a predisposing role in the development of alcoholism. In response, Enoch Gordis, head of the National Institute on Alcohol Abuse and Alcoholism, and his colleagues stated in an editorial in the *Journal of the American Medical Association* (April 18, 1990) that "it is highly unlikely that the same gene or genes confer vulnerability in all families." And so the debate continues.

There is significant doubt that Blum's results will be replicated; only further research will tell. Yet children of alcoholics have four times the likelihood of becoming alcohol abusers themselves. Could this all be nurturing, social learning, and modeling at work? Other research has discovered that in electro-encephalogram findings, subjects exposed to alcohol who have relatives who abuse alcohol differ from controls in P3 brain wave amplitudes (Watterlond, 1983).

DISEASE CONCEPT

The etiology of addictive behaviors, such as alcoholism, goes beyond diagnostics and therapeutics to include politics. The disease concept of alcoholism has been debated for years. Some view it as the medicalization of a social or behavioral problem, and others view it as a worthwhile, destigmatizing model for understanding. Gordis (1989) differentiates those who episodically misuse alcohol as categorized under "alcohol abuse," while others who are alcohol dependent are seen as having a "disease," for there is a predictable course, and a set of specific, identifiable symptoms.

Fingarette (1990) argues that there is no scientific basis to such a concept, for no consistent pattern or single cause exists. He gives the example that "alcohol is used in many so-called 'primitive' societies, but their drinking patterns are not [the same as] ours, and what we call alcoholism does not exist among them before contact with Europeans. That would not be true if alcoholism were a disease caused by chemical and neurological effects of drinking in conjunction with individual genetic vulnerability" (p. 5).

The debate turned political when it went to the U.S. Supreme Court in a case concerning the Veterans Administration regulation to view alcoholism not as a disease but rather as "willful misconduct." McNulty (1987) reported that a National Council on Alcoholism paper stated that alcoholism should not be discriminated against when there are other behaviors that cause disease that go with impunity: "Cigarette smoking may lead to lung cancer, respiratory illness and hypertension; eating patterns may affect the progress of diabetes; and improper diet or lack of exercise may contribute to the development of heart disease" (1989, p. 6).

On April 20, 1988, the Court ruled "that the VA's definition of 'primary alcoholism' as being the result of 'willful misconduct' does not violate the Rehabilitation Act of 1973, which prohibits discrimination on the basis of handicaps" (Holden, 1988, p. 597). It was a close four-to-three opinion. However, the Court did not actually deal with or render a decision as to whether it accepted the disease concept of alcoholism. The Court's opinion was complexly worded: "If Congress had intended . . . that primary alcoholism not be deemed 'willful misconduct' . . . Congress most certainly would have said so" (1988, p. 597).

EPIDEMIOLOGY

To parallel Arther Jensen's view on intelligence to addictive etiology, it is easier to measure than to define. Barring questionable methodology, there is relatively little debate as to statistical rates and epidemiology of substance abuse. In 1987 Shearer quoted from the *Statistical Bulletin* of Metropolitan Life Insurance Company:

1. Among the nation's adults, 67 percent consume alcohol regularly.
2. The apparent per capita consumption of alcohol in the United States is 2.65 gallons per year.
3. The District of Columbia ranked first in the apparent consumption of alcohol, with an annual rate of 5.34 gallons per person; Nevada at 5.19 gallons; New Hampshire, 4.91 gallons; Alaska, 3.86 gallons; and California and Wisconsin both at 3.19 gallons.
4. The lowest state was Utah, at 1.53 gallons per person (1987, p. 16).

Kolata (1988, p. 37) reports that there are approximately 10 million severe alcoholics and between 7 million and 8 million alcohol abusers. This is estimated to cost $119 billion annually. Barnes (1988, p. 1729) notes that the National Institute on Drug Abuse reported that there are 5,000 new cocaine abusers each day; 6 million are regular users, and between 200,000 and 1 million are compulsive users. A hopeful trend lies in a slight decrease in marijuana use among high school seniors—from 40.6 percent in 1985 to 36.3 percent in 1987, and for cocaine use, from 13.1 percent in 1985 to 10.3 percent in 1987.

Beyond the sole problem of substance abuse are the secondary issues. For example, 65 percent of spouse beatings, 55 percent of physical child abuse, 65 percent of murders, and 88 percent of knifings occur when the perpetrator is intoxicated (Kent, 1990, p. 11).

In 1988, Surgeon General C. Everett Koop reported to the nation's 51 million tobacco users that nicotine is as addictive as cocaine or heroin. Moreover, it results in the deaths of 300,000 Americans each year.

Although this book does not focus on international issues, it is nevertheless important to look at some other countries' experiences. The Dutch, for example, use "a get-soft approach in which the government essentially tolerates casual drug use while providing users with copious amounts of health information and advice" (Holden, 1990). Their approach treats drug addictive behaviors as a public health concern rather than a criminal problem. However, the degree of their population's use is not as severe as in the United States. This fact in and of itself, however, raises curious questions of cause and effect.

Alcoholism in the Soviet Union is a marked problem. Their version of moonshine, called *samogen*, worsens the problem and parallels illicit drug use in the United States: The problem is so widespread that the Politburo assigned the anti-alcoholism campaign as its highest priority (Holden, 1989).

Addictive and wreckless behaviors go hand in hand. For instance, sexual addictions along with intravenous drug use act to maintain the epidemic spread of human immunodeficiency virus (HIV). The deadliness of addictive behaviors often is not immediately seen. The ravaging effect of acquired immune deficiency syndrome is dramatic only in its terminal phases, when it is too late for good judgment, self-control, and prevention. Addictive-related behaviors in tandem with HIV create an unprecedented lethal synergism. The defensive symptom of denial becomes deadly. It is our most important public health danger.

INTERVENTION AND OUTCOME

Issues of treatment are addressed in the appropriate chapters. Generally, however, various pharmacological interventions are being increasingly used. Disulfiram (Antabuse) is a classic pharmacobehavioral therapy in alcohol addiction. Clonidine is being used in opiate withdrawal and detoxification. Monoamine oxidase inhibitors (MAOIs), typically used as antidepressants, can be used in alcoholism treatment. Carbamazepine, an anticonvulsant, is being used in cocaine addiction. Flupenthixol Decanoate, an antidepressant and antipsychotic medication, looks hopeful in treating crack smokers. Desipramine (an antidepressant) and bromocriptine (an anti-Parkinsonian drug) also show some promise in treating cocaine addictions. Sertralene, mazindol, buspirone, and chlorpromazine are all being empirically examined for their potential applicability in the pharmacotherapy of addiction. But when all the dust clears, there are no medical cures.

Clinical readers are more likely concerned with other interventions, leading us back to the controversy noted at the beginning of this introduction: What effects change in treating addictive disorders? There is no easy answer; how could there be? If internationally recognized experts cannot agree on the etiology or a model of understanding, how could a consensus be reached regarding treatment? The last word has yet to be written concerning treatment efficacy. There are so many contaminants and conflicts in the variables to be examined. Control groups usually cannot be ethically employed in examination or most quasi-experimental designs, and longitudinal studies are fraught with dropouts.

Early studies' findings are quite disturbing. William R. Miller stated in the July 1986 issue of the *American Psychologist* that inpatient versus outpatient treatment showed little difference in successful outcomes. Helen Annis's work showed little difference in long- versus short-term lengths of stay versus day treatment versus outpatient programs. Furthermore, she notes, neither type of treatment nor its intensity acts as a good predictor of patient outcome.

In 1980 the Institute of Medicine's position was that "the best predictor of patient outcome is the patient'' (Holden, 1987, p. 21). Although this may sound sarcastic or useless, there is a grain of truth in it. Holden notes that ''researchers say we now have a fairly good picture of who will do well, regardless of the treatment. People with jobs, stable relationships, minimal psychopathology, no history of past treatment failures, and minimal involvement with other drugs'' (1987, p. 21). This area, fortunately, is a site of ever-increasing research. A multitreatment approach individually tailored to the patient's needs is where the future of addictions treatment and research should be directed if we are to effect change.

Toward this end the handbook provides an eclectic review of leading trends advanced by specialists in the addiction fields. Readers will find dual emphasis placed on substance abuse disorders and eating disorders. Addiction in this respect covers the biological as well as psychosocial causes underlying tolerance and the problems raised by addiction among families and special populations.

The handbook also examines addiction as an integrative discipline involving multidisciplinary interventions rather than one approach. Readers will find its theory and methodology particularly sympathetic to advancing ideas in systems psychology, following the imperative for comprehensive short-term treatments that are inexpensive, affect all family members, and effectively prevent relapse. Finally, all treatment strategies considered in this book directly derive from applied clinical research. Students and practitioners can garnish techniques from each chapter, safely assuming the techniques have passed rigorous tests of scientific scrutiny.

REFERENCES

Barnes, D. M. (1988). Drugs: Running the numbers. *Science, 240,* 1729–31.
Fingarette, H. (1990). We should reject the disease concept of alcoholism. *Harvard Medical School Mental Health Letter, 6* (8), pp. 4–6.
Gordis, E. (1989). The disease concept of alcoholism. *Psychiatric Hospital, 20* (4), 151–52.
Holden, C. (1987). Is alcoholism treatment effective? *Science, 236,* pp. 20–27.
Holden, C. (1988). Supreme Court denies plea of alcoholic vets. *Science, 240,* p. 597.
Holden, C. (1989). Soviets seek U.S. help in combating alcoholism. *Science, 246,* pp. 878–79.
Holden, C. (1990). Getting stoned the healthy way. *Science, 249,* p. 120.
Kent, D. (1990). A conversation with Claude Steele. *Observer,* pp. 11–17.
Kolata, G. (1988). Alcoholic genes or misbehavior. *Psychology Today, 5,* 34–37.
Marshall, E. (1988). Drug wars: Legalization gets a hearing. *Science, 241,* 1157–59.
McNulty, T. J. (1987, December 6). Court case tests perception of alcoholism. *Chicago Tribune,* p. 6.
Shearer, L. (1987, May 10). How much do we drink? *Parade Magazine,* p. 16.
Vance, M. U. (1988). Drug decriminalization. *Science, 246,* p. 1102.
Watterlond, M. (1983). Telltale metabolism of alcoholics. *Science, 83,* pp. 72–76.

_____ *Part I*

Theories and Approaches

Behavioral Systems Approach

DOUGLAS H. RUBEN

Recent inquiry into methods of treating alcohol and drug abuse have been frustrated by the same conclusion: "Does the person really change?" Naturally the goals of abstinence, of sobriety, invoke all sorts of personal commitment to change—from alcohol or drug consumption to life patterns. Altering interpersonal, social, occupational, and recreational variables dismantles the vicious cycle of repeated addiction developed over a period of time. But what does this accomplish? The goal of fully disinfecting an addict's world of cues and urges is to prevent relapse; or is the goal simpler: to modify specific addictive behaviors at the root of the problem? Both are credible goals. Systems therapists subscribe primarily to the first goal, whereas behavioral therapists focus on the second. Which school of therapy is on the right track?

This chapter addresses a critical need to identify elements from each school of thought that empirically promise a valid treatment methodology. Consider the behavioral camp. Pure applied behavioral analysis, a forerunner to behavioral therapy, already has outlived its limited efficacy on the complex levels of problems facing chronic addicts. The unit of analysis is simply too small. Calls for expansion of the stimulus $\longrightarrow$ response boundary initiated quite early, with Gibbs (1979) and Mishler (1979) leading the reformation. Opening up the field to larger boundaries also meant adopting an ecologically based approach to addiction. This prompted behaviorists to examine social system variables toward establishing new methods in hopes of discovering new scientific laws. However, few, if any, of these ambitious behavioral systems pioneers cared to consider what already existed in social systems theory. Were the systems compatible? Was behavioral systems theory similar to, say, Bronfenbrenner's developmental systems model?

Usually the answers to these questions remained unknown. Except for rare comparisons published in nonmainstream behavioral journals (e.g., Foster & Hoier, 1982), behaviorists largely did not know what a bona-fide systems theory really involved. Recently an undertaking to advance systems psychology (e.g., Smith, Mountjoy & Ruben, 1983; Reese & Parrott, 1986; Ruben & Delprato, 1987) has made some headway but not enough to overcome current ignorance. This chapter hopes to fill the void by presenting tenets of each systems theory contributing to the integrated-field or ecobehavioral approach to substance abuse. Sections follow an evolutionary path starting with general systems theory. Levels of systems theory derived from this step cover sections on ecosystem, social exchange theory, applied behavioral systems, and ecobehavioral approach.

GENERAL SYSTEMS THEORY

General systems theory (GST) aims to describe patterns and processes in a wide range of phenomena that are the same across disciplines and across levels of complexity and organization. It is mainly descriptive and qualitative, focusing on how a system evolved or prescribing what is necessary for that system to survive. Systems begin with an input that is processed by the system on its way to becoming an output. The process of transformation through the system is governed by rules of transformation, frequently called feedback. Types of feedback regulate stability and allow the system to evolve through constant change. All objects in the system are reciprocally interdependent, causing changes in one person or object to have specific and broad consequences for other persons or objects interfaced in the system.

The basic assumption underlying GST is that time, energy, and space are properties of organization. Balance among these properties varies with different levels of *feedback* and *control*. Miller (1972), for example, proposed four particular levels affecting families: simple feedback, cybernetic control, morphogenesis, and reorientation or conversion.

Simple feedback is a typically circular process in which inputs to a system convert into outputs, producing a complete feedback loop (also called a *positive feedback loop*). Should the loop be delayed, disrupted, or diverted, causing separation between inputs and outputs, then it is called a *negative feedback loop*. In addictive family relationships, loops translate into communicative messages exchanged between significant players such as between parents or parent and child. Lack of communication means any input from children or nonaddict parent is lost. The resulting negative loops distance family members and foster distrust.

At level 2, *cybernetic control,* the output of a system returns to a monitoring or inspection modality wherein adults judge it as correct or incorrect based on criteria or *meta-rules*. Criteria established and promulgated by the family may act as the standard for comparison. On a family level, this means a child's grades "return" to stand trial against his parents' meta-rules of expectations. Failure to meet their criteria forces the child's grades (input) to be corrected before that child again can interact with external systems (the school). Before starting a new marking period, in other words, the child must suffer reprehensible consequences for poor grades. That way, cybernetically, his future grades (input) will reflect the family standards.

Morphogenesis, the third level, is an ideal situation. Here the monitoring system recognizes that its meta-rules are defective and must undergo change to prevent repetition of bad output. In theory, this means that families reflect on their values, morals, and expectations toward a revision that best fits a child's realistic abilities. Alcoholic families, however, would never partake in morphogenetic transitions because they require self-exploration, self-admission of mistakes, and self-correction. Disclosure of vulnerability threatens the insecurity of family members, and they may bypass this level, only to seek outside authority on how to change the system.

Reorientation or conversion, the last level, is what this system is for. The main goal here is confrontation of the goals and principles governing a system. By dramatically altering a faulty system, input and output signals can resume a balanced flow with a positive loop. On a practical level, radical systemic changes rendered internally require members of the system to be objective to solve problems. Dysfunctional families cannot do this; this is why they seek the authority of therapists or experts upon whom they can lay the burden of changes. Shirking responsibility backfires when the authority figure recommends systemic changes that are resisted by the family.

FIRST LEVEL OF BEHAVIORAL SYSTEMS: ECOSYSTEM APPROACH

Ecology is the science that studies interactions between living organisms and their environment. No living organism exists in isolation. The basic unit of organism-environment interaction resulting from the complex interplay of living and nonliving elements in a given area is called an *ecosystem* (Evans, 1956; Micklin, 1973). The ecosystem concept is central to human ecology—the study of ecosystems as they affect or are affected by human beings. In its application to the family, emphasis is on families as systems interdependent with their natural physical-biological, human-built, and social-cultural settings. This perspective emerged in the latter part of the nineteenth century, a period of social reform, urbanization, industrialization, and concern about the health and welfare of families. It reemerged in the 1960s with increased trends toward viewing psychological phenomena from a holistic and systems perspective.

Ecosystems can be used to study a wide range of problems related to families and their relationships with various environments and diverse levels and kinds of external systems (Andrews, Bubolz & Paolucci, 1980; Hook & Paolucci, 1970). It is appropriate for families of different structures, ethnic, or racial backgrounds or in different life stages and circumstances. Focus is upon individual family members as well as on the family as a whole, taking into account ways that families blend the many tasks and functions transacted in their daily lives.

Ecological framework offers an eclectic approach to examine interrelationships and interactions. Theories from psychoanalytic, behavioral, and developmental systems, among others, can be adapted to ecological concepts for inspection of system changes. Despite this flexibility, all underlying assumptions of ecosystems begin with the basic premise that the parts and wholes of families operate reciprocally with each other. Decisions, activities, and essentially all psychosocial and physical-biological functions are interdependent and cannot be considered in isolation (cf. Herrin & Wright, 1988; Wright & Herrin, 1988). Ten other core assumptions regarding family ecosystems follow from this premise (cf. Bubolz & Sontag, in press):

1. In family ecology the properties of families and the environment, the structure of environmental settings, and the process taking place within and between them must be viewed as interdependent and analyzed as a system.

2. As human groups, families are part of the total life system, interdependent with other forms of life and the nonliving environment.

3. Families are semi-open, goal-directed, dynamic, adaptive systems. They can respond, change, and develop and can act on and modify their environment. Adaptation is a continuing process in family ecosystems.

4. All parts of the environment are interrelated and influence each other. The natural physical-biological environment provides the essential resource base for all of life; it is affected by the sociocultural and human-built environment and also influences these environments.

5. Families require interactions with multiple environments.

6. Families are energy or transformation systems and need matter-energy for maintenance and survival, for interactions with other systems, and for adaptive, creative functioning. Information organizes, activates, and transforms matter-energy in the family system.

7. Interactions between families and environments are guided by two sets of rules: immutable laws of nature, which pivot around the capacity of the natural environment to supply energy and other essential resources and to process materials and waste, and human-derived rules such as social norms and values, allocation of resources, role expectations, and distribution of power.

8. Environments do not determine human behavior but pose limitations and constraints, as well as possibilities and opportunities, for families.

9. Families have varying degrees of control and freedom with respect to environmental interactions.

10. Decision making is the central control process in families, which directs actions for attaining individual and family goals. Collectively, decisions and actions of families have an impact on society, culture, and the natural environment.

Empirical tests of the human ecosystem model are relatively scarce, and they usually are extensions of research on existing systems models. Dadds (1987), for example, evaluated abusive children using an ecological model similar to Bronfenbrenner's (1979, 1986). This model has four systems revolving around the child:

1. Microsystem, a pattern of activities, roles, and interpersonal relations experienced by the developing child in a given setting.
2. Mesosystem, which comprises the interrelations among two or more settings in which the developing child actively participates, such as school, church, and peers.
3. Exosystem, which refers to one or more settings not involving the developing child as an active participant but where the events occurring are affected by what happens in the setting containing the developing child.
4. Macrosystem, referring to consistencies at the level of subculture or the culture as a whole, along with belief systems or ideology underlying such consistencies.

Dadds examined the relationship between family variables and child behavior, particularly that of oppositional disorders. Ecologically she showed that aggression is a function of three events: (1) it is determined by a network of subsystems that form the components of more complex systems, (2) at each level components are interdependent in the way they function, and (3) each level is affected by the dynamics of levels above and below it. This coalesces with Bronfenbrenner's (1979) micro-macrosystems model. Identified as causes of the behavioral problem were traitlike behaviors and the child's repertoire of deficits and excesses. Factors acting on the child included interactions of the child with primary caregivers and reaction to disruptive environment. Factors within the families acting upon parent and child included maladjustment of family members (as in case of stepparenting or having a second child), mental illness in the family, and marital instability. Finally, community impacts described included a decline in the extended family, urbanicity versus rural isolationism, and working parents.

In addictive families, the ecosystem reads like a blueprint. The *microsystem* consists of dysfunctional dynamics within the family household. Dynamics range from poor hygiene of children and disorganized, dirty, living quarters, to parental mistreatment. The *mesosystems* are rare and inconsistent, regulated by the monopolizing parents who prevent outsiders from learning about problems at home. But there are many *exosystems* affected by addicted families. For example, friends of the family and the extended family alert to the child's adversities may be conspiring to confront the parents or rescue the child. School counselors, as one type of conspirator, frequently discover family abuse and take responsibility, informing protective services or another social welfare agency that there is a need for intervention. The *macrosystem* supports moral beliefs about child rearing, about not drinking around children, and about seeking advice from authority.

Pitfalls of Bronfenbrenner's (1977, 1979) model primarily stem from its hypothetical structure. Attempts by Belsky (1980, 1984) to operationalize it, however, have been beneficial in explaining the etiology of child maltreatment. Belsky (1984) traced parental functioning back to contextual sources of stress and support, functions of support, and parenting deficits. Though clinically intriguing, this analysis is still too speculative and draws validity by comparing itself to the rigorously crafted scientific experiments in behavioral research with aggressive children (e.g., Ammerman & Hersen, 1990; Patterson & Reid, 1984).

SECOND LEVEL OF SYSTEMS: SOCIAL EXCHANGE APPROACH

At the second level of systems theory evolution are operational refinements of the human ecosystem that examine specific as well as holistic interpersonal (interorganismic) interaction. One prominent model illustrating this approach is the *social exchange model* (Burgess & Huston, 1979; Ekeh, 1974; Heath, 1976; Simpson, 1972). Social exchange proposes that social and interpersonal relationships operate according to economic principles of profit and loss. Economy or "family economy" builds on the concept that resources are valuable commodities, transferable between family members or outside families. Transfer of human resources determines the worth of that family relationship. Resources include not only such material forms as money, time, energy, and productive skills but also nonmaterial forms, such as love, loyalty, pride, and status.

Several researchers have developed conceptual typologies for personal and interpersonal resources. Rettig (1985) focused on two typologies: economic exchange behavior and social exchange behavior. Economic exchange behavior involves two-way or reciprocal transfer of objectively measured resources or services. Relationships between two parties depend on this equal or near-equal investment. Social exchange behavior involves subjectively measured resources or services transferred between two parties.

Foa and Foa (1974, 1980) linked these two typologies toward developing a more comprehensive resource exchange model. They proposed six essential resources within this model required to maintain familial equilibrium:

1. Love
2. Status
3. Information (exchange or advice)
4. Money (as currency)
5. Goods (tangible products)
6. Services (performed for one another)

All six resources address the underlying issue of whether individual life and family satisfaction fluctuate depending on dyadic gains and losses. Essentially, does one family member (giver) earn dividends on how he invests his own resources in another family member (receiver)? Does each family member reap equal shares of those dividends? To answer these questions, consider the following assumptions about any exchange in a family.

First, reciprocal needs develop chronologically through logical stages of personality or behavioral changes along a continuum of time. This assumption basically proposes that needs evolve and differentiate in a hierarchy or sequential growth in relation to the four-stage developmental schema by Foa and Foa (1980). Naturally different needs as a child or parent may also depend on such adaptive factors as success and failure of personal growth. How the environment receives or refuses the services and goods of family members may limit or even diversify Foa and Foa's stages. The order and formation of resource classes are not automatic.

Second, all resources function as external or internal rewards or costs. Foa and Foa argue that exchangeable resources function to a degree either to facilitate or hinder relationships. Services, status, goods, love, money—all possess properties internally or externally influential upon recipients or consumers and thereby must, like the environment, shape the behavior of that recipient. Following this conditioning view, some resources seem to encourage action without much personal experience, whereas others require direct experience of the recipient with that resource for action to occur. Love, for instance, to which infants readily respond, supposedly is inherently reinforcing and unlearned. Money and services—more universal and concrete—exert control over people by virtue of learning about their rewarding outcomes. What is missing, however, is a mechanism or system by which unlearned rewards and losses transform into learned rewards and losses.

Third, reciprocal resources transfer via concrete-symbolic or particularistic-universal modalities. Resources are plotted along two polar coordinates according to Foa and Foa's (1980) model. The concrete-symbolic continuum describes that certain resources are tangible, confrontable, and overtly transmitted between people, such as goods and services. Status, love, and parlingual behaviors transfer along less conspicuous routes, usually illustrated by words or remote outcomes. Feelings generated from receiving a job promotion or being in a position of authority are at times inarticulate but nonetheless strong. These are symbolic. When exchanges depend on "who" transfers resources—that is, when givers and takers affect the quality of resources—that exchange is particularistic. Exchanges where the resource value is desirable or undesirable regardless of giver (for example, in the case of money) are universal.

Finally, laws or principles of human behavior govern rules on reciprocity of rewards and losses and the production of human happiness. Of all the assumptions implied, none stirs up positivistic overtones as great as claiming that exchange is orderly. Foa and Foa (1980) attempt levity by saying that "resource

exchanges can be likened to a game in which participants give and take resources from one another'' (p. 93). However, this is no game at all. Reference
to ''game'' simply disguises the brute reality that social exchange theory follows basic principles of operant and respondent conditioning.

On a global level, exchange theory also directly provides rules or laws governing the orderliness of human behavior and social expectations. Foa and Foa
(1980, pp. 93–94) summarize these governing laws in 13 rules they call ''rules
of the game,'' which describe transactions and their predictable outcomes based
on gains and losses:

1. The larger the amount of resource possessed by a person, the more likely it is to
   be given to others.
2. The smaller the amount of a resource possessed by a person, the more he is likely
   to take it away from others.
3. The nearer two resources are, the more likely they are to be exchanged with one
   another.
4. The nearer to love a resource is, the more likely it is to be exchanged with the
   same resource. Love is exchanged for love; money is rarely exchanged with money.
5. The nearer to love a resource is, the narrower is the range of resources with which
   it is likely to be exchanged.
6. For resources closer to money, the amount lost by the giver tends to approach the
   amount gained by the receiver (so that one's gain is the other's loss).
7. When a resource is not available for exchange, it is more likely to be submitted by
   a less particularistic than by a more particularistic one.
8. The simultaneous transmission of love and another resource increases the value of
   this other resource or facilitates its transmission.
9. Taking away any resource (other than love) produces a loss of love.
10. The optimal range (neither too little nor too much) of a resource is narrowest for
    love and increases progressively for resources closer to money.
11. In the absence of exchange, the decrease in the amount of love possessed decreases
    and is greater for resources closer to love.
12. Other conditions being equal, the probability of occurrence of a given exchange is
    contingent upon the institutional setting in which it may take place.
13. The probability of love exchange is higher in small groups. The opposite is true for
    money.

These rules of the game offer 13 trends observed in human resource exchanges
that identify probabilities or likely causes given contingent relationships between proximity, amount, and frequency of resources and the vested interest of
receivers.

Underlying these propositions are basic ''economic trends'' in addiction families that shed light on why Foa and Foa's (1980) rules of the game seem

plausible. They answer the question, "Why do dysfunctional families engage in an exchange?"

1. *There are multiple buyers and sellers.* For any resource or number of resources, multiple family members may vie for sharing interest or investment in that resource.
2. *There is a requirement for perfect information (consumers need accurate information to compare products, investments, and so forth).* Family members do not blindly request goods and services on transfer. They first inspect, assess, and weigh gains and losses among resources to determine the degree of trust and safety before making a choice.
3. *Margin utility is based on maximizing profit.* Choice is calculated and depends on the least sacrifice of resources juxtaposed by the greatest gain potential. Parents may speculate "on margin" by restricting or delaying rewards to children who misbehave; premature investment (attention) may ruin the product (the child may begin a tantrum), whereas delayed investment (attention when the child is quiet) may show a greater profit return (the child's on-task behavior is restored and increased).
4. *Conditions must be predictable.* Social exchange implies a "market economy." As such, exchange theory anchored in uncertainty would misdirect participants. Family members must at least partially predict and control outcomes for their own purposes of planning, organizing, and selecting choices; otherwise, exchange mechanisms deteriorate. Ambiguity of exchange distorts prediction, reduces probability of risk by family members, and leads to family decay.
5. *Household production presupposes a connection between consumption and utility.* Essentially this proposition claims a family resource must be "useful." Nonmaterial or material goods and services transferred all share properties of being needed by the family or part of regular routines or interactions such that their deprivation would disrupt the family cycle. Examples range from food (for mealtime) to love and affection.
6. *Household is a homogeneous entity.* Disparity of values and needs on a macroeconomic level yields diversity of products. The more selective a community is, the greater is the variety for accommodation. In a family, homogeneity ensures more unanimity among resources; it ensures that resources stand a better chance of equitable exchange among all family members and thereby that family cohesion is stronger.
7. *Economic activities require time for acquisition, consumption, utilization, and expenditure (waste).* Human exchange, like human conditioning, is a temporal process. Slow or fast rates of exchange depend on whether the resource is already in a state for consumption and utilization. Love and affection, for example, require very little prerequisite ability for transfer, whereas permitting driving privileges to a child does require preexisting or acquired skills in operating an automobile. In that case, resource transfers are contingent. Contingencies may also include how the child plans on utilizing the car and projected waste (of gas).

THIRD LEVEL OF BEHAVIORAL SYSTEMS: APPLIED BEHAVIORAL SYSTEMS APPROACH

The third level of behavioral systems links naturalistic with social sciences. This model consists of scientifically valid concepts applied to everyday human interaction that help predict and control outcomes of addictive behavior. Two types of conditioning principles dominate the research: respondent and operant. Respondent conditioning refers to pairings or association between stimuli, between responses, or between stimuli. Operant conditioning consists of responses shaped by the "contingent" outcomes or consequences following behavior. Increases or decreases in behavior depend on whether consequences are reinforcers or punishers and are influenced by the schedule of consequences administered.

In operant conditioning, definitions of reinforcement and punishment usually vary by their positive or negative effect on the behaving person. Put simply, distinctions between reinforcement and punishment can be represented as follows. For *positive reinforcement,* present something (usually pleasant) to a person immediately following his (appropriate or inappropriate) behavior, and that behavior will increase in the future. For *negative reinforcement,* remove or take away something (usually unpleasant) from a person immediately following his (appropriate or inappropriate) behavior, and that behavior will increase in the future. For *positive punishment,* present something (usually unpleasant) to a person immediately following his (appropriate or inappropriate) behavior, and that behavior will decrease in the future. And for *negative punishment,* remove something (usually pleasant) from a person immediately following his (appropriate or inappropriate) behavior, and that behavior will decrease in the future.

Strengths of the operant and respondent models largely derive from controlled experimental analyses of behavior in laboratory and field applications. Since the early 1960s, evidence on principles of conditioning has passed the test of replication and generalization and has widespread assimilation into schools, institutions, and clinical settings.

Evidence also is extensive in family addiction research. Newlin's (1987) analysis of why sons of alcoholics become alcoholics employed basic operant and respondent conditioning principles. Newlin described the sequential steps of conditioning leading sons of alcoholic parents to explore, drink, and develop drinking habits. Pavlovian conditioning explained how sons of alcoholics increased their autonomic arousal around "elicitive" cues and thereby increased tolerance to alcohol consumption levels. The model proposed that tolerance of alcohol represents the development of a conditioned response to drug cues that inhibits natural (unconditioned) responses to reject alcohol (because alcohol is not a natural body-producing chemical).

FOURTH LEVEL OF SYSTEMS: ECOBEHAVIORAL OR INTEGRATED-FIELD APPROACH

This final step unifies systems analysis with scientific or positivistic principles of behavior. Traditional stimulus⟶response (learning) theory broadens its boundaries by merging with an ecosystems approach. To achieve this goal, two issues are covered. First, let us consider the parameters of a new behavioral system using an integrated-field approach. Second, benefits of combining integrated-field (ecobehavioral) and social exchange models are proposed for clinical application to family addiction.

Ecobehavioral Approach

Recently there has been an expansion of the unicausal behavioral model to a systems approach (Midgley & Morris, 1988; Wahler & Fox, 1981). Russo's (1990) presidential address to the Association for the Advancement of Behavior Therapy (AABT), for example, marks a crucial turning point in behavioral therapy. He argued that multiple factors must be considered in both research and clinical endeavors. Enlarging the unit of analysis from single to complex stimulus-response connections echoes the sentiments of many behaviorists (Biglan, Glasgow & Singer, 1990; Morris, 1988) who support a contextualist approach. Such an approach promotes a field-theory concept following Aristotle's interactionism and Dewey and Bentley's (1949) transactionalism. It replaces the artificial distinction between behavior and stimulus. Principles of field theory describe human behavior naturalistically where stimulus and response constitute the overall transaction of events. Human behavior, in other words, is part of a process in a field of connected things and events, all reciprocally dependent.

Much of the history of field thinking can be traced to the early writings of J. R. Kantor (1888–1984), who essentially challenged the existing psychological constructs of mind and body and the formalization of intrapsychic dynamics (Kantor, 1959, 1970, 1976; Lichtenstein, 1984; Moore, 1984; Parrott, 1984; Smith, 1973, 1976, 1984). According to Kantor (1969), the psychological field is "the entire system of things and conditions operating in any event taken in its available totality. It is only the entire system of factors which will provide proper descriptive and explanatory materials for the handling of events. It is not the reacting organism alone which makes up the event but also the stimulating things and conditions, as well as the setting factors" (p. 371).

Field thinking is unusual for a learning theory. It rejects heredity, environment, mind, cognition, stimuli, reinforcers, independent variables, and so on as exclusive controlling forces in behavior. In fact, behavior itself must be totally redefined as an event. Such events not only involve actions of an active organism but also the stimulating objects, media of contact between organism and environment, functional stimulus and response attributes, and attending setting factors, all of which define the psychological field. Antecedents and consequences are one among many interactive parts of the whole. Reinforcement, punishment, conditions of deprivation, pharmacologic interactions, and response properties more closely resemble kinetic energy in machinery. There are no singular units of action per se but rather the synthesis of many larger aggregates of action (Thompson & Lubinski, 1986). For Kantor, as with other avant-garde field theorists, these fundamental units of a behavioral system act in constant motion along a time continuum.

Adaptations of the integrated-field perspective are evident in numerous recent clinical developments (Delprato, 1987; Ruben, 1984, 1986; Upson & Ray, 1984). Among these are theoretical and experimental applications concerning aging (Herrick, 1983a, 1983b; Ruben, 1990a), anthropology and sociology (Herrick, 1974; MacRoberts & MacRoberts, 1983), child development (Bijou, 1976; Wahler, House & Stambaugh, 1976), substance abuse (Ruben, 1989, 1990b, in press), and methodological designs (Ray & Delprato, 1989). A systems alternative attests to the advancing potential of using a larger unit of applied behavioral analysis as a conceptual scheme over traditional systems theory, human ecology, or traditional clinical models.

A case in point is the work by Wahler (Wahler, 1975; Wahler, Berland, Coe & Leske, 1977; Wahler & Hann, 1987). Wahler helped inspire a movement called *ecobehaviorism,* essentially concerned with applying behavioral principles to marital and family problems within an integrated-field or ecological framework. Ecology, by definition, was different from a human ecology explanation. The term referred to a larger boundary or field of analysis wherein the same functions of responses and stimuli occurred but the effects were spread over time and involved multiple sequences of behavior and continuous, reciprocal exchanges of human-to-human contact. Delprato (1986; Delprato & McGlynn, 1986) later categorized these interdependent response patterns into two types: concurrent response patterns, when responses occur simultaneously (for example, when talking, walking, and using gestures happen simultaneously), and sequential response patterns, responses in a chain link that depend on each for sources of reinforcement as well as from antecedents and consequences.

Ecobehaviorism thus is exclusively concerned with the reciprocal interactions of people and objects with which they come into contact. There are three parts of this conceptual relationship within the field originally introduced by Kantor. The first part is the *stimulus.* Actions of the objects that may be other persons or events are conventionally referred to as stimuli. These stimuli consist of physical construction, of form as described by physical measurement, and of function. The stimulus function, or "meaning," is how a stimulus affects a person's interaction with it. To say that the sharp edge of a blade cuts the sandwich in half is describing a stimulus function.

The second part consists of *responses.* Three ways can describe a person's interacting with stimuli: the person's *equipment* or repertoire, which describes internal and external biological structure and the functioning of the individual; the *response form,* or organized form or structure of behavior that may be described by physical measurement; and the *response* function, in which reasons for behavior are based on the results or outcomes produced by interacting with stimuli. To say that a sharp edge of the knife cut a sandwich the person ate is describing the reason, or function, of the knife-cutting responses.

Setting events are the third part. They are the contextual conditions and may exist as internal, biological conditions (e.g., chemical imbalance, fatigue, in-

Event or Field Boundary

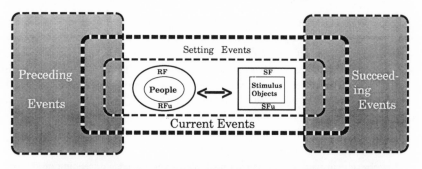

Time Continuum

RF =   Response Form
RFu =   Response Function
SF =   Stimulus Form
SFu =   Stimulus Function

Figure 1.1
Interaction of Stimuli and People in a Succession of Fields

jury) and as external environmental conditions, both physical-chemical (e.g., the weather, room temperature, noise) and social-cultural (e.g., classrooms, play yards, household). The critical aspect of setting events is that they influence the function of stimuli and of responses. For example, drinking parents who ignore their children at the babysitter's house is vastly different from ignoring their children when the whole family is at the home, or, worse, at the bar.

Interactions between people and stimuli are continuous in a succession of different segments, or *fields* (Figure 1.1). The field boundary is permeable across time as people and objects undergo change and the environment remains in constant motion. Transmission from one field to another is not like walking from one room into another. It is more like shifting position in a chair while in the same room. Each body movement constitutes a new field or segment different from the one before it, despite obvious similarities in responses and stimuli. Over time, this procession of fields moves through essentially three different time zones: past or preceding events, current events, and future or succeeding events.

Together the total environment is an integrated field comprising continuous, permeable interactions of people, objects, and setting events. Field thinking is not so new, but the science provided by examining stimuli and responses within a system is new. To begin, then, consider three sets of postulates underlying an integrated-field (ecobehavioral) system, all of them preparing clinicians with directives on dealing with addictive clients.

Postulates Defining the Science of Ecobehaviorism:

1. Ecobehaviorism is the enterprise of interacting with specific things and events, which leads to a definite and precise orientation with respect to those things and events. The investigator is part of the field.
2. Ecobehaviorism concerns the existence and identity of things and events of their components and the relationship between either the components of things and events or between the things and events themselves.
3. Ecobehaviorism is not concerned with existences or processes that transcend the boundaries of scientific enterprises. This includes invented concepts or unproved ideas beyond the events under investigation.
4. Ecobehaviorism requires specialized instruments and methods depending on the specific characteristics of events studied and the specific problems formulated about them.
5. Ecobehavioral analyses are evolutional; they are cumulative and corrigible. They are completely free from all absolutes, ultimates, or universals.
6. Ecobehavioral applications constitute the basis for scientific prediction and control.

Postulates of Events and Transactions in Integrative-Field (Ecobehavioral) Model:

1. Ecological events consist of multifactor fields.
2. Ecological events are interrelated with social as well as with biological and physical events.
3. Ecological events are evolved from ecological behavior.
4. Ecological events involve the participation of a total person (organism), not merely special organs or tissues.
5. Ecological events are ontogenetic (they originate in the lifetime of particular individuals).
6. Ecological events are continuous.
7. Ecological events consist of interrelated factors that do not admit nonscientific determiners (psychic, mythical powers, explanatory fictions).
8. Ecological events consist of stimuli and responses that contain symmetrical and reciprocal functions.
9. Ecological events contain setting events that operate as inhibiting or facilitating conditions in behavior segments.
10. Individual development consists of the evolution of ecological fields.

Therapeutic Postulates:

1. The ability to prescribe interventions depends on an analysis of total events.
2. The analysis of total events consists of identifying response and stimulus connection, setting events, and principles of behavior governing these connections.

3. The readjustment to fields involves reeducation.

4. Factors entering in therapy involve not only psychological but also biological, social, domestic, economic, educational, and other features of the individual's life circumstances.

The study of human ecology can duplicate natural (not social) sciences in investigating systemic phenomena. An illustration of this approach appears in the next section on combining ecobehavioral with social exchange theory.

Ecobehavioral Application to Family Addiction

An ecobehavioral systems view of family addiction considers behaviors, setting events, and biological factors in causing a problem. Consider the clinical scenario that follows. Addicted parents who neglect or mistreat their children reciprocally destroy their own lives, and the entire family system gradually deteriorates. Exactly where should the analysis of causes start? Predicting the variables that cause this systemic family deterioration is not always easy. Griffore and Phenice (1988) recently made this attempt. They traced ecological impacts on human development, in part following Bronfenbrenner's (1979) model and Aristotle's model of causality. Creatively they attributed disruptions in the flow of activity patterns and energy transfer in multilevel (ecobehavioral) systems to material, formal, efficient, and final causes. However, these four types of causes were too inexact for scientific predictions on how systems changed.

An alternative proposal is to advance the predictability of social exchange theory along with the principles of reinforcement and punishment. This poses interesting possibilities considering that Foa and Foa's (1980) model explicitly describes interactional outcomes of resources between a giver and receiver. Their rules of the game stipulate gains and losses, just as operant contingencies stipulate reinforcers and punishers. In both cases, the reciprocal exchange transacted determines whether those affected by the exchange will repeat their actions (increase the probability of their behaviors) or inhibit their actions (decrease the probability of their behaviors) in the future.

Combining both systems begins with a change in terminology. Let us substitute some words from Foa and Foa's list of rules with behavioral terms. Love, money, status, and other positive resources equal "rewards" (reward exchanges). Physical abuse, verbal abuse, and hate will constitute negative resources, equal to "punishers" (punishing exchanges). The quality and quantity of resources can be described by measurable properties such as frequency, duration, magnitude, and intensity. The exchange itself is either response contingent or response noncontingent. If it is response contingent, resources may occur on a schedule or for something specific that giver and receiver do. If it is response noncontingent, no schedule or order of exchange exists (it is arbitrary, random), and it has nothing to do with what giver or receiver are doing.

With these changes in mind, consider the following revised rules of the game for a comprehensive ecobehavioral systems theory:

Reward Exchanges: The outcomes increase the probability of either giver's or receiver's actions.

1. The more amount (frequency and intensity) of rewards given by one person, the less amount of rewards returned by another person.
2. The less amount of rewards given by one person, the more amount of punishers returned by another person.
3. The more rewards are taken away after they are given, the higher amount of punishers returned by another person.
4. When rewards are absent, it is more likely that receivers demand substitutes or dispense punishers in return.
5. The more rewards are given response contingently, the faster the rewards are returned by the receiver.
6. The more rewards are given response noncontingently, the slower that rewards are returned by the receiver, but the higher is the demand for rewards by receiver.

Punishing Exchanges: The outcomes decrease the probability of either giver's or receiver's actions.

1. The more amount (frequency and intensity) of punishers given by one person, the less amount of rewards returned by another person. And there is a greater probability of punishers returned by receiver. Where there have been many punishing exchanges, the receiver may avoid the exchange entirely.
2. The less amount of punishers given by one person, the more amount of punishers is given by another person.
3. The more punishers are taken away after they are given, the higher amount of rewards is returned by another person, to avoid future recurrence of punishers.
4. When punishers are absent, there is a high amount of rewards given by receivers, to avoid future recurrence of punishers.
5. The more punishers are given response contingently, the more amount of punishers is returned by another person.
6. The more punishers are given response noncontingently, the fewer punishers or rewards are returned by the receiver. Where there have been many punishing exchanges, the receiver may avoid the exchange entirely.

Simultaneous and Delayed Exchanges (Transmissions) of Rewards and Punishers: The outcomes increase or decrease the probability of either giver's or receiver's actions based on the timing of rewards and punishers.

1. When more rewards and fewer punishers are transmitted simultaneously, it is likely that a receiver will react to the punisher and return with a punisher.

2. When fewer rewards and more punishers are transmitted simultaneously, it is likely that a receiver will react to the punisher and return with a punisher.

3. When equal amounts of rewards and punishers are transmitted simultaneously, it is likely that a receiver will react to the punisher and return with a punisher.

4. When rewards are given followed by punishers (within 30 minutes), it is likely that a receiver will react to the punisher and return with a punisher.

5. When punishers are given followed by rewards (within 30 minutes), it is likely a receiver will react with neither punisher nor reward.

Clinical Warning Signs of Family Addiction

By revising Foa and Foa's rules, exchanges take on a new meaning of prediction and control. In therapy, for instance, the objective is predicting pathologic tendencies and controlling their chance of recurrence in family and interpersonal relationships. Clinicians working with addictive families and even adult children of alcoholic families are particularly attentive to family pathology and rely on all instruments of prediction to help family members identify, prevent, and manage duress. Clinical control depends on detecting warning signs of family decay in advance of the dysfunction. Once they are spotted and isolated, therapy stands a chance of helping members to strike a balance in communication and increase rewarding exchanges.

What are the warning signs that can be detected? Early indicators of family addiction are plentiful and clearly deal with parent and child. From the perspective of the child, certain patterns may arise based on the revised rules of exchange and become very noticeable to observers. Teachers, like clinicians, are likely to discover warning signs over time rather than from isolated episodes. Developing warning signs may take one of three forms: behavioral deficits, behavioral excesses, and avoidance behaviors.

A behavioral deficit means the child's actions fall below standard levels or that he lacks important skills for dealing with demands of the age group—for example:

1. Behavior is slow.
2. Behavior takes much effort to complete.
3. The child wants little or no feedback on the behavior.
4. The child has difficulties relating to his behavior.
5. The behavior attracts sympathy in other people, or people do the behavior for him.
6. The child is easily agitated if confronted with the deficiency.
7. The child is easily distracted or diverted or the child procrastinates (seems lazy).
8. The child will avoid or escape situations where he must do the deficient behavior.

A behavioral excess occurs when the child reacts in ways beyond the normal amount for his age group. Defined criteria for this pattern usually include the following:

1. Behavior is rapid.
2. Behavior takes much effort to complete.
3. The child demands much feedback on his behavior.
4. The behavior repels people's attention after awhile.
5. The child is preoccupied with that behavior or talks much about it.
6. The child is aggressive if the feedback on his behavior is delayed.
7. The child is noncompliant or argues a lot.

Avoidant behavior under most circumstances means the child is afraid. He anticipates criticism, rejection, failure, or any punishment so regularly or is so self-critical that attempts at good behavior pose monumental hazards. The following signs are typical:

1. The child is scared to behave in general around other people.
2. The child is selective about his words and actions.
3. The child reacts slowly, in small amounts, or has difficulty with behavior.
4. The child delays reacting or wishes to be excused quickly when pressed to respond in certain ways.
5. The child cries easily or is highly intimidated.
6. The child feigns illness or has frequent stomachaches and headaches.
7. The child refuses to try new behavior or be creative.
8. The child sneaks around or does the requested behavior when others are gone.

Children afflicted by deficits, excesses, or avoidance develop unspoken rules about the addictive family that prevent communication at home and that will likely sabotage therapy unless they are spotted. Such rules as "it's not okay to talk about problems" and "be perfectionistic" haunt the child's self-image in the context of his system. With this revised exchange theory, clinicians now have a better edge on the complex family system to trace, locate, predict, and control problems in individual family members and as a unit.

A second advantage of ecobehavioral thinking is preservation of scientific integrity. Therapy focusing on abstinence works diligently to alter life-style patterns and biological urges. Too commonly, however, traditional system interventions try global warfare against these combative forces of drug and alcohol use. They end up taking a shotgun approach, scattering advice to as many different components of the field as possible—some directed to the client, some to the family, some to the social network. The goal is to strike as fast and at as many sensitive areas as possible before the abuse worsens. In few cases, these scattered efforts hit targets, are coordinated, or share common denominators that give cohesion to therapy. Ecobehavioral interventions, by contrast, are cohesive by following the canons of good science. With tenets of prediction and control, specific patterns of behavior in family exchanges become operationally observable and measurable and thus are easy targets for correction once family members implement concrete strategies.

The ecobehavioral way is not simply a new popular psychology doomed for extinction after a year or two, not another passing phase of quick-fix schemes aimed at superficially solving individual, marital, and family problems. It is instead the hallmark of innovative natural science long sought after by dissatisfied behaviorists, displeased with the narrow scope and expired usefulness of the Skinnerian three-term contingency, and floundering systems therapists who search desperately for empirically valid support for their theories and methods. Ecobehavioral systems provide direct answers for both camps. How far ecobehaviorism evolves into the future mainstream of clinical disciplines depends entirely on its research growth and further theoretical development by dedicated scientists.

REFERENCES

Ammerman, R. T. & Herson, M. (1990). *Treatment of family violence: A sourcebook.* New York: John Wiley & Sons.

Andrews, M. P., Bubolz, M. M. & Paolucci, B. (1980). An ecological approach to study of the family. *Marriage and Family Review, 3,* 29–49.

Belsky, J. (1980). Child maltreatment: An ecological integration. *American Psychologist, 35,* 320–35.

Belsky, J. (1984). The determinants of parenting: A process model. *Child Development, 55,* 83–96.

Biglan, A., Glasgow, R. E. & Singer, G. (1990). The need for a science of larger social units: A contextual approach. *Behavior Therapy, 21,* 195–215.

Bijou, S. (1976). *Child development: The basic stage of early childhood.* Englewood Cliffs, N.J.: Prentice-Hall.

Bronfenbrenner, U. (1977). Toward an experimental ecology of human development. *American Psychologist, 52,* 513–31.

Bronfenbrenner, U. (1979). *The ecology of human development.* Cambridge: Harvard University Press.

Bronfenbrenner, U. (1986). Ecology of the family as a context for human development: Research perspectives. *Developmental Psychology, 22,* 723–42.

Bubolz, M. M. & Sontag, M. S. (forthcoming). Human ecology theory. In P. Boss, W. Doherty, R. LaRossa, W. Schumm & S. Steinmetz (eds.), *Sourcebook of family theories and methods: A contextual approach.* New York: Plenum.

Burgess, R. G. & Huston, T. L. (1979). *Social exchange in developing relationships.* New York: Academic Press.

Dadds, M. R. (1987). Families and the origins of child behavior problems. *Family Relations, 26,* 341–57.

Delprato, D. J. (1986). Response patterns. In H. W. Reese & L. J. Parrott (eds.), *Behavior science: Philosophical, methodological, and empirical advances* (pp. 61–113). Hillsdale, N.J.: Lawrence Erlbaum Associates.

Delprato, D. J. (1987). Developmental interactionism: An integrative framework for behavior therapy. *Advances in Behaviour Research and Therapy, 9,* 173–205.

Delprato, D. J. & McGlynn, F. D. (1986). Innovations in behavioral medicine. In M. Hersen, R. M. Eisler & P. M. Miller (eds.), *Progress in behavior modification*, vol. 20 (pp. 67–122). Orlando, Fla.: Academic Press.

Dewey, J. & Bentley, A. F. (1949). *Knowing and the known*. Boston: Beacon Press.

Ekeh, P. P. (1974). *Social exchange theory*. Cambridge: Harvard University Press.

Evans, F. (1956). Ecosystem as the basic unit in ecology. *Science, 123*, 1127–28.

Foa, E. G. & Foa, U. G. (1974). *Societal structures of the mind*. Springfield, Ill.: Charles Thomas.

Foa, E. G. & Foa, U. G. (1980). Resource theory: Interpersonal behavior as exchange. In J. Gergen, L. Greenberg & A. Willis (eds.), *Social exchange: Advances in theory and research*. New York: Plenum.

Foster, S. L. & Hoier, T. S. (1982). Behavioral and systems family therapies: A comparison of theoretical assumptions. *American Journal of Family Therapy, 10,* 13–23.

Gibbs, J. C. (1979). The meaning of ecologically oriented inquiry in contemporary psychology. *American Psychologist, 34,* 127–40.

Griffore, R. J. & Phenice, L. (1988). Causality and the ecology of human development. *Psychological Record, 38,* 515–25.

Heath, A. (1976). *Rational choice and social exchange*. Cambridge: Cambridge University Press.

Herrick, J. W. (1974). Kantor's anticipations of current approaches to anthropology. *Psychological Record, 24,* 253–57.

Herrick, J. W. (1983a). Interbehavioral perspectives on aging. *International Journal of Aging and Human Development, 16,* 95–123.

Herrick, J. W. (1983b). The road to scientific ageism. In N. W. Smith, P. T. Mountjoy & D. H. Ruben (eds.), *Reassessment in psychology: The interbehavioral alternative* (pp. 269–75). Washington, D.C.: University Press of America.

Herrin, D. A. & Wright, S. C. (1988). Precursors to a family ecology: Interrelated threads of ecological thought. *Family Science Review, 1,* 163–84.

Hook, N. & Paolucci, B. (1970). The family as an ecosystem. *Journal of Home Economics, 62,* 315–18.

Kantor, J. R. (1959). *Interbehavioral psychology*. Granville, Ohio: Principia.

Kantor, J. R. (1969). *The scientific evolution of psychology* (Vol. 2). Chicago: Principia.

Kantor, J. R. (1970). An analysis of the experimental analysis of behavior. *Journal of the Experimental Analysis of Behavior, 13,* 101–8.

Kantor, J. R. (1976). The origin and evolution of interbehavioral psychology. *Revista Mexicana de Analisis de la Conducta, 2,* 120–36.

Lichtenstein, P. E. (1984). Interbehaviorism in psychology and in the philosophy of science. *Psychological Record, 34,* 455–75.

MacRoberts, M. H. & MacRoberts, B. R. (1983). An interbehavioral and historico-critical examination of anthropology, ethology and sociology. In N. W. Smith, P. T. Mountjoy & D. H. Ruben (eds.), *Reassessment in psychology: The interbehavioral alternative* (pp. 297–325). Washington, D.C.: University Press of America.

Micklin, M. (1973). Introduction: A framework for the study of human ecology. In M. Micklin (ed.), *Population, environment and social organization* (pp. 2–19). Hillsdale, Ill.: Dryden Press.

Midgely, B. D. & Morris, E. K. (1988). The integrated field: An alternative to the behavior-analytic conceptualization of behavioral units. *Psychological Record, 38,* 483–500.

Miller, J. G. (1972). *Living systems.* New York: John Wiley & Sons.

Mishler, E. G. (1979). Meaning in context: Is there any other kind? *Harvard Educational Review, 49,* 1–19.

Moore, J. (1984). Conceptual contributions of Kantor's interbehavioral psychology. *Behavior Analyst, 7,* 188–96.

Morris, E. K. (1988). Contextualism: The world view of behavior analysis. *Journal of Experimental Child Psychology, 46,* 289–323.

Newlin, D. B. (1987). Alcohol expectancy and conditioning in sons of alcoholics. *Advances in Alcohol and Substance Abuse, 6,* 33–57.

Parrott, L. J. (1984). J. R. Kantor's contributions to psychology and philosophy: A guide to further study. *Behavior Analyst, 7,* 169–81.

Patterson, G. R. & Reid, J. B. (1984). Social interactional process in the family: The study of the moment by moment family transactions in which human social development is embedded. *Journal of Applied Developmental Psychology, 5,* 237–62.

Ray, R. & Delprato, D. J. (1989). Behavioral systems analysis: Methodological strategies and tactics. *Behavioral Science, 34,* 81–127.

Reese, H. W. & Parrott, L. J. (eds.). (1986). *Behavior science: Philosophical, methodological, and empirical advances.* Hillsdale, N.J.: Lawrence Erlbaum Associates.

Rettig, K. (1985). Conceptual issues for integrated economic and social exchange theories. *Journal of Consumer Studies and Home Economics, 9,* 43–62.

Ruben, D. H. (1984). Major trends in interbehavioral psychology from articles published in "The Psychological Record" (1937–1983). *Psychological Record, 34,* 589–617.

Ruben, D. H. (1986). The "interbehavioral" approach to treatment. *Journal of Contemporary Psychotherapy, 16,* 62–71.

Ruben, D. H. (1989). Behavioral predictors of alcoholics: A "systems" alternative. *Alcoholism Treatment Quarterly, 5,* 137–62.

Ruben, D. H. (1990a). *The aging and drug effects: A planning manual for medication and alcohol abuse treatment of the elderly.* Jefferson, N.C.: McFarland & Company.

Ruben, D. H. (1990b). Interbehavioral approach to treatment of substance abuse: A "new" systems model. *Alcoholism Treatment Quarterly, 7,* 47–61.

Ruben, D. H. (in press). *Family addiction: An analytical guide.* New York: Garland Press.

Ruben, D. H. & Delprato, D. J. (eds.). (1987). *New ideas in therapy: Introduction to an interdisciplinary approach.* Westport, Conn.: Greenwood Press.

Russo, D. C. (1990). A requiem for the passing of the three-term contingency. *Behavior Therapy, 21,* 153–65.

Simpson, R. L. (1972). *Theories of social exchange.* Morristown, N.J.: General Learning Press.

Smith, N. W. (1973). Interbehavioral psychology: Roots and branches. *Psychological Record, 23,* 153–67.

Smith, N. W. (1976). The works of J. R. Kantor: Pioneer in scientific psychology. *Revista Mexicana de Analisis de la Conducta, 2,* 137–48.

Smith, N. W. (1984). Fundamentals of interbehavioral psychology. *Psychological Record, 34,* 479–94.

Smith, N. W., Mountjoy, P. T. & Ruben, D. H. (eds.). (1983). *Reassessment in psychology: The interbehavioral alternative.* Washington, D.C.: University Press of America.

Thompson, T. & Lubinski, D. (1986). Units of analysis and kinetic structure of behavioral repertoires. *Journal of the Experimental Analysis of Behavior, 46,* 219–42.

Upson, J. D. & Ray, R. D. (1984). An interbehavioral systems model for empirical investigation in psychology. *Psychological Record, 34,* 497–524.

Wahler, R. G. (1975). Some structural aspects of deviant child behavior. *Journal of Applied Behavior Analysis, 8,* 27–42.

Wahler, R. G., Berland, R. M., Coe, T. D. & Leske, G. (1977). Social systems analysis: Implementing an alternative behavioral model. In A. Rogers-Warren & S. F. Warren (eds.), *Ecological perspectives in behavior analysis.* Lanham, Md.: University Park Press.

Wahler, R. G. & Hann, D. M. (1987). An interbehavioral approach to clinical child psychology: Toward an understanding of troubled families. In D. H. Ruben & D. J. Delprato (eds.), *New ideas in therapy: Introduction to an interdisciplinary approach* (pp. 53–78). Westport, Conn.: Greenwood Press.

Wahler, R. G., House, A. E. & Stambaugh, E. E. (1976). *Ecological assessment of child problem behavior.* New York: Pergamon Press.

Wahler, R. G. & Fox, J. J. (1981). Setting events in applied behavior analysis: Toward a conceptual and methodological expansion. *Journal of Applied Behavior Analysis, 14,* 327–38.

Wright, S. D. & Herrin, D. A. (1988). Ecology, human ecology, and the study of the family: Part 2. *Family Science Review, 1,* 253–82.

2

Family Systems Approach

THOMAS C. TODD AND ANTHONY W. HEATH

This chapter explores a variety of family systems models for the understanding of addictive behavior, with particular reference to chemical dependency and eating disorders. Although at times practitioners refer to a family systems view of a particular problem, in actuality there are various family systems interpretations of a given problem such as addictive behavior. These systems perspectives share similarities but also have differences, which have important implications. Although the focus of this chapter is not primarily on treatment, the treatment implications of the different family systems approaches will be discussed briefly.

In a recent review of family therapy approaches to the treatment of addictive disorders, Heath and Stanton (1991) noted that over a dozen books and innumerable articles have been written on the subject of "families under the influence" (cf. Elkin, 1984). In this chapter, we have organized the many contemporary approaches taken by family therapists into three categories in order to highlight the salient ideas of major family therapy contributors: historical, function of the symptom, and postfunctional. We will present an integrative summary of all of the approaches in order to show how they can be sensibly integrated.

THE HISTORICAL APPROACHES

Some of the most influential family systems views of addictive behavior, particularly in the area of chemical dependency, have placed emphasis on historical factors that continue over many generations. Two major family pioneers are notable in this regard: social worker Virginia Satir and Dr. Murray Bowen.

The Contributions of Virginia Satir and Sharon Wegscheider

Virginia Satir was a family therapy pioneer who left behind a strong humanistic legacy. Her most notable contribution to the family systems understanding of chemical dependency has come through her work on identifying typical family roles, particularly as outlined in her book, *Peoplemaking* (Satir, 1972). Satir emphasized that in all families, members take on distinctive roles, but in dysfunctional families, such as families of alcoholics, these roles can become imprisoning stereotypes. She identified five major roles that she believed captured most of the important variations: computer, blamer, placater, rescuer, and distracter. In spite of the rather pejorative sounding names, the roles were not seen as inherently pathological. Only rigidly stereotyped roles were considered problematic.

Sharon Wegscheider-Cruise translated and popularized Satir's work for the chemical dependency field in her book, *Another Chance* (Wegscheider, 1981). She related the development of stereotypic roles in relationship to family members' attempts to manage the behavior associated with substance abuse. In Wegscheider's view, each family member develops a characteristic role in the family dance around alcohol or drug use: dependent, enabler, hero, scapegoat, lost child, and mascot, most of which correspond closely to roles described by Satir.

Like Satir, Wegscheider believes that the first step toward breaking free from rigid roles is for family members to become more clearly aware of them. After identification and awareness, family members can play with these roles through techniques such as family sculpting and family drawings and begin to experiment with new behavior that departs from the expected role. Because of the ease with which family members can understand these roles, this framework has become an important part of family education in many chemical dependency treatment programs. These programs typically accept the notion that becoming aware of these roles and having a conscious intention of changing this behavior will be instrumental in leading to change.

The Contributions of Murray Bowen

Murray Bowen, another family therapy pioneer, is known for his emphasis on the importance of triangular relationships in the family system. He emphasized the importance of looking at such triangles over a span of several generations, and he expressed the belief that the behavior and position of individual family members could be predicted with considerable accuracy by examining these patterns. One of the most important tools in this work is the multigenerational family genogram, which provides a schematic map of family relationships over several generations (McGoldrick & Gerson, 1985).

In the chemical dependency field, the genogram often provides dramatic evidence of addictive patterns existing over many generations. This not only includes highlighting patterns of chemical dependency in many family members over several generations but also patterns of repeated marriage to chemically dependent individuals and patterns of caretaking professional choices, such as nursing.

Another key dimension in the Bowenian analysis of family systems is in the area of overfunctioning and overresponsibility versus underfunctioning and underresponsibility (Bepko & Krestan, 1985). In this view, all families show a tendency toward complementary patterns of overfunctioning and underfunctioning. This includes relationships both within a generation (e.g., husband overfunctions and wife underfunctions) and across generations (e.g., mother overfunctions in relationship to underfunctioning irresponsible child). Bowenian practitioners believe that they can predict patterns of mate selection on this dimension, as well as the likely repercussions throughout the system, if a previously overfunctioning individual begins to function more normally, or an underfunctioning member begins to act responsibly.

The Bowenian approach emphasizes a mixture of insight and behavioral change. Here the family genogram becomes a conceptual tool not only for the therapist but also for increased understanding on the part of the family. This is seen as helping families to identify previously unconscious patterns of mate selection or parenting so that they can begin to break those patterns and accommodate to the resulting changes. The genogram is also used to help family members target particular kinds of change in their family relationships, which then can be implemented with the help of a therapist.

APPROACHES EMPHASIZING THE FUNCTION OF THE SYMPTOM

A good deal of important work in the addictions field, particularly having to do with chemical dependency and eating disorders, is based on the notion that the primary symptom (chemical dependency or an eating disorder) has come to serve an important function in the family system. This does not mean that families have deliberately produced the symptom, consciously or unconsciously; instead, it is based on the idea, often supported by observable facts, that the symptom is both maintained by the family system and plays a role in maintaining the existing pattern of family interaction. This reciprocal relationship between the symptom and the family system needs to be identified and changed for the symptom to be alleviated and for the family system to function on a stable basis without an addicted member.

The Family Life Cycle

Like many others in the family therapy field (e.g., Carter & McGoldrick, 1989), Salvador Minuchin and Jay Haley have considered life cycle transitions to be critically important in understanding family dysfunction. Many well-functioning families encounter difficulty when faced with critical life cycle transitions, such as the addition or loss of a family member. In his book *Leaving Home*, Haley (1980) placed emphasis on the life cycle stage of young adults' developing independence and leaving their nuclear families. Haley included drug addiction in young adults as one of the symptoms that seems to relate closely to the life cycle stage of leaving home. Substance abuse often solves a life cycle dilemma for the family. The young person serves a key role in the family, such as stabilizing the parents' marriage. Staying involved with the family but being drug addicted allows this person to achieve a semblance of independence while continuing to provide a focus for the parents. Therapy is seen as a process of removing this function and freeing the family to launch the young person successfully.

Todd (1988) took the Haley model further in three important directions in discussing life cycle issues in substance abuse. First, he acknowledged that substance abuse may play a variety of functions in life cycle transitions for the family system, distinctions that were critically important for successful treatment. Adolescent drug experimentation as an expression of rebellion and autonomy is quite different from a life-style of chronic drug use in a young adult who was never successfully launched. Drug and alcohol use could also be triggered or escalated by life cycle stages such as the empty nest or retirement. Second, a distinction was made between the life cycle transition present at the time of initiation of serious substance use as compared with life cycle stage currently facing the family during treatment. While a 35-year-old heroin addict who is married with children might seem to be a functioning adult, close analysis frequently reveals that heavy substance use has persisted since high school and young adulthood, preventing true independence from being successfully achieved. Finally, as is frequently noted in the substance use field, addiction and recovery also have a characteristic developmental cycle, so that decisions about appropriate treatment need to take the stage of addiction or recovery into account.

The Contributions of Stanton and Todd

In the early 1970s M. Duncan Stanton, Thomas C. Todd, and their associates at the Philadelphia Child Guidance Clinic launched an ambitious study of family factors and family treatment of heroin addiction in young adult males. Despite complications involved in working with the methadone maintenance program and despite being limited by the funding agency to ten sessions of family therapy, the project was radically successful in getting chronic heroin addicts off both legal and illegal drugs and functioning productively.

Stanton, Todd, Heard, Kirschner, Kleiman, Mowatt, Riley, Scott, and Van Deusen (1978) conducted an extensive analysis of the function of heroin addiction in the family system. They saw heroin addiction as a paradoxical solution to a number of developmental dilemmas for the addict and his family. It allowed the addict to maintain a regressive closeness to his mother and family yet allowed him to feel distant; it allowed aggression on the part of the addict to be viewed as a function of the drug use; it allowed the addict to have sexual experiences that did not suggest disloyalty to the family; and it allowed the addict to form relationships outside the family, which, because they were drug related, were seen as evidence of incompetence and dependence rather than separation. Many other factors, which vary from case to case, influence and perpetuate addiction. Stanton et al. (1978) have argued that a thorough understanding of family addictive processes requires a careful analysis of family functioning and the role of drug use within individual families.

The Stanton and Todd team used a structural-strategic therapy model based heavily on the work of Minuchin and Haley to use the resources of the family to promote rapid and lasting change. (See Stanton & Todd, 1982, for details of their conceptual model of treatment.) Their understanding of the role of symptoms in maintaining the family system helped to guide focused interventions to block this function and find other healthy alternatives, at least in this population. Because the symptoms were heavily entrenched, it proved difficult to remove the function of the symptom without provoking a significant crisis (Mowatt, Heard, Steier, Stanton, & Todd, 1982). Nevertheless, therapy proved successful when the therapist was active and framed an addiction-related crisis as a crisis for the whole family. With significant support, families resolved these crises together and emerged with a healthier organization that did not revolve around substance use.

The Psychosomatic Families Project

No account of family systems views of addictive behavior would be complete without a discussion of the work of Minuchin and his group on the family treatment of eating disorders. This work focused on anorexia nervosa and culminated in a number of publications (Minuchin, Baker, Rosman, Liebman, Milman, & Todd, 1975), including the classic book *Psychosomatic Families* (Minuchin, Rosman, & Baker, 1978). There are important similarities and differences between this work on psychosomatic families and the discussion of the treatment of drug addiction, which also emanated from the Philadelphia Child Guidance Clinic and was also influenced by the work of Minuchin.

The conceptual model of psychosomatic families (Minuchin et al., 1975) was an early attempt to extend models of anorexia nervosa and other physical symptoms to an open systems model. A generic open systems model was compared to a medical model, a psychodynamic model, and the behavioral model. The ultimate open systems model included a number of factors shared with other models, which were linked in a system of reciprocal feedback. Extrafamilial stresses were seen as affecting both the vulnerability of the child to become symptomatic and the family organization. The vulnerability of the child not only influenced family organization but also was exhibited in the endocrinological and biochemical systems of the child. The child's symptoms were seen as a complex by-product of both family functioning and the individual physiological functioning of the child. Finally, the child's symptoms were seen as influencing the family organization and functioning directly and indirectly to the identified patient. In addition to the research group's work with anorexia nervosa, this model was also seen as applicable to psychosomatic problems of juvenile diabetes and intractable asthma.

The model proposed by the Minuchin group was not a strict family model in that it posited a level of biological vulnerability on the part of the child who ultimately became symptomatic. To produce psychosomatic symptoms in a family, however, two additional factors are needed beyond the vulnerability of the child: a set of characteristics of the family environment and a specific role played by the symptomatic child. Extensive evaluation of families with psychosomatic children (compared to other families with a child with diabetes or other physical symptoms) was conducted using structured family tasks and a stress-inducing family diagnostic interview. Not only were the results of these interventions obvious in the videotapes of family transactions, but they were reflected in physiological measurement obtained by studying the free fatty acids of the patient and the patient's parents.

Four characteristics of overall family functioning were identified from these systematic observations. No one of these characteristics taken alone was sufficient to trigger and reinforce psychosomatic symptoms; however, the combined cluster of transactional characteristics was felt to be descriptive of the family processes that encourage symptom formation:

1. *Enmeshment,* which refers to extremes of proximity and intensity with overinvolvement and poorly differentiated boundaries among family members.

2. *Overprotectiveness* in the psychosomatic family, shown throughout the family in a high degree of concern of family members for each other's welfare. This concern was not limited to the identified patient or to the area of illness.

3. *Rigidity,* seen in a heavy commitment to maintenance of the symptom. Compared to effectively functioning families, these families seemed poorly equipped to deal with life cycle changes and transitions or with fluctuating demands of the tasks of daily problem solving.

4. *Lack of conflict resolution,* in which most psychosomatic families showed very limited tolerance for the expression of open conflict, with even low levels of criticism or disagreement triggering protective responses. In a small minority of families, there

were also examples of chronic unresolved conflict. Conflict in these families would be expressed but never seemed to go anywhere.

The vulnerability of the child and the general characteristics of the family seemed an incomplete explanation of the psychosomatic functioning of a particular child. Under conditions of stress and conflict, the role of the symptomatic child became clear in helping the family system deal with conflict that seemed toxic to the overall system, particularly a conflict between the parents. Several patterns were identified that describe the role of the symptomatic child in moderating the conflict between the parents. Most typically, parents unable to deal with each other directly unite in protective concern for the sick child, avoiding conflict by *protective detouring.* In some families the child was recruited into a *stable parent-child coalition.* Psychosomatic families also showed a third pattern, *triangulation,* in which both parents competed openly and vigorously for an alliance with the symptomatic child. This pattern is extremely stressful to the child; it typically produces high levels of physical symptoms and is unstable, typically leading to the emergence of protective detouring or stable parent-child coalition. A final mechanism for involving a child in parental conflict is comparatively rare with psychosomatic families; *scapegoating* or *detouring attacking* appears in behaviorally disordered diabetic children and in families with drug-abusing offspring, preventing parental conflict by allowing parents to unite by criticizing and attacking one of the children. This pattern is not seen in psychosomatic families because it conflicts with the parents' view of the child as sick and their associated commitment to a high level of protectiveness.

Structural family therapy as practiced by Minuchin's group has proved to be highly effective in working with psychosomatic families. This is particularly true for anoretic girls and their families. In order to see the family functioning clearly and obtain some leverage for structural change, it is often necessary to induce a crisis in the family, usually by having the family eat lunch together in a therapeutic session. Once the patterns of characteristic family functioning are exhibited, the therapist works to counteract them. This therapeutic approach, described much more completely in *Psychosomatic Families,* includes explicitly challenging each of the family characteristics listed. In addition, an effort is made to remove the symptomatic child from his role in managing parental conflict.

THE POSTFUNCTIONAL APPROACHES

Among the theorists who hold a systems view of the therapy process are those who have historically argued against the idea that symptoms serve functions. These systems theorists and therapists have long objected to the common assumption that symptoms are caused by ''deeper,'' more important problems or processes. In the realm of addictive disorders, they reject the premise that addictive behavior exists because of personality faults, historic traumas, literal or metaphorical illness, marital problems, hierarchy infractions, or similar therapeutic or diagnostic explanations.

The pioneers of this group of countercultural theorists are the representatives of the Brief Therapy Center of the Mental Research Institute (MRI) in Palo Alto, California (e.g., Watzlawick, Weakland & Fisch, 1974; Fisch, Weakland & Segal, 1982). More recently, the MRI has been joined by two other groups of theorist-practitioners: Steve de Shazer's solution-focused therapy and Michael White's cybernetic therapy.

MRI Brief Therapy

The MRI brief therapy approach has its origins in the pioneering work of anthropologist Gregory Bateson, hypnotist Milton Erickson, and revolutionary psychiatrist Don Jackson. In 1967, these men and several others began a research project designed to investigate what worked and did not work in psychotherapy. Unwilling to let their work proceed without evidence of rapid success, they set a ten-session limit on the therapy provided in the experimental Brief Therapy Center.

Today MRI therapists still value efficiency in resolving client problems. Therapy is strictly focused on resolving the problem presented by "customers" of therapy or those who clearly request the assistance of the therapist. Problems are defined clearly and behaviorally, and therapy is considered complete when the problem has been resolved.

It is important to understand that MRI therapy is both nonnormative and nonpathological. It is nonnormative in the sense that therapists do not impose standards of family structure or communication on clients. Problems are considered to exist only when and as clients perceive them. It is nonpathological in that clients are seen as caught up in unhelpful or unsatisfactory interactional patterns. Nothing is seen to be wrong with clients, and they are not diagnosed in the usual sense of the word. Instead, clients are thought to be doing the best that they can to solve their problems.

The essential description of problem formation in the MRI model is simple. MRI theory suggests that an everyday difficulty becomes a problem when attempts to resolve the problem fail. As more and more efforts are made to solve the problem, these attempted solutions themselves begin to aggravate the situation. Soon it is the attempted solutions that perpetuate and maintain the problem. Thus, for MRI therapists, the problem is the attempted solutions being used by the clients. Therapy therefore is entirely focused on blocking more of the same attempted solutions and finding a different and effective solution for the original problem, which often requires a totally different approach.

When MRI therapists consider addictive behaviors, they seek specific behavioral definitions of problems, avoid causal (e.g., disease) explanations of problems, and work with those concerned to find new and effective solutions to the problems presented. Every client is seen as unique, as is every problem. Terms like *alcoholic, codependent, drug addict, child of an alcoholic, anorectic,* and *bulimic* are considered too abstract and too pejorative to be used as problem definitions. Furthermore, when such words are used to explain troublesome events, actions, or behavior, they are seen as obscuring issues of interpersonal influence and responsibility and distracting everyone from solving the problems at hand (Heath & Ayers, 1991).

de Shazer's Solution-Focused Brief Therapy

Steve de Shazer, Insoo Kim Berg, and their colleagues have run the Brief Family Therapy Center (BFTC) in Milwaukee since 1977 and have more recently created a new approach to brief therapy, which they call *solution-focused brief therapy* (de Shazer, 1982, 1985, 1988, 1991). Solution-focused therapy, developed on the conceptual foundation laid by the MRI group, focuses on behavioral exceptions to the problems of clients. Based on the idea that there are exceptions to every problem or times when clients have solved their problems temporarily, solution-focused therapists act to build on these exceptions. For example, they might ask an addicted client to describe what happens when he overcomes the urge to use drugs and then help him to use the same strategies at other times.

The focus on success distinguishes this model. Instead of attending to problems, solution-focused therapists draw attention to solutions and to the behaviors that promote them. In place of questions about problems, there are questions about past and current successes and plenty of praise for things clients have done well (Berg & Gallagher, 1991). In the example, the solution-focused therapist would lavish praise on the drug addict for the self-control he had exercised and help him to use the same approach to overcome future urges to use drugs.

Another interesting distinction drawn by de Shazer and his colleagues concerns the talk that occurs in the therapy room. To appreciate this distinction, it is helpful to listen to a therapy session, noticing how much of the time is devoted to client reports about the problem(s) and how much of the session is spent in discussion of changes that have occurred for the client(s). In most therapy sessions, it seems as if talk centers on the former.

De Shazer, like many other family therapists, believes that we all mentally construct our lives through interaction with others, through communication. These constructions, or cognitive maps, are represented in language. Problems and solutions are maps as well; change occurs when maps are revised, often through dialogue.

Gingerich, de Shazer, and Weiner-Davis (1987) have observed that therapists promote change when they elicit "change talk," which occurs when clients talk about goal or action-related things. Thus, for solution-focused therapists, the goal for every session is to encourage clients to talk about change so that they develop new understandings of their worlds, leading to new experiences (de Shazer, 1988).

Michael White's Cybernetic Therapy

Michael White, a family therapist in Adelaide, Australia, shares the interest of de Shazer and others in clients' constructions and the processes of cognition (Durrant & Coles, 1991). In addition, he has borrowed from the work of anthropologist Gregory Bateson and the systems theorists. Thus, the family is viewed as a system governed by the cognitive abilities of its members.

White, like the MRI group, argues that problems develop when a chance event, accident, or mistake provokes families to respond, and their response(s) aggravate the situation. Seeing the situation as worsened, the family members respond again—in the same way—and the situation becomes worse. This process, called *deviation-amplifying feedback* or *vicious cycles,* inevitably produces blame, guilt, despair and defeat, and symptoms. It continues because family members are restrained by the way they see the problem; they are unable to see the situation differently to find their ways out.

A therapist's job is to help clients adopt new beliefs and presuppositions about their problems. The therapist must propose a different view of the problem and encourage the family to recognize it as different: "The juxtaposition of such new descriptions against the family's old or restrained description invites them to draw distinctions and it is these distinctions that trigger discoveries" (Durrant & Coles, 1991, p. 145).

In dealing with a drug addict or alcoholic, the therapist might learn, for example, that the family saw the problem as outside the control of the addict but within the control of the other family members. This view tends to produce behavior that is forgiving of misbehavior and slips on the part of the addict and critical of the sober members. Thus, transgressions are forgiven, and blame is assigned to and assumed by all others. The therapist's job, according to White, is to pose an alternative view of the situation that could be understood by the family and lead to different behavior on everyone's part.

INTEGRATIVE SUMMARY

There are a number of promising signs, but it may be premature to state unequivocally that family therapists have entered a new era of integration. While this integrative spirit may not yet be universal, we will integrate some of the diverse ideas presented in the previous sections. Although all of the ideas explored in this chapter fall within the broad rubric of family systems therapy, the different theories are based on assumptions that differ considerably and that can make integration difficult. Moreover, we have our own biases, which in-

evitably influence our selection of assumptions we find comfortable and therapeutic techniques we find useful.

The historical approaches of Bowen and Satir have shown promise as part of
a psychoeducational approach to families with a substance-abusing member.
Such families typically have difficulty understanding the behavior of the substance abuser, as well as their own role in dealing with the abuser. The Bowenian and Satir models are clearly useful in this regard.

Bowen's work places substance use in historical context. For most substance
users, it is easy to find evidence of a pattern of substance use and abuse that
extends back over multiple generations. Counselors and family members have
found this observation helpful when confronting a substance user who denies a
problem. Once the substance user has agreed to enter treatment, the historical
perspective can also help family members to be less blaming of the individual
substance user, since they can see the substance use as part of a historical
tradition.

Family members can also see their behavior in a similar historical perspective, since it is not at all uncommon for spouses of substance abusers to have
a family history containing a parallel tradition of marriage to alcoholics and
drug abusers and often a pattern of choosing caregiving professions. Satir's
work on family roles can help family members to accept the idea that they play
a part in the family dance. Seeing the family interaction as akin to a dance or
a mobile with counterbalancing roles helps family members to understand their
part in the interaction without feeling blamed. It also helps them to understand
why recovery may be destabilizing to the family unless they learn new patterns
of interaction.

The MRI theorists hold that it is important not to equate function with blame.
In this view, having substance abuse acquire functional utility in a family is
seen as somewhat of a historical accident of accommodation that occurred as
the family continued to do the best it could. This differs from an extreme
functional position, which often seems to imply, for example, that parents recruit a drug-addicted child in order to solve the problems of their marriage and
that they may find a new recruit if one child becomes abstinent.

One key variable in assessing the utility of a functional model or the MRI
model seems to be the degree of chronicity of the substance abuse. It is our
belief that when substance abuse has persisted in a family over a long period
of time, family members have adapted to the substance use and have found
themselves caught up in stereotypic patterns of behavior around the substance
use. Often the initial patterns began as problem-solving efforts, but they typically have acquired a life of their own. In this view, direct efforts to convince
family members to change often fall on deaf ears, and it is important to give
family members credit for good intentions. The link here to Michael White's
work is also obvious, since his work seems most appropriate with longstanding
problems. He believes that patients and families inevitably exhibit increasingly

stereotypic behavior as the problem persists. This certainly matches our experience with chronic drug problems, where both the addict and family members feel compelled to continue to exhibit the same behavior and attempt solutions that are "more of the same."

The MRI model is also helpful in sorting out the complexity of typical substance cases. It places heavy emphasis on determining who is a "customer" and exactly what that customer is willing to buy. This is extremely important in a field where typically the person who seeks treatment is not the person who has the symptoms. The MRI model also alerts the therapist to the likelihood that a number of paid or unpaid helpers are interacting with the substance user and the family in ways that are presumed to be helpful but often have the unintended consequence of maintaining the problem. This model offers guidelines on how to approach such helpers and find diplomatic ways of viewing their efforts, which can help to persuade them to change their tactics.

The solution-focused work of de Shazer and his colleagues, such as Selekman and Weiner-Davis, offers a refreshing antidote to the pessimistic predictions that abound in the substance abuse field. This approach allows a stance toward patient and families that does not presume denial, resistance, and power struggles. Especially with cases that are less chronic, it is often possible to build on positive changes, using the techniques devised by de Shazer and his colleagues. Adopting the positive mind-set of this approach is also important, since otherwise positive changes may go unnoticed or be dismissed as trivial.

Todd and Selekman (1991a) have offered a number of integrative principles for working with families with a substance-abusing adolescent member. Probably the most important consideration, which is particularly important with families of substance-using young people, is having parents establish clear control in the family and the importance of eliminating hierarchical confusion. Once techniques such as those promulgated by Haley have been used to put the parents in charge, it is then frequently possible to move to a much more positive solution-oriented approach. At the opposite extreme, there are also times when no techniques that push for change seem helpful. The symptoms seem well entrenched in these families, who have often gone through a long series of relationships with helpers and agencies. A number of techniques may be possible to help the therapist avoid a rigidly pro-change position. These can be mild techniques such as the constructivist work of Anderson and Goolishian (1988), or they can include sharpening the dialogue and the debate around the merits of change versus stability (Papp, 1980) and the reflecting teamwork of Andersen and his American colleagues (Andersen, 1987; Lussardi & Miller, 1991). In extreme cases, an explicitly paradoxical approach may be the treatment of choice (Todd, 1981).

Finally, we believe that while recovery may be a lifelong affair, we do not promote a lifetime of therapy. This can involve some apparent conflict with the Alcoholics Anonymous (AA) philosophy, which suggests that alcoholism and addiction are lifelong conditions that require a lifelong commitment to twelve-step programs. Our observation is that there seems to be a natural life cycle to involvement with AA and other self-help programs, which for many people is much longer than the typical course of therapy but still limited (Todd, 1988). Many patients who have extremely positive experiences with AA decrease their involvement radically after a year or two of sobriety; even the stalwarts of the program often seem to cut back and want to move on to other issues after six or seven years.

Regardless of treatment philosophy and regardless of the treatment components, we believe that it is important for the patient and the family to give themselves ample credit for positive change when treatment is ending. Positive changes too frequently are attributed entirely to outside agencies—hospitals, therapists, the AA program—and they can become quite fragile when a patient begins to slip. We want the family to feel considerable pride and ownership toward the positive changes of the substance user. They also function to provide a safety net against future substance abuse. We help them to identify the positive changes that they can make and to consolidate what they have learned in treatment. This can include explicit training in relapse prevention and having the family go through drills to plan the handling of possible slips and relapses. Clients are best left with a message that they have accomplished a great deal, but it would not be a sign of failure if they needed to reenter treatment briefly in the future.

While we conclude this chapter with these integrative principles, they certainly do not represent the final word in the evolution of family systems approaches to addiction. We hope that readers will find them useful, and, more important, we hope that this chapter will give readers a sense of the rich contributions made to the understanding and treatment of addiction by family systems theorists and therapists.

REFERENCES

Andersen, T. (1987). The reflecting team: Dialogue and meta-dialogue in clinical work. *Family Process, 26* (4), 415–28.

Anderson, H. & Goolishian, H. (1988). Human systems as linguistic systems: Some preliminary and evolving ideas about the implications for clinical theory. *Family Process, 27* (4), 371–95.

Bepko, C. & Krestan, J. A. (1985). *The responsibility trap: A blueprint for treating the alcoholic family.* New York: Free Press.

Berg, I. & Gallagher, D. (1991). Solution focused brief treatment with adolescent substance abusers. In T. Todd & M. Selekman (eds.), *Family therapy approaches with adolescent substance abusers* (pp. 93–111). Boston: Allyn & Bacon.

Bowen, M. (1978). *Family therapy in clinical practice.* New York: Jason Aronson.

Carter, B. & McGoldrick, M. (eds.) (1989). *The changing family life cycle: A framework for family therapy* (2d ed.). Boston: Allyn & Bacon.

de Shazer, S. (1982). *Patterns of brief therapy.* New York: Guilford Press.

de Shazer, S. (1985). *Keys to solutions in brief therapy.* New York: Norton.

de Shazer, S. (1988). *Clues: Investigating solutions in brief therapy.* New York: Norton.

de Shazer, S. (1991). *Putting difference to work.* New York: Norton.

Durrant, M. & Coles, D. (1991). Michael White's cybernetic approach. In T. Todd & M. Selekman (eds.), *Family therapy approaches with adolescent substance abusers* (pp. 137–75). Boston: Allyn & Bacon.

Elkin, M. (1984). *Families under the influence: Changing alcoholic patterns.* New York: Norton.

Fisch, R., Weakland, J. & Segal, L. (1982). *The tactics of change: Doing therapy briefly.* San Francisco: Jossey-Bass.

Gingerich, W., de Shazer, S. & Weiner-Davis, M. (1987). Constructing change: A research view of interviewing. In E. Lipchik (ed.), *Interviewing* (pp. 21–32). Rockville, Md.: Aspen.

Haley, J. (1976). *Problem solving therapy.* San Francisco: Jossey-Bass.

Haley, J. (1980). *Leaving home: The therapy of disturbed young people.* New York: McGraw-Hill.

Heath, A. (1981). Responses to the response. *Underground Railroad, 2* (4), 2.

Heath, A. & Ayers, T. (1991). MRI brief therapy with adolescent substance abusers. In T. Todd & M. Selekman (eds.), *Family therapy approaches with adolescent substance abusers* (pp. 49–69). Boston: Allyn & Bacon.

Heath, A. & Stanton, M. D. (1991). Family therapy. In R. Frances & S. Miller (eds.), *Clinical textbook of addictive disorders* (pp. 406–30). New York: Guilford.

Lussardi, D. J. & Miller, D. (1991). A reflecting team approach to adolescent substance abuse. In T. C. Todd and M. Selekman (eds.), *Family therapy approaches with adolescent substance abusers* (pp. 226–40). Boston: Allyn & Bacon.

McGoldrick, M. & Gerson, R. (1985). *Genograms in family assessment.* New York: Norton.

Minuchin, S. (1974). *Families and family therapy.* Cambridge: Harvard University Press.

Minuchin, S., Baker, L., Rosman, B., Liebman, R., Milman, L. & Todd, T. (1975). A conceptual model of psychosomatic illness in children: Family organization and family therapy. *Archives of General Psychiatry, 32,* 1031–38.

Minuchin, S., Rosman, B. & Baker, L. (1978). *Psychosomatic families: Anorexia nervosa in context.* Cambridge: Harvard University Press.

Mowatt, D. T., Heard, D. B., Steier, F., Stanton, M. D. & Todd, T. C. (1982). Crisis resolution and the addiction cycle. In M. D. Stanton et al., *The family therapy of drug abuse and addiction.* New York: Guilford.

O'Hanlon, W. & Weiner-Davis, M. (1989). *In search of solutions: A new direction in psychotherapy.* New York: Norton.

Papp, P. (1980). The Greek chorus and other techniques of paradoxical therapy. *Family Process, 19,* 45–57.

Satir, V. (1972). *Peoplemaking.* Palo Alto, Calif.: Science and Behavior Books.

Segal, L. (1981). Segal's response. *Underground Railroad, 2* (4), 2–3.

Stanton, M. D., Todd, T. C., Heard, D. B., Kirschner, S., Kleiman, J. I., Mowatt, D. T., Riley, P., Scott, S. M. & Van Deusen, J. M. (1978). Heroin addiction as a family phenomenon: A new conceptual model. *American Journal of Drug and Alcohol Abuse, 5,* 125–50.

Stanton, M. D., Todd, T. C. & Associates (1982). *The family therapy of drug abuse and addiction.* New York: Guilford.

Stanton, M. D. & Todd, T. C. (1982). The therapy model. In M. D. Stanton, T. C. Todd & Associates, *The family therapy of drug abuse and addiction*. New York: Guilford.

Todd, T. C. (1981). Paradoxical prescriptions: Applications of consistent paradox using a strategic team. *Journal of Strategic and Systemic Therapies, 1* (1), 28–44.

Todd, T. C. (1988). Developmental cycles and substance abuse. In C. Falikov (ed.), *Family transitions: Continuity and change over the life cycle*. New York: Guilford.

Todd, T. C. & Selekman, M. D. (1991a). Beyond structural-strategic family therapy: Integrating other brief systemic therapies. In T. C. Todd and M. D. Selekman (eds.), *Family therapy approaches with adolescent substance abusers*. Boston: Allyn & Bacon.

Todd, T. C. & Selekman, M. D. (eds.) (1991b). *Family therapy approaches with adolescent substance abusers*. Boston: Allyn & Bacon.

Watzlawick, P., Beavin, J. & Jackson, D. (1967). *Pragmatics of human communication: A study of interactional patterns, pathologies, and paradoxes*. New York: Norton.

Watzlawick, P., Weakland, J. & Fisch, R. (1974). *Change: Principles of problem formation and problem resolution*. New York: Norton.

Wegscheider, S. (1981). *Another chance: Hope and health for the alcoholic family*. Palo Alto, Calif.: Science and Behavior Books.

3

Psychoanalytic Approach to Addictive Disorders

ALAN M. JAFFE

EARLY ROOTS

Early in the history of psychoanalytic thinking, addictions were considered to represent a regressive expression of instinctual strivings that took the form of habitual pleasure-seeking behavior. The symptoms described as the behavioral pattern of the addicted individual are organized at the unconscious level to replace the threat of instinctual; these are pleasure-pain mechanisms (Freud, 1905, 1960; Abraham, 1926; Fenichel, 1945). This chapter reviews roots and contemporary psychoanalytic models of addiction. The focus is on advances in the discipline of concern to clinicians. It explores the foundations of Freudian thinking, examines components of treatment, and presents a case illustration of an alcoholic and compulsive eater from a psychoanalytic perspective.

Addictive behavior was understood as a fixation at stages of development, such as oral for eating disorders and compulsive drug and alcohol use and phallic for compulsive sexual behavior. The psychotherapeutic work with patients followed the standard procedure for the treatment of the general neurotic population manifesting a compulsive symptom picture. The early work stressed the importance of viewing compulsive symptoms as an important piece of a larger defense system organized to ward off unpleasant affect unsuccessfully managed any other way. Psychoanalysts today continue to accept and build upon these theories regarding addictions as a symptom/defense (Silber, 1974; Vaillant, 1983; Wurmser, 1984).

With the introduction of "self" psychology, there has been a shift from viewing compulsive behavior not as a defense resulting from conflict but rather as a deficient formation of the self, lacking cohesion and unable to provide its own comfort. This early deficit leads to narcissistic disturbance in later life, thus creating a need for an artificial self-soothing agent. This process ultimately develops into a maladaption, which can assume the form of an addiction (Kohut, 1971, 1977; Kernberg, 1975). Both the conflict and deficit approaches offer a correct and compatible understanding of the psychological underpinnings of addiction.

Probably the most valid criticism of early analytic treatment was the inflexibility of early analysts in approaching addictive problems. The reluctance of early analysts to deviate from a classical psychoanalytic posture, which emphasized a totally nondirective environment for the patient, made treatment difficult and often frustrating for both doctor and patient. Psychoanalytic work does not involve directing the individual toward making specific choices in his life, and this holds true across all schools of psychoanalytic thought; however, in current practice, certain therapeutic interventions of a direct nature are made solely for the purpose of preserving the integrity of the treatment. If, for example, an individual is preventing the analytic process, then it is necessary for detoxification before treatment can start (Jaffe, 1983). Other interventions can be employed to set the stage for a successful psychoanalytic treatment, such as inpatient hospitalization and behavior modification.

Both the traditional conflict model and the more recent self-deficit model should be considered in the successful treatment of an addicted individual. Rather than being viewed as incompatible, they should be considered in tandem; early childhood deficits and poor internalization of soothing mechanisms cause the creation of neurotic defenses, which must then be analyzed and properly worked through to achieve a healthy adjustment.

THE WORKING ALLIANCE

A good working alliance is the foundation of any successful psychoanalytic treatment. In the therapeutic setting, the working alliance describes the strength of the relationship between the analyst and the patient. Through this collaborative effort, both can effectively allow the unconscious material to be expressed in their structured therapeutic relationship. Many therapists fail to appreciate the amount of special attention and deliberation involved in creating and maintaining a strong alliance. The working alliance determines the ability of the analyst-patient relationship to tolerate struggle; that is, it describes the level of trust the patient experiences for the therapist. This grows out of several responses on the part of the therapist to respect the subjective reality of the patient. Emphasis is on the subjective because it is essential the patient trust the analyst to see and tolerate the patient's experience of self in the world as he sees it:

From the vantage point of the patient's unconscious neurotic processes and psychological organization, they represent his attempts at maintenance of the status quo. They protect the patient against conscious awareness of unacknowledged and unpleasurable elements within his own psychic life, and they promote and sustain the continuing search for fulfillment of inappropriate drives, fantasies and relationships. (Dewald, 1982, p. 48)

By the time the addicted patient reaches the analyst's office, he has developed a long history with people in the world at large who are incapable of understanding (and therefore untrustworthy and critical of) the patient's defenses (drug use, overeating, purging, or any other compulsion). The analyst is in the unique position of creating an alliance with the patient based on a true appreciation of the patient's defenses as seen in an adaptive context, even though they are wholly inadequate:

Even at times when the patient himself recognizes that his behavior may be in opposition to the vowed wish for psychological maturation and change, the unconscious adaptive and anxiety-reducing functions of behavior may take precedence over the wish for maturation and growth. (Dewald, 1982, p. 48)

Let us consider an example of alliance building in the early treatment of an alcoholic. A husband initially reports that his reason for treatment is that his wife has threatened separation if he does not seek help. His presenting problem is not that he has a drinking problem because at his level of defensive functioning (denial), he does not experience it that way. What he is perceiving is a family that does not understand him and, in particular, a wife who nags him too much about his drinking. No one in his family is able to accept his version of reality or validate his perceptions of what is happening in their home environment because they are experiencing it quite differently.

During the course of history taking, it may be abundantly clear to the analyst that the patient in fact does have a serious drinking or drug problem. Patients commonly minimize and misrepresent the amount of drinking, drug use, and other addictive behaviors during an initial interview (Gedney, 1984). The analyst is appropriately more concerned about first validating the perceptions of the patient as a way of building the alliance in what will lead to longer-term growth. The assumption is this: The analyst-patient relationship will follow the same futile pattern as other relationships in the patient's life if the analyst makes the mistake of attacking the patient's defense structure (like so many others who have been unable to reach him). Before the patient's defenses can tolerate letting the analyst assume a trusted position in his life, that trust must be earned over time. The first way to accomplish this is for the analyst to demonstrate that he is not an agent of the defense-attacking outside world but rather someone whose primary task is to see the world through the eyes of the patient. Threatening the patient's autonomous expression could ultimately lead him into a negative therapeutic reaction (Jaffe, 1981). The result of proper validation is that the patient feels understood and capable of a working therapeutic alliance with a trusted analyst.

ANXIETY AND DEFENSE

Great care is taken in psychoanalytic treatment to be sensitive to the patient's defensive functioning. These ego defenses, although they appear primitive at times, serve an important adaptive purpose: protecting the conscious portion of the psyche from becoming overwhelmed by thoughts and accompanying feelings that are difficult to integrate and threaten effective living. The analyst's responsibility is to be acutely aware of the nature and purpose of the defenses at all times and to work around them until the alliance is sufficiently strong to sustain an interpretation of them. This approach is especially necessary in the treatment of addicted individuals, whose defenses are particularly brittle. To tamper with the defense too quickly will cause the patient to flee from treatment or leave him flooded with anxiety, unable to achieve insight into himself, and all the more eager to resurrect defenses of the past. That is why, in psychoanalytic treatment, the patient determines the content and pace with which treatment proceeds:

The patient determines the subject matter of the analytic hour. This rule is a corollary of that other one, that we must always work with "living reality." What does not interest the patient cannot be forced upon him . . . for who must operate at that point where the affect is actually situated at the moment. (Fenichel, 1941, p. 44)

There must be respect of the patient's resistance to breaking down his defenses and an appreciation that the defenses will not be relaxed before the patient is ready. To increase anxiety is to exacerbate the addictive symptom, as Slochower (1987) demonstrated in her research on overeating. The addicted individual utilizes addiction as an adjunct to his defense structure. His ego defenses along with the addictive behavior provide a strong affect defense against experiencing the signal anxiety and the subsequent thoughts and feelings that lie beneath the repression barrier. Wurmser (1984–85) suggests this defense is largely to ward off superego conflicts in addition to a "return of repressed."

When the addictive behavior is removed, the result is a significant increase in two kinds of anxiety. The first, *withdrawal anxiety,* is unique to the physiologically addicted person who undergoes biochemical changes during withdrawal of a substance. In psychoanalytic thinking this is also considered objective anxiety because it represents a real threat to the individual's survival. The second form of anxiety, *neurotic anxiety,* results from a perceived threat of a breakdown of ego defenses, allowing for repressed ideas and affects to enter into conscious awareness. Although psychiatric nomenclature is often lacking in specificity (Eysenck, Wakefield & Friedman 1983), there are psychometric data to support the linkage of addictive behavior, neuroticism, and accompanying anxiety. For example, the Minnesota Multiphasic Personality Inventory, a frequently researched objective personality inventory, has been used to establish that certain personality types, particularly those with neurotic traits, are frequently associated with addictive symptom patterns (Friedman, Webb & Lewak, 1989).

ANALYZING THE TRANSFERENCE

Children come into the world without expectations on how they will be treated by others. Their phylogenetic structure causes them to engage in certain reflexive responses. They arrive as strangers to a new world without any interactive history. They do not know whether the world is friendly, hostile, fair, rational, arbitrary, reasonable, or cruel. Only through interactions with others do they arrive at a developed set of expectations of self and others. Their interaction with the world and their evolving expectations begin to develop at the moment they arrive on the scene. It is not necessary for any verbal exchange to take place for children to begin to learn about the world.

The following example illustrates how easily expectations are formed. Imagine two girls, Rachel and Leah, born to two sets of parents in the same hospital on the same day. Although constitutionally different, both share a limited interactive history by virtue of their limited experience with the outside world. From the moment they are born, however, their ontogenetic history begins. Let us examine how transference develops as a result of differences in child rearing by looking first at the relationship between Leah and her mother.

Leah's mother is overly concerned that her baby be properly fed and healthy. She believes that her baby does not know instinctually what is best for her and must rely entirely on parental discretion to provide the necessary nourishment. This is reflected in her feeding style, force feeding Leah every two hours whether or not Leah expresses any interest in eating. She keeps the nipple in Leah's mouth until she consumes the amount that the mother predetermined. At times when Leah is either satiated or uncomfortable and wishes to pull her mouth away from the nipple, the mother forcibly pushes the nipple back into place. Even when Leah cries, her mother insists that she continue feeding and forces the nipple back until the child passively submits.

Rachel's mother behaved in quite a different way toward feeding. Rachel's mother fed her on demand. This mother came to the feeding situation with no preconceived ideas about how much her child should eat. Instead, she waited for natural cues that her daughter was hungry (such as rooting and crying) and then provided nourishment. When Rachel fussed during a feeding, her mother withdrew the nipple and attempted to comfort her. If Rachel was no longer eating, her mother would not force her to continue.

Two babies are offered different approaches to feeding, and the beginnings of disparate worldviews immediately develop. Let us imagine that these babies were visitors from another planet sent to spend one month on earth and then called back to report their findings. Granted, their breadth of experience is limited mostly to interaction with the nipple (mother), but this forms the basis of their understanding of the world as they know it. Leah would describe the world as a place where one is expected to accommodate the demands of unsympathetic external forces. It is a world that is experienced as basically hostile because one is immediately placed in an adversarial position with the environment. It is a place where one feels helpless to reduce comfort and is expected to submit passively to an insensitive and all-powerful authority. Leah's experiences are generally characterized as helpless, overwhelming, frustrating, and resigned to insensitivity.

Rachel's report is quite different. She describes the world as a pleasant place where needs are quickly gratified and discomfort is promptly remedied by powerful benevolent forces. She finds it to be exceptionally responsive and eager to accommodate her wishes. This creates in her feelings of effectiveness and competence in a world where people are reliable and basically kind.

These examples illustrate the early development of worldview (the child's expectations of others and general philosophical outlook on the basic nature of humanity). It is well known and appreciated in pyschoanalytic study that these early and persistent encounters with primary caregivers give form to interaction patterns that continue throughout life. These patterns continue even though an individual will come in contact with others (e.g., teachers, relatives, and neighbors). The reason is explained by the principles that govern ego organization and accompanying personality development. Once organized, the ego defines the world in a way that is consistent with its initial impressions of it. It is highly resistant to the integration of information that contradicts its original worldview. The ego continues to assign a perception based on original conclusions drawn about the nature of human interaction. What makes this such a fascinating process to observe is not only the ego's prepotent disposition toward experiencing people in a particular way but the relentless quest to seek out and associate with others who by their actions support this original worldview position. This makes the position airtight and serves to reduce anxiety in the conscious portion of the ego by maintaining predictability.

Transference is the continuation of early expectations, perceptions, and behavioral patterns that an individual brings to every relationship. In psychoanalysis, the transference emerges in the context of the therapeutic relationship and can be analyzed so that the patient can discover the origins and nature of his early conflicts. Because a person's worldview pervades every idea, verbalization, and action, it is impossible to conceal it in any relationship. It is common for people to seek out others who will reinforce their general outlook and the interactive patterns that follow. Early conflicts continue to be expressed in the transference with others who make up the individual's world. This becomes especially noticeable in the life-styles of alcohol and drug addicts, who surround themselves with those who behave similarly.

Transference plays a central role in treatment. It offers an opportunity to engage in a relationship that serves as a type of human laboratory within which the transference is illuminated and analyzed. The patient agrees to become a subject of study in an educational pursuit designed to uncover the underpinnings of the subject's personality development. The transference derives from the core of the individual's psychic structure and is activated in a therapeutic (or any) relationship. Transference is virtually indistinguishable to the patient. Observing one's own transference is analogous to seeing the forest from the trees. It is virtually impossible to achieve awareness of it independently, without benefit of an objective person capable of maintaining an alliance and providing the proper interpretation at the critical time, which aids the person in becoming aware of the transference phenomena:

This new fact which we thus recognize . . . is known by us as *transference*. We mean a transference of feelings on to the person of the doctor, since we do not believe that the situation in the treatment could justify the development of such feelings. We suspect, on the contrary, that the whole readiness for these feelings is derived from elsewhere, that they were already prepared in the patient and, upon the opportunity offered by the analytic treatment, are transferred on to the person of the doctor. (Freud, 1977, p. 442)

The degree to which the patient rejects or resists the analyst's attempt to analyze the transference is termed *transference resistance*.

The first awareness of transference usually occurs as a revelation that one's parents do not represent the paradigm for all adults. For example, it is common for a patient to report, "I never realized that all fathers didn't drink," or "I never thought that any parents took an interest in the details of their children's social life." That type of realization opens up the individual to a greater understanding of the causal relationship that exists between early childhood experiences and addictive patterns formed later in life. Helping a patient to become aware of transference phenomena usually ensures continued motivation, self-wonderment, and confidence in the analytic method. At this point in the treatment, the entire process begins (perhaps for the first time) to make perfect sense to the patient. Until this time, the patient's commitment to treatment may be maintained by blind faith or the immediate comfort that the patient experiences by the soothing presence of the analyst.

SELF: FROM SYMPTOM TO OBJECT

In psychoanalytic treatment, the therapist, once engaged in an active working alliance, can assume the position of an idealized object for the patient; that is, the patient can assign certain defensive powers to the analyst to help soothe the patient in the face of anxiety. Since the threat of anxiety is so great (most addicted individuals believe they cannot live without their symptom of choice), the working alliance must be quite strong, and the analyst must be perceived as someone who begins to approximate strength, reliability, and the defensive power of the patient's addition:

The nature of the object relations of the drug-dependent patient is such that he craves to be unified with an ideal object, but at the same time dreads it. He thus becomes addicted to acting out the drama of fantasy introjection and separation from the drug. There is a corresponding intrapsychic defect; certain essential functions related to nurturance are reserved for the object-representation. The objective of therapy is to permit the patient to extend this conscious self-recognition to all of himself, thereby freeing him from the need of the placebo effect of the drug as a means of gaining access to his alienated parts and functions. (Krystal, 1977, p. 98)

The analyst must engage the patient in a relationship that serves to be uniquely accepting and empathic. Through this encounter, the patient may develop a greater sense of trust in his ability to acquire emotional nourishment from others in exchange for the temporary and ultimately destructive soothing that is derived from an addictive symptom. The natural process of growth and development that occurs when an individual is actively registering, processing, and integrating his world becomes seriously arrested during the addictive process. This process must be set into motion again through the work of the analysis. At first, the patient exhibits little trust in this process since it was originally found to be inadequate and abandoned in favor of an addictive defense. It must be assumed that the patient is psychically overwhelmed during the initial period of abstinence from the addictive symptoms.

The ego functions necessary to accomplish the negotiations of impulses have been effectively operating artificially prior to abstinence from the symptom. Demands on the ego are to mediate, integrate, organize, and defend against impulses. The flooding of anxiety, fears, and feelings of being overwhelmed comes about as a signal that the ego verges on losing equilibrium. Previously the addiction fortified the ego defenses and created an artificial homeostasis; during abstinence, the analyst must provide the external fortification of ego defense to allow the patient to make a transition from symptom to object (person).

At this point in the treatment, the patient resumes an approximation of the early parental relationship that empathically failed him. Without the use of the addictive symptom, the patient experiences the reawakening of childhood's overwhelming emotions, anxiety and vulnerability. It is through the mastery of a manageable frustration and anxiety that the infant and child develop a sense of inner resourcefulness for providing adequate self-soothing and frustration tolerance. Early in life, this is achieved through repetitive contact with parents (particularly the mother) in which actual soothing is provided physically and verbally. The child learns that he possesses the ability to withstand unpleasant sensations by utilizing the parents' methods and strategies (defenses), which eventually become his own. This process is known as *transmuting internalization* (Kohut, 1977). Transmuting internalization (self-soothing) is accomplished only when the child is forced to cope with the manageable frustrations that will inevitably occur. "What are the wholesome self-object processes that build up the healthy self? We see them as occurring in two steps. First, a basic intuneness must exist between the self and its self objects (parents). Second, self object failures of a non-traumatic degree must occur. We refer to the results of such failure of self objects of childhood as 'optimal frustrations' '' (Kohut, 1984, p. 70).

When frustrations are overwhelming for the child and result in a faulty connection between mother and child because of neglect or inconsistent communications (especially during the time of the child's discomfort), several problems occur. First, the child learns that the world is unresponsive and unreliable and cannot be counted upon for soothing.

Second, since the individual recognizes that he has not accomplished the necessary internalization of self-soothing capacity, he continues unconsciously to seek something in his external world that can be taken into himself to satisfy the previously unsuccessful internalization. This is not the case in which one or both parents were addicted during the child's development. In that situation, the child actually introjects the parents' methods (addiction) for managing discomfort. This accounts for why such a high incidence of addiction follows family lines.

Third, the child and subsequent developed adult is limited in his ability to register, analyze, and integrate his world through meaningful contact with others. Instead, the child, and later the adult, compulsively turns to his symptoms of choice. In other words, the individual is limited in his capacity for object relatedness.

Finally, the individual is resistant to giving up an addictive symptom for the promise of personal growth that never before had been realized by way of a dependent relationship (parent-child).

It should be apparent why the recapitulation of the early parent relationship in the context of analysis has its challenges. The analyst must constructively deal with the patient's resistance until the patient can view his world more accurately by working through the unresolved issues in the analytic relationship. The analytic relationship offers the patient an opportunity to repeat an earlier time in his psychological development and correct the maladaptive defensive organization that has produced the addiction. This successful transition from addiction to improved human relatedness with the analyst becomes generalized to the world at large.

MAKING THE UNCONSCIOUS CONSCIOUS

In order to understand analytic work, it is necessary to appreciate the role that the unconscious plays in maintaining the maladaption of the addictive process. The defenses fortified by the addictive behavior exist in order to ward off anxiety, which is the signal that unpleasant ideas and accompanying affect are pushing their way into consciousness. This push upward is motivated by the psyche to free up countercathected energy required to allow the repressed material to continue to reside in the unconscious domain. This energy used to hold on to the repressed material at the unconscious level is not available to the psyche for application in other more constructive activities, such as working, creating, and loving. As long as these threatening ideas reside at the unconscious level, they drain energy, seek symbolic expression, and control the individual. The work of the analysis is to help the patient loosen up and free the unconscious material into consciousness so that he can exert greater control over his life.

Psychotherapists observe how the addict's defense of denial prevents the individual from becoming aware of disturbing realities concerning the nature of his self-destructive behavior and other painful realities that predate the onset of the addiction. Although the realities of this patient's life may be more than apparent to an objective observer, the patient is unable to see it. That which the patient cannot integrate into his conscious awareness is termed *unconscious*. The inexperienced or overly zealous therapist is likely early in treatment to insist the patient see what is so obvious to the therapist (and the patient's family). This is often attempted through the use of confrontation. Unfortunately, this method serves to mobilize the defenses against the therapist and the unconscious material that he is seeking to illuminate. The defenses will break down and allow the protected unconscious material to emerge only as the patient can tolerate integrating these ideas with a manageable amount of anxiety. The analyst's job is to monitor and, to the extent that he can, modulate an improvement in the patient's general outlook on life, because for the first time he can trust the process of growth itself. This is what is often referred to as a spiritual awakening in twelve-step programs. The patient's existence is directed away from simply maintaining a habitual pattern of behavior to avoid the ensuing anxiety, instead learning to confront and understand the historical basis for anxiety, thereby freeing himself from the chains of his past.

The analyst always attempts to be aware of the patient's level of anxiety. Too much anxiety causes the patient's defenses to form an impasse, or the patient discontinues treatment. When there exists too little tension or anxiety, especially early in treatment, the patient can lose motivation for continuing in therapy.

INTERPRETATION

Interpretation involves helping the patient to understand his current behavior as a product of past and current relationships and situations. It is the tool that the analyst uses to help loosen unconscious material to make it available to the patient's conscious mind. The reason it is termed "interpretation" is that the unconscious thought process is inaccessible unless there is an effective ambassador serving as translator between the unconscious and the conscious domains. To be a successful translator, the analyst must be familiar with the particular conscious thought process of the individual and be especially knowledgeable of the unique ways in which the individual conceptualizes himself and the world. It is a process analogous to an ambassador's serving as liaison between two countries that differ in philosophical and cultural traditions and practices. Unless the ambassador is well acquainted with the customs of a foreign country, it is too easy for him accidentally to commit a social faux pas or fail to communicate an important message.

Analysts in training commonly make interpretations that are either too early or too deep based on a limited understanding of the patient's concept of self (Fenichel, 1941). These interpretations are not only rejected out of hand but create a rift between analyst and patient that may prove to be insurmountable and impossible to repair. It is not unusual to hear psychotherapists who practice outside the analytic schools of thought to complain that psychoanalysis is a modality of treatment that takes too long to achieve its goals. But responsible and conscientious psychoanalysts do not risk the patient's progress by making assumptions about his internal life before understanding how the patient views his world and himself in it.

Most effective interpretations are offered to the patient in a spirit of honest inquiry, stressing the collaborative effort between patient and analyst to explore and uncover hidden truths that lie below the surface of the patient's repression barrier. Therefore, the patient is always offered the opportunity to express his separateness by rejecting an interpretation (Jaffe, 1981). The seasoned analyst will make the analytic setting a comfortable place for the patient to take issue with any interpretation if the patient is inclined to do so. In keeping with this position, it is desirable that interpretations be made tentatively or in the form of a question—for example, "Could it be that . . . ," "Perhaps . . . ," or "I wonder if . . . ." These qualifiers permit the patient to respond at his level of comfort with the timing and depth of the interpretation. It is important that the analyst assess the patient's tolerance to accept a particular form of an interpretation. Selecting the correct form of an interpretation should not be underestimated; the key to a successful analysis usually lies in the analyst's ability to be exquisitely sensitive to the limits of the patient's tolerance for interpretive intervention at any time. "When one makes an impact, they do so not because we are so omniscient or omnipotent, but most likely because we have had the good sense to read the patient's signals correctly and tell him what he is ready to hear" (Basch, 1980, p. 145). If the interpretations are accurate, they provide the substance from which the patient is able to achieve independent insight into the forgotten and hidden secrets of his own being by someone who has been listening carefully.

The pitfalls that are unique to the addicted patient tend to be associated with the anxiety level the patient is experiencing in treatment. An accurate interpretation is experienced not only as an "aha" event for the patient but is also taken as empathic soothing by the analyst of the patient. When the anxiety level is not maintained at a manageable level, either because there is an insufficient amount of soothing or because of other internal facts, the individual is more likely to resort to his earlier defense against the anxiety, the addiction. With nonaddicted patients, this concern is not as immediately threatening to the well-being of the patient and the treatment. In all cases, it is necessary to be in tune with the patient's anxiety level at all times before attempting an interpretation.

CASE STUDY

This brief case study concerns an alcoholic and compulsive eater from a psychoanalytic perspective.

The Beginning of Treatment

Mr. A. made an appointment for an evaluation because his drinking, eating, and depression had increased over the previous two years. Just prior to coming in, he could not find the motivation to go to work and sat drinking and over-eating in his house for almost a week. At the suggestion of his wife, he made an appointment to see if something could be done to help him out of his condition. He had no prior history of treatment.

During the initial appointment, Mr. A. reported being unable to control his eating and drinking; he felt desperate and stated that if he were permitted to return home, he would continue to drink and become more depressed. Hospitalization was offered to help him detoxify from the alcohol and provide a safe holding environment. He readily accepted and was taken to the hospital, where he was evaluated and admitted to an open substance abuse unit for three weeks. Mr. A. began seeing me for individual psychoanalytic psychotherapy twice weekly while in the hospital and then three times per week after discharge.

During the initial sessions of psychoanalysis, Mr. A. expressed an urge to resume drinking and asked for help in abstaining. At first, I asked if he would be willing to attend Alcoholics Anonymous (AA) meetings, but he flatly refused, saying that he would consider virtually all measures except AA. When inquiry was made as to why he refused to attend AA, he said he was unaware of any specific reason, only that he did not like "those kind of people," whom he described as being "religious fanatics who are critical and judgmental," although it appeared to the staff that his contact with them was positive on the inpatient unit. It appeared to me that this perception involving religious fanaticism was transference laden and defensive, so I avoided confronting it at that time.

Patient History

Mr. A. was born in Canada in 1930. His father, a minister by profession, was 38 years old at the time of his birth; his mother, a housewife, was 26. The family moved to southern California two years after his birth. An only child, Mr. A. grew up in a semirural area of California and attended public schools.

The patient's father, who died when Mr. A. was 23 years old, was described as a strict disciplinarian. He was remembered as being "moralistic and critical" and although very concerned about punishing Mr. A. for misbehaving, rarely, if ever, physically controlled him. Instead, he would discuss with his son the sinful nature of his son's behavior. Consequently, the patient developed a strong sense of morality and accompanying guilt. Active as the community church leader, his father spent a great deal of time with other people and away from the house. Mr. A. was taught to be the man of the house in his father's absence, and it was stressed that he (like his father) must be an example to the community.

The mother, who died when the patient was 34 years old, was described as being emotionally volatile and unpredictable. Mr. A. recalled being unable to know from one hour to the next how his mother was feeling and thus how she would behave. Mr. A. recalled that his parents argued constantly as he grew up. In particular, his father frequently complained about his wife's appearance and the general upkeep of the house. Mr. A. vividly remembered the mother's screaming at the top of her voice in response to his father's criticisms.

Mr. A.'s first memory dates back to when he was 8 years old. In school, a liquid wax candy broke in his pocket, but before asking for an explanation, his teacher publicly accused him of having urinated in his pants. He recalls feeling humiliated, which was followed by ridicule from his classmates.

Mr. A. was quite tall and large (obese) for his age but experienced a great dilemma when physically confronted by peers. Although fighting was commonplace in grade school, he was always afraid that he would be punished by his father or that because of his great size he would seriously injure his challenger. Denying ever provoking a physical fight, he remembers almost always walking away from them. However, one day when he was 10 years old, a smaller boy cajoled him into fighting back. The boy suffered a broken jaw and had to be taken to the hospital. When Mr. A. was taken home he was severely punished with a belt by his father. He does not ever remember fighting again after that episode.

Mr. A. always excelled academically. He was an A student and described himself as always well behaved. Throughout elementary school, he never had more than one friend at a time and did not participate in any team sports. At the age of 14, his father caught him smoking a cigarette behind the house. Mr. A. remembers that at first his father began to lecture him but began to sob uncontrollably and could not finish talking. Mr. A. continued to smoke cigarettes thereafter but felt guilty for years.

After attending college for a short time, his only friend joined the army to go to Korea, and he followed. After basic training, he requested placement in a technical job, which served to isolate him significantly. It was during the time Mr. A. was in the army that he began to binge drink. Always responsible, his drinking took place during his time off, and it was often necessary for someone to bail him out of jail on the weekend.

When he returned home, he met a woman 18 years old and married her within a month. This woman was part Indian, and Mr. A's father strongly objected to the marriage. It lasted for less than a year, with his wife's running off with another man. Two years later, his father died, and shortly after Mr. A. left California for a job in Chicago, against his mother's wishes and requests.

After living in Chicago for a few years, he met and married his second wife, in a marriage that lasted seven years. The separation occurred for unknown or vague reasons, according to Mr. A., except that they began "drifting apart." At the end of the marriage, they had a son, who is now 23 years old. Eight years later, Mr. A. was married again to his current wife, twelve years his senior.

Dynamic Formulation

Impulsivity was always a problem for Mr. A., and he continued to be concerned that he would "lose control of his anger and hit someone." This especially created concern for him when he was frustrated, criticized, or humiliated by another person. To deal with the threatening impulses to express his aggression in destructive ways, he drank alcohol, ate compulsively, and utilized the defense of intellectualization. In this way, he was able to intellectually minimize or rationalize conflictual situations to avoid having to experience his aggressive and rageful impulses, wishes, and accompanying fears.

Intellectually defensive in his approach to people and problems, Mr. A. was overly controlled and lacking spontaneity. His intonation was often void of affect, his emotional experience of the world virtually unavailable to him. He attempted to maintain distance from intimacy but was left feeling alienated and socially isolated. It was difficult for him to get close to another person, including me.

Mr. A. grew up in a family that provided a distorted and impoverished view of reality. His father was critical, moralistic, and verbally punitive. As a result, he incorporated a strict and overbearing superego, which prohibited the expression of aggressive impulses because to do so was considered primitive and subsequently was punished. AA was experienced early on as a paternal transference object easily associated with his father's church in Mr. A.'s childhood. In the transference, AA was perceived as possessing all of the negative attributes of his father. Eventually this was interpreted, and Mr. A. was able to understand it. However, this is a case that clearly demonstrates that to have insisted Mr. A. attend AA would have been contraindicated and would have destroyed the therapeutic relationship. All treatment modalities, including AA, must be evaluated on an individual basis and assigned relative value according to dynamic issues at hand. Anxiety associated with the expression of impulses was compounded when, as the result of his anger, Mr. A. sent a fellow class-mate to the hospital. From early on, he repressed any aggressive wish, impulse, or fantasy. In order to manage these impulses, he developed a keen intellect that helped him to circumvent his overwhelming emotional experience. This defensive strategy did not sufficiently inhibit the impulses' expression into his consciousness because it appeared as signal anxiety. Finally, he attempted to eliminate the anxiety by using alcohol.

The patient's identification was with his father, but he experienced intense feelings and ambivalence toward him. On the one hand, the father was seen as strong, worthy of respect, and emotionally stable (at least more than the mother); on the other hand, he was critical, arbitrary, and punitive. Unable to resolve the ambivalence, the patient felt guilty and afraid of his own strength and afraid that the expression of his own impulses would be followed by moral condem-nation and disastrous consequences. His admiration of his father was mixed with rage for having been so frequently criticized by him. This led to Mr. A.'s attempt to avoid awareness of his own human shortcomings and rationalize away mistakes that he made.

Early in the treatment Mr. A. demonstrated difficulty forming a working alliance because of all the negative paternal transference aroused by the therapy situation. He was unable to tolerate even the most shallow interpretation, taking it to be criticism. In general, he has had difficulty accepting caring from others, and he prefers to be alone. Caring relationships ultimately come to be perceived as critical and hurtful, and so to maintain distance, he drank. He ate exces-sively to make himself less attractive to others.

Despite the difficulty he experienced with his father, Mr. A. did rely on this parent to provide a fair amount of consistency and stability. His mother was apparently disturbed in this area. She was unable to provide basic mothering because she was emotionally unstable, labile, and generally erratic in her treat-ment of her son. Mr. A. remembered when he was a boy that his mother cried uncontrolled for long periods of time without stopping while intermittently screaming and cursing at him. He recalled being frightened and confused dur-ing these periods. He became frightened and overwhelmed by intense feelings in general. Although he could not recall the source of this information, Mr. A. reported hearing that his mother was "terrified" of giving birth. It can be reasonably assumed that the responsibility of taking care of an infant was over-whelming for his mother and that she was unable to soothe him properly. In the absence of necessary nuturance and soothing from his mother early in his life, the patient never achieved the transmuting internalization necessary for adequate self-soothing.

Mr. A. remained deeply frustrated by ungratified dependency needs. In his relationships with women, he has assumed a passive-aggressive position. He appears very needy and yet unable to accept caring from them (reenacting his relationship with his mother). During treatment, it was revealed that his maternal transference caused him to view women as objects who take from him, and he denied that they have anything to offer him except instability.

As an only child, Mr. A. remembered feeling isolated during much of his childhood. Although he did have one friend most of the time, he always felt alienated from the social mainstream in school. He felt envious of children who were more comfortably involved but compensated by participating more actively in solitary kinds of sports. This mode of relating to others persisted over time. Before treatment, he did not identify with the group (his current contemporaries) and referred to himself as an outsider. In therapy, he became aware of how this position served to maintain distance so as not to risk getting closer to the old disappointments and rage so typical of his childhood. He joined two social organizations and made new friends.

Mr. A.'s size also affected the way in which he perceived himself. Much larger than all of his classmates, he recalled being treated with ridicule by his peers and expected to behave more like an adult to the point that friends of the family commented how being in his presence was like being with an adult. He assumed the behavior of a much older person but secretly resented being inhibited from expressing himself as a child. This strengthened his intellectualized defense against his true feelings, offering no opportunity to understand and integrate more primitive impulses typical of his true age.

Earlier in the treatment Mr. A. would perceive much of what I had to say as being disapproving, even though it was neutral. His apparent perception (transference) of me changed quite frequently during the first year from being critical to kind, demanding to uncaring, from wanting to control me and cause me to feel guilty and ashamed to being totally disinterested in me. It took almost two years before he was able to acknowledge that he was in a meaningful therapeutic relationship and was able to recognize that many of his perceptions of me were the result of transference derived from earlier experiences in his life. At the end of four years he was still sober, at the fiftieth percentile for weight, in his own business, more aware of the emotional dimension of his existence, and significantly less conflicted in life. It was at that time that we mutually agreed to terminate treatment.

REFERENCES

Abraham, K. (1926). The psychological relation between sexuality and alcoholism. *International Journal of Psychoanalysis, 7,* 2.

Basch, M. (1980). *Doing psychotherapy.* New York: Basic Books.

Dewald, P. (1982). Psychoanalytic perspectives on resistance. In P. L Wachtel (ed.), *Resistance* (pp. 45–69), New York: Plenum Press.

Eysenck, H. J., Wakefield, J. A. & Friedman, A. F. (1983). Diagnosis and clinical assessment: The DSM III. *Annual Review of Psychology, 34,* 167–93.

Fenichel, O. (1941). *Problems of psychoanalytic technique.* New York: Psychoanalytic Quarterly.

Fenichel, O. (1945). *The psychoanalytic theory of the neuroses.* New York: Norton.

Friedman, A. F., Webb, J. T. & Lewak, R. (1989). *Psychological assessment with the MMPI.* Hillsdale, N.J.: Lawrence Erlbaum Associates.

Freud, S. (1905). Three essays on the theory of sexuality. *Standard edition,* (vol. 7). London: Hogarth Press, 1953.

Freud, S. (1960). *The ego and the id.* New York: W. W. Norton.

Freud, S. (1977). *Introductory lectures on psychoanalysis.* New York: W. W. Norton.

Gedney, M. (1984). The alcoholic in dynamic psychotherapy. *Issues in Ego Psychology, 7,* 11–17.

Ghaffari, K. (1987). Psychoanalytic theories on drug dependence: A critical review. *Psychoanalytic Psychotherapy, 3,* 39–51.

Jaffe, A. (1981). The negative therapeutic reaction. *Psychotherapy: Theory, Research and Practice, 18,* 313–19.

Jaffe, A. (1983). Alcoholism psychotherapy: The problem of the procrustean bed. *International Journal of Eclectic Psychotherapy, 2,* 49–58.

Kernberg, O. F. (1975). *Borderline conditions and pathological narcissism.* New York: Jason Aronson.

Kohut, H. (1971). *The analysis of the self.* New York: International Universities Press.

Kohut, H. (1977). *The restoration of the self.* New York: International Universities Press.

Kohut, H. (1984). *How does analysis cure?* Chicago: University of Chicago Press.

Krystal, H. (1977). Self and object representation in alcoholics and other drug dependence: Implications for therapy. In *NIDA Research Monograph Series: Psychodynamics of Drug Dependence, 12,* 89–99.

Silber, A. (1974). Rationale for the technique of psychotherapy with alcoholics. *International Journal of Psychoanalytic Psychotherapy, 3,* 28–47.

Slochower, J. (1987). The psychodynamics of obesity: A review. *Psychoanalytic Psychology, 4,* 145–61.

Vaillant, G. (1983). *The natural history of alcoholism: causes, patterns and paths to recovery.* Cambridge: Harvard University Press.

Wurmser, L. (1984–85). The role of superego conflicts in substance abuse and their treatment. *International Journal of Psychoanalytic Psychotherapy, 10,* 227–58.

Wurmser, L. (1984). More respect for the neurotic process: Comments on the problem of narcissism in severe pathology, especially the addictions. *Journal of Substance Abuse Treatment, 1,* 37–45.

Part II

Assessment of Addictive Disorders

4

Assessment of Substance Abuse: An Integrated Approach

MARGO M. JACQUOT

As the field of chemical dependency treatment has evolved, assessment of these disorders has evolved as well. Moral and social attitudes in the 1980s brought treatment of alcohol- and drug-related disorders to the forefront. These new attitudes altered how issues of substance abuse were perceived by professionals and laypeople alike. Addictions became known as primary disorders in themselves rather than simply symptoms of some deeper psychopathology. Addiction was defined as primary, chronic progressive disease that would prove fatal if left untreated.

Assessment at first collected data on tolerance levels, progression, losses related to consumption of substances, changes in attitude, and behavior and performance in all areas of existence. Essentially the asssessor examined the extent to which substance abuse impaired the person's ability to function emotionally, socially, in a legally responsible manner, physically, financially, spiritually, and as a functional participant within the context of a family and community. The information obtained was relatively clear-cut and focused on drinking and drug use only, with the goal of helping people to develop a twelve-step foundation that would aid them in remaining clean and sober. Exploration of intrapsychic conflict, family of origin issues, and other issues was generally discouraged. The belief was that drug addicts and alcoholics needed to attend to first things first. The assumption was that if a person became and remained chemical free, attended self-help meetings, and worked the twelve steps of Alcoholics Anonymous (AA) to the best of his or her ability, intrapsychic conflict, family of origin issues, depression, and other life difficulties would eventually dissipate.

Assessment and treatment steps became more complex, however, and new problems face this once-simple methodology. This chapter considers factors making it complex and that intefere with accurate assessment.

THEORETICAL MODELS AND BELIEF SYSTEMS

If a clinician's personal belief system views substance abuse and dependence as self-medicating behaviors connected to underlying symptomatology, assessment and treatment will bear out that bias. This line of thinking remains quite popular today and is more commonly known as the medical model. It assumes that patients present symptoms of an underlying physical or psychological disorder. If the cause of the problem is treated and cured, the symptoms will disappear.

Clinicians believing that substance abuse and addiction are the result of learned behavior acquired by watching parents or other models abuse substances will listen with an ear sensitive to those issues. Social learning theory, and specifically the concept of modeling or vicarious learning, helps to describe these phenomena. It is assumed that eventually some people intraject these models and incorporate these behaviors into their own behavioral patterns. In such cases, people will themselves abuse drugs and alcohol.

Other clinicians subscribe to a very different model for viewing substance abuse disorders. The disease concept of alcoholism, a common yet controversial model, assumes a very different set of criteria for the etiology of addiction. The disease concept developed following the acceptance of alcoholism as a disease by the American Medical Association in the 1950s. A disease must meet specific criteria before being labeled as such. These include evidence of cause, signs and symptoms, course, outcome, and treatment.

While many clinicians may agree with the application of the other criteria, the issue of cause is at the core of most controversy. Cause has remained difficult to define, although several theories attempt to explain it. Twin studies, for example, exploring tetrahydroisoquinolyn (THIQ), and endorphin and enkephalin studies have been quite prevalent in theories explaining cause. Also recent research indicates that a recessive gene carried a predisposition to addiction. Clearly some phylogenetic component plays a role.

Signs of biologically based disturbances that generally emerge in advanced stages of the disease are commonplace. Alcoholics may experience cirrhosis of the liver, pancreatitis, rhinophyma (excessive growth of the subcutaneous tissue of the nose), and ataxia, to name a few. Symptoms, on the other hand, tend to be universal for all alcoholics and drug addicts and can be broken down into early, middle, and late stages of the disease. Many variations of what was originally described as a Jellinek Chart contain symptom clusters outlined according to Jellinek's research. Symptoms are progressive, downhill, and principally irreversible as long as the person continues drinking. Cessation of alcohol and temporary sobriety may arrest the progression but only until the person resumes drinking. At that point, they pick up where they left off. Untreated stages of alcoholism lead to death (due to overdose or automobile or household accidents), insanity, or institutionalization (jail, psychiatric hospitalization, or medical hospitalization).

The problem with disease-oriented providers is they assess with an ear sensitive only to organic pathology. They tend not to examine issues of intrapsychic distress, family of origin issues, chemically based depressions, and external contingencies—that is, the effects of the environment, developmental factors, or learning. While the disease treatment concept holds promise for many people, the reasons for its efficacy remain ambiguous. Research indicates that the statistics for recovery are low, and factors identified for recovery are inconsistent. Too many people relapse to drug and alcohol use patterns, and for reasons undetected by the disease model.

Concerns regarding declining recovery rates resulted in another shift within the field of addictions assessment. Many treatment centers have looked objectively at available models and discovered that it is improbable that a single theory will apply to all patient populations. People are complex, and the reasons behind the behavior tend to be equally varied and complex. Consequently, treatment centers now integrate issues of psychopathology and substance abuse, forming dual diagnosis treatment units.

Dual diagnosis means that a person is suffering from concurrent psychiatric and substance abuse disorders. While some view the psychopathology as primary and substance abuse as secondary, the two are equally important for assessment, treatment, and recovery. Alcoholic illness cannot be divided into parts. Unlike many organic pathologies, behavior is not reducible into small, isolated units and analyzed for treatment. Sequences and patterns of behavior lack this molecular advantage because they are ongoing, transactional, and part of an integrated system. Seclusion of one part of alcoholic illness, medical or behavioral, loses precious information on etiology and produces misleading diagnoses.

The model for alcohol assessment presented here subscribes to the dual diagnosis approach that substance abusers concurrently suffer from psychopathology.

THE ASSESSMENT PROPER

A thorough, accurate assessment requires knowledge of both psychopathology and substance use disorders. Assessment is an ongoing process that begins with the initial contact with the client and continues throughout the course of treatment. Two interviews are scheduled to acquire necessary data for treatment planning. Minimally, the clinician needs to meet with the client and significant others separately. If time allows, meeting with each significant person in the client's life is suggested. However, as agency or hospital funding diminishes, so do the luxuries that time provides. Consequently, we will assume that two sessions are adequate for data collection.

The following categories of questions are required for a thorough assessment:

Interview with Client

1. Client's perception of the problem.
2. Client's perception of family and friends' perception of the problem.
3. Client's perception of how he sees the world now.
4. Client's perception of how he saw the world as a child, adolescent, and/or adult.
5. Client's perception of significant life events.
6. A chronology of drug and alcohol use beginning with initial exposure and ending with last exposure.
7. Client's perceptions of changes in functioning and consequences of drug and alcohol use.
8. Client's perception of the benefits of continued and discontinued use of substances.

Interview with Significant Other

1. Significant other's perception of the problem.
2. Significant other's perception of the client's perception of the problem.
3. Significant other's perception of how he sees the world and the client's world now.
4. Significant other's perception of how he saw the world and the client's world as a child, adolescent, or adult.
5. Significant other's perception of significant life events in the life of the client.
6. A chronology of client's abuse of substances (as the significant other knows it).
7. Significant other's perception of changes in the client's functioning or consequences of drug and alcohol use, including changes in the relationship between the client and significant others.
8. Significant other's perceptions of benefits of continued or discontinued substance abuse for self and user.

One traditional facilitator for information collection is using clinical tools. These diagnostic instruments are based on standardized norms to compare patient scores in clustered groups such as percentile ranks and character disorders. Advantages of testing are numerous and largely expedite decisions regarding basic psychopathology or parameters of drug use behavior. However, the disadvantages of testing are equally numerous. Validity and reliability issues aside, standardized questionnaires or surveys do not measure complex interactional factors of addiction. Drug-taking data are better left to formal interviews where the assessor can probe addiction factors relative to the client's unique circumstances and background.

Clinical interviewing is not entirely invincible either. Therapist morals, values, and therapeutic orientation prejudice client information and may weaken the veracity of the facts presented. Even recorded answers cannot completely free confounding variables. Efforts to reduce bias by having two or more interviewers and agreeing beforehand on definitions of pathology are powerful precautions and easy to implement. Another alternative is designing a list of uniform questions asked by all therapists of their patients from the category of questions already listed: perceptions of the problem; perceptions of significant others' perception of the problem; perceptions of how patients see their world right now; perceptions of how patients saw their world as a child, adolescent, and adult; patients' perceptions of significant life events; chronology of drug and alcohol use; perception of changes in functioning; and perception of benefits from continued or discontinued use.

Perceptions of the Problem

The purpose of this section is to examine whether the client believes he or she has a problem with substance abuse. Frequently, people seek help when they are faced with potentially losing something if they continue using substances. The general mind-set is not, "How can you help me stop using drugs and alcohol?" but rather, "How can you teach me not to get in trouble with my substance abuse?" For many clients, substance abuse has proved to be adaptive behavior that serves a powerful purpose in their lives—more powerful than even they are aware.

Sample questions include the following:

Who or what caused you to come see me now?

Whose decision was it for you to come today?

How do you think your use of substances played in to this decision?

How would you describe the difference between a social drinker, drug user, a person with a drug or alcohol problem, and an alcoholic or drug addict?

Based on these categories, where do you see yourself, and why?

The assessment process is an opportune time to begin educating the client regarding substance abuse. Clients may surround themselves with friends or family members who use drugs and alcohol and whose lives are as bad as or worse than their own. Consequently, the client's perception of the world becomes skewed, and he begins to believe "everyone" uses as much as he does.

Clients need to be taught the differences separating social users, problem users, and severe addiction:

Social user: Uses substance infrequently, knows limits, stops at those limits, and almost always follows this predictable pattern of drug monitoring.

Problem user: Drinking and drug use have caused problems in the user's life.

Addicted user: Drinking and drug use continue despite physical and psychological consequences. Once consumption starts, the person cannot or does not want to stop. A secondary consequence is awareness of the addiction among caring, significant others.

Clearly this is an extremely simplistic model; however, it can be quite effective in planting the seed that not everyone sees their drug and alcohol use as clients do.

Perceptions of Significant Others' Perceptions of the Problem

Questions regarding perceptions of others aid in identifying several factors. They facilitate uncovering who is important in this person's life, who has enabled and opposed the behavior; who may facilitate and hinder the recovery process, and what is the structure of these relationships. In addition, this information is useful in constructing the assessment of significant others.

Sample questions include the following:

Who is the most important person in the world to you, and why?

Who else is important, and why?

Who do you like the least right now, and why?

Who in your life knows you use drugs or drink? How do they feel about your use?

Who have you been able to keep it a secret from? How and why?

If [most important person] were here right now, what would he [she] say about you and your drug use?

How would other people in your life describe you and your drug use?

Perception of How Clients See Their World Right Now

Questions within this category elicit the client's perception of how well or how poorly he believes he is currently doing in life, and why. Client answers generally are sparse and favor more control over life situations than actually exists. Refusal to admit problems happens for two reasons. First, disclosure of problems implies the necessity for change, which can be difficult even when it is positive. Most drug and alcohol users do not view change as positive, particularly if that change includes sacrificing substances. Second, clients have an inaccurate perception of problems. Problems arise, by definition, when substance abuse interferes with the person's daily life—whether realized by the user himself or by others alerting him to it. Users doubting this interference may ignore observations by trusted people. They mistakenly consider that their real problem is tolerating the faulty and annoying accusations of being chemically dependent.

Sample questions to ask regarding the client's status include these:

If you had to describe the quality of your life in three words, what would they be?

What is going well right now, and why?

What is not going well, and why?

What do you enjoy doing, and why?

If you could do anything with the rest of your day, what would that be?

Perception of How Clients Saw Their World as a Child, Adolescent, and Adult

It is important to take a life history utilizing a developmental, systemic model. As time allows, one needs to explore briefly how the client feels about his life as a whole. Questions within this section highlight where intrapsychic distress may have occurred and identify any history of familial substance use and abuse. In addition, answers provide information targeting when behavioral deterioration began.

Sample questions include the following:

In Childhood

What was it like growing up in your house?

Where and with whom did you live?

If you lived with your mother, what was your relationship like with her?

If you had a stepmother, what was your relationship like with her?

If you had a father, what was your relationship like with him?

If you had a stepfather, what was your relationship like with him?

If you had brothers and/or sisters, what were your relationships like with them?

If you had friends, what were they like?

What were other people like who lived in your house or neighborhood?

If you had to choose three words to describe your childhood, what would they be?

In Adolescence

What is/was it like being an adolescent?

What did/do you like the most/least?

How do you think your parents feel/felt about your getting older and more independent?

What are/were your relationships like with your parents?

Do/did you date? How is/was it?

What changed from the time you were a child?

What three words describe your adolescence?

In Adulthood

What is it like being an adult?

What do you like most/least about being an adult?

Who is responsible for your bills, laundry, cleaning, and so forth?

What are your relationships like with people now?

Have your relationships changed in any way over the past few years? If so, why?

If you had to use three words to describe your adulthood, what would they be?

Perception of Significant Life Events

Determining whether substance abuse is a reactive process in the client's life can be facilitated by a series of questions and by gathering information regarding the client's repertoire of coping skills and level of affective connection to self and others. In addition, this line of questioning will provide necessary information for connecting substance use and abuse with real life consequences.

Sample questions include the following:

What has happened in your life that has been difficult and painful for you? If clients are unable to generate lists on their own, examples may include death or illness of a family member; divorce (parents, grandparents, self); loss (jobs); a move from a home or neighborhood that was unwanted; breakup from friend, boyfriend, or girlfriend; accidents; injuries; and so forth.

How did you feel when these events occurred, and what did you do with those feelings?

How did other people in your life deal with these events?

How do you believe these events affected your life (ability to feel, trust, hope, etc.)?

Who supported, comforted, and helped you through the difficult times?

How did they do so?

Are there any leftover resentments?

Describe the happiest, most fulfilling event of your life and what you did to celebrate.

Describe the most painful event in your life and what you did to cope with the pain.

Chronology of Drug and Alcohol Use

Information describing the chronology of substance abuse is crucial to assessment; it is also the most difficult information to obtain. Abusers tend to be less than truthful regarding the onset and frequency of use (if they admit use at all). Guarded answers accompany defenses or rationalizations on why their episodic drug use is normal and that their physical drug tolerance is minimal. Underestimating tolerance effects partly is due to clients' normalizing their problem. Clients also underestimate tolerance because, after suffering through withdrawal repeated times, withdrawal symptoms no longer traumatize them. In their opinion, withdrawal is manageable, whereas for nonrepeated users, a single withdrawal imprints horribly negative memories.

Given that most repeated users are tolerant to withdrawal symptoms, therapists must find a way to sharpen a client's recollection. Asking questions two or three times in different ways may be helpful, as is being patient. Another option is to use metaphors for clarification. One metaphor I use follows:

Have you ever tried to put together a jigsaw puzzle? Well what happens if you are missing pieces? Most people get down on the floor and search, or they look under the box, and so on. Do you think it takes more time to assemble a puzzle if you have all the pieces or if you are missing a few? [Unless they are not listening, they cannot help but follow the logic.] That's right; it is quicker if you have all of the pieces. What we are doing today is attempting to put together the pieces of the puzzle of your life. Then we can quickly help things in your life begin to change for the better so you may not have to lose _____. If you do not give me all of the pieces, or in this case the entire story, it will take much longer to get things back in order. The choice is yours.

A statement such as this is firm yet not punitive. It reaffirms that the clinician is on their side and that, while clients may not be ready to change, disclosure is the first step to limiting further losses.

Once disclosure occurs, directing the client to recall major pieces of history can be cumbersome. Let the following categories guide the interview from general to specific clinical facts:

History and pattern of drug/alcohol use

Signs and symptoms

History and pattern of drug/alcohol use and that of significant others

Psychiatric history

Treatment history

Legal history

Spiritual history

Medical history

Financial history

Sexual history

Assessment of support network

Many of these categories are required by accrediting bodies and will provide a thorough assessment for treatment planning.

History and Pattern of Drug/Alcohol Use

When describing patterns of alcohol and drug use, clients tend to emphasize what they have not done rather than what they have done. Opening with a statement such as the following may be helpful: "Often when I ask people about their drug use, they are inclined to talk about what they have not done rather than what they have done. We will be able to complete the assessment much more quickly if we stick to what you have done.'' A just-the-facts approach facilitates the process as well.

The goal of these questions is to elicit information relative to amount and frequency of drug and alcohol use. Open each category of questions with, "Have you *ever* used certain drugs?" A worksheet, such as shown in Exhibit 4.1, is helpful for recording answers.

Signs and Symptoms

While several taxonomies indicate signs and symptoms of abuse, for the purpose of this section the terms *early, middle,* and *late* stages will be used to indicate progression.

The hallmark of the *early stage* is that the user has discovered that drugs or alcohol provide some form of relief—from stress, self-consciousness, day-to-day worries, or pain. Escape from miseries using mind- or behavior-altering substances at first produces innocent patterns of addiction. Patterns that repeat, worsen in terms of higher drug intake and deterioration of self-control, and cause irreparable social damage evolve through the following signs and symptoms:

Blackouts: Substance-induced memory lapses lasting moments to hours. The person functions without remembering.

Prestress drinking/using: Using substances to bypass or alleviate stress.

Using to achieve a desired effect: Substances that cause a high, sedated, or altered elevation in mood.

Development of tolerance: The user requires more of a substance to achieve the same effect.

Sneaking and/or hiding drinks or drugs: The deliberate deception of drug using and drinking habits to avoid or escape unwanted reactions from significant others.

Preoccupation with use: Spending more and more time thinking about and planning drinking and drugging.

Loss of interest in previously satisfying activities: Withdrawal from or apathy toward daily routines, personal gratifiers, or efforts to generate new interests.

Taking more and more chances and risks: Health risk taking and social audacity seem out of control. A previously passive person releases inhibitions in language or physical actions. Feelings of invincibility increase as success at risk taking expands into more dangerous risks.

Beginning to ignore consequences: Loss of sensitivity, remorse, and fear that accompany increased potential for risk-taking actions. Actions resulting in punitive consequences are disregarded as the person conspires to repeat the risk action less cautiously.

Becomes defensive about drinking or using when confronted: The user, refusing to accept powerlessness or seek professional assistance, perceives confrontation as people "controlling him" and "exposing vulnerability."

Exhibit 4.1
Worksheet to Determine Amount and Frequency of Drug Use

Substance	First used	Last used	Average Amount	Frequency

Alcohol _____
(beer,wine, wine coolers, hard liquor - straight/mixed)

Cannibas_____
(joints, bowls, bongs, hashish, hashish oil)

Cocaine_____

Hallucinogens _____
(LSD [acid], PCP [angel dust], mushrooms, ecstacy, happy stick [marijuana laced with PCP or embalming fluid]

Amphetamines _____
(diet pills, speed, caffeine pills, caffeine, uppers, black beauties)

Barbiturates _____
(sleeping pills, tranquilizers, downers, phenobarbitol)

Inhalants   _____
(glue, gasoline, paint, White-Out, markers, butane, rush, solvents, aerosols, nitrates, hydrocarbon, nitrous oxide, amyl nitrate, hair spray)

Opiates   _____
(opium, Demerol, talwin, methadone, codeine)

Prescription _____
medication
(xanax, painkillers,Tylenol 3/4, Darvocet)

Over the   _____
counter medication
(water pills, diet pills, cough syrup, cold medicine, allergy medication)

tobacco   _____
(cigarettes, chewing tobacco, cigars, pipe)

other   _____

Criminal violations: The user risks actions that increase physical liability and potential for crime. Violations against property, persons, and self using a vehicle or during social interaction start to require police intervention. Driving under the influence of alcohol or drugs, truancy, spouse abuse, bar fights, and related disturbances enter the user in the criminal justice system.

Indicators of the *middle stage* of dependency are that users suffer losses directly related to their substance abuse. Many users are unable to connect problems in their life to their abuse of substances. Perhaps they are intentionally being deceptive, but it is more likely they are oblivious to the problem. They also have been under a self-medicated state long enough to disturb, distort, or obliterate cognitive and affective sensitivity to effects of loss. The following symptoms are measurable indexes of the middle stage:

Loss of control. Users cannot accurately predict if their using will be a controlled or out-of-control episode. They do not need to be out of control each time they use.

Others notice drug- or alcohol-using behavior. Significant bystanders observing the progression of illness make comments to the user about quitting and seeking help. Users have more difficulty concealing drug and alcohol habits.

Increased rationalizations for use. The user justifies substance abuse, blaming it on overwhelming obligations, responsibilities, and unfair expectations he believes he must live up to.

Use is more frequent. Daily or weekly increases in alcohol and drug intake are proportional to higher amounts consumed.

Mixes drugs and alcohol indiscriminantly. Combinations of drugs and alcohol are frequent, dependent, and become part of the ritual. Drinking after cocaine use, for example, first eases drug diminishment effects and thereafter is an automatic step in the sequential cocaine-taking pattern.

Ignores warning signs of physical and social dangers. The client dismisses dangers to the body, such as cirrhosis or respiratory suppression.

Emotional instability and lability. Fluctuation of mood swings is continuous. The client loses his temper more frequently and may become abusive.

Experiences problems in major life areas. Addiction interrupts home, school, work, and legal, financial, physical, and spiritual areas of the person's life.

Steals and engages in other behavior previously seen as abhorrent. Risk-taking behaviors not only are abnormal but also hypocritical for the user's personality.

Friends all drink and use drugs. Social groups form that entirely are drinkers or participate in drinking or drug-using activities.

Diminished feelings of guilt occur. Minor, infrequent feelings of remorse disappear after drinking or medicated by drug use.

Resentments and blaming increase. Egocentric needs for immediate gratification that are not met cause conflict. Users resent or act aggressively toward persons preventing, delaying, or interrupting drinking or drug-using opportunities.

Lies and/or hollow promises increase. User does not do what he says. Consistency between actions and words deteriorates due to impulsive social actions and unpredictable substance abuse habits.

Uses to enhance pleasure. Drug use or drinking functions as a lubricant to slide risk behaviors through the abuser's history of fears and shame. Enhanced risks usually involve sexuality, fist fights, and parental, spouse and peer confrontations.

Relationships become increasingly impaired. Friendships and employee relationships deteriorate rapidly as the user's selfish demands imbalance the control and consequently exploit the trust.

Onset of physical withdrawal symptoms. Organic or physical dependence on drugs or alcohol instantly causes withdrawal symptoms in between use and during attempts at abstinence.

May contemplate suicide. Faced with declining resources, the drug or alcohol abuser may threaten or attempt self-harm, believing it would free others from inconvenience.

Late stages of substance abuse personify the stereotype of what most people typically imagine from chronic inebriety or drug abuse. Deterioration in all major life areas is evident. Once a person progresses to this stage, the chances of recovery greatly diminish. Characteristic symptoms at this level include the following:

Uses substances to wake up and go to sleep. Insomnia is relieved by overmedication. Frequency of sleep also enables the user to escape confrontation of daily problems.

No longer cares what they consume and in desperation will consume hair spray, shaving lotion, and even poisons, in an attempt to achieve an effect. Indiscriminate drug and alcohol use reflects uncontrolled cravings and intolerance to withdrawal symptoms.

Physical addiction is apparent. Withdrawal syndrome apparent in middle stages now progresses to organic impairment, possibly causing Korsakoff's or related psychosis.

Person uses not to feel good but to avoid feeling bad. Tension reduction and arousal are less incentives than is preventing withdrawal symptoms. Repeated, excessive consumption delays, diminishes, or overcomes severe physical reactions.

Daily or frequent episodic use destroys social, emotional, familial, financial, physical, and spiritual areas of life. By now the corrosion of family dynamics has caused irreversible damage, resulting in separation, divorce, loss of custody, rejection from friends, and isolationism.

Feelings of insanity and depression arise. Loss of control, emotional stability, and family and peer support destroys life ambition and creates feelings of victimization. Helplessness also leads substance abusers to abandon hope, abandon commitments, and stop grooming and other personal daily living skills. Diminished life interest usually is the first sign of being suicidal, coupled by other signals, such as unbearable withdrawal symptoms, illness, organ loss or impediment, and physical pain brought on by polymorbidity.

History of Drug/Alcohol Use and That of Significant Others

This section aids in solidifying what the client's learning experiences have been relative to substance use and abuse. It is important to clarify the purpose that drugs and alcohol serve in the home, since for some families, there are religious and cultural norms defining use of substances, and alcohol in particular. Discovered as well are learning experiences concerning abstinence and recovery from substances. Ways in which clients observe others cease abusing substances will color their perceptions on altering their own behaviors. The rating scale in Exhibit 4.2 is a guideline for the collection of attitudes and behavioral rules regarding substance use, abuse, and abstinence.

Many clients raised in an alcoholic or drug-abusing home are quite proud of their ability to survive. It is crucial to help them clarify that no one emerges from a dysfunctional home without some dysfunction themselves. If they have difficulty identifying ways in which they were affected, ask them to describe how they think life might have been different if some family member did not use substances. This also helps set the stage for altering their thinking that substance abuse is not necessarily ''normal'' behavior.

General Psychosocial History: Self and Significant Others

Taking inventory of historical information faces hurdles of poor reliability, inaccurate details, and reporter bias. Clients, including their significant others, are poor historians at recalling precipitants or placing events in proper chronological contexts. The most memorable events are ones that traumatically shook the historian, caused irreparable damage to the family system, or continue to upset the balance. Aberrances described are usually the extremes—excesses or deficiencies—omitting periods of sobriety, abstinence, or healthy adjustment. Finally, historians have an ulterior motive for reporting data: to change the exploitive abuser. Because they are victims of the abuser, historians bias accounts of drug use patterns from the perspective of those family members hurt by the client in order that treatment for the client seems imperative. Despite these obstacles, data collection must glean as many facts from fiction as possible.

A checklist, such as Exhibit 4.3, is helpful to sort through this information from both client and significant others, including subjective impressions. The checklist should cover history of psychiatric disorders, treatment history, legal history, spiritual history, physical history, financial history, sexual history, and history of support network.

Because some of the questions are personal and sensitive, it is important that clinicians assess their own comfort level prior to asking them. Even the most sensitive questions are crucial in pulling together all of the pieces of a person's life so that both client and clinician can examine the problem in its entirety. Viewing the written report can help the client understand that drug and alcohol use eventually permeates every facet of life.

Exhibit 4.2
Rating Scale on Attitudes toward Substance Abuse

Scale for Rating:
1. Abstainer
2. Occasional/ light/ social
3. Moderate / social
4. Frequent/ heavy
5. Abuser
6. Chemically dependent (active)
7. Chemically dependent (nonactive or recovering)
8. Does not know

Family member	Use rating	Current use	Future use
mother	_____	_____	_____
father	_____	_____	_____
sister(s)	_____	_____	_____
brother(s)	_____	_____	_____
step mother	_____	_____	_____
step father	_____	_____	_____
grandmother	_____	_____	_____
grandfather	_____	_____	_____
aunt(s)	_____	_____	_____
uncle(s)	_____	_____	_____
cousin(s)	_____	_____	_____

What were your family's attitudes regarding drug and alcohol use (socially, legally, religiously, culturally?_____

Has anyone in your family ever attempted to stop using? yes _____ no ___

If so, who? _____

Did anyone in your family ever seek inpatient/outpatient treatment?

yes _____ no ___

If so who? _____

Did anyone in your family ever attend self-help meetings (AA, NA, Al-Anon)?

yes _____ no ___

If so, who and what? _____

How do you feel their use and/or recovery affected your life? _____

_____

Exhibit 4.3
Checklist on Client's History

Psychiatric Disorders

1.   Have you ever been diagnosed as having a psychiatric disorder (depression, suicidal ideation, anxiety, hyperactivity, eating disorder, etc.) ?

                                                                      yes_____ no _____

2.   If so, what and When?_____

Hospitalization? _____

Medication? _____

3.   Has anyone in your family ever been diagnosed as having a psychiatric disorder?

If so, who, what, and when?_____

Hospitalization? _____

Medication?   _____

Treatment History

Have you ever been treated for substance abuse (DUI remedial education, inpatient/ outpatient treatment)?   yes _____ no _____

If so, when and where? _____

How did treatment come to pass? _____

Have you ever attended self-help meetings (AA,NA,CA)? _____

Did you find this helpful ?   yes _____ no_____

Explain _____

Legal History

Have you ever been arrested?   yes _____ no _____

If so, describe the offense(s). _____

Are you currently on probation or parole?   yes _____ no _____

Were you ever on probation or parole?   yes _____ no _____

What offense(s) led to probation or parole? _____

Exhibit 4.3 (continued)

Have any of your offenses been alcohol/drug related?　　yes _____ no___

If so, what? _____

Have you ever been arrested for DUI?　　　　　　yes _____ no__

If so when and where? _____

Number of prior DUI offenses _____

Have you ever had your drivers license suspended or revoked?

　　　　　　　　　　　　　　　　yes_____ no___

If so, when, why and for how long? _____

Have you ever engaged in alcohol or drug-related activities that could have gotten you

arrested, but did not?　　　　　　　　yes _____ no____

If so, what? _____

Spiritual History

Have you found that your ability to hope has changed?　　yes _____ no_

How did your family view religion when you were growing up?_____

_____

How do you feel about your religious upbringing? _____

What were your family's values and morals? _____

Do you still ascribe to their moral code and value system? _____

The most important moral or value in my life is_____

Prior to drinking and using drugs the most important moral or value in my life

was?_____

How do you believe drinking or drug use altered your morals/values/ belief systems?

_____

Physical History

Have you ever injured yourself, been involved in an accident (automobile or

household), or been involved in a physical fight while under the influence?

　　　　　　　　　　　　　　　yes ____ no ____

If so, what, and when? _____

Exhibit 4.3 (continued)

How would you describe your general health? _____

How has your health changed since you began using drugs/alcohol?_____

_____

Has your physician ever mentioned that you have:

gastrointestinal problems	yes_____ no_____
ulcers	yes_____ no_____
an enlarged liver/pancreas	yes_____ no___
elevated biliruben level	yes_____ no_____
increased heart rate	yes_____ no_____
changes in blood cell count	yes_____ no_____
urinary tract disorders	yes_____ no_____
reproductive difficulties	yes_____ no_____
respiratory disorders	yes_____ no_____

other _____

Did your physician ever suggest that these problems may be connected with

drinking or drug use?   yes_____ no_____

Have you been honest with your doctor about your

alcohol/drug consumption?   yes_____ no_____

Have you ever become defensive when your physician suggested a connection between

physical problems and substance use ?   yes_____ no_____

Do you believe that you would be in better physical health if you ceased using drugs/

alcohol?   yes_____no _____

Financial History

Are you currently employed?   yes _____ no_____

How much of your weekly income is spent on drugs/alcohol? _____

Have you ever sold belongings or stolen to obtain money to replace or supplement your

income?   yes _____ no___

Exhibit 4.3 (continued)

How frequently did you need to do so due to drug/alcohol use? _____

How far are you currently in debt? _____

If you had to estimate, how much money have you spent on drugs/alcohol or related

functions (parties, DUIs, substances, olives, mixers, court fees, hospital bills, etc.)?

_____

What would you like to do with that money if you had it now?_____

_____

How concerned are you with your current state of financial affairs?_____

_____

Sexual History

Are you currently sexually active?   yes____ no____

With one person or multiple partners?_____

Do you ever place yourself at risk of suffering consequences from your sexual behavior

(contracting diseases, unwanted pregnancy)   yes___ no___

Have you ever been unfaithful to your significant other?   yes ___ no___

If so, were any of these times associated with drug/alcohol use?

                                                          yes ___ no___

Do you believe drugs/alcohol enhance sexual experiences? yes ___ no ___

Has your ability to perform sexually ever been impaired due to alcohol/drug use?

                                                          yes ___ no__

Has anyone ever attempted to have sex with you without your consent?

                                                          yes ____ no__

If so who? _____

Has anyone ever taken advantage of you sexually while you were under the influence

of drugs/alcohol?   yes____ no__

Has anyone in your family ever attempted to have sex with you?

                                                          yes ____ no__

Do you believe this person was under the influence of drugs or alcohol at the time?

                                                          yes ____ no__

Exhibit 4.3 (continued)

If so, did you ever tell anyone?   yes ____ no__

Why or why not? _____

How did the person respond?_____

Do you have contact with this person currently? _____

How do you believe you were able to survive? _____

_____

History of Support Network

Who will support you if you decide to change your drug/alcohol use patterns?

_____

Who might stand in your way (intentionally or unintentionally) as you attempt to

become clean and sober? _____

Why? _____

How can you go about enlisting help from family and friends without getting them to

do your work for you? _____

Will you attend self help meetings (AA,NA, CA)?_____

If not, why?_____

Do you know how to go about finding self-help meetings? _____
What is the first thing you need to do to begin making changes in your
life?_____

Perception of Changes in Functioning

By the time the assessment reaches this point, the seed has been planted that drug and alcohol use is a problem. Realization of its dangers and its intrusive impact on family and friends is unsettling. Clients may react in one of three ways: (1) defensively disputing facts and denying blame for familial dysfunctions; (2) reflectively asking questions, showing introspection, and probing etiologic details underlying progression of the abuse; or (3) nonanalytically conceding to the powerlessness, responsibility, and fault others place on him. Agreement with others' complaints by no means ensures genuine remorse for substance abuse or commitment to therapy. That is why providers should ascertain the cognitive and affective status of clients after initially taking the social and psychiatric history.

Sample questions may include the following:

Given all that we have discussed thus far, how do you believe your abuse of drugs/alcohol has affected your life?

If you had it to do over again, what consequences would you reverse?

If you continue to abuse drugs/alcohol, what kind of future can you look forward to?

Perception of Benefits from Continued or Discontinued Use

The goal here is to help the client begin to see that healthy changes in behavior may change the quality of his life as well.

Sample questions include the following:

What do you get out of using drugs or drinking alcohol?

What are the benefits of continued use?

How likely do you believe it is that the quality of your life will improve if you continue using?

Describe in detail how your family and friends will feel about your continued use.

Sample questions for discontinued use include the following:

How would your life be different if you stopped using?

Do you believe your life would be better or worse if you stopped using?

What would you most like to see change in your life that may require you to cease abuse of substances to achieve?

How will your family and friends feel if you stop using?

Are there friends you sell drugs to who depend on your continual supply or use for their own habits?

CONCLUSION

A thorough, accurate assessment of substance abuse disorders is crucial to develop comprehensive treatment plans. Assessment covering biological as well as psychosocial factors in early, middle, and late stages of abuse are necessary components for extensive client case histories. The process described in this chapter may be utilized in sections or in its entirety based on the clinician's discretion. All major life areas need to be covered, however.

The more we do something, the easier it becomes. This is true for assessment of substance abuse as well. Remaining nonjudgmental and composed throughout the assessment facilitates the process and frees the client up to receive the educational dimension that the assessment process provides. A thorough assessment teaches clients as much about themselves as clinicians learn about clients.

5

Diagnosing Alcoholism: Toward a Multisource Approach

AMY LAUDERBACK LEE

Alcoholism ranks as one of the most prevalent psychiatric disorders, as evidenced by the numbers of people seeking treatment for its effects (Tarter, Arria, Moss, Edwards & Van Thiel, 1987). However, finding an accurate and objective diagnostic method for alcoholism has been a challenge to both researchers and clinicians. There is little continuity between studies in the criteria and methods used to label individuals as alcoholic. Researchers have assigned the diagnosis of alcoholism to subjects who were in treatment for alcoholism (Calder & Kostyniuk, 1989; Wright & Obitz, 1984), who were in concordance with diagnostic criteria for alcoholism (Jacob & Leonard, 1986; Hegedus, Alterman & Tarter, 1984), or who gave a self-diagnosis of alcoholism (Werner, 1985; Marcus, 1986). These broad approaches diminish the consensus regarding how alcoholism should be defined, and for both researchers and clinicians (Baird, Burge & Grant, 1989), the definition for alcoholism can become confused and fraught with inconsistencies; therefore, a uniform system for diagnosing alcoholism is needed. However, questions have also been raised regarding the validity of a diagnostic category of alcoholism (Tarter et al., 1987). Perhaps the diversity of diagnostic approaches represents the actual diversity within the category of alcoholism, and rather than a distinct category of alcoholism, there exists a continuous system of alcoholic disorders.

Alcoholism has been called a multidimensional system of subjective, behavioral, and biochemical components (Kivlahan, Sher & Donovan, 1989). As a multidimensional system, alcoholism could be characterized by differing degrees of pathology along each dimension, with different individuals having different sets of symptoms. A fuller appreciation of the multidimensional nature of alcoholism has begun with many assessment methods, but a greater emphasis on the components is needed. This review illustrates the utility of examining the different dimensions through multiple sources when diagnosing alcoholism. The emphasis will be placed on the strengths and limitations of some diagnostic approaches and on developing a multisource diagnostic system.

PROFESSIONAL RATINGS FOR DIAGNOSING ALCOHOLISM

Rating systems are composed of criteria that define alcoholism as a distinct category. These approaches have been developed largely for the purpose of reducing problems with reliability of diagnosis. Providing researchers and clinicians with clearly defined inclusion and exclusion criteria has been a method used to reduce variability in the diagnosis of alcoholism. As a result, rating systems have specific criteria required for diagnosis. The concept of a multidimensional alcoholism with differing degrees of severity is only beginning to be addressed with such criteria.

Two approaches used in research and clinical practice are the Criteria for the Diagnosis of Alcoholism (CDA: National Council on Alcoholism, 1972) and the criteria for substance use disorders in the *Diagnostic and Statistical Manual of Mental Disorders III* (DSM-III: American Psychiatric Association, 1980) and III-R (DSM-III-R: American Psychiatric Association, 1987). Both approaches use criteria that must be present in some combination for the diagnosis of alcoholism to be valid. Both also consider alcoholism to be a distinct category of disease. The systems differ in that the CDA divides criteria into two symptom dimensions, physiological/clinical and behavioral/psychological/attitudinal, with temporal and severity levels also included. The DSM versions contain criteria for alcohol abuse and alcohol dependence, describing alcohol dependence as a more severe and chronic pattern of use. The DSM-III-R also made several improvements on the DSM-III by including severity ratings and more specific symptom criteria across behavioral, psychological, and physical dimensions. Both the CDA and the DSM approaches can be extremely useful to clinicians because they attempt to include criteria that address the different dimensions affected by alcoholism; however, both also require categorizing individuals with different symptom sets and levels of severity.

The problem of information loss associated with categorial approaches to defining alcoholism is somewhat improved upon with the CDA and DSM approaches; however, it remains evident that the diversity of alcoholic disorders is not completely appreciated when the label of alcoholism is assigned. For example, Tarter and associates (1987) found little construct validity for the DSM-III criteria for alcohol abuse when compared with self-reported severity of alcohol use in males in treatment for alcoholism. In order to account for the diversity of people with this diagnosis, they suggest a more dimensional approach to defining alcoholism where individuals would fall on a continuum of alcoholic disorders. In another example, Brooner, Templer, Svikis, Schmidt, and Monopolis (1990) found three factors common to alcoholics and exhibited in different combinations, suggesting that separate individuals can differ along a continuum of alcoholic symptoms.

The problem of differences in judgment across clinicians brings into question whether outside professionals should be the primary source of diagnosis. There is some evidence supporting the use of other diagnostic sources in addition to clinical judgment. Baird, Burge, and Grant (1989) found that 4.3 percent of a large sample of hospital patients were reported by their physicians to be alcoholic, but retrospective classification estimated that 15.9 percent of the patients were alcoholic. Similarly, clinicians classified fewer people as alcoholic than did the Michigan Alcoholism Screening Test (Otto & Hatt, 1988). Lack of uniformity in the criteria used by clinicians may have contributed to the inconsistencies.

The problem of inconsistency of diagnosis may also be due to differing perceptions of what constitutes an alcohol problem among different populations. Leavy and Dunlosky (1989) surveyed undergraduates and faculty at two midwestern colleges and found that the groups viewed alcohol use differently; personal consumption patterns, demographics, age, and gender-related attitudes can affect the determination of what is considered problem drinking. The assessment of problem drinking is a subjective process for laypersons and may be a subjective process with professionals as well. Inconsistent clinical judgments could perhaps be reduced by using other diagnostic methods.

SELF-REPORT MEASURES

A number of self-report scales have been developed for the assessment of alcoholism. Typically they aim to categorize individuals as alcoholic given certain response patterns, through either a questionnaire format or an interview format. The measures considered here are: the Alcohol Dependence Scale (ADS), the MacAndrew Alcoholism Scale (MAC), the Michigan Alcoholism Screening Test (MAST: Selzer, 1971) and variations on it, and the Rutgers Alcohol Problem Index (RAPI: White & Labouvie, 1989).

Alcohol Dependence Scale (ADS)

Derived from the Alcohol Use Inventory, the Alcohol Dependence Scale (Skinner & Allen, 1982) was formed with the notion that with greater severity of alcohol dependence, there is greater coherence among elements characterizing alcoholism. Therefore, severely abusive alcohol use patterns could indicate problems along other dimensions as well. For example, Skinner and Allen (in Kivlahan, Sher & Donovan, 1989) found a positive relationship between the ADS and alcohol-related social consequences, alcohol consumption, psychopathology, and physical symptoms. Kivlahan et al. (1989) did not find the same strong relationships. Also, predictive validity of the ADS was questioned. For example, ADS scores did not predict attrition from inpatient treatment, self-reported alcohol consumption, or duration of aftercare involvement (Kivlahan et al., 1989). Therefore, the ADS assumption that with more severe alcohol dependence the disorder becomes more unidimensional appears questionable, and the predictive utility seems limited.

MacAndrew Alcoholism Scale (MAC)

The MAC is a 49-item self-report questionnaire used for the assessment of alcoholism that queries information seemingly irrelevent to the alcoholism diagnosis. The MAC is based on a cluster of items from the Minnesota Multiphasic Personality Inventory (MMPI) that MacAndrew found to be characteristic for alcoholics. MacAndrew wanted to create a subtle measure that would resist faking and so deliberately removed two items from the scale that referred to drinking. Therefore, the items do not directly ask about drinking, drinking-related behaviors, or consequences of drinking but were theoretically thought to tap characteristics of alcoholic personalities (Graham, 1987). However, the MAC may have become limited by attempts to measure too many aspects of personality without measuring dimensions usually associated with alcoholism.

The MAC has been tested with different diagnostic groups, with results raising some questions about its validity. Apfeldorf and Hundley (1981) used the MAC with patients diagnosed alcoholic, with psychiatric patients, and with controls to determine whether the scale would distinguish among the groups, though amounts of drinking varied within each group. The MAC did identify the alcoholics as the highest-scoring group and the psychiatric patients as the lowest-scoring group. However, Apfeldorf and Hundley pointed out that the MAC seemed most useful only when the primary diagnosis was alcoholism because it did not identify psychiatric patients who were also heavy drinkers. Their findings suggest that the MAC may not be valid for individuals with dual diagnoses.

In another test of construct validity, Schwartz and Graham (1979) used the MAC with males and females from alcoholic, antisocial, and general psychiatric groups. Their results showed that the MAC differentiated the female alcoholics from the other psychiatric groups but not the male alcoholics. Through factor analysis, Schwartz and Graham found that the MAC's sensitivity to adequate social functioning was important for differentiating alcoholics from other groups. Similarly, Preng and Clopton (1986) concluded that the MAC may not discriminate between alcoholics and antisocial personalities. In addition to these validity problems, Graham (1987) warns of a cultural bias when the MAC is used with blacks. Blacks tend to obtain elevated scores on the MAC and have a higher false-positive rate than whites (Graham, 1987). Therefore, its lack of relevance to alcoholism may make the MAC less useful than other measures.

Michigan Alcoholism Screening Test (MAST)

The MAST (Selzer, 1971) is a self-report measure for identifying alcoholics that has advantages over both the ADS and the MAC. The MAST is a 25-item self-report measure administered in a structured interview format. It broadly surveys drinking behaviors and social and familial consequences of drinking. Designed to be sufficiently neutral in order to allow for truthful responding, it has spurred the development of several related measures. The MAST has been found to satisfy basic psychometric requirements for reliability, validity, and internal consistency (Hotch, Sherin, Harding & Zitter, 1983), but researchers have questioned aspects of its validity.

In testing the validity of the MAST, Selzer (1971) was disappointed when the MAST identified just over half of subjects convicted of either driving under the influence (DUI) or drunk and disorderly conduct (D&D), when it had identified 98 percent of hospitalized alcoholics. He suggested that some of the DUI and D&D group members may have been concealing an alcohol problem. In fact, Otto & Hall (1988) determined that when instructed to give MAST responses that would prevent detection of their alcoholism, alcoholics were able to avoid detection. Consequently, they suggested using a validity scale with the MAST, or as part of the MAST, to identify people who may try to "fake good." Otto & Hall's suggestion is an attempt to deal with the MAST's underidentification of alcoholics who are reluctant to reveal their problems with alcohol.

Zung (1984a, 1984b) has addressed the construct validity of the MAST. Using a short form of the MAST, Zung (1984a) found high false-positive and false-negative rates when compared with psychiatric diagnosis. However, psychiatric criteria for the diagnosis of alcoholism may not always be consistent or useful. In another study, Zung (1984b) searched for personality correlates of the MAST using a personality inventory but was unable to find any personality factors that accounted for a significant amount of MAST variance. He concluded that to establish the MAST's construct validity, personality correlates need to be found. Zung succeeded in raising possible problems with the construct validity of the MAST, although there is no conclusive evidence regarding whether clinicians' diagnoses of alcoholism are accurate or whether there are certain personality types for alcoholism.

Another construct validity problem cited with the MAST is the lack of attention to time and duration of the substance abuse. The MAST asks only about current problems with alcohol. Consequently, it does not adequately identify cases where alcohol use is currently under control (Rounsville, Weissman, Wilber & Kleber, 1983). Rounsville et al. found that the MAST did not differentiate opiate addicts who were currently using alcohol from those who were not. They stated the importance of being able to identify past and present problems with alcohol, especially with opiate addicts, who may be at risk for alcoholic relapse when in treatment for other drugs.

The MAST has been found by most researchers to be reliable over time but to have some problems with validity. Many suggestions have been made to improve the MAST's validity. However, the MAST remains one of the better self-report measures available to diagnosticians due to its direct questions about alcohol-related problems. Because the MAST has proved useful as a screening device, attempts to improve identification of alcoholics have resulted in the development of a version with time-related questions, self-administered versions, and versions for the identification of alcoholic parents.

In an attempt to measure the temporal aspects of alcoholism, Magruder-Habib, Harris, and Fraker (1982) created the Veterans Alcoholism Screening Test (VAST) from the MAST. They used 24 MAST questions and added time-related queries. The VAST is an attempt to distinguish what Magruder-Habib et al. call "past" from "present" alcoholism. When they used the VAST with general medical outpatients, they found that it was a more accurate and valid measure of alcoholism than the MAST. Development of the VAST added to the dimensions already measured by the MAST, increasing its validity.

Self-administered versions of the MAST have been developed for easier screening of patients in medical facilities. Hotch, Sherin, Harding, and Zitter (1983) used a self-administered MAST in a family practice center and obtained a score distribution similar to those found with the interview form of the MAST. Another self-administered version of the MAST, retitled the Self-Administered Alcoholism Screening Test (SAAST), has adequately identified alcoholics in medical clinic settings, with sensitivity rates from 90 to 95 percent using the full 35 items or 96.4 to 99.4 percent with a 9-item version developed from discriminant analysis (Davis, Hurt, Morse & O'Brien, 1987). The SAAST has had similar success in identifying alcoholics in a Mexican medical sample, with similar items having the strongest discriminating power (Davis, de la Fuente, Morse, Landa & O'Brien, 1989).

Rutgers Alcohol Problem Index (RAPI)

The methods discussed thus far have been designed for diagnosing adult alcoholics, but problems with alcohol are not restricted to adults; identifying adolescents with alcohol problems is also a concern. The RAPI was designed by White and Labouvie (1989) for assessment of adolescent problem drinking. Alcohol dependence scales are more appropriate for older subjects because of the long-standing nature of the alcoholic symptoms and consequences. With the RAPI, they try to assess problem patterns of alcohol use in young people. Their work addresses the idea that alcoholism not only affects multiple dimensions of human experience but may also take different forms at different ages.

Two issues arise regarding the self-report measures discussed thus far. First is whether responses from subjects are truthful. Self-report measures, in general, are susceptible to less-than-truthful responses from subjects due to social desirability or self-deception (Selzer, 1971). For example, Morrow-Tlucak,

Ernhart, Sokol, Martier, and Ager (1989) found that women who drank more during pregnancy underreported their alcohol use while they were pregnant, apparently due to the social stigma attached to drinking during pregnancy. Rychtarik, Tarnowski and St. Lawrence (1989) also found false reporting when they obtained reports of marital adjustment from married male alcoholics and their wives. The husbands reported their marriages to be significantly more satisfying than did their wives. Rychtarik et al. reasoned that it was either social desirability or self-deception by the alcoholics that led to the disparate responses. Blum, Roman, and Bennett (1989), in surveying a sample representative of a census population in Georgia, found that people broadly accepted alcoholism as an illness but also believed alcoholism was the result of moral weakness. These results suggest that alcoholism is considered something to be hidden in our society, and therefore alcoholics may attempt to conceal their alcohol problems when responding to self-report questionnaires.

The second issue is that self-report instruments may be less than reliable measures of alcoholism. One solution is to expand the parameters of variables evaluated. Using the observations of family members has been one method for validating a clinician's assessment. Various measures for use with children of alcoholics exist that could be very useful in this capacity.

INFORMANT MEASURES

Questionnaires that assess a child's perceptions of parental impairment due to alcohol are usually used for identifying children of alcoholics (COAs) for research or treatment. Children are keenly aware of when their own needs are not met and can accurately assess whether a parent has been made unavailable to them due to alcohol consumption. In research samples, estimated COA rates range from 15 to 21 percent (Berkowitz & Perkins, 1988). Approaches that identify COAs may also be useful for diagnosing their parents when used in combination with other methods. Descriptions of some of the measures follow.

The first set of approaches are questionnaires for identifying COAs. One questionnaire is the Short Michigan Alcoholism Screening Test (SMAST), adapted to address either mother's or father's drinking-related behaviors and named the M-SMAST or F-SMAST, respectively. Sher and Descutner (1986) administered the F-SMAST to college-aged sibling pairs and found that the F-SMAST was reliable across siblings, with total score the most reliable measure across siblings. These results suggest that obtaining an assessment of parental alcoholism from COAs can provide useful information. More research is needed to determine whether the adapted SMAST is effective for identifying most COAs.

A more commonly used questionnaire is the 30-item Children of Alcoholics Screening Test (CAST) developed by Jones (1981; cited by Pilat & Jones, 1984/85). The CAST can be used to identify children of alcoholics by measuring feelings, attitudes, perceptions, and experiences related to a parent's drinking. The test items were formulated from actual experiences shared by clinically diagnosed COAs. The CAST is suitable for use with people from 9 years of age to adulthood. In addition, it has been shown to be reliable, valid, and to have good internal consistency (Pilat & Jones, 1984/85). Pilat and Jones used the CAST with high school students and identified over 25 percent as having alcoholic parents. Another study (Pilat & Jones, 1984/85) used the CAST with mental health professionals and obtained a similar percentage of COAs. Although Pilat and Jones have found the CAST to be a useful identification device for COAs, one could argue that it is flawed because it may not identify COAs who may be affected by their parent's alcoholism but whose parent no longer drinks. Abstinence from alcohol does not end the pathology of the alcoholic and the alcoholic family. In fact, Biek (1981) notes that family tensions often increase when the problem drinker abstains. Therefore, a large population of COAs who are affected by their parents' alcoholism may not be identified by the CAST. For example, Claydon (1987) showed that the CAST underidentified the COA population in a sample of college freshmen because of its emphasis on parental drinking. Claydon administered the CAST and asked direct questions regarding whether a parent was alcoholic. He found that using a direct question, along with the CAST, identified almost 5 percent more COAs than with the CAST alone. Together, the CAST and direct questions allowed for identification of a fuller range of COAs.

The discussions of both the CAST and the adapted forms of the SMAST suggest the importance of gaining information about the multiple dimensions of alcoholism through COAs. Although we have no information regarding the validity of the F-SMAST, we do know that there are problems with the MAST's ability to identify alcoholics. The CAST also appears limited in its capacity to identify the full range of children with alcoholic parents. It was suggested that some direct questions regarding parental alcoholism may improve the CAST. The multidimensional nature of parental alcoholism may possibly be assessed with a single question or a short interview.

Single-question methods use a question, such as, ''Has the drinking of either parent ever caused a problem for you?'' (Biek, 1981) to determine whether an individual should be designated a COA. These methods identify pecentages of COAs similar to more involved questionnaires, such as the CAST, without underidentification (Berkowitz & Perkins, 1988). For example, Berkowitz and Perkins used a single question to identify COAs among college students and adults in a local community and validated the method with 12 CAST items. The researchers asked subjects whether a parent ''may have had or may have an alcohol abuse problem'' to which 18 percent answered yes. Not only did the authors identify a percentage of COAs consistent with past research, but all of the COAs identified by the single question answered at least half of the 12 CAST items affirmatively, compared to almost none by the non-COAs.

In another example, DiCiccio, Davis, and Orenstein (1984) were able to identify COAs from groups of seventh through twelfth graders using the question, ''Have you ever wished that either one or both of your parents would drink less?'' They reported identifying more COAs with this method than with the traditional ''amount of parental drinking'' method. These authors encourage using methods that address the child's peception of parental drinking but acknowledge that information about the amount of parental drinking may also be needed. A single question that ascertained a child's perceptions of a parent included more information than a child's report about parental drinking habits alone. Therefore, single-question methods appear to be very useful due to their ease of administration and accurate identification rates.

For researchers and clinicians who want to gather explicit information regarding the COAs experience with their parent but want to avoid the underidentification associated with the CAST, Biek (1981) suggests administering a screening test with the question, ''Has the drinking of either parent created a problem for you?'' and conducting a short, semistructured interview. She found that the interview identified more COAs than the single question had, especially those who had been reluctant to disclose their parent's problem. Biek reasoned that the interview was better because of the trust the interviewer could establish with the teenager and because the questions more directly considered the entire life experience of the child. Using the interview approach seems superior to the single-question method in order to encourage more disclosure in some COAs. However, the single-question method remains a useful tool for screening general populations because of the implied multidimensionality and quick administration.

The methods described for identifying children of alcoholic parents are another reminder of the diversity of the alcoholic population. Each approach tries to encompass as many dimensions of the disorder as possible. The single-question methods appear effective for general screening and may be enhanced by specific queries about stressors or life circumstances. Because the CAST has similar to less effective identification rates and takes longer to administer, it seems to be less preferable than a single question with some additional queries. Due to its open-ended format, a single question could be stated so that a child could answer affirmatively about a parent who has or had problems with alcohol and has or has not been officially diagnosed alcoholic. Therefore, use of a single question for screening, with additional queries regarding the effects of parental alcoholism on the COA, can provide useful insights into parental alcoholism and can be an important addition to the diagnosis of alcoholism.

CONCLUSIONS

One of the goals of this review was to develop a diagnostic system for defining alcoholism. The ideal situation for diagnosing alcoholism is all three types of diagnostic approaches used in combination: professional ratings, a self-report measure, and an informant measure. Used separately, each approach has limitations, but used together they can compensate for one another (see Table 5.1).

Of the professional rating systems, the DSM-III-R is probably the best known

Table 5.1
Summary of Measures for the Diagnosis of Alcoholism

Measures	Format	Focus	Strengths	Limitations
Professional Ratings				
CDA	Criteria	Symptoms	Systematic and includes many dimensions	Judgment may vary across clinicians
DSM-III/III-R	Criteria	Symptoms	Systematic and includes many dimensions	Judgment may vary across clinicians & construct validity
Self-Report Measures				
ADS	Questionnaire	Alcohol use	Concurrent validity Internal consistency	Predictive validity
MAC	Questionnaire	Personality	Reliability and resists faking	Construct validity
MAST	Interview	Consequences of drinking	Reliability and direct approach.	Predictive and construct validity

				Predictive and construct validity.
VAST	Interview	Added temporal queries to MAST.	Reliability and improved construct validity	
SMAST	Questionnaire	See MAST		
SAAST	Questionnaire	See MAST	Useful for identifying alcoholics in medical settings and across cultures	
RAPI	Interview	Adolescent drinking.	Exclusively for adolescents	Reliability? Validity?
Informant Measures				
F-SMAST/ M-SMAST	Interview	Parental alcoholism.	Reliable across siblings	See MAST
CAST	Questionnaire	Parental alcoholism	Reliability Validity	May underidentify
Single Questions	Question	Parental alcoholism	More accurate identification rates	
Short Interview	Interview	Experience of COA	Especially identifies reluctant COA's	

and most widely used in the United States. Although there have been improvements, a future revision could clarify the meaning of the term *alcoholism* within its system. Also, a continued movement toward a dimensional system would serve diagnosticians well. For example, the CDA approach of listing physical and clinical symptoms and psychological, behavioral, and attitudinal symptoms on two separate tracks is an example of such a dimensional system. A better approach might include each type of symptom as a separate dimension and a tally of symptoms per dimension, without the necessity of classification into a category. Other dimensions that should be included are duration of disturbance and severity of disturbance. A dimensional approach would provide a descriptive quality and could be useful for determining types of alcohol-related disorders.

Among the self-report measures reviewed, the most inclusive measure appears to be the Veterans Alcoholism Screening Test (VAST) (Magruder-Habib et al., 1982). Because the VAST has adapted the MAST by including a temporal dimension, it can distinguish between alcoholics who are currently using alcohol and those who are not. Both recovering and using alcoholics have suffered the effects of alcoholism, and both groups should be considered in determining the pathology of alcoholism. Also, a researcher or clinician should consider the age of the person assessed and perhaps use a measure like the Rutgers Alcohol Problem Index (White & Labouvie, 1989) with younger persons. At least one other source of information may be needed with these self-respect approaches in order to control for social desirability or self-deception.

The last group of approaches were those designed for identifying children of alcoholics. Of these methods, a single question, such as, "Have you ever thought that your parents may have had or may have an alcohol abuse problem?" (Berkowitz & Perkins, 1988) can be useful for screening or identifying COAs. Questions regarding general stressors and the effects of parental alcoholism on the COA could be used as a follow-up. In terms of diagnosing the parent, this method could serve as validation for the other two approaches.

Each type of approach described in this chapter has merits and faults. Used together, the methods can provide substantial amounts of information. Each could be used separately but would not provide a full description of the alcoholic disorder. There may, however, be occasions when using just one of the systems would be appropriate, such as using an informant measure to identify COAs for research purposes. A comprehensive multidimensional system that considers not only the perceptions of the alcoholic but also of family members should be the ultimate goal of a diagnostic approach to alcoholism.

REFERENCES

American Psychiatric Association (1980). *Diagnostic and statistical manual of mental disorders* (3d ed.). Washington, D.C.: APA.

American Psychiatric Association (1987). *Diagnostic and statistical manual of mental disorders* (3d ed. rev.). Washington, D.C.: APA.

Apfeldorf, M. & Hundley, P. J. (1981). The MacAndrew Scale: A measure of the diagnosis of alcoholism. *Journal of Studies on Alcohol, 42,* 80–86.

Baird, M. A., Burge, S. K. & Grant, W. D. (1989). A scheme for determining the prevalence of alcoholism in hospitalized patients. *Alcoholism: Clinical and Experimental Research, 13,* 782–85.

Berkowitz, A. & Perkins, H. W. (1988). Personality characteristics of children of alcoholics. *Journal of Consulting and Clinical Psychology, 56,* 206–9.

Biek, J. E. (1981). Screening test for identifying adolescents adversely affected by a parental drinking problem. *Journal of Adolescent Health Care, 2,* 107–13.

Blum, T. C., Roman, P. M. & Bennett, N. (1989). Public images of alcoholism: Data from a Georgia survey. *Journal of Studies on Alcohol, 50,* 5–14.

Brooner, R. K., Templer, D., Svikis, D. S., Schmidt, C. & Monopolis, S. (1990). Dimensions of alcoholism: A multivariate analysis. *Journal of Studies on Alcohol, 51,* 77–81.

Calder, P. & Kostyniuk, A. (1989). Personality profiles of children of alcoholics. *Professional Psychology: Research and Practice, 20,* 417–18.

Claydon, P. (1987). Self-reported alcohol, drug and eating-disorder problems among male and female collegiate children of alcoholics. *Journal of American College Health, 36,* 111–16.

Davis, L. J., de la Fuente, J-R., Morse, R. M., Landa, E. & O'Brien, P. C. (1989). Self-Administered Alcoholism Screening Test: Comparison of classificatory accuracy in two cultures. *Alcoholism: Clinical and Experimental Research, 13,* 224–28.

Davis, L. J., Hurt, R.D., Morse, R. M. & O'Brien, P. C. (1987). Discriminent analysis of the Self-Administered Alcoholism Screening Test. *Alcoholism: Clinical and Experimental Research, 11,* 269–73.

DiCiccio, L., Davis, R. & Orenstein, A. (1984). Identifying the children of alcoholic parents from survey responses. *Journal of Alcohol and Drug Education, 30,* 1–17.

Graham, J. R. (1987). *The MMPI: A practical guide* (2d ed.). New York: Oxford University Press.

Hegedus, A., Alterman, A. & Tarter, R. (1984). Learning achievement in sons of alcoholics. *Alcoholism: Clinical and Experimental Research, 8,* 330–33.

Hotch, D. F., Sherin, K. M., Harding, P. N. & Zitter, R. E. (1983). Use of the self-administered Michigan Alcoholism Screening Test in a family practice center. *Journal of Family Practice, 17,* 1021–26.

Jacob, T. & Leonard, K. (1986). Psychosocial functioning in children of alcoholic fathers, depressed fathers and control fathers. *Journal of Studies in Alcohol, 47,* 373–80.

Kivlahan, D. R., Sher, K. J. & Donovan, D. M. (1989). The Alcohol Dependence Scale: A validation study among inpatient alcoholics. *Journal of Studies on Alcohol, 50,* 170–75.

Leavy, R. L. & Dunlosky, J. T. (1989). Undergraduate student and faculty perceptions of problem drinking. *Journal of Studies on Alcohol, 50,* 101–7.

Magruder-Habib, K., Harris, K. E. & Fraker, G. G. (1982). Validation of the Veterans Alcoholism Screening Test. *Journal of Studies on Alcohol, 43,* 910–26.

Marcus, A. M. (1986). Academic achievement in elementary school children of alcoholic mothers. *Journal of Clinical Psychology, 42,* 372–76.

Morrow-Tlucak, M., Ernhart, C. B., Sokol, R. J., Martier, S. & Ager, J. (1989). Underreporting of alcohol use in pregnancy: Relationship to alcohol problem history. *Alcoholism: Clinical and Experimental Research, 13,* 399–401.

National Council on Alcoholism (1972). Criteria for the diagnosis of alcoholism. *Annals of Internal Medicine, 77,* 249–58.

Otto, R. K. & Hall, J. E. (1988). The utility of the Michigan Alcoholism Screening Test in the detection of alcoholics and problem drinkers. *Journal of Personality Assessment, 52,* 499–505.

Pilat, J. M. & Jones, J. W. (1984/85, Winter). Identification of children of alcoholics: Two empirical studies. *Alcohol Health and Research World,* 27–36.

Preng, K. W. & Clopton, J. R. (1986). The MacAndrew Scale: Clinical applications and theoretical issues. *Journal of Studies on Alcohol, 47,* 228–35.

Rounsville, B. J., Weissman, M. M., Wilber, C. & Kleber, H. D. (1983). Identifying alcoholism in treated opiate addicts. *American Journal of Psychiatry, 140,* 764–66.

Rychtarik, R. G., Tarnowski, K. J. & St. Lawrence, J. S. (1989). Impact of social desirability response sets on the self-report of marital adjustment in alcoholics. *Journal of Studies in Alcohol, 50,* 24–29.

Schwartz, M. F. & Graham, J. R. (1979). Construct validity of the MacAndrew Alcoholism Scale. *Journal of Consulting and Clinical Psychology, 47,* 1090–95.

Selzer, M. L. (1971). The Michigan Alcoholism Screening Test: The quest for a new diagnostic instrument. *American Journal of Psychiatry, 127,* 89–94.

Sher, K. J. & Descutner, C. (1986). Reports of paternal alcoholism: Reliability across siblings. *Addictive Behaviors, 11,* 25–30.

Tarter, R. E., Arria, A. M., Moss, H., Edwards, N. J. & Van Thiel, D. H. (1987). DSM-III criteria for alcohol abuse: Associations with alcohol consumption behavior. *Alcoholism: Clinical and Experimental Research, 11,* 541–43.

Werner, E. (1985). Resilient offspring of alcoholics: A longitudinal study from birth to age 18. *Journal of Studies on Alcohol, 47,* 34–40.

White, H. R. & Labouvie, E. W. (1989). Towards the assessment of adolescent problem drinking. *Journal of Studies on Alcohol, 50,* 30–37.

Wisnieski, N. M., Glenwick, D. S. & Graham, J. R. (1985). MacAndrew Scale and socio-demographic correlates of adolescent alcohol and drug use. *Addictive Behaviors, 10,* 55–67.

Wright, M. & Obitz, F. (1984). Alcoholics' and nonalcoholics' attributions of control of future life events. *Journal of Studies in Alcohol, 45,* 138–43.

Zung, B. J. (1984a). Reliability and validity of the short Michigan Alcoholism Screening Test among psychiatric inpatients. *Journal of Clinical Psychology, 40,* 347–50.

Zung, B. J. (1984b). Correlates of the Michigan Alcoholism Screening Test among DWI offenders. *Journal of Clinical Psychology, 40,* 607–12.

6

Assessment of Eating Disorders

JOHN L. LEVITT

Clinicians are finding an increasing number of clients who exhibit symptoms indicative of either an eating disorder or some aspect of a disordered eating pattern. Indeed, they are discovering that clients are presenting eating disorders exhibiting a wide variety of eating disorder symptom patterns (Garfinkel & Garner, 1982; Garner & Garfinkel, 1988; Hsu, 1990; Lacey, Dip & Birtchnel, 1986). Therapists now treat problems that they may have once believed were either distinctly different from, unrelated to, or distantly related to an eating disorder. Yet eating disorders are commonly found in association with many other disorders. In reviewing the literature on bulimia, Johnson and Connors (1987) found that several studies suggest that bulimics "experience a variety of impulse difficulties, including stealing, substance abuse, and suicidal behavior" (p. 58). Bass and Davis (1988), for example, suggest several ways that problematic eating behaviors function for sexual abuse survivors; survivors of sexual abuse may overeat in order to numb their feelings, to self-nurture, or to protect themselves. Anorectics may "falsely believe that if they don't grow breasts, develop full hips, become curvy, they won't be attractive, and then no one will force them into being sexual" (p. 218) and that vomiting for bulimics is a way of saying "No!"

Putman (1989) and Ross (1989) have found that eating disorders are common in cases of multiple personality disorders (MPDs). Ross found in a series of 236 cases of MPD that 16.3 percent had been previously diagnosed as having an eating disorder:

I think that this is a gross underestimate of the prevalence of pathological eating behavior in MPD, which must be present in over 50 percent of the cases, and probably over

75 percent. Eating disorders are one of the hierarchically lower disorders within chronic trauma disorder and are related to sexual abuse in general . . . and to MPD in particular. (p. 171)

Woods and Brief (1988) have discussed at length the similarities between eating disorders and other addictions. They suggest that certain individuals are predisposed to employ drug or alcohol dependencies as protective mechanisms to guard against personal threat. For a variety of reasons, however, certain people turn to food rather than drugs or alcohol.

Although it is unclear whether the rise in the quantity of eating-disordered clients or clients presenting with disordered eating patterns is due to an actual increase in numbers or to the improved awareness and evaluative skills of clinicians, it is essential for professionals to be armed with sufficient expertise in the assessment of these disorders. This chapter explores aspects of the assessment process that occurs between an eating-disordered client and the clinician who seeks to understand and treat that client.

ASSESSMENT AND DIAGNOSIS: AN OVERVIEW

Assessment is a mutual interactional process that occurs between a clinician and a client system. The client system, also referred to here as the client, represents all those individuals, settings, and events related to the client and his or her problem. It has been described as a "complex information-gathering process that provides the data for case decision making" (Pinkston, Levitt, Green, Linsk & Rzepnicki, 1982, p. 113). Assessment can also serve to introduce the client to the treatment process and may even be therapeutic in and of itself.

The process of assessment provides the clinician with the opportunity to develop an awareness of and understanding about the client as a person, the client's reason(s) for seeking help, the client's goals and objectives, and the general nature of the problem(s) as it affects the client's overall functioning (Levitt, in press). The clinician has the task of guiding the assessment in a way that will result in the development of an effective treatment plan. The therapist is not only organizing the assessment process, taking in the immediate as well as unique needs and characteristics of the client and his eating disorder, but developing an overall treatment strategy that will result in a reduction of the eating disorder symptoms and improve general functioning. To simplify this relatively complex organizational process somewhat, the clinician is essentially involved in three interrelated functions: collecting, sorting, and analyzing information that will guide intervention.

Characteristics of the Assessment Process

The Relationship. Assessment is based on the development of a relationship. In this assessment process, the clinician must often ask uncomfortable and sometimes intrusive questions in order to develop a comprehensive understanding of the client's problem situation. For the individual client, who may be in crisis, suffering considerable emotional pain, or feeling overwhelmed or out of control regarding eating, food, and weight patterns, the initial experience with the professional may be characterized by fear and dread. Clients often long for someone who can both understand their situation and might be able to assist them in regaining some degree of control in their lives. Clearly, assessment requires both technical skills in collecting information and great therapeutic skill in managing the relationship.

Ongoing Nature. The process of assessment occurs throughout the therapeutic relationship. Although many clinical texts identify phases of treatment (e.g., assessment, intervention, termination), these phases are more for heuristic than practical value. For assessment to have any real value, it must be available for reformulation as new information and experience surfaces. The treatments, the client, and the various aspects of the client's interpersonal and intrapersonal environments will continually interact: "A resultant implication is that the assessment process is not static; rather, it is a dynamic process" (Donovan & Marlatt, 1988, p. 15).

Mutuality. The very context of developing a therapeutic relationship entails mutual interaction between clinician and client. In therapy, the development of the relationship itself may affect the assessment process. For example, a female client may be wary of sharing with a male therapist private information about the way she sees and experiences her body, which may be directly related to her eating disorder. She may deliberately omit, distort, or even lie about various aspects of the eating disorder in order to protect herself from becoming too vulnerable to the therapist. The therapist will then have inaccurate information about the eating disorder condition and might also misinterpret the client's fears as part of an underlying affective disorder or personality characteristic.

The important point here is that the assessment process is a mutual one and that the client is also engaged in collecting, sorting, and analyzing information about the therapist, as well as the general context of treatment. The style and skills that the client employs to collect, sort, and analyze information about the therapuetic context and then how the client uses that information may have a significant impact on the clinician's assessment.

A Nontheoretical Base. The assessment of conditions directly related to eating disorders or patterns of disordered eating is considered here to be unrelated to any specific theory base. While there have clearly been shown to be relationships between eating disorders and depression, personality factors, and familial functioning (e.g., Blinder, Chaitin & Goldstein, 1988; Garner & Garfinkel, 1988, Hsu, 1990; Minuchin, Rosman & Baker, 1978) there has generally been a focus on the description of eating disorders as clinical entities (Williamson, 1990). Bruch (1973) and others (e.g., Garfinkel & Garner, 1982) have reviewed various etiological perspectives related to the development of an eating disorder. Shaw and Garfinkel (1990) write, "The field has progressed rapidly, with a widespread agreement on diagnostic criteria based on signs and symptoms, and an appropriate de-emphasis on etiology as a form of classification, particularly as pathogenesis is inferred largely rather than known'' (p. 546).

The focus on eating disorders as clinical entities, or syndromes, is primarily due to the lack of specific causal information or data that indicate which factors are associated with what kind of an eating disorder, to what degree, and with what impact. For example, Garner and Garfinkel (1988) discussed contemporary concerns regarding both the diagnosis between and within eating disorder categories. Rosen, Murkofsky, Steckler, and Skolnick (1989) found that anorectics, bulimics, and bulimic anorectics differed on the symptoms of interoceptive awareness, maturity fears, and ineffectiveness as measured by the Eating Disorder Inventory (EDI) (Garner, Olmsted & Polivy, 1983). Noring et al. (1989) found that patients with eating disorders differed in terms of ego functioning. They were able to identify four subgroups that differed primarily in terms of ego strength and potential prognosis.

The eating disorder literature is replete with outcome studies illustrating the variability of characteristics within and between the categories of eating disorders. Indeed, even in 1982, Garfinkel and Garner emphasized the growing heterogeneous nature of the eating-disordered population. They pointed out that it was no longer useful to conceptualize eating disorders as discrete categories or diagnoses but rather to see them as a continuum of symptoms and symptom clusters. Consequently, while clinicians will employ their own theoretical understandings within their assessment schemata, a primary focus of assessment (and intervention as well) must be on those characteristics directly associated with disturbed and disordered eating patterns.

Collecting, Sorting, and Analyzing Information. The underlying functions in the assessment process are collecting, sorting, and analyzing the information obtained from the client. These functions continuously interact and affect one another.

The function of collecting information is related to two further processes: identifying the domains to be evaluated and measuring elements within each domain. While the general DSM-III-R criteria for the diagnosis of anorexia nervosa and bulimia nervosa (APA, 1987) appear to have enhanced validity and reliability (Shaw & Garfinkel, 1990, p. 546), the number of subclinical or "partial syndrome" cases that may be incorporated under the DSM-III-R criteria for Eating Disorders Not Otherwise Specified may in fact be more numerous than the primary eating disorder categories themselves (Shaw & Garfinkel, 1990; Szmuckler, 1985). Consequently, identification of which domains to be assessed needs to be concerned foremost with the conditions and sequelae of the eating disorders themselves.

Eating disorders are clearly related to and influence an individual's general life situation. Assessment must also examine various areas of functioning, as well as any particular conditions that the client exhibits (e.g., anxiety, depression). While the diversity of an individual's functioning will need to be tapped and examined, the evidence today as to which areas are more or less relevant to eating disorders is quite scarce and sometimes even contradictory. Although there is a growing body of information, clinicians must often rely on their own theoretical perspectives as to which area(s) should be emphasized (e.g., cognitive, behavioral, affective). Some predisposing, precipitating, and maintaining factors that have been found to be relevant in the assessment and treatment of eating disorders (Garfinkel & Garner, 1982; Johnson & Connors, 1987; Levitt, 1987) may provide some general focuses for assessment:

Predisposing factors

Developmental, intrapsychic

Familial

History of physical or sexual abuse

Cultural

Social, peers

Genetic or physiological

Precipitating factors

Crisis or trauma events

Developmental passage points

Dieting sequelae

"Addiction syndrome"

Maintaining factors

Biological sequelae secondary to the eating disorder

Biological and interpersonal classically conditioned psychophysiological responses

Biological and interpersonal operantly conditioned responses

Intrapsychic dynamics

Cultural metaphors of illness

Cognitive distortions and styles of reasoning and thinking

Societal networking

Levels of coping and problem-solving skills

Presence of chemical dependency/addiction

The second area relevant to collecting information is the measurement of the domains. Measurement means being able to place a numerical estimate on a certain characteristic. There are various means by which numerical estimates can be obtained. In general, authors suggest that one use as many different ways of measuring as possible in order to give the fullest picture of the client situation (see Corcoran & Fisher, 1987, for further information).

Whenever feasible, *direct behavioral observation* by the clinician of the client's behavior is preferable. Given the private nature of eating disorders, however, this is often not possible. Even when hospitalized, clients are unlikely to demonstrate openly either their disordered behaviors or their rituals. Also, areas of guilt, self-image, moods, and others are not readily directly observable. In these cases, the use of collateral contacts (family, friends) and indirect tools may prove useful.

Client verbal reports supply information about the client's situation as best as the client can recall. This information may be fraught with mistakes, is susceptible to the client's moods, and may be unreliable. For the person with an eating disorder, an anecdotal report is based on memories obtained during instances when she may be behaviorally disordered. On the other hand, the client verbal report may reflect the client's perceptions and is readily available and easily incorporated into the clinical session.

Client logs increase the accuracy of the client report and extend measurement to the home situation; these are structured diaries about certain areas of the client's functioning (such as food, calories, mood, or cognition). During episodes of loss of control or reporting information representing vulnerable areas for the client, accuracy may be limited. Nevertheless, logs are frequently used in the areas of weight management and eating disorders in order to attempt to structure information collecting (Williamson, 1990).

Self-anchored rating scales, constructed between the clinician and the client, generally focus on estimates of symptom intensity and have some degree of face validity due to client specificity. They are developed by having the client select a problem area, and an informal rating scale (e.g., 1 to 10) is used to estimate the relative intensity or frequency of the symptom. These scales are then repeated over time. They are useful for regularly assessing areas such as mood and self-concept and have the added benefit of being uniquely developed for and with each client.

Standardized measures are tests, scales, inventories, and indexes that are derived empirically and have been found to measure a condition(s) reliably and validly. They are often useful for giving relatively accurate criterion information but may sometimes be difficult to administer or intrude in the general development of clinical rapport.

Many clinicians use their *observations within the session* to give evaluative data as to how the client is progressing. While this is one type of useful information, it is limited. It assumes that how the client interacts within the session is an actual representation of her behavior outside the session and that this interaction is directly related to the eating disorder. Both assumptions need to be carefully evaluated for each client. In addition, it cannot be overemphasized that the only way to evaluate whether the eating disorder is improving, worsening, or remaining the same is to examine directly aspects of the eating disorder itself.

Sorting and analyzing information are two interconnected processes. Sorting refers to the various steps involved in taking information derived from possibly disparate sources and placing it into a useful, accessible condition. This is often an exercise in classification, and while clinicians are usually not label bound, all use some explicit or implicit sorting mechanism. For example, almost all clinicians will be able to discuss the client in terms of affect/mood, eating and general behavioral functioning, and cognitive distortions or reasoning styles. These categories or conditions provide an organizational scheme that may be used for further assessment and reassessment of the client condition.

Analyzing information allows the clinician to be able to diagnose, or categorize, the client condition as well as to give a general meaning to the overall client situation. Developing a sense of "meaning" regarding the eating disorder allows the clinician to understand the nature of the eating disorder and its unique connection to the client as an individual. It is at this point that the clinician's theory of human functioning, nature and development of problems, and meta-psychology may be incorporated. Clinicians need to be careful to continue to evaluate the client's eating disorder and specific aspects of functioning and not to begin to use their theoretical constructs as the principal material for assessment.

A Note about Diagnosis

The assessment of an eating disorder is a complex process. Often, however, therapists are required to apply a diagnostic label to the general client condition. This label is a shorthand method of identifying and communicating to others about a group of symptoms. Although a client is certainly more than a group of related symptoms, by using a label professionals are able not only to communicate with each other but may locate a relevant body of literature and various community services that are useful for that clinical condition (Levitt, in press).

In the area of eating disorders, there are three general *Diagnostic and Statistical Manual of Mental Disorders III* (DSM-III-R) categories that are frequently employed (APA, 1987). Another, compulsive overeating, is increasingly being used (Williamson, 1990):

Anorexia nervosa, characterized by a severe weight loss (greater than 15 percent of expected weight), fear of weight gain or becoming obese, a disturbance in the way one sees and/or experiences one's body, and an absence of menstrual cycles. Other characteristics often associated with but not necessary for the diagnosis are hyperactivity, difficulties with concentration, mood changes, and a reduced capacity to tolerate cold.

Bulimia nervosa, characterized by eating large amounts of food (binging), using purgatives (vomiting, laxatives, exercise, etc.), losing control over eating, and regular bulimic episodes (at least two per week for three months). Other associated symptoms are mood changes, secretiveness, other impulsive behaviors (e.g., compulsive shopping), and sleep difficulties.

Eating disorder not otherwise specified, a category for any combination of symptoms
that do not neatly fall into one of the other two categories. Shaw and Garfinkel (1990)
suggest that clinical cases may more frequently fall into this category than either of
the ones cited above.

Compulsive overeating, characterized by the consumption of large amounts of food when
not hungry, the experience of a loss of control when eating, nonuse of purgatives,
and emission of these behaviors over an extended period of time. Other features are
secret eating, moodiness, depression, sleep difficulties, and having food and/or eating
interfere with normal functioning.

It is important to note that diagnostic criteria are still quite limited. Indeed,
even the definition of what constitutes a binge is unclear (Rossiter & Agra,
1990). More important, Russell (1988) points out that

diagnosis should obviously go further than the mere cataloguing of disparate symptoms.
The aim is that of identifying something more meaningful: an underlying morbid process, associated with a regular pattern of symptoms, presumably brought about by a
specific cause or causes. . . . It is highly desirable that a diagnosis should point the
way to the solution of practical issues, such as the optimum choice of treatment and the
accurate prediction of the clinical outcome. (p. 4)

THE ASSESSMENT PROCESS

The development of an assessment process begins long before the clinician
ever sees an eating-disordered client. Assessment processes are developed at
the time that the clinician either decides to work with eating-disordered populations or needs to develop an understanding of those conditions. Sometimes
clinicians who have been treating other disorders (such as depression) simply
interpret the disordered eating as secondary to or as a consequence of the other
disorder. Thus, assessment of the eating disorder patterns is left largely unat-
tended and only cursorily examined. Often how clinicans tend to treat disorders
will determine how they assess them. In other words, the clinician's particular
orientation toward how one psychologically develops and resolves problems in
general determines the assessment process without emphasis on the uniqueness
of the disorder in question. In this situation, if the clinician holds a developmental orientation toward psychopathology and believes that the way these
problems are resolved is through the long-term therapeutic relationship, then
the assessment focus might well be on the relationship context, with little emphasis on collecting, sorting, or analyzing specific information related to the
eating disorder.

There is a continuous growth in the body of literature on eating disorders
and their connections to individual functioning. Although most authors stress
the need to have a broad understanding of the individual's psychological and
personality dimensions (Garner & Garfinkel, 1984; Johnson & Connors, 1987),
virtually all writers today emphasize a comprehensive assessment of the eating

disorder itself. It becomes vital for clinicians to develop an awareness of their theoretical and practical biases in order to provide effective treatment to individuals with eating disorders. Although eating disorders are certainly found in conjunction with other problems, eating disorders represent unique and distinct entities that require careful, comprehensive assessment for any treatment to be successful (Hsu, 1990).

The Telephone Contact

Assessment usually begins at the time of the first telephone contact. Sometimes clients have been previously assessed and referred by another professional.

The client informs the clinician (or the clinican's representative—that is, the intake person) about the nature of services being sought. The client is often calling to obtain information about the clinician's (or, often the case today, the "program's") availability, therapeutic orientation, fees, treatment options, appointment times, and so forth. The clinician has an opportunity to begin to learn about the client: her name and other general identification material, the general nature of the problem, and, from her requests and vocal tone, the emergent nature of her situation. The client is obtaining information at the same time about the clinician: vocal tone, style, goals, and methods of helping. This exchange is important for setting up the foundation of the following face-to-face assessment sessions.

Initial Meeting

Generally, the initial assessment process takes place within the first five face-to-face sessions. When the client and clinician meet in the first session, information is gathered about the client's immediate emotional and physical condition. Levitt (in press) points out that it is important for the therapist to be sensitive to client fears because,

while this is a regular experience for the therapist it is often a time of considerable uncertainty for the client. Many clients often feel ashamed or uncomfortable about their eating disorder, and they may feel physically ill as well. So the therapist's first goal is to collect information about the "presenting" condition while providing support and reassurance so that further information may be collected.

The initial assessment task is to exchange general information beginning with what brought the client to seek help and what precipitated that decision. Changes in the immediate physical condition, variations in the nature, degree, intensity, or frequency of the elements of the eating disorder, increased difficulty in daily functioning, changes in the social or familial context, familial insistence to seek help, and so forth may be fruitfully explored.

In addition to the reasons for seeking help, a sense of the client's awareness of and orientation toward treatment is an important area for exploration. Eating-disordered clients have often had previous therapy experiences with differing therapeutic orientations and styles. The clients have also had varying responses to those experiences, which they bring to the treatment situation. It is similarly important, therefore, to ascertain their personal goals for treatment. What they wish to accomplish, to what extent, and ideas they might have for how to attain those goals are pertinent in order to assess client-therapist fit.

In this initial opportunity to observe the client, the clinician can scan the client's physical appearance in order to evaluate physical pallor and tone. It is vital for even nonmedical therapists when working with eating-disordered clients to develop a hunch about the client's physical well-being. Clients are often reluctant to discuss the intimate nature of their problem openly but therapists are continuously assessing the congruence between what the clients say and how they appear.

What is important here is that not only are specific features of the eating disorder being explored but also their various affects on the client's functioning. Understanding the eating disorder and in what way it has been assimilated into the client's life provides a great deal of information about not only the eating disorder but the person of the client as well. Since all information here is obtained through clinician-client interaction and exchange, the client and the clinician may benefit from the conjoint sorting process and together develop a realistic appraisal of the disorder.

Hsu (1990) recommends that the following areas be examined in the evaluation of the eating disorder: weight and diet history, eating patterns, menstrual and sexual history, mental state, social and developmental history, previous treatment, medical history and physical examination, and family history. Levitt (in press) suggests a somewhat different arrangement of domains to be assessed, with emphasis placed first on the immediate character of the eating disorder. Although any area affecting the client's current functional situation needs to be evaluated, a number of general areas of an eating disorder may be usefully assessed.

The *history of the eating disorder* includes information about when the eating disorder began, the situational variable that led to the onset along with the precipitant(s), any changes in the pattern of the disorder throughout its duration, and, importantly, the function and significance of the disorder to the client.

The area of *weight patterns* includes information about past, current, and client goal weights, any relevant history of being overweight or references of being fat, determination of realistic weight given the client's height and physical structure, and assessment of the client's psychological and emotional connections to weight.

In exploring the client's *dieting history and weight control methods,* the clinician is primarily interested in the client's characteristic styles or patterns of losing weight or maintaining lost weight. In particular, the clinician is examining for duration, severity, variation, degree and intensity, and potential harm of those methods. Minimally, evaluation will consider the parameters of fasting, vomiting, purgatives, exercise, and formal and informal diet programs.

Eating behavior is an important area. Eating is a relatively complex series of interconnected biopsychosocial behaviors and events. In order to assess these behaviors and events, the clinician needs to look to the client to give relevancy for one area over another. At the least, however, the clinician will want to obtain information about any recent changes in eating patterns, food selectivity and restrictions, overt ritualistic behaviors, the quantity and quality of the foods selected, choice of setting(s) and social contexts, and the various meanings attached to the above.

Since most therapists are not medical doctors, they should always work conjointly with a physician trained in the area of eating disorders who will determine the client's *physical condition* by performing relevant physical exams and laboratory tests. Yet to work with eating-disordered individuals, even nonmedical clinicians need to be sensitive to the general physical condition of the client. These include changes in the condition of the skin, hair, or nails, obvious swollen glands, dental changes, client experience of chilling or becoming unusually cold, hyperactive or hypomanic behaviors, or the appearance of looking tired, fatigued, or ill.

The area of psychological functioning is extremely broad and requires a great deal of time to understand. In the initial stages of assessment of the client's *psychological condition,* the clinician is interested in areas related to current functioning: the client's capacity for present orientation and the evaluation for any overt psychotic or organic condition, difficulties with concentration or memory, sleep disturbances, changes in sexual interest, presence of overwhelming anxiety, panic, or phobias, fatigue or lethargy, level of depression, and degree of body image distortion.

Clearly, the clinician will spend at least the first few sessions gathering these data. If the client appears in any imminent physical danger, these areas may need to be more thoroughly explored in the first session and more inclusive material obtained later. Once the characteristics of the eating disorder have at least been surveyed, further assessment will focus on identifying the client's unique style of coping with his or her world and the contextual relationship to the eating disorder. A number of areas are useful to explore.

In the area of *cognitive style,* the clinician is interested in understanding the client's learning style and limitations, capacity for introspection, and her style of cognitive distortion (e.g., mind reading, all-or-nothing thinking, denial, minimization).

Body image is an extremely important area to be evaluated because the degree of body image distortion has been found to be associated with prognosis (Garfinkel & Garner, 1982). Thus, the degree of body image distortion, as well as the nature and degree of the client's satisfaction or dissatisfaction with certain parts of her body and the ways the body (parts) appear and are experienced, is essential in any assessment.

Self-concept is a vital area to explore. Bruch (1973) talked extensively about the anorectic's paralyzing sense of ineffectiveness as being a primary feature of the illness. Others (e.g., Johnson & Connors, 1987) have also discussed the lack of experienced initiative and autonomy of the bulimic. Consequently, the client's experience of self—her sense of worthwhileness and worthiness, perception of capacity to be valued by others, and belief in her capacity to change and make changes in her environment—are important.

A review of the client's *developmental history* can be quite important in order to understand the development and progression of the illness. Although some of this material may have been examined in taking the history of the eating disorder, the premorbid context and any relevant information may be useful for treatment. This is particularly true if there is a history of residence changes, illnesses, divorce, physical or sexual abuse, or other overt trauma.

Clients with eating disorders often develop ineffective and sometimes chaotic or self-destructive *interpersonal relationships*. Since the therapist is also developing a relationship with the client, aspects of their relating are important. The clinician will want to explore the number, pattern, nature of friendships and intimate relations, along with the client's experience of trust, closeness, and feelings of competency within the various significant relationships.

Family history is an important area to be explored because much of what the client exhibits may be related to the familial context (Minuchin, 1978). Particularly relevant is any history of alcoholism or drug abuse, mental or physical illness, physical or sexual abuse, the nature of the relationships with each family member, and the ways day-to-day situations, as well as difficult family problems or events, were managed.

These, then, are the general areas to be assessed as they relate to eating disorders. The goal is to survey these domains and emphasize, organize, and articulate the more client-relevant ones and then assimilate them. This should result in a dynamic picture of the client problem system. Since an essential task that must also be accomplished during these sessions is to engage the client and the client's family in treatment, great care must be taken to pace the sessions and listen respectfully to the verbal and nonverbal information as the client system presents it. In general, exploratory questions should be asked directly and honestly and received in an open, compassionate, and patient manner. In the chapter appendix, the Eating Disorders Assessment Protocol (Levitt, 1988) is presented; it provides one structured format for interviewing the client and some possible ways to phrase questions.

ASSESSMENT TOOLS AND MEASURES

In addition to exploratory questions and areas, there are a variety of tools and measures available for obtaining information about eating disorder symptoms and related client characteristics. These tests or instruments may give the clinician additional or supporting information about the client and may be introduced any time in the assessment process.

Structured Interview Formats

Several instruments have been developed for the purpose of conducting research or as a result of clinical experience that provide a relatively structured format, or protocol, for the assessment of eating disorders. The general purpose of these instruments is to guide the assessment process and aid in the organization of information. Most of these tap relatively similar areas although from slightly different perspectives. Three of these are presented here.

The Diagnostic Survey for Eating Disorders—Revised (DSED-R; Johnson, 1984; Johnson & Connors, 1987) is a standardized instrument designed to investigate various aspects of anorexia and bulimia. Divided into 12 sections, the instrument surveys areas of body image, eating and weight history, demographic factors, and others. The instrument is quite complete and appears to have been developed for the purposes of conducting research.

The Eating Disorders Assessment Protocol (EDAP; Levitt, 1988) was created out of clinical experience to help inexperienced eating disorder clinicians develop a systematic way of organizing the assessment process. The EDAP provides guidelines for obtaining information within the session through client-therapist interaction.

The Interview for Diagnosis of Eating Disorders (IDED; Williamson, 1990) is a relatively brief instrument designed to diagnose the conditions of anorexia, bulimia, compulsive overeating, and obesity. All of the questions are based on the DSM-III-R criteria for eating disorders (except compulsive overeating and obesity), which Williamson discusses.

Rapid Assessment Instruments

The rapid assessment instruments (RAIs) are a category of measures that are standardized paper-and-pencil instruments, can be easily filled out by a client quickly, are relatively easy to administer and score by the clinician, and are able to give a generally accurate picture of a client's condition at one or multiple periods of time (Levitt & Reid, 1981). While essentially self-report instruments, RAIs have the advantage of structuring the reporting process, applying a numerical estimate(s) to the condition that can be evaluated over time, and frequently have been designed to possess cutting scores that provide another source of information indicating the presence of a significant level of the problem. Building on the concept of the RAIs developed by Levitt and Reid, Corcoran and Fisher (1987) point out that RAIs have the following advantages: accessibility, disclosure, comparability, efficiency, and neutrality. Corcoran and

Fisher also explain in some detail how to administer the tools and have pains-takingly included a variety of the actual instruments in their work.

Assessment of Eating Disorder Symptoms

A number of instruments have been developed to aid clinicians in assessing the symptoms of the eating disorders themselves. These instruments are easily administered paper-and-pencil tests that result in a numerical estimate of var-ious symptom clusters. The purpose of these tools is to inform the clinician of the type of symptom, its severity and intensity, and its relationship to other related eating disorder symptoms. Descriptions of some of these tools follow:

Bulimia Test (BUILT), a 32-item test to target individuals with bulimic disorders (Smith & Thelen, 1984).

Binge Eating Scale (BES), a 16-item test to measure components of binge eating, es-pecially for obese individuals (Gormally, Black, Daston & Rardin, 1984).

Binge Scale, a 9-item test to measure binge eating components associated with bulimia (Hawkins & Clements, 1980).

Compulsive Eating Scale (CES), an 8-item test to measure compulsive eating associated with obesity (Kagan and Squires, 1984).

Concern over Weight and Dieting Scale (COWD), a 14-item test to assess concerns over weight and dieting as they relate to eating disorders (Kagan & Squires, 1984).

Eating Attitudes Test (EATS), a 40-item test to identify and assess attitudes associated with anorexia nervosa (Garner & Garfinkel, 1979).

Eating Disorder Inventory (EDI), a 64-item measure to assess psychological and behav-ioral components found in common between anorexia and bulimia (Garner, Olmsted & Polivy, 1983).

Eating Questionnaire—Revised (EQ-R), (1987) a 15-item instrument used as a symptom checklist to measure the DSM-III criteria for bulimia (Williamson et al., 1987).

Goldfarb Fear of Fat Scale (GFFS), a 10-item test that measures fears of becoming fat (Goldfarb, Dykens & Gerrard, 1985).

Hunger-Satiety Scales (H-SS), two 9-item measures for research on anorexia that looks at the capacity to discriminate hunger and satiety (Garfinkel, 1974).

Internal Versus External Control of Weight Scale (IECW), a 5-item instrument to mea-sure the degree to which individuals see that the capacity to lose weight is under their control (Tobias & MacDonald, 1977).

Restraint Scale (RS), a 10-item test that measures the ability to restrain one's eating (Herman, 1978).

Assessment of Specific Problematic Symptoms

There are many areas of a person's functioning that have been reported in the literature as being associated with eating disorders that the clinician might also wish to examine. These might arise during the course of treatment, for example, when a particular affective state becomes overt, such as depression or anxiety. In other cases, the clinician might want another source of information about a client's world of internal experience such as self-image, attitude toward the family, or other attitudes, values, or beliefs. The eating disorder literature is replete with numerous instruments covering virtually anything that clinicians have been able to conceptualize and operationalize. To cover them all would be beyond the scope of this work. There are, however, several problem areas that have been frequently discussed in connection with eating disorders, and instruments to assess them have been developed:

Anxiety

Fear of Negative Evaluation (FNE) (Watson & Friend, 1969).

Self-Rating Anxiety Scale (SAS) (Zung, 1971).

State-Trait Anxiety Inventory (STAI) (Spielberger, Gorusch & Lushene, 1970).

Depression

Beck Depression Inventory (BDI) (Beck, 1967).

Generalized Contentment Scale (GCS) (Hudson, 1982).

Self-Rating Depression Scale (SDS) (Zung, 1965).

Family Attitudes

Child's Attitude towards Father (CAF) (Hudson, 1982).

Child's Attitude towards Mother (CAM) (Hudson, 1982).

Family Environment Scale (FES) (Moos, 1974).

Index of Family Relations (IFR) (Hudson, 1982).

Obsessive-Compulsive Traits

Maudsley Obsessional-Compulsive Inventory (MOCI) (Hodgson and Rachman, 1977).

Obsessive Compulsive Scale (OCS) (Gibb, Bailey, Best, and Lambrith, 1983).

Assessment of Personality and Other Psychological Problems

Clinicians will often want a broad-based assessment of a client's general symptom presentation or general personality characteristics. These measures give the clinician another avenue for understanding the client's private world and giving a picture of the client's symptom configuration. Following are but a few of the possible measures:

General Symptom Evaluation

Symptom Checklist-90 (Derogatis & Cleary, 1977).

Personality Characteristics

Borderline Syndrome Index (BSI) (Conte, Plutchik, Karasu & Jerrett, 1980).

Minnesota Multiphasic Personality Inventory (MMPI) (Hathaway & McKinley, 1951).

Millon Clinical Multiaxial Inventory (MCMI) (Millon, 1982).

SPECIAL ISSUES IN ASSESSMENT

Sometimes in the assessment of eating disorders, the clinician encounters special problems or issues that have to do with the unique nature of eating disorders and the settings and individuals involved with the assessment. In order to be prepared, the clinician needs to be aware of these situations to obtain the most accurate assessment of the client system as possible.

Various settings will support the assessment of eating disorder features. Some of these include inpatient and outpatient eating disorder and compulsive disorder programs. In other settings, however, where the eating disorder is viewed as a manifestation of an underlying pathological process, the aspects of the eating disorder may be viewed as less important, and thorough assessment and monitoring might even be thought of as placing too much emphasis on them. In these cases, therapists are faced with a difficult decision: whether to assess and monitor behaviors where the setting is unsupportive. In this perspective, it is as important to assess and monitor the client's eating disorder condition as any other condition. In settings where this is not openly supported, informal assessment methods, such as client self-report and the clinician monitoring of food intake and weight, are vitally important. While accuracy and reliability may be lost, the advantages in obtaining some information will continue to allow the therapist to evaluate whether improvement is occurring.

In other instances, there will be settings where staff are untrained in not only how to assess eating disorder conditions but may be uneducated in even the general area of eating disorders. In this situation, the clinican needs to educate the staff about eating disorders in general and then gradually train them to use increasingly complex assessment methods. It is important not to overwhelm the staff with the intricacies of both the aspects of eating disorders and the assessment processes.

Eating disorders are by their very nature private and hence secretive disorders. Often clients are embarrassed or ashamed about their behaviors and struggle with sharing with a stranger their lack of being able to control not only their eating but often many other aspects of their lives. Additionally, the clients may often be engaging in socially unacceptable behaviors, such as shoplifting, or behaviors that others might find abhorrent, such as vomiting into plastic bags in their bedroom. It is important for the clinician to be sensitive to the private aspects of the disorder and not to expect too much too soon. While it is my experience that most clients answer direct, honest questions as truthfully as possible, there may well be some information, or aspects of previously discussed information, that will be shared only later as trust and experience grow.

There are also individual characteristics of both the client and the therapist that may affect the assessment process. Williamson (1990) speaks of the difficulties of assessing the resistant client: "the patient may often attempt to deceive the person(s) conducting the evaluation. . . . the patient may often minimize or negate any report of affective distress regarding weight gain, eating 'normally,' or binge eating" (p. 101). Clearly, given the private nature of eating disorders and the ways in which the disorders become integrated into the individual's interpersonal and intrapersonal systems of functioning, denial and resistant behaviors might well be viewed as integral to the disorder. Rather than taking the view of resistance where the client actually is fighting the assessment or recovery process, resistance might be more usefully viewed as part of the disorder and, consequently, an area requiring evaluation in each client. Rather than seeing resistance as something that belongs to a specific kind of client (the one who fights or actively refuses assessment and treatment), resistance might be seen on a continuum and be expected. Thus, resistance itself becomes a regular part of the assessment process; therapists may avoid negatively labeling clients who have greater difficulty accepting help, and "assessment control struggles" might be avoided.

Of course, there are clients who are not ready or are unwilling to accept assistance. If the therapist carefully assesses the client's reasons for requesting treatment and the client's personal goals, then this should become apparent and be addressed early on. For clients whose physical integrity is in jeopardy, in-depth assessment will be less necessary initially, and focus can be placed on areas necessary to regain a relatively healthy status (caloric intake, laboratory parameters, weight, etc.). Later, if the client is willing, other areas may be assessed more comprehensively.

Finally, therapists themselves may be influenced by the clients and their disorder. Johnson and Connors (1987) refer to this as countertransference and discuss three general areas affecting all therapists and two specific areas of countertransference for both males and females. In general, they suggest that sharing society's obsession with thinness, revulsion at the binge/purge behavior (or similarly with the anorectic's restricted eating/weight avoidant behaviors), and impatience with the client's refusal to change may all affect the therapeutic process. For female therapists, envy of the patient or having an eating or weight problem themselves can also serve to impair the efficacy of treatment. Male therapists need to be aware, according to Johnson and Connors, of difficulties in developing an empathic connection with female clients and with potential concerns about the intrusiveness of body-related explorations. While these potential areas of countertransference concern were not originally presented by Johnson and Connors (1987) in relation to assessment, it is easy to see how they might be equally applicable to the assessment process. It is essential that while the clinician is assessing and monitoring the client system, the therapist is also attuned to the therapist-client system and the ways the clinician himself is being affected during the assessment process. Then the material obtained will most accurately and thoughtfully reflect the client condition.

CONCLUSION

Despite the plethora of data in the eating disorder literature, more information remains unknown than is known. This is also true of eating disorder assessment.

We are still unsure of what causes or even what maintains the disorder, though we have some ideas. It is unclear today, for example, why certain individuals in a family develop an eating disorder and others do not. We lack certainty as to what occurs in dieting that leads to the onset of the disorder and why it occurs in some individuals and not in others. There seems to be some potential relationship between eating disorders and affective disorder, but the data are unclear as to the connection, the strength of the connection, the synergistic effect of the interactions, and the most useful way to evaluate these conditions. Clearly, those differences and relationships would have a significant impact on our choice of assessment domains.

Assessment of eating disorders needs to become a more regular and systematic process for all therapists so that we are able to share information more readily and provide the most effective, caring treatment that benefits the client.

REFERENCES

American Psychological Association (1987). *Diagnostic and statistical manual of mental disorders* (3d ed. rev.). Washington, D.C.: American Psychiatric Association Press.

Bass, E. & Davis, L. (1988). *The courage to heal: A guide for women survivors of child sexual abuse.* New York: Harper & Row.

Beck, A. T. (1967). *Depression: Clinical, experimental, and theoretical aspects.* New York: Harper & Row.

Blinder, B. J., Chaitin, B. F. & Goldstein, R. S. (eds.) (1988). *The eating disorders: Medical and psychological bases of diagnosis and treatment.* New York: PMA Publishing Group.

Brownell, K. D. & Foreyt, J. P. (1986). *Handbook of eating disorders: Physiology, psychology, and treatment of obesity, anorexia, and bulimia.* New York: Basic Books.

Bruch, H. (1973). *Eating disorders: Obesity, anorexia nervosa, and the person within.* New York: Basic Books.

Conte, H. R., Plutchik, R., Karasu, T. & Jerrett, I. (1980). A self-report borderline scale: Discriminative validity and preliminary norms. *Journal of Nervous and Mental Disease, 168,* 428–35.

Corcoran, K. & Fisher, J. (1987). *Measures for clinical practice: A sourcebook.* New York: Free Press.

Derogatis, L. R. & Cleary, P. (1987). Confirmation of the dimensional structure of the SCL-90: A study in construct validation. *Journal of Clinical Psychology, 33,* 981–89.

Emmet, S. E. (ed.) (1985). *Theory and treatment of anorexia nervosa and bulimia: Biomedical, sociocultural, and psychological perspectives.* New York: Brunner/Mazel.

Garfinkel, P. E. (1974). Perception of hunger and satiety in anorexia nervosa. *Psychological Medicine, 4,* 309–15.

Garfinkel, P. E. & Garner, D. M. (1982). *Anorexia nervosa: A multidimensional perspective.* New York: Brunner/Mazel.

Garner, D. M. and Garfinkel, P. E. (1979). The eating attitudes test: An index of the symptoms of anorexia nervosa. *Psychological Medicine, 9,* 273–79.

Garner, D. M. & Garfinkel, P. E. (eds.) (1984). *Handbook of psychotherapy for anorexia nervosa and bulimia.* New York: Guilford Press.

Garner, D. M. & Garfinkel, P. E. (eds.) (1988). *Diagnostic issues in anorexia nervosa and bulimia nervosa.* New York: Brunner/Mazel.

Garner, D. M., Olmsted, M. P. & Polivy, J. (1983a). The eating disorder inventory: A measure of the cognitive/behavioral dimensions of anorexia nervosa and bulimia. In P. L. Darby, P. E. Garfinkel, D. M. Garner & D. V. Coscina (eds.), *Anorexia nervosa: Recent developments* (pp. 173–84). New York: Guilford Press.

Garner, D. M., Olmsted, M. P. & Polivy, J. (1983b). Development and validation of a multidimensional inventory for anorexia nervosa and bulimia. *International Journal of Eating Disorders, 2,* 15–34.

Gibb, G. D., Bailey, J. R., Best, R. H. & Lambrith, T. T. (1983). The measurement of the obsessive compulsive personality. *Educational and Psychological Measurement, 43,* 1233–37.

Goldfarb, L. A., Dykens, E. M. & Gerrard, M. (1985). The Goldfarb fear of fat scale. *Journal of Personality Assessment, 49,* 329–32.

Gormally, J., Black, S., Daston, S. & Rardin, D. (1984). The assessment of binge eating severity among obese persons. *Addictive Behaviors, 7,* 47–55.

Hathaway, S. & McKinley, J. (1951). *MMPI manual* (rev. ed.). New York: Psychological Corporation.

Hawkins, R. C. & Clements, P. F. (1980). Development and construct validation of a self-report measure of binge eating tendencies. *Addictive Behaviors, 5,* 219–26.

Herman, C. P. (1978). Restrained eating. *Psychiatric Clinics of North America, 1,* 593–607.

Hodgson, R. J. & Rachman, S. (1977). Obsessional-compulsive complaints. *Behaviour Research and Therapy, 15,* 389–95.

Hsu, L. K. G. (1990). *Eating disorders.* New York: Guilford Press.

Hudson, W. W. (1982). *The clinical measurement package: A field manual.* Chicago: Dorsey Press.

Johnson, C. (1984). The initial consultation for parents with bulimia and anorexia nervosa. In D. M. Garner and P. E. Garfinkel (eds.), *Handbook of psychotherapy for anorexia nervosa and bulimia.* New York: Guilford Press.

Johnson, C. & Connors, M. E. (1987). *The etiology and treatment of bulimia nervosa: A biopsychological perspective.* New York: Basic Books.

Kagan, D. M. & Squires, R. L. (1984). Eating disorders among adolescents: Patterns and prevalence. *Adolescence, 19,* 15–29.

Lacey, J. Hubert, Dip, A. Harte & Birtchnell, S. A. (1986). Bulimia—towards a rational approach to diagnosis and treatment. In Felix E. F. Larocca (ed.), *Eating disorders: Effective care and treatment* (pp. 107–28). St. Louis, Mo.: Ishiyake EuroAmerica.

Larocca, F. E. F. (ed.) (1986). *Eating disorders: Effective care and treatment.* St. Louis, Mo.: Ishiyake EuroAmerica.

Levitt, J. L. (1987 October). *Multiple problems—Drugs, alcohol, and food.* Paper presented at American Association of Eating Disorders Counselors Annual Conference, Orlando, FL.

Levitt, J. L. (in press). Assessment of eating disorders. In *Eating disorders: A reference handbook*. Phoenix: Oryx Press.

Levitt, J. L. (1988). Eating disorder assessment protocol. In *Annals of Clinical Research* (pp. 53–62). Des Plaines, Ill.: Forest Foundation Press.

Levitt, J. L. & Reid, W. J. (1981). Rapid assessment instruments for practice. *Social Work Research and Abstracts, 17,* 13–19.

Millon, T. (1982). *Millon clinical multiaxial inventory* (2d ed.). Minneapolis: National Computer Systems.

Minuchin, S., Rosman, B. L. & Baker, L. (1978). *Psychosomatic families: Anorexia nervosa in context*. Cambridge: Harvard University Press.

Moos, R. (1974). *Family environment scale manual*. Palo Alto, Calif.: Consulting Psychologists Press.

Norring, C. Sohlberg, S., Rosmark, B., Humble, K., Holmgren, S. & Nordquist, J. (1989). Ego functioning in eating disorders: Description and relationship to diagnostic classification. *International Journal of Eating Disorders, 8,* 607–22.

Pinkston, E. M., Levitt, J. L., Green, G. R., Linsk, N. L. & Rzepnicki, T. L. (1982). *Effective social work practice: Advanced techniques for behavioral intervention with individuals, families, and institutional staff*. San Francisco: Jossy-Bass.

Putman, F. M. (1989). *Diagnosis and treatment of multiple personality disorders*. New York: Guilford.

Rosen, A. M., Murkofsky, C. A., Steckler, N. M. & Skolnick, N. J. (1989). A comparison of psychological and depressive symptoms among restricting anorexic, bulimic anorexic, and normal-weight bulimic patients. *International Journal of Eating Disorders, 8,* 657–63.

Ross, C. A. (1989). *Multiple personality disorder: Diagnosis, clinical features, and treatment*. New York: John Wiley and Sons.

Rossiter, E. M. & Agras, W. S. (1990). An empirical test of the DSM-III-R definition of binge. *International Journal of Eating Disorders, 9,* 513–18.

Russell, G. M. (1988). The diagnostic formulation in bulimia nervosa. In David M. Garner and Paul E. Garfinkel (eds.), *Diagnostic issues in anorexia nervosa and bulimia nervosa* (pp. 3–25). New York: Brunner/ Mazel.

Shaw, B. F. & Garfinkel, P. E. (1990). Research problems in the eating disorders. *International Journal of Eating Disorders, 9,* 545–55.

Smith, M. C. & Thelen, M. H. (1984). Development and validation of a test for bulimia. *Journal of Consulting and Clinical Psychology, 52,* 863–72.

Spielberger, C. D., Gorusch, R. L. & Lushene, R. E. (1970). *Manual for the state-trait anxiety inventory*. Palo Alto, Calif.: Consulting Psychologists Press.

Szmuckler, G. I. (1985). The epidemiology of eating disorders. *Journal of Psychiatric Research, 12,* 143–54.

Tobias, L. L. & MacDonald, M. L. (1977). Internal locus of control and weight loss: An insufficient condition. *Journal of Consulting and Clinical Psychology, 45,* 647–53.

Watson, D. & Friend, R. (1969). Measurement of social-evaluative anxiety. *Journal of Consulting and Clinical Psychology, 33,* 448–57.

Williamson, D. A. (1990). *Assessment of eating disorders: Obesity, anorexia, and bulimia nervosa*. New York: Pergamon Press.

Williamson, D. A., Davis, C. J., Goreczny, A. J., McKenzie, S. J., & Watkins, P. C. (1987). The eating questionnaire—revised: A new symptom checklist for bulimia. In P. A. Keller and L. G. Ritts (eds.), *Innovations in clinical practice: A sourcebook* (pp. 321–26). Sarasota, Fla.: Professional Resource Exchange.

Woods, S. C. & Brief, D. J. (1988). Physiological factors. In Dennis M. Donovan and G. Alan Marlatt (eds.), *Assessment of addictive behaviors* (pp. 296–322). New York: Guilford Press.

Zung, W. K. (1965). A self-rating depression scale. *Archives of General Psychiatry, 12*, 63–70.

Zung, W. K. (1971). A rating instrument for anxiety disorders. *Psychosomatics, 12*, 371–79.

APPENDIX: EATING DISORDERS ASSESSMENT PROTOCOL

The Eating Disorders Assessment Protocol (EDAP) has been developed as a way of helping me organize my thinking around how to develop an understanding of individuals who present with some form of eating disorder. It was developed also in response to requests from students and practitioners participating in my classes and workshops who were eager to learn about this population but had few guidelines to help them. Indeed, there had been very few structured interview formats developed, and most of these were for the purpose of obtaining research-based information about the eating disorder. Other instruments were surveys or questionnaires. Few tools existed to help the clinician explore and understand the individual who had an eating disorder. The EDAP was designed to help with this problem.

The EDAP is designed to be an assessment protocol, that is, to guide the assessment and understanding process—not to determine what it should be or to limit it. Hence, it was structured to be relatively broad in scope and allow clinicians to explore and obtain relevant information from individuals from any age group or with any eating disorder problem area. It is relatively atheoretical in orientation and covers a wide spectrum of both the eating disorder itself and an individual's general functioning. For example, the EDAP includes weight, eating behaviors and habits, physical systems, psychological systems, and family history and family systems. It provides a sound foundation from which clinicians may expand inquiry according to their theoretical orientation, setting requirements, and specific client needs.

Included in the general protocol is the Quick Assessment Form (EDAP-QAF), designed to provide clinicians with a brief, simple, and efficient guide to determine the presence and, to some degree, the severity of an eating disorder. The QAF was developed to review some of the most pertinent clinical areas around the eating disorder itself. Once the presence of an eating disorder is determined, the general EDAP may be used.

The EDAP was not intended to replace complete medical or psychological assessments. It provides a somewhat standardized format for information and data collection. It may also serve as a diagnostic guide in that the questions are often presented as "practitioner statements" for clinicians who are learning interview skills or would like some help in phrasing specific questions. Clinicians are, of course, free to use their own words and phrasing, and discussion with clients should be as natural and comfortable for all parties as possible. Spaces are provided for client responses as well as for clinician impressions from which other explorations may be made.

Administration of the EDAP or the EDAP-QAF is probably best done informally in order to avoid rote questioning and overlooking useful client-specific information. Not every question or problem area must, or perhaps even should, be covered to the same extent and in the same way with each client. Experience using the EDAP with well over 150 clients in both inpatient and outpatient settings suggests that the greater the flexibility the clinician employs with the EDAP, the more useful and elaborate the clinician's data collection and understanding of the client.

The information collected is primarily useful for client-clinician person/problem understanding and treatment planning and may be used for evaluating the general efficacy of service provision. Although specific factual information is available and may be abstracted from the protocol, its intent is not research oriented. Information therefore is not designed to be normed or tallied, but, rather, it is to be incorporated into an overall narrative or summary evaluation of the client's status. It is hoped that the EDAP will help clinicians collect useful information about people with eating disorders more consistently, effectively, and with a better understanding of clients in their context.

EATING DISORDERS ASSESSMENT PROTOCOL (EDAP)

Name:_____ DOB:_____ Sex:_____

Address:_____ Phone:_____

Referral Source:_____ Date:_____

Occupation:_____ Height:_____

Marital Status:_____ Religion:_____

Children (ages & sex):_____

Personal Physician:_____ Income:_____

Person to Contact In Emergency:_____

Reason for Requesting Assessment:_____

What brings you here now? _____
_____

Could you please describe your problem? _____
_____
_____

If we agree to work together what would you like to see
changed by the time we terminate? _____
_____
_____

What have you tried in the past that has seemed to be
useful/not useful? _____
_____
_____

Are there any people you feel are particularly relevant or
important to your recovery? Who are they and how are they
important? _____
_____
_____

Do you feel that your problem has been improving, staying the same, or getting worse in the last month? Has anything been happening in your life that you think might be useful in helping us to understand this situation? _____
_____
_____
_____

Weight
   1. What is your current (today's) weight? _____

   2. Have there been any recent changes in your weight?
     Yes No   Please describe:_____
     _____

     A) Weight for last 4 days: _____, _____, _____, _____
     B) Weight one week ago today: _____
     C) Weight two weeks ago today: _____

   3. What is the most you have ever weighed? _____
     When was that? _____

   4. What is the least you have ever weighed? _____
     When was that? _____

   5. At what weight do you feel you function best at?
     _____ What leads you to think this? _____
     _____

   6. What would you like to weigh now? _____

   7. How often do you weigh yourself per day now? _____

   8. When do you weigh yourself?
     A) What times? _____
     B) After meals? _____
     C) After exercise? _____
     D) Other? _____

   9. How do you think others react to your weight?

    1 2 3 4 5 6 7 8 9 10
  not very   very
    upset   upset

   10. How do you feel about your present weight?

```
1  2  3  4  5  6  7  8  9  10
not very                 very
  upset                  upset
```

Eating Behavior

1. How often per day do you normally eat? _____

2. At what times do you normally eat? _____

3. Where do you typically eat your meals? _____

4. With whom do you typically eat? _____

5. Are there any special foods or food groups that you
   dislike or refuse to eat? _____
   _____

6. Are there any special foods or food groups that you
   specially like to eat? _____
   _____

7. Are there any particular ways or styles in
   which you eat that you have noticed are different
   from other people? _____
   _____

8. Describe three meals that you typically eat in a day:
   _____ __
   _____
   _____

9. How much of the day do you spend thinking about
   eating?
   A) less than 10%
   B) 10%-30%
   C) 30%-60%
   D) 60%-90%
   E) more than 90%

10. Binging habits. When did you begin binging?_____

   A) Do you consume large quantities of
      food (binge) in a

brief
or
extended   period of time?

B) How often do you binge? _____

C) What is the most number of binges you have done
in one day? _____

D) What are the average number of binges you have
had: today? _____
       last 2 days? _____
       last 2 weeks? _____
       last month? _____

E) In the last month how many days have you gone
without binging? _____

F) Where do you normally binge? _____
_____
_____

G) When do you normally binge? _____
_____

H) Describe 2 different binge episodes: _____
_____
_____
_____

I) How do you feel before, during. and after a binge?
before:_____
during:_____
after:_____

J) What does a binge "mean" to you? _____
_____
_____

11. Vomiting Habits. Do you ever force yourself to vomit
or behave/create circumstances that lead you to
vomit?
                Yes

                No

A) When did you begin vomiting?_____

B) How often do you vomit? _____

C) What are the most number of times you have vomited
   in one day? _____ When was that?
   _____

D) How many times have you vomited on average: today?
   _____
   last two days? _____
   last two weeks? _____
   last month? _____

E) In the last month how many days in a row have you
   gone without vomiting? _____

F) Where do you typically vomit? _____
   _____

G) When do you typically vomit? _____

H) Describe two different episodes of vomiting. ___
   _____
   _____
   _____

I) How do you feel before, during, and after
   vomiting?
   before: _____
   _____
   _____

   during: _____
   _____
   _____

   after: _____
   _____
   _____

J) What does vomiting "mean" to you? _____
   _____
   _____

12. Laxative/ipecac habits. Do you take, or began
    taking, laxatives or ipecac for the purpose of
    controlling of affecting your weight or body image?

Yes

No

A) When did you first start taking laxatives_____
_____ or ipecac?_____

B) How many laxatives, or how much ipecac, do you
frequently take in one day? _____ How many
do you take at one time? _____

C) What are the most number or amount of laxatives
or ipecac you have taken in one day? _____
When? _____

D) How many laxatives/ipecac have you taken:

today? _____
yesterday? _____
two days ago? _____

E) What brand of laxatives/ipecac do you typically
take? _____

F) When do you usually take the laxatives/ipecac?

_____

G) Where do you usually take the laxatives/ipecac?

_____

H) Have you noticed any side effects from taking the
laxatives or ipecac?
physical side effects? _____

_____

emotional side effects? _____

_____

I) Describe how you feel before, during, and after
you take the laxatives or ipecac:
before: _____
during: _____
after:_____

J) Please discuss the importance that laxatives or
ipecac "mean" to you:_____

_____
_____

13. Diuretic and/or diet pill habits. Do you take
diuretics or diet pills for the purpose of
controlling your weight, hunger, or body image?

      diuretics   yes   no

      diet pills   yes   no

      both   yes   no

A) When did you first start using diuretics_____
_____ or diet pills? _____

B) How many diuretics or diet pills do you typically
take in one day? _____ How many do you take
at one time? _____

C) What is the most number of diuretics or diet
pills you have taken in one day? _____ When?
_____

D) What brand of diuretics or diet pills do you
usually take?
_____

E) How many diuretics or diet pills have you taken:

      today? _____
      yesterday? _____
      two days ago? _____

F) When do usually take the diuretics or diet
pills?_____
_____

G) Where do you usually take the diuretics or diet
pills? _____
_____

H) Have you noticed any side-effects from taking
the diuretics or diet pills?
physical side effects? _____
_____
emotional side effects? _____

I) Descibe how you feel before, during, and after
you take the diuretics or diet pills:
before:_____
during:_____
after:_____

J) Discuss the importance that diuretics or diet
pills have for you: _____
_____
_____
_____

14. Do you use binging, vomiting. laxatives/ipecac, or
diuretics/diet pill in combination? _____
How? _____
_____
_____

Physical Systems

1. How have you been feeling lately?

A) Excellent
B) Good
C) Fair
D) Poor

2. How have you been feeling recently as compared to
what you consider to be your normal physical
condition? (e.g., the last 10 days compared to 6
months ago)

A) Excellent
B) Good
C) Fair
D) Poor

3. Have you been having any problems with the following
areas?

			started	stopped
mouth	Y	N	_____	_____
lips	Y	N	_____	_____

gums	Y	N	_____	_____
teeth	Y	N	_____	_____
throat	Y	N	_____	_____
stomach	Y	N	_____	_____
moving bowels	Y	N	_____	_____
urinating	Y	N	_____	_____
muscle cramps	Y	N	_____	_____
dry skin	Y	N	_____	_____
headaches	Y	N	_____	_____
sweats	Y	N	_____	_____
shortness of breath	Y	N	_____	_____
heart palpitations	Y	N	_____	_____
blood in bowels	Y	N	_____	_____
blood in urine	Y	N	_____	_____

4. Do you (client or practitioner) notice bilaterally swollen glands on the side of the neck? (i.e., chipmunk facies)?

Y   N

5. Do you (client or practitioner) notice any significant effects on the teeth or mouth?

A) Changes in color (e.g., grayish color due to stomach acid)?

Y   N

B) Erosion from placing objects in the mouth?

Y   N

6. Do you (client or practitioner) notice swelling or cracking in the corners of the mouth or lips (i.e., cheilosis)?   Y   N

7. Do you (client or practitoner) notice calloused knuckles (from vomiting)?

Y   N

8. Do you (client or practitioner) notice changes in hair (i.e., hair loss, dry)?

Y   N

9. Do you (client or practitioner) notice changes in the skin or nails (e.g., cracking or splitting)?

Y   N

10. Menstrual cycle problems?
   A) When was your last menstrual cycle? _____
   B) Any recent changes in your menstrual cycle?
   Y   N
   If so, describe_____
   _____

   C) Describe a typical menstrual cycle:
   physically_____
   _____

   emotionally_____
   _____

   D) What was your weight at your last cycle? _____

11. Have you been having any of the following
    difficulties?
   started   stopped

   anxiety or panic attacks   Y   N _____   _____

   sleep disturbances:
      going to sleep   Y   N _____   _____
      sleep interrupted   Y   N _____   _____
      early awakening   Y   N _____   _____
      nightmares   Y   N _____   _____

   experiencing severe cold
      or chilling easily   Y   N _____   _____

   difficulty with memory   Y   N _____   _____

   difficulty concentrating   Y   N _____   _____

   fatigue or lethargy   Y   N _____   _____

   sexual difficulties:
      interest   Y   N _____   _____
      performance   Y   N _____   _____

12. Have you been experiencing any other physical
    problems not previously discussed?

   Y   N
   If so, please discuss:_____
   _____

13. Have you ever been hospitalized for any reasons?
If so, please describe where, when, and for how long
and for what condition:

_____

_____

_____

14. Are you presently under the care of a physician,
chiropractor, or any helping professional? If so,
please state who they are, for what are you being
treated, and give a telephone number where they can
be reached. _____

_____

_____

_____

Psychological Systems

Individual:

1. Any recent changes in school or work performance?
Describe:_____

_____

_____

2. Any observed or reported withdrawal from friends or
or family? Describe:_____

_____

_____

3. Describe client's affect:
expression of affect:_____

_____

experience of affect:_____

_____

4. How does client receive any sense of emotional
accomplishment from her life other than from
manipulating food or aspects of her body?_____

_____

_____

5. What is client's present cognitive capacity (e.g. is
client able to process logical thoughts or feelings
or is client's thinking confused, rigid, delusional
or result in clients becoming flooded or overwhelmed
etc.)? Describe:_____

_____
_____

6. What is client's normal or typical cognitive
   capacity? Describe:_____

_____

7. Describe client's reasoning styles (examples):

   A) Black and white thinking
   B) Overgeneralization
   C) Magnification
   D) Reading others' minds
   E) Selective focus on negative
   F) Personalization
   G) Minimization/denial

8. Body awareness and body image:

   A) How do you physically describe yourself? _____

   _____
   _____

   B) What do you think others see when they look at
      you? _____

   _____

   C) Please rate the following areas according to the
      degree to which you are satisfied or dissatisfied
      by circling the number representing the closest
      answer. These are:

   very   somewhat
   satisfied = 6   dissatisfied = 3

   mostly   mostly
   satisfied = 5   dissatisfied = 2

   somewhat   very
   satisfied = 4   dissatisfied = 1

   Hair   6   5   4   3   2   1
   Face   6   5   4   3   2   1
   Eyes   6   5   4   3   2   1

Nose	6	5	4	3	2	1
Lips	6	5	4	3	2	1
Teeth	6	5	4	3	2	1
Cheeks	6	5	4	3	2	1
Skin	6	5	4	3	2	1
Hands	6	5	4	3	2	1
Arms	6	5	4	3	2	1
Shoulders	6	5	4	3	2	1
Chest	6	5	4	3	2	1
Breasts	6	5	4	3	2	1
Stomach	6	5	4	3	2	1
Hips	6	5	4	3	2	1
Buttocks	6	5	4	3	2	1
Genitals	6	5	4	3	2	1
Thighs	6	5	4	3	2	1
Knees	6	5	4	3	2	1
Calves	6	5	4	3	2	1
Ankles	6	5	4	3	2	1
Feet	6	5	4	3	2	1
Figure	6	5	4	3	2	1
Height	6	5	4	3	2	1
Weight	6	5	4	3	2	1

D) How does client describe and/or experience her internal feelings or sensations of:

hunger_____

anger_____

fatigue_____

pain_____

other feelings_____

_____

_____

_____

9. Do you (client or practitioner) observe hyperactivity? Y   N

A) When is the client likely to be hyperactive?_____

_____

B) How does being hyperactive seem to function for the client? _____

_____

10. Self-concept

A) What is the client's subjective experience of
self? _____

_____

_____

B) What is the client's perception of her capacity
for change? _____

_____

C) Does client believe herself deserving of change,
of being cared for, or being worthy of having an
improved life? _____

_____

_____

D) What is the client's perception of her capacity
to:

be loved and cared for? _____

_____

love and care for others? _____

_____

11. What are the client's primary defenses (e.g.,
projection, denial, reaction formation sublimation,
intellectualization, rationalization)? _____

_____

_____

_____

_____

12. Interpersonal relationships (other than family)

A) How many relationships are there and what is the
client's degree of achieving closeness, trust,
intimacy, being assertive, and feeling effective
within them? _____

_____

_____

B) What is the nature of the client's past
relationships and what is the pattern of the
interaction? _____

_____

_____

_____

C) How long do the relationships last on average? ___

_____

shortest_____

longest_____

D) How does client feel about.those relationships and
what is her perception of what was successful and
what was less successful about them? Also, how
and to what degree does the client own
responsibility about the relationship? _____

_____

_____

_____

_____

_____

E) What was the nature of the bond in
present primary relationships?_____

_____

_____

past primary relationships?_____

_____

_____

Family History and Rehtionships

1. Family history

A) Is there a family history of:

alcoholism_____

sexual abuse_____

physical abuse_____

incest_____

mental illness_____

physical illness_____

B) Have any of your immediate family members been
hospitalized? What for? _____

_____

_____

2. Present living circumstances

A) Who lives with the client?_____

_____

B) What is the client's support system like? _____

_____

C) How and what ways does the client interact with
her family? _____

_____

_____

3. How does the client feel about her relationship with:

mother_____

_____

father_____

_____

siblings_____

_____

extended family_____

_____

_____

4. What was/is it like for the client to attempt to
separate/individuate within the family?_____

_____

_____

5. What is the nature of the client's level of
affiliation within the family?_____

_____

_____

6. Briefly describe any presenting "family problems" or
observations:_____

_____

_____

_____

_____

Family System

1. Family structure:

A) Describe the parenting system:

who is in control?_____

_____

how is control implemented?_____

_____

who provides the support and nurturing?_____

_____

how is support and nurturing provided?_____

_____

who provides the direction for parenting?_____

_____

how is the direction provided?_____

_____

how are "rules established"?_____

_____

how is conflict handled and resolved?_____

_____

how is information exchanged?_____

_____

B) Describe the marital system:

what are the primary feelings demonstrated in the
dyad?_____

_____

how are these feelings demonstrated?_____

_____

how is conflict handled and resolved_____

_____

_____

how is information exchanged?_____

_____

what is the nature of the sexual relationship in
terms of frequency and quality_____

_____

_____

how is affection demonstrated?_____

_____

how are daily living requirements handled?

_____

_____

who is, or tries to be, responsible for the
marriage?_____

_____

C) Describe the sibling system:

how independent are the siblings?_____

_____

how is conflict demonstrated and resolved?_____

_____

_____

how is affection demonstrated?_____

_____

how do siblings receive and use direction?_____

_____

2. Family Style

A) How does the family show affection?_____

_____

B) How do family members respond to and resolve
conflict?_____

_____

C) How does the family experience fun or liesure?____

_____

_____

D) What are the family members' methods of
communicating?_____

_____

_____

E) Are family members:

enmeshed?_____

_____

disengaged?_____

_____

chaotic?_____

_____

F) What are "triangles" of relationships that are
   exhibited with the family?_____

_____

_____

General Information

Name:_____ DOB:_____ Sex:____

Address:_____ Phone:_____

Referral Source:_____ Date:_____

Occupation:_____ Height:_____

Marital Status:_____ Religion:_____

Children (ages & sex):_____

Personal Physician:_____ Income:_____

Person to Contact In Emergency:_____

Reason for Requesting Assessment:_____

How long have you had your problem and what brings you here
now? _____
_____

Could you please describe your problem? _____
_____
_____

Do you feel that your problem has been improving, staying the
same, or getting worse in the last month? Has anything been
happening in your life that you think might be useful in
helping us to understand this situation? _____
_____
_____

Review of Symptoms

   1. What is your height? _____

2. What is your current (today's) weight? _____ Any recent
changes?_____

   most weight_____ when_____

   least weight_____ when_____

3. Ideal Body Weight (IBW)= _____ (use formula below)

   females - #100 for 5 feet +
       #5 for each inch   add 10% for large bones
                             add 0% for medium bones
   males - #100 for 5 feet +   minus 10% for small bones
       #6 for each inch

4. If you are losing weight how are you doing this?_____
   _____

5. Do you binge?

           no   yes

               how often per day?_____

6. Do you vomit

           no   yes

               how often per day?_____

7. Do you use laxatives or ipecac

           no   yes

               how many do you take? _____

               how often do you take them?_____

8. Do you use diet pills or diuretics

           no   yes

               how many do you take?_____

               how often do you take them?_____

9. Do you get cold easily?

        no   yes

10. Do you have trouble with memory or concentration?

        no   yes

11. Are you having any physical problems?

mouth, lips, throat	no	yes
stomach	no	yes
bowels	no	yes
urinating	no	yes
muscle cramps	no	yes
headaches	no	yes
sweats	no	yes
chest discomfort	no	yes
dizziness	no	yes

12. Is your menstrual period regular?

        no   yes

When was your last period?_____

13. How often and for how long do you exercise?_____
_____

What kind of exercise(s)?_____

14. How have you been feeling emotionally lately?_____
_____

15. Have you been finding yourself becoming increasingly:

        sad/crying_____

depressed_____

anxious_____

isolated/withdrawn_____

feeling out of control_____

16. Please briefly describe how you see your body_____

_____

17. To what degree do you feel that you are able to control
or change these symptoms?_____

_____

18. If we agree to work together what would you like to see
changed by the time we terminate?

_____

_____

_____

19. What have you tried in the past that has seemed to be
useful/not useful? _____

_____

20. Are there any people you feel are particularly relevant
or important to your recovery? Who are they and how are
they important? _____

_____

_____

_____

_____

_____

past primary relationships?_____

_____

_____

PART III

Treatment of
Addictive Disorders

7

Smoking Modification: Research and Clinical Application

NORMAN HYMOWITZ

This chapter deals with the issues of cigarette smoking and its modification. Cigarette smoking is considered to be the most important preventable cause of mortality in American society (USDHHS, 1989). It is a key etiologic risk factor for heart disease, cancer, and non-neoplastic broncopulmonary disease (USDHHS, 1989). Much progress has been made in combating smoking since the first surgeon general's report (USPHS, 1964), and, for the first time in many decades, the prevalence of smoking among adult Americans has dropped below 30 percent (USDHHS, 1989). Despite this progress, cigarette smoking remains an important challenge to the medical, behavioral, and public health communities. Relatively more smokers are smoking 25 or more cigarettes per day (heavy smoker) than ever before, certain minority groups have not responded as well as whites to the antismoking campaign (USDHHS, 1989), and the prevalence of smoking in Third World countries has been increasing at an alarming rate (Skirrow, 1986).

The process of helping people quit smoking is a complicated one, involving the interaction between behavioral and pharmacological factors. Nicotine is the drug that most likely accounts for cigarette smoking's addicting potential (Henningfield, 1986). The past conditioning and learning history of the smoker, as well as prevailing psychological factors, also must be taken into consideration (Sacks, 1986). It is likely that these same kinds of factors enter into the understanding and treatment of other forms of addiction and substance abuse.

Two unique features of cigarette smoking are that it is legal, as is alcohol, and that even low-level exposure to smoking can be very harmful (USDHHS, 1989). Whereas modest and social uses of alcohol may be acceptable and not life threatening, daily use of cigarettes increases the risk of life-threatening disease. Because of the danger that smoking presents, it is important for clinicians to be familiar with public health issues, as well as particular clinical interventions.

All of the studies described in this chapter are examples of clinical application research on cigarette smoking. All were carried out by my colleagues and me at the New Jersey Medical School during the past two decades. Some of the studies have been completed, and the major findings and implications are reviewed and discussed. Others are underway. Each, however, addresses the issue of bridging the gap between clinical intervention and public health impact. For that reason, they are of particular importance to clinicians interested in intervention on cigarette smoking and drug abuse in general.

THE MULTIPLE RISK FACTOR INTERVENTION TRIAL (MRFIT)

The MRFIT was a national collaborative randomized clinical trial for the prevention of coronary heart disease mortality (MRFIT Group, 1976).[1] Subjects were high-risk but otherwise healthy men, aged 35 to 57 at the start of the six-year trial. Twenty-two clinical centers participated nationwide, with a subject pool of 12,866 men.

Participants were assigned randomly to one of two groups: a special intervention (SI) group, for which modification of coronary risk factors (hypertension, elevated serum cholesterol, cigarette smoking) was provided by the clinical centers, and a usual care (UC) group, who were referred to their usual source of medical care for treatment of risk factors. Approximately 64 percent of SI and UC men smoked cigarettes at the start of the trial, and they smoked an average of 34 cigarettes per day.

Intervention

The risk factor intervention program consisted of three phases: initial intervention, extended intervention, and maintenance (Benfari & Sherwin, 1981). During initial intervention, participants and their wives or homemakers were invited to participate in 10 to 12 weekly sessions of a group program aimed at lowering serum cholesterol through dietary management, controlling high blood pressure (weight loss, sodium restriction, and pharmacologic therapy), and stopping smoking. The groups sought to increase awareness, provide knowledge, and facilitate behavioral change (Benfari, 1981). Although the MRFIT was a large public-health-oriented study, intervention strategies were clinical in nature, involving intensive therapy with individual patients, alone and in groups.

Participants who successfully lowered their risk factors entered maintenance; those who did not entered extended intervention, which included individual counseling and formal groups, both of which focused on one risk factor at a time. All participants returned to the clinical center annually for physical examination. Participants returned every four months for monitoring and data collection purposes and more often for intervention and follow-up (Benfari & Sherwin, 1981).

The group program combined educational, medical, and behavioral strategies to help smokers quit smoking. Films and group discussion dealt with the health hazards of smoking, the particular risk smoking posed to each participant in the group, and potential benefits to be gained by stopping smoking. Many of the take-home smoking and health brochures available today (USDHHS, 1989) follow a similar strategy of presenting the facts, helping smokers personalize their own risk, and emphasizing the benefits gained from stopping smoking.

Participants were encouraged to monitor their smoking behavior, to note when and where they smoke, to gain insight into stimulus conditions associated with smoking, and to learn about the functional or reinforcing value of each cigarette. Gradual change procedures were implemented to prepare smokers for a group quit date. Quit-smoking strategies (carry cigarettes in a different place, switch brands, take a new route to work, etc.) and behavioral contracts were used to help specify specific behavioral change strategies (e.g., no smoking in the car, fill car ash tray with candy mints, pull car over and get out of the car if you must smoke). These strategies helped smokers break seemingly automatic behavioral patterns, learned associations between stimuli and smoking, and the acquired physiological dependence on cigarettes. Only positive behavioral strategies were employed; pharmacologic adjuncts were not used. Relaxation training, dietary management, and mild exercise recommendations were integral features of the program (Hymowitz, 1982). Acquisition of active relapse-prevention strategies, taught through films, group problem solving, and behavioral rehearsal, helped ex-smokers guard against relapse.

Maintenance included a number of activities aimed at helping participants sustain reduction in risk (Benfari & Sherwin, 1981), including group reunions, the buddy system, telephone follow-up, periodic reviews of medical and risk status, social events for participants and wives or homemakers, and health fairs. The goal was to help participants maintain risk reduction for the six years of follow-up so that the benefit of lowered risk of coronary heart disease death would accrue.

Results

The reported quit rate for SI men was 43.1 percent at year 1 and 50 percent at year 6 (Hymowitz, 1987). These rates were significantly superior to those for UC: 13 percent and 29 percent, at years 1 and 6, respectively. When serum thiocyanate, a breakdown product of hydrogen cyanide, was used as an objective measure of cigarette smoking, somewhat more modest estimates of smoking cessation were obtained (Hymowitz, 1987). At year 6, the thiocyanate-adjusted quit rates for SI and UC were 46 percent and 29 percent, respectively.

Discussion

Several features of the MRFIT data merit discussion. Most of the SI quit smoking during the first year of the program, during initial intervention, while quitting among UC was more evenly distributed over the six years of the trial. This latter finding is in keeping with a secular trend toward adult smoking cessation in the United States over the same time period (USDHHS, 1989). Of the SI smokers who reported not smoking at year 1, over 60 percent continued to report smoking cessation at each follow-up visit through year 6 (USDHHS, 1987). These data are in marked contrast to reports available in the literature at the time the MRFIT was initiated that indicated that 70 to 80 percent of successful quitters relapsed within one year (Hunt & Bespalac, 1974).

It is likely that the MRFIT group intervention, secondary intervention, and maintenance programs account for the fine long-term performance of the SI smokers. The long-term success rates generally are superior to those of shorter studies reported in the literature, but they are consistent with outcome data reported by other clinical trials of disease prevention in the United States and elsewhere (Hymowitz, 1987). These findings document the value of clinical behavioral interventions, show that initial smoking cessation success need not be comprised by high rates of relapse, and demonstrate the importance of embedding intervention programs within a long-term context, in this case, a six-year clinical trial for heart disease prevention. Psychologists who work with smokers in other settings must consider the issue of follow-up and long-term contact, perhaps building follow-up into their treatment plan from the start.

Variables that influenced smoking cessation in the MRFIT men also are of interest. For SI, men who were older, had more education, had higher expectations of quitting at the start of the study, had quit smoking in the past, and smoked fewer cigarettes per day at baseline were more likely to quit smoking during the six-year trial (Hymowitz, Sexton, Shekelle, Ockene & Grandits, in press). Lighter alcohol drinkers and men with fewer friends who smoked were also more likely to quit, but these relationships were not statistically significant after adjusting for other variables. Race, marital status, smoking status of spouse, life events, and the score on the Jenkins Activity Survey (JAS) did not influence SI smoking cessation (Hymowitz et al., in press).

The likelihood of quitting for UC smokers was also influenced (in the same direction as for SI) by age, education, past quitting history, and number of cigarettes smoked (Hymowitz et al., in press). Alcohol, number of life events, and the presence of a wife who smoked were significantly and negatively related to smoking cessation in UC men on univariate as well as multivariate analyses (Hymowitz et al., in press).

It is possible that the group intervention helped to buffer SI men against the adverse impact of life events and smoking spouses. The buffering effect of intervention also may account for the finding that the adverse effects of alcohol did not emerge as an independent predictor of smoking cessation for SI upon multivariate analysis but did emerge for UC. Clinicians in practice who undertake the task of helping patients stop smoking would do well to address variables that otherwise would hinder the smoking cessation efforts.

Alcoholic drinks per week at baseline served as an independent predictor of relapse (the return to smoking) in both SI and UC participants. For UC, education, number of life events, and past success in quitting also served as independent predictors of relapse (Hymowitz et al., in press). These variables did not influence relapse in SI men. The difference between the SI and UC may be accounted for by the efficacy of the group intervention program and maintenance strategies. The differential effects of life events and education on UC and SI illustrate the importance of preparing smokers to cope with stress and selected conditions that increase the likelihood of relapse.

Past quitting was related to relapse in UC but not SI men (Hymowitz et al., in press). Possibly long-term intervention and follow-up helped break the quit-relapse cycle of SI men. Among UC men, who were not offered the special intervention program, the quit-relapse cycle, so prevalent in the smoking and drug abuse literature, continued.

Another aspect of the data is of special interest to the substance abuse community. For SI and UC, heavy smokers and those who reported at the start of the study that they never quit smoking in the past were significantly less likely to quit smoking than light smokers or those who reported that they quit smoking in the past (Hymowitz et al., in press). The year-6 quit rate for SI light smokers (less than 25 per day) was 63 percent, while the quit rate for heavy smokers (more than 25 per day) was 36 percent. For UC, the quit rates were 46 percent and 23 percent for light and heavy smokers, respectively (Hymowitz et al., in press). These findings suggest that the behavioral, educational, and medical intervention strategies used in the MRFIT were most effective for the lighter, perhaps less physically dependent smokers than for the heavier, and thereby more addicted, smokers.

According to Henningfield (1986; Henningfield & Jasinski, 1988), cigarette smoking, like other forms of drug dependence, involves the interaction of pharmacologic and nonpharmacologic factors in which the relative contribution of each factor may vary. It is conceivable that the smokers who benefited most from the MRFIT intervention program were those for whom dependence on nicotine played a less important role in maintaining their smoking behavior. In view of the fact that most behavioral interventions are more effective for light than heavy smokers (USDHHS, 1989), there is a real need, from both clinical and public health perspectives, to develop intervention strategies that are more effective for heavy smokers.

Nicotine-replacement strategies (Pomerleau & Pomerleau, 1988) may be particularly helpful to heavy smokers. In addition to following standard behavioral recommendations for smoking cessation and relapse prevention, heavy smokers may benefit from nicotine polacrilex gum, a nicotine-containing gum marketed by Merrell Dow under the name Nicorette (USDHHS, 1988). Smokers are instructed to chew nicotine gum instead of smoking, reducing the withdrawal symptoms that make life so uncomfortable for some smokers when they abstain from smoking (Russell, 1986). In 3 to 6 months, the nicotine substitute is gradually withdrawn, leaving the ex-smoker totally nicotine free (cf. Russell, 1986).

Nicotine replacement strategies may be a useful adjunct to interventions in clinical and public health settings (Pomerleau & Pomerleau, 1988). They make intuitive sense, and initial reports indicate that Nicorette may enhance long-term quit rates over and above quit rates obtained by behavioral interventions alone (Schwartz, 1987). While some investigators report that Nicorette is more helpful to heavy than to light smokers (Fagerstrom, 1984), others (DeWit & Camic, 1986) have failed to confirm this. Clearly, the specific effectiveness of nicotine replacement for the heavy and/or addicted smoker remains an important issue for research. Had Nicorette been available for use among SI heavy smokers, it is possible that many more of them would have been able to quit smoking, thereby helping to lower their risk of coronary heart disease death.

THE SMOKING CESSATION REDUCTION ACTION PROGRAM (SCRAP)

The MRFIT showed that it is possible to help large numbers of smokers quit smoking and remain abstinent for a long period of time. The intervention, however, was extremely labor intensive. Group intervention programs typically were conducted by smoking specialists, usually doctoral-level clinicians. Extended intervention and maintenance activities involved individual counseling and a myriad of other forms of face-to-face encounters. This form of intervention, although effective from the clinical point of view, falls somewhat short from a public health point of view. Few skilled therapists are available to accommodate the great numbers of smokers in need of treatment, and few, if any, environments can devote the energy and resources needed to help sustain abstinence in the manner of the MRFIT. An important challenge to the behavioral and public health communities is to explore the utility and efficacy of other settings and programs for long-term intervention on cigarette smoking. It is also important to determine whether lay therapists can be trained to carry out the intervention, thereby extending greatly the reach of the clinical intervention.

Among these other settings, work sites offer unique features that make them useful for long-term intervention programs. Workers return to the work site, day after day, for many years, providing an opportunity for intervention and follow-up on smoking and other drugs of abuse. It is possible to offer a vast array of programs, allowing workers to select forms of intervention most suitable to their needs. Furthermore, if a worker is unsuccessful in one program, there is always the hope that the next program will prove more effective. This is particularly important for intervention on cigarette smoking because smokers may quit smoking many times and try a variety of programs before they finally succeed (Schwartz, 1987).

Intervention

The SCRAP is a comprehensive work site–based smoking cessation program with three interacting components: a group quit-smoking program, health education activities, and policies for restricting smoking at the work site.[2] In an effort to make the program more generalizable and cost-effective, volunteer employees of participating work sites were trained to conduct the group program and to carry out health education and other activities with relatively little professional supervision. In addition, the volunteers served as important resources to their sites for the future.

The group quit-smoking program was modeled after the MRFIT, consisting of an orientation session, eight 2-hour group sessions, and periodic group reunions. Similar educational and behavioral strategies for smoking cessation were employed. The group program was offered at no cost to employees at each of six participating work sites, usually during nonworking hours. Three of the sites offered the health education and smoking policy protocol, and three did not. This allowed assessment of whether the additional activities enhanced the long-term effectiveness of the group intervention. The hypothesis was that the policy restrictions and health education activities would improve the long-term effectiveness of the group program, leading to significantly superior sustained quit rates at the full SCRAP sites as compared to the SCRAP group-only sites.

Each of the three work sites randomly assigned to the full SCRAP condition instituted policies for restricting smoking at work. The smoking regulations were publicized in work site newsletters and handout material. One of the three group-only SCRAP sites also implemented smoking regulations, a growing trend in New Jersey and elsewhere around the country (USDHHS, 1989).

The full SCRAP sites also carried out a number of health education and public health–oriented quit-smoking activities. Employee health areas distributed material on smoking and health, self-help smoking cessation brochures, and signs and buttons so that smokers could stop smoking on their own and/or create their own smoke-free environments. Employee health physicians were advised how to counsel employees who smoke, and they followed guidelines provided by the American Heart Association's Heart at Work Kit (USDHHS, 1989). Formal evaluation of the effects of mobilizing the employee health area for smoking intervention was not carried out; however, record-keeping logs showed that over 300 smokers at the full SCRAP sites were counseled in the employee health areas during the three years of the study.

Additional activities included participation in the Great American Smokeout, Heart Month, and High Blood Pressure Month. For each of these occasions, numerous brochures and self-help material were distributed, and expired-air carbon monoxide was measured to help smokers personalize the risk of smoking (cf. Hymowitz, 1980). In the three years of the study, over 3,000 pieces of material were distributed at the three work sites for the Great American Smokeout alone, and over 500 expired-air carbon monoxide tests were completed on smokers. In addition, newsletter articles on smoking and how to stop appeared quite frequently, and the health education activities served as an important mechanism for referring smokers to the group program.

All of the lay smoking therapists acquired the necessary behavioral skills to conduct the SCRAP group quit-smoking program, although none had ever conducted a quit-smoking group in the past. Each therapist subsequently conducted a minimum of two groups during the three-year program. The therapists were males and females, blacks and whites, and included nurses, personnel staff, administrative personnel, and one employee who also served as the on-site alcohol counselor. Landow (1987) has shown that lay therapists can be as successful as professionals in helping smokers quit smoking. The SCRAP study supports this contention.

Two hundred fifty-two smokers participated in the group program, of whom 63 percent were female and 34 percent were minorities (mostly blacks and Hispanics). The average age of participants was 42 years. They smoked an average of 27 cigarettes per day, and over 88 percent reported that they had quit smoking in the past. Most participants (80 percent) listed concern for health as the main reason for wanting to stop smoking, and the majority (of participants who quit in the past) listed coping with stress (41 percent) or "craving" (30 percent) as the main reason they returned to smoking. Official data collection visits were scheduled at 4, 8, and 12 months, and expired-air carbon monoxide served as an objective measure of smoking. No discrepancies between reported smoking and carbon monoxide levels were observed.

Results

The initial end-of-treatment and 12-month quit rates were virtually identical for participants at the full SCRAP and group-only sites. For participants who attended at least the first three sessions of the group program, the end-of-group quit rate was 54 percent, a figure that compares favorably with the MRFIT (Hughes, Hymowitz, Ockene, Simon & Vogt, 1981). Dropouts were a problem at some of the sites, accounting for a range of end-of-group quit rates from a low of 25 percent to a high of 80 percent. The quit rate for all participants combined, including dropouts, was 41 percent. Women and minorities were as successful at stopping smoking as white males. Employee travel demands were a significant problem at some sites, leading to the development of self-help materials specifically designed for frequent travelers. Fifty percent of the initial quitters in the full SCRAP condition remained abstinent through the 12-month follow-up visit. Forty-seven percent of the initial quitters in the group-only condition remained abstinent. The sustained abstinence rates did not differ for the full SCRAP and group-only SCRAP sites.

The sustained abstinence rate is quite satisfactory for a public health–oriented program such as SCRAP, although intuitively one might have expected a greater effect on maintenance of the health education activities and work site regulations on smoking. Moreover, the quit rates are not superior to those obtained in other settings. It is possible that three years is too short a time to create a context within which the long-term effectiveness of the group intervention program is enhanced. It is also possible that more salient and robust aspects of normal work site settings overshadowed the influence of the additional activities. Group reunions and social support were present at all six sites, and the fact that group members returned to work every day, where they come into contact with other participants as well as the employee therapist, may have served as added incentives to remain abstinent. One of the three group-only SCRAP sites introduced work site regulations on smoking during the course of the study, and all three group-only sites participated in the Annual Great American Smokeout.

SCRAP data also show that those who smoked the most cigarettes, those who never quit in the past, and those who reported experiencing intense withdrawal symptoms the last time they stopped smoking for 24 hours or more were the least likely to stop smoking at the end of group and at 12 months. These findings are consistent with those of the MRFIT, and they add to the importance of incorporating interventions that are more effective for the smokers in whom tobacco dependence assumes the highest priority.

Work sites provide an important forum for reaching Americans and promoting good health. They are a fertile area for future research and clinical application. Clinicians and practitioners have an important role to play as consultants, counselors, and investigators. Depending on the nature of the work site, clinicians may wish to offer group cessation programs, accept individual smokers on a referral basis, or implement health promotional interventions that affect the entire employee population.

PULMONARY MEDICINE SMOKING PROJECT (PMSP)

The SCRAP extended the MRFIT group intervention approach to a more public health–oriented model by training lay therapists to conduct the program, utilizing health education activities and self-help materials to reach the many smokers who do not attend the group program, and by attempting to create a milieu in which the long-term impact of the group could be enhanced. SCRAP was carried out at the work site, where large numbers of employees can be accommodated in an environment conducive to long-term intervention and follow-up. Skilled clinicians can similarly extend their scope to public health settings by becoming part of a broader referral network for smoking cessation and by serving as consultants to sites where skills in training and supervising others to intervene on smoking may come into play.

Hospitals represent another setting where large numbers of smokers can be reached, although opportunities for intervention are less than ideal. Physicians, nurses, and staff are quite busy, and patient stays usually are too short for extensive counseling for smoking cessation. However, hospitalized patients who smoke are at serious risk of disease, and they demand our attention.

University Hospital is an inner-city teaching hospital associated with the New Jersey Medical School in Newark. The patient population is predominantly black and Hispanic, and the patients are of low socioeconomic status (SES) as measured by income or level of education. Poor and uneducated blacks and Hispanics have responded less well to the antismoking message compared to other segments of the population, leading to the likelihood that in the future, persons of lower SES will account for a disproportionate number of smokers and smoking-related diseases (Novotny, Warner, Kendrick & Remington, 1988).

The PMSP focused on patients admitted to the hospital with a primary pulmonary diagnosis and who did not test positive for the human immunodeficiency virus.[3] Those with a history of cigarette smoking within a month of admission to the hospital were included in the study. Since patients in University Hospital's Pulmonary Unit are not allowed to smoke and in view of the relationship between smoking and pulmonary disease, it seemed reasonable to ask whether patients continue to remain abstinent upon discharge. Preliminary analyses of the data for over 100 patients (Passannante, Hymowitz, Sia, Soya, Gupta & Reichman, 1989) suggest that as many as 90 percent return to smoking shortly after discharge. In view of the clear relationship between smoking and lung disease (USDHHS, 1989) and the presence of national survey data suggesting that close to 90 percent of adults believe that smoking causes emphysema and 86 percent of all adults believe that smoking causes chronic bronchitis (USDHHS, 1989), these relapse data are little short of astonishing.

The follow-up survey is continuing, and questions concerning beliefs about the relationship between cigarette smoking and diseases of the lung have been added. An intervention program for relapse prevention has also been initiated. Patients are assigned to one of two groups: a Usual Care (UC) control group and a Special Intervention (SI) experimental group. The latter receives a self-help relapse-prevention kit prior to discharge.

Intervention

The self-help kit contains a host of material to help smokers remain abstinent upon discharge. In short, it takes what is known about relapse prevention and packages it in a carry-home kit. Included in the kit are: (1) information about the relationship between smoking and diseases of the lung, as well as other health effects; (2) behavioral strategies to monitor urges to smoke and stimuli and conditions associated with them; (3) cognitive and behavioral strategies for coping with urges and high-risk relapse situations (cf. Shiffman & Wills, 1985); (4) instructions and audiotape for several forms of relationship training; (5) diet and exercise advice; and (6) buttons, posters, and signs for creating a smoke-free environment at home.

Results

The study, which has only recently started, is in the mold of public health interventions. Educational and behavioral materials known to be effective in clinical encounters are packaged so that large numbers of high-risk patients may utilize them with minimal professional supervision. Whether self-help strategies will be sufficient to prevent relapse in this hard-core smoking population remains to be seen. At best, this study represents an important first step, and additional studies may address ways of improving the kit and further reducing relapse. Physician advice and counseling, as well as an in-hospital cessation program, perhaps using Nicorette, may improve long-term cessation rates. However, serious limitations in the availability and time of physicians and in the opportunity for follow-up represent important obstacles to more labor-intensive efforts.

It is estimated that 60 to 70 percent of adult smokers in the United States visit a health care facility in any given year (USDHHS, 1989). It is important for psychologists and other mental health professionals to work closely with physicians and health care facilities as consultants and resources for referral. Skilled clinicians can play an important role by training other health care professionals to identify and assist smokers and to utilize various treatment modalities to help their patients stop smoking. The PMSP focused on a particularly hard-core smoker, the pulmonary patient who continued smoking up to the most recent hospitalization. Other patient populations may be more responsive to smoking intervention. By taking advantage of clinical opportunities, health care practitioners may have a dramatic impact on smoking cessation from clinical as well as public health perspectives.

GRADUATED EXTERNAL FILTERS

Most smokers are aware that smoking is harmful to their health, and a majority state that they would like to quit smoking (USDHHS, 1989). Approximately 2 percent per year succeed, most making a number of attempts before reaching their goal (USDHHS, 1989). Nearly half of all living adults who ever smoked have quit (USDHHS, 1989), and most quit on their own (Fiore, Novotny, Pierce, Giovino, Hatziandrev, Newcomb, Surawicz & Davis, 1990). At this time, fewer than 30 percent of adult Americans smoke cigarettes, a marked decline from several decades ago (USDHHS, 1989).

Despite considerable progress, a growing appreciation that cigarette smoking is harmful, and a trend toward quitting smoking, well over 50 million Americans continue to smoke (USDHHS, 1989). In view of the fact that less than 10 percent of them will ever receive intense therapy for quitting smoking and most smokers state that they prefer to try to quit smoking on their own (USDHHS, 1989), it is necessary to facilitate self-initiated quitting through the use of self-help minimal intervention strategies. This may take the form of brief advice from a physician or other health practitioner, a self-help brochure or manual, or a commercially available product aimed at helping smokers quit smoking while minimizing the need for professional assistance. One commercially available quit-smoking aid is the graduated filter system, One Step at a Time. It is a smoking withdrawal product marketed in the United States by Teledyne Water Pik (Hymowitz, Lasser & Safirstein, 1982).[4]

Intervention

One Step at a Time is a four-step, 8-week, stop-smoking system consisting of four progressively stronger external plastic filters. According to the manufacturer, Filter 1 filters approximately 25 percent of tars and nicotine, and Filter 4 filters approximately 90 percent. Smokers advance from one filter to the next in 2-week steps and quit smoking in 8 weeks. If they are not successful, they may continue to use Filter 4, commercially available separately, to achieve a "safer" level of smoking.

One hundred thirty men and women, aged 35 or above and with no history of using the filter system, were assigned randomly to one of three experimental conditions: group 1, quit smoking on own; group 2, placebo filters; and group 3, One Step at a Time. The placebo and real filters were identical in appearance and were similarly packaged. Participants in groups 2 and 3 were instructed in the use of the filters, assigned a quit date in 8 weeks, and scheduled for their second visit within a week after their quit date. Participants in group 1 were similarly scheduled for visit 2 after 8 weeks, but they were asked to quit smoking on their own. All participants were scheduled to return to the center every 3 to 4 months for the next 12 months (visits 3–6) for assessment, monitoring, and additional testing (cf. Hymowitz, Lasser & Safirstein, 1982).

Results

At visit 2, the quit rates for groups 1, 2, and 3 were 21, 14, and 26 percent, respectively. Smoking cessation was confirmed objectively by measurement of expired-air carbon monoxide. The differences among groups were not statistically significant.

Participants in groups 1 and 2 who did not quit at visit 2 were given One Step at a Time, assigned a new quit date, and followed in 8 weeks at visit 3. Three additional smokers in group 1 quit smoking for the first time at visit 3 following use of One Step at a Time, which they received at visit 2. Six of the 11 smokers who quit smoking for the first time at visits 4, 5, and 6 did so following use of Filter 4 (Hymowitz, Lasser & Safirstein, 1982).

While the study did not provide unequivocal support for the efficacy of the filter system, several features of the study merit discussion. Subjects readily used the filter, and 22 percent of the subjects given the actual filter system at visit 1 were abstinent through visit 6. This one-year quit rate obtained with a minimal-intervention, commercially available filter system compares favorably with the long-term cessation effects of intensive group and individual therapy, as well as with the use of nicotine substitution therapy (Schwartz, 1987).

It is possible that, when combined with more comprehensive behavioral interventions, the filter systems would prove an important adjunct, leading to superior long-term quit rates. Clearly, research with nicotine gum suggests that it is most effective when combined with behavioral interventions (Schwartz, 1987). Private practitioners and counselors may want to explore the use of commercially available products within the context of more comprehensive treatment. Case reports of the outcome of such initiatives would be an important contribution to the literature.

While the quit rate obtained with the filters was not superior to that obtained when subjects were asked to quit smoking on their own, it is still possible that the filters can play an important role in the antismoking arena. At any given time, individuals may find themselves more or less ready at least to try to quit smoking (cf. Prochaska and DiClemente, 1983). Since it is relatively unlikely that such individuals will seek out a therapist to help them quit smoking, there may be considerable advantage to having a diverse array of self-help products and techniques readily available for use by the public.

SMOKING-DETERRENT LOZENGE

Another self-help minimal intervention product that may have utility for smoking cessation is a product that contains silver acetate (cf. Malcolm, 1986). Available commercially in Europe as over-the-counter products Tabmit and Respaton, the silver in the gum or lozenge interacts with the smoke in cigarettes to cause a metallic taste, which most smokers perceive as highly aversive, causing the smoker to eliminate the cigarette. Like Antabuse therapy, the key is for the smoker to use the silver acetate throughout the day to deter smoking.

Silver tends to accumulate in the body, and sufficient buildup causes argyrism, a bluish tint to organs of the body, including the skin. Thus, only a limited amount of silver acetate can be used; standard therapy calls for no more than six pieces of silver-containing gum or lozenge per day for 3 weeks. At this point, the lozenge has been shown to be only minimally effective, with no long-term follow-up data reported in the literature (Schwartz, 1987).

Intervention

The study underway at the New Jersey Medical School employs a modified silver acetate lozenge that contains only 2.5 mg of silver, as opposed to the standard 6 mg in other silver products, but which provides a deterrent response for close to 2 hours per lozenge.[5] Thus, it is possible for users to employ more of the lozenge and avoid the problem of argyrism. We are investigating the efficacy of the lozenge for smoking cessation in a double-blind placebo controlled trial with a 3-month follow-up and two objective measures of cigarette smoking, expired-air carbon monoxide and saliva cotinine. If efficacy is demonstrated under these conditions, a larger clinical trial with 12 months of follow-up will be proposed.

Results

The study is still in progress. Initial cessation data for 78 subjects are available for report, although the 3-month follow-up data are incomplete. The initial quit rate for 39 subjects assigned randomly to the actual lozenge condition was 31 percent and that for subjects assigned to placebo, 26 percent. This difference is not statistically significant. However, we did encounter a compliance problem: many subjects were fearful of argyrism, others did not want to experience the noxious taste, and still others preferred to try to quit smoking on their own. Thus, only 64 percent of subjects assigned to the actual lozenge condition and 62 percent of subjects assigned to the placebo condition used the product.

When the data are examined for subjects who used the product only, the efficacy of the lozenge for at least initial smoking cessation emerged. Forty percent of the subjects who used the actual lozenge quit smoking. The quit rate for subjects assigned to the actual lozenge condition but did not use the lozenge was 17 percent. Statistical comparison shows that the difference between the two approaches statistical significance ($p = .093$; 1-tailed Fisher's exact test), and the doubling of the quit rate for lozenge users suggests that the lozenge may have clinical utility. For subjects assigned to placebo, it made little difference whether they complied with the instructions. The quit rate for subjects who used the placebo was 25 percent and for those who did not, the quit rate was 27 percent. Final evaluation of the study must await completion of the 3-month follow-up.

In addition to clinical efficacy, the initial quit data showed that side effects and argyrism were not a problem, and smokers in the actual lozenge condition experienced a noxious taste when they smoked soon after lozenge use. Otherwise, the lozenge had a pleasant taste.

Hence, it is possible that the 2.5 mg smoking deterrent lozenge may have an important role to play in the antismoking arena. Behavioral studies have shown that aversion therapies, such as rapid smoking and hot, smoky air, each of which produce a foul taste as well as nausea, are among the most effective techniques for producing initial smoking cessation (Schwartz, 1987). The smoking-deterrent lozenge seems to work by a similar conditioning mechanism. Clearly it is not for everyone. It may have some efficacy and may facilitate cessation in motivated smokers. It may also be of considerable use as an adjunct to more intensive group and individual therapy and, as such, add to the clinician's armamentarium.

THE COMMUNITY INTERVENTION TRIAL (COMMIT)

The COMMIT is a national collaborative clinical trial involving 22 cities in the United States and Canada (Cancer Letter, 1988).[6] The COMMIT is a public health trial that uses a community organization approach to modify smoking in entire communities. Each of 11 participating clinical centers identified two cities, ranging in size from 50,000 to 150,000 people, which were similar in sociodemographic and other features but were far enough apart geographically so that they did not overlap in media. Following collection by telephone surveys of baseline smoking information, the 11 pairs of communities were randomly assigned to intervention and comparison or control conditions. In New Jersey, Paterson serves as the intervention community and Trenton as the comparison community.

Intervention

The intervention phase of COMMIT started in 1988 and will last four years; during that time, each intervention community will implement a standard protocol for smoking intervention. Each intervention community will form a community board, which will oversee community mobilization and implementation of a community smoking control plan. Staff hired from the community will work with the board and its task forces to carry out smoking interventions, in each case working closely with existing structures and organizations to ensure community involvement and ownership.

The smoking control activities are organized according to channels through which the smokers can be reached (Cancer Letter, 1988). The major channels are health care settings, work sites and other organizations, schools and youth, and public education and media. Within each channel, a variety of activities will be carried out, ranging from introducing smoke-free policies and clinical group cessation programs to more public health–oriented self-help strategies. Within the Health Care Channel, for example, physicians may refer smokers to an American Cancer Society stop-smoking program, or they may utilize the American Academy of Family Physicians smoking kit (USDHHS, 1989) to counsel smokers. Training programs will be carried out to prepare physicians and dentists to counsel smokers and to use Nicorette gum, if they choose. Other key health site activities are setting up waiting room displays of no-smoking materials, participation in the American Cancer Society's Great American Smokeout, and establishing smoke-free health care in the community.

Results

While the outcome of COMMIT will not be known for many years, process variables suggest that the study is off to a good start. Community boards and task forces have been mobilized, and the community-based intervention is being carried out at each site. The main objective of the intervention is to encourage smoking cessation in large numbers of people and to create an antismoking milieu in the community. Community trials such as COMMIT aim to achieve a synthesis of awareness, educational, motivational, and behavioral strategies (Hymowitz, 1987). It is necessary to influence opinions and attitudes, to move people from a position of not contemplating change to one of trying to quit (cf. Prochaska & DiClemente, 1983), and to provide skills and techniques to facilitate cessation, either on one's own or with professional assistance.

It is anticipated that COMMIT will serve as a model for how other cities and communities might mobilize their resources to combat smoking and other health problems in the future. The key is to coordinate activities, using existing channels and resources, and produce a combined effect that is greater than any one approach alone. Private practitioners and clinicians no doubt will play a leadership role in their own communities. They may serve as expert consultants and trainers, therapists, and public health advocates. They may extend their network, volunteer for other community endeavors, such as assisting with media programming, or join a community board to oversee and guide the community intervention. Cigarette smoking is a major public health problem, and while the individual therapist always will have an important role to play, there is a need to consider ways of joining in total community intervention efforts. It is hoped that COMMIT will provide guidance on how this can be accomplished. Outcome data from the trial will be available in 1995.

CONCLUSION

Cigarette smoking and smoking cessation are complex processes that involve an interplay of behavioral and pharmacologic factors. Considerable progress against smoking has been made, and nearly half of all living adults who ever smoked have quit (USDHHS, 1989). Much work still remains. Smoking is responsible for more than one of every six deaths in the United States (USDHHS, 1989), and many smokers require assistance in stopping, whether in a clinical or public health context.

Clinical applications research provides insights into the kinds of settings in which educational, behavioral, and, perhaps, pharmacological interventions on smoking may be applied. Psychologists, by the nature of their training, are most comfortable with a clinical approach. This entails labor-intensive involvement with individuals or groups of smokers, generating, it is hoped, a relatively high quit rate. Talented clinicians no doubt can attract a steady flow of smokers to their offices, and they can readily extend their impact or reach by working in close association with medical and work site settings, perhaps participating in a referral network and training others to assist them.

Imaginative public health endeavors also present important opportunities for impact and practice. To enter this domain, clinicians must adjust their expectations and the way in which they think about behavioral change. Lesser quit rates are acceptable so long as larger numbers of smokers can be affected. Mass media presentations, for example, may yield cessation rates of only 5 percent (Flay, 1987). However, if they affect, say, 25,000 people, their public health impact may be great.

Studies such as the MRFIT indicate that successful long-term intervention on smoking is possible, and the success rates generated may be well worth the effort. The use of nicotine-replacement strategies, external filters, and smoking-deterrent lozenges may improve success rates, bringing the science of smoking cessation to the point that clinicians can be quite optimistic about their ability to help their patients stop smoking. Yet as a society, we may still be far from eliminating cigarette smoking as a public health menace. The challenge before the clinical psychological community is to bridge the gap between clinical and public health arenas, extending successful clinical interventions so that they can be brought to bear on the health of the larger public.

SCRAP represents an important step in this direction; it extended the MRFIT smoking intervention program to a new setting in a cost-effective and generalizable manner. The PMSP is also in keeping with the public health agenda. It represents an attempt to package clinical interventions so that smokers may carry them out themselves. While additional work will be required to refine the relapse prevention kit and strengthen its impact, the value of this rehabilitative effect on pulmonary patients should prove gratifying.

COMMIT represents the culmination of several decades of clinical intervention research and sets the pace for community intervention in the 1990s. It takes state-of-the-art interventions, which have been effectively carried out by clinicians, physicians, work sites, schools, and the media, and brings them together in a total community program. Each intervention began in the clinical arena. Subsequent research documented its effectiveness in other settings and modes of delivery. Can these interventions be implemented by the community to produce a significant public health impact? If so, COMMIT will serve as an important model for intervention for other communities in the future.

Clinical psychologists have much to contribute to public health initiatives such as COMMIT. They can extend their referral network, serve as consultants, and take an active role in packaging their interventions. Innovative films, bibliographic material, and computer programs are available (USDHHS, 1989), showing that clinicians are not reluctant to join the fray. The surgeon general has extended the challenge of creating a smoke-free society by the year 2000 (USDHHS, 1989). Clinical psychologists will play an important role in meeting the challenge. As they extend their scope from clinical to public health settings, their contributions will become even greater.

NOTES

1. This research was supported, in part, by National Heart, Lung, and Blood Institute (NHLBI) contract No. N01-HL-3-3104 to Norman L. Lasser.

2. This research was supported, in part, by a grant from the American Heart Association, National Center to the author.

3. This research was supported, in part, by National Heart, Lung, and Blood Institute (NHLBI) Preventive Pulmonary Academic Award (I-K0007-HL-02095-02) to Lee B. Reichman.

4. This research was supported, in part, by a grant from Teledyne Water Pik to the author.

5. This research was supported, in part, by National Heart, Lung, and Blood Institute (NHLBI) grant No. SBIR GRANT L R43 HL42738-01 to Michael Fey and Norman Hymowitz.

6. This research was supported, in part, by National Cancer Institute Contract No. NO1-CN-64099 to the author.

REFERENCES

Benfari, R. C. (1981). The Multiple Risk Factor Intervention Trial (MRFIT) III. The model for intervention. *Preventive Medicine, 10,* 426–42.

Benfari, R. C. & Sherwin, R. (1981). The Multiple Risk Factor Intervention Trial after 4 years: A summing up. *Preventive Medicine, 10,* 544–46.

Cancer Letter (1988). COMMIT, massive anti-smoking effort moving into implementation. *Cancer Letter, 14,* 3–6.

De Wit, H. & Camic, P. M. (1986). Behavioral and pharmacologic treatment of cigarette smoking: End of treatment comparisons. *Addictive Behavior, 11,* 331–35.

Fagerstrom, K. O. (1984). Effects of nicotine chewing gum and follow-up appointments in physician-based smoking cessation. *Preventive Medicine, 13,* 517–27.

Fiore, M. C., Novotny, T. E., Pierce, J. P., Giovino, G. O., Hatziandreu, E. J., Newcomb, P. A., Surawicz, T. S. & Davis, R. M. (1990). Methods used to quit smoking in the United States. *Journal of the American Medical Association, 263,* 2760–65.

Flay, B. R. (1987). Mass media and smoking cessation: A critical review. *American Journal of Public Health, 77,* 153–60.

Henningfield, J. E. (1986). How tobacco produces drug dependence. In J. K. Ockene (ed.), *The pharmacologic treatment of tobacco dependence: Proceedings of the World Congress, November 4–5, 1985* (pp. 19–31). Nashua, N.H.: Puritan Press.

Henningfield, J. E. & Jasinski, D. R. (1988). Pharmacologic basis for nicotine replacement. In O. F. Pomerleau & C. S. Pomerleau (eds.), *Nicotine replacement: A critical evaluation* (pp. 35–61). New York: A. R. Liss.

Hughes, G. H., Hymowitz, N., Ockene, J. K., Simon, N. & Vogt, T. M. (1981). The Multiple Risk Factor Intervention Trial (MRFIT). Intervention on Smoking. *Preventive Medicine, 10,* 476–500.

Hunt, D. A. & Bespalec, D. O. (1974). An evaluation of current methods of modifying smoking behavior. *Journal of Clinical Psychology, 30,* 431–38.

Hymowitz, N. (1980). Personalizing the risk of cigarette smoking. *Journal of the Medical Society of New Jersey, 77,* 579–82.

Hymowitz, N. (1982). The Multiple Risk Factor Intervention Trial: A four year evaluation. *International Journal of Mental Health, 11,* 44–67.

Hymowitz, N. (1987). Community and clinical trials of disease prevention: Effects on cigarette smoking. *Public Health Reviews, 15,* 45–81.

Hymowitz, N., Lasser, N. L. & Safirstein, B. H. (1982). Effects of graduated external filters on smoking cessation. *Preventive Medicine, 11,* 85–95.

Hymowitz, N., Sexton, M., Shekelle, R., Ockene, J. K. & Grandits, G. Relationship between baseline variables and smoking cessation and relapse in MRFIT smokers. *Preventive Medicine,* in press.

Landow, H. O. (1987). Lay facilitators as effective smoking cessation counselors. *Addictive Behavior, 12,* 69–72.

Malcolm, R. (1986). Silver acetate gum as a deterrent to smoking. *Chest, 90,* 107–11.

Multiple Risk Factor Intervention Trial Group (1976). The Multiple Risk Factor Intervention Trial (MRFIT). *Journal of the American Medical Association, 235,* 825–27.

Novotny, T. E., Warner, K. E., Kendrick, J. S. & Remington, P. L. (1988). Smoking by blacks and whites: Socioeconomic and demographic differences. *American Journal of Public Health, 78,* 1187–89.

Passannante, M. R., Hymowitz, N., Sia, A., Soya, D. G., Gupta, T. & Reichman, L. B. (1989). *Smoking relapse rates among pulmonary patients.* Paper presented at the meeting of the American Public Health Association, Chicago.

Pomerleau, O. F. & Pomerleau, C. S. (1984). Neuroregulators and the reinforcement of smoking: Towards a biobehavioral explanation. *Neuroscience and Biobehavioral Reviews, 8,* 503–13.

Pomerleau, O. F. & Pomerleau, C. S. (1988). *Nicotine replacement: A critical evaluation.* New York: A. R. Liss.

Prochaska, J. O. & DiClemente, C. C. (1983). Stages and processes of self-change of smoking: Toward an integrative model of change. *Journal of Consulting and Clinical Psychology, 51,* 390–95.

Russell, M. A. H. (1986). Conceptual framework for nicotine substitution. In J. K. Ockene (ed.), *The pharmacologic treatment of tobacco dependence: Proceedings of the World Congress, November 4–5, 1985* (pp. 90–107). Nashua, N.H.: Puritan Press.

Sacks, D. P. L. (1986). Nicotine polocrilex: Clinical promises delivered and yet to come. In J. K. Ockene (ed.), *The pharmacologic treatment of tobacco dependence: Proceedings of the World Congress, November 4–5, 1985* (pp. 120–40). Nashua, N.H.: Puritan Press.

Schwartz, J. L. (1987). *Review and evaluation of smoking cessation methods: United States and Canada, 1978–1985.* U.S. Department of Health and Human Services, Public Health Service, National Institutes of Health (NIH Publication No. 87-2940).

Shiffman, S. & Wills, T. A. (1985). *Coping and substance abuse.* New York: Academic Press.

Skirrow, J. *Strategies for a smoke-free world.* Edmonton: Alberta Alcohol and Drug Abuse Commission, 1986.

U.S. Department of Health and Human Services (1987). *Smoking and health. A national status report.* Public Health Service, Centers for Disease Control (DHHS Publication No. (CDC) 87-8396).

U.S. Department of Health and Human Services (1988). *The Health consequences of smoking: Nicotine addiction. A report of the Surgeon General.* U.S. Department of Health and Human Services, Public Health Service, Centers for Disease Control, Center for Health Promotion and Education, Office on Smoking and Health (DHSS Publication No. (CDC) 88-8406).

U.S. Department of Health and Human Services (1989). *Reducing the health consequences of smoking: 25 years of progress. A report of the Surgeon General.* U.S. Department of Health and Human Service, Public Health Service, Centers for Disease Control, Center for Chronic Disease Prevention and Health Promotion, Office on Smoking and Health (DHHS Publication No (CDC) 89-8411).

U.S. Public Health Service (1964). *Smoking and health. Report of the Advisory Committee to the Surgeon General of the Public Health Service.* U.S. Department of Health, Education and Welfare, Public Health Service, Center for Disease Control (PHS Publication No. 1103).

8

Treatment of Alcohol and Drug Abuse

DOUGLAS H. RUBEN

Recent advances in substance abuse treatment methodology (Goldberg & Sto-lerman, 1985; Hester & Miller, 1989; Monti, Abrams, Kadden & Cooney, 1989; Schuckit, 1989) clearly demonstrate the increasing imperative for effec-tive, short-term interventions. Behaviorally treating substance abusers, espe-cially following detoxification, has been effective for two reasons. First, goal identification is more specific, and consequently goal attainment is predictably higher. A second reason deals with counselor accountability. Levels of com-petency among providers can be tested when interventions are more measur-able. This comports with initiatives by many state offices on substance abuse that are developing counselor credentialing systems (e.g., Arneson, Ruben & Husain, 1984).

Recognition of these strengths is only the first step. The second step is hav-ing definite guidelines for multiple interventions. Reviews of clinical method-ology on addictions unfortunately limit specification of exact steps to single strategies (e.g., aversion therapy) and remain unclear about sequential strate-gies (e.g., Bellack & Hersen, 1985). Use of multicomponent or comprehensive designs already is commonplace for many behavioral disorders (e.g., self-in-jury, encopresis, habits). However, addictive disorders lack this advantage.

This chapter offers one step toward a solution. Components of a behavioral systems approach (Ruben, 1983, 1989a, 1990b; see also Chapter 1) are exam-ined in the order of their application. Each component outlines essential or relevant features for quick reference by practitioners.

RATIONALE AND BASIC METHODOLOGY

The assessment and treatment components are based on two premises. The first is modern systems and ecological and interactional thinking, that is, a recognition that all people do what they do because of their history of interactions with surrounding conditions; this includes their individual psychological and biological histories. The second premise is that training is constructional. Goldiamond (1974) first proposed this approach to replace the exclusive goal of behavioral modification of eliminating problematic behaviors. Different from eliminative approaches, constructional approaches focus on teaching new skills, with emphasis on reinforcement technology. Delprato's (1981, 1987) discussion of least alternatives to treatment implies six instructions for treatment methodology:

1. Therapy is equivalent to training.
2. Therapy is continuous rather than isolated to the treatment session.
3. Social aspects behind the referral are addressed.
4. Therapy is preventive. If it is an intervention, prevention components are built in as safeguards against relapse (relapse prevention).
5. Therapy is naturalistic in the sense that it does not appear to be therapy to the casual observer.
6. Therapy is constructive by emphasizing that the goal is to develop alternative behavioral patterns to replace those patterns of the client prone to psychological and physical dependency.

On a practical basis, these six instructions immediately materalize in the form of general strategies expected to appear in all assessment and treatment phases. The basic "method," in other words, contains four areas of focus.

First is *naturalistic arrangement*. Changes discussed or introduced in therapy should be "programmed" or tailored for immediate appiication in the client's natural environment. Frequently significant others are called into the session to help with the treatment plan or carrying out certain applications. Contrived or temporary restructuring of the client's world will only delay progress and may mistakenly encourage relapse once the temporary system erodes. Instead, changes are introduced that have enough basis to remain strong over time.

Second is *specification of desired or target behaviors*. This may vary with individual orientation to therapy. However, many problems can result from the fact that therapists forget to specify in precise terms what is functional for the client. Once the goals and subgoals or objectives are defined, clearly presenting the exact target behaviors may include verbal description, modeling, written description, or analogue description, involving the use of audio or video equipment to simulate or give feedback to the behavior desired.

Feedback is the third area. Problems may arise because the client was not given precise feedback regarding the appropriateness or inappropriateness of particular actions. Feedback typically is verbal from the therapist or an appointed monitor in the client's natural environment. Constructive feedback is crucial and contains what the client did correctly, how the achievements related to the goals or objectives, what the client forgot to do, and instruction, modeling, and imitation on how to do it, and an assignment for trying out new skills.

Last is *monitoring*. Regularly scheduled sessions keep the training current and will alert the therapist to pitfalls, problems, contraindications, or other side effects based on the client's self-report or other reports of progress.

MAJOR ELEMENTS OF SUBSTANCE ABUSE ASSESSMENT

Assessing clients for outpatient substance abuse treatment (Dendy, Cooper & Cantwell, 1977; Ryan, Arneson, Popour & Ruben, 1984) covers a large domain. However, factors universal to behavioral assessment involve such preliminary client criteria as readiness for treatment, rationality for treatment, resources for treatment, and responsibilities for treatment.

Client readiness is assessed by understanding why a person came to treatment, as indicated by the following questions:

- What brought the client to treatment: Family pressure, legal pressure, peer pressure, street pressure, job pressure, or financial pressure? Why is there an immediacy?
- What brought the client to this program? Consider his preferred treatment, expectations, and beliefs and attitudes about therapy.
- What is the client's previous treatment experience? Consider previous attempts at treatment, types and duration of treatment, consequences of treatment, satisfaction with treatment, reasons for termination, and particular elements of treatment helpful to client.
- What are the social factors affecting therapy? Consider family factors, adverse family conditions (drug abuse, alcoholism, criminality, abuse, etc.), separations/divorce, previous confinement (jail, institution, etc.), and the individual's psychological history.

Client rationality is assessed by determining the emotional stability or status relative to the chemical dependency in question. Variables to detect in this decision include:

- Extreme mood states. Consider depressed, elevated, and mixed moods.
- Suicide potential. Consider situational clues (e.g., abrupt unemployment, divorce, family death), depressive clues (e.g., insomnia, apathy, poor concentration, low self-esteem), verbal clues (e.g., statements about death, suicide, helplessness), and behavioral clues

(e.g., previous suicide attempt, sudden recovery from depression, buying a gun, sudden resignation from groups, jobs).

- Impulse control. Consider the client's control over urges and impatience, time to anger, driving record, control over food (e.g., frequent diets, eating disorders), and smoking or other addictive habits.
- Potential for violence. Consider whether the client ever harmed anybody, has a history or record of homicide or assault, is motivated to commit physical attacks, or is sadomasochistic.

Client resources and responsibilities are determined by a closer look at his:

- Economic status. Consider the nature of his current job (if employed), previous job history, previous education and training, attitudes toward work, nature of income, and domestic responsibilities.
- Relationship with other agencies. Consider assistance from welfare agencies, vocational rehabilitation, unemployment, and the Veterans Administration.
- Social support system. Who are the significant others? What are the quality, duration, or present status of the relationships? Are his friends people of the same or opposite sex? What are his sexual orientation and marital status?

COMPONENTS OF SUBSTANCE ABUSE TREATMENT

Basic goals typically fit into seven categories for outpatient therapy: drug use, medical help, legal problems, psychological problems, living arrangements, social support systems, and coping skills. Attention to these goals begins with the treatment orientation. Treatment orientation is generally dependent on the therapist's expertise with a certain model or school of psychology. A variety of appropriate short-term models of therapy have been effective in substance abuse counseling, but their efficiency possibly can be improved if there is a uniform order of the components. *Components* refer to prescribed steps or phases in the treatment process enabling the client proper exposure to basic prerequisites for sobriety or drug elimination. Whether a therapist's training is behavioral, humanistic, or psychodynamic, elements of each component derive from the behavioral (social learning theory) model. Components are recommended in serial order, starting with cues and urges and ending with relapse prevention. The description of each component provides an overview of relevant variables for application.

Component 1: Cues and Urges

Generally addicts in recovery or repeated offenders receive instructions and rules about not to use chemicals, and consequently they believe abstinence is the result of "willpower." In this component, emphasis is on the fact that abstinence is not due to willpower but instead depends on learned counterreactions to highly susceptible conditions. These conditions are physical and psychological and are called *cues*. The client's susceptibility is known as an *urge*. Awareness of cues and urges alerts the client to the potential of a drinking problem based on objective facts.

A cue is anything that occurs right before the person feels either the temptation to drink or has the opportunity to drink. Many of the cues are hidden. Cues may be visual, olfactory, tactile, audible, or social; they are receptive by all basic senses. Most cues are external. Properties of cues are the things paired or associated with the cues in a drug experience. Once paired with the drug experience, the cues remain strong. For example, if heroin use is done in a house with plants, every time the client is around plants, he might feel the "temptation" (urge) to use heroin. This client may be in a green-painted room and also feel the urge (known as "metaphorical extension"). Further, people may talk about plants even in the absence of plants, and the urge will be strong. Conditioning of cues works in these ways.

Urges are physical cravings or desires felt privately. Biologically, the body grows accustomed to certain substances and then craves more of them, known as tolerance. Urges are also "opportunities for drug use," although actual drug use may not occur. Urges pass through a series of three stages of development (Figure 8.1). Over time, urges grow stronger with the amount of certain substances and frequency of their administration. Initial experience of withdrawal and expectation of effects is the threshold stage. Muscular contractions and glandular secretions signal this stage. Urges that increase in intensity finally reach a pivotal or "peak" point, where tension may explode outward in aggressive actions or in erratic and unusual forms of behavior (same pattern happens in poor anger control). As minutes pass, the urge will subside and allow the client to regain composure over the cues.

The steps involved in urge-cue learning occur in this recommended order:

1. Explain cues and urges to client.

2. Identify exemplar cues for the client and how urges intensify.

3. Assign homework of identifying cues and urges.

4. In subsequent steps, teach client to prevent submission to urges by using a timer set to 10 to 15 minutes to delay behavior, removing self from cues that signal urges, relaxing for relief of muscular tension during urges, and identifying if significant others contribute to cues and urges.

Component 2: Belief Systems

Perspectives on drinking and drug abuse typically are fraught with irrational or distorted thinking, engendered from childhood, current situations, or family and social relationships. One way or another, they are learned and transformed into personal rules, values, and beliefs that bias the client's expectations and

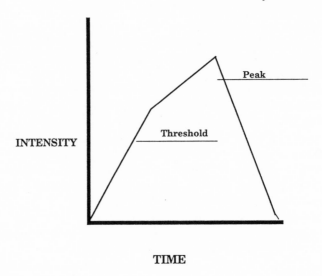

TIME

Figure 8.1
Urge Chart

understanding of other people, addiction, and related psychological problems (e.g., legal, anger, depression) (Hayes, 1989). Focus on these irrational beliefs, also called impure inferences, is the first way to draw attention to these misperceptions. How to eliminate impure inferences (irrational beliefs) and replace them with healthy alternatives is open to many short-term approaches. The best, with some variation, is Ellis's Rational-Emotive Therapy, but other approaches are acceptable (Ellis & Grieger, 1977; Ellis & Harper, 1975; Ruben, 1989b; Ruben & Ruben, in press). Essentially the therapist follows two steps.

The first step is to identify that what the client views are events. It seems as if these events trigger urges or anger (or some other behavior) like a reflex, when these events are innocuous. What actually causes the reaction are the thoughts in between the events and the client's reactions. Explain that when events are clear—we have all the details about them—usually we know how to react. When they are unclear—we do not know why they happen or what the person's motives are (reasons unknown)—then we guess; we speculate about them. Guesses are based on three sources of information: the past ("in the past when this has happened, it has happened because . . ."), "if it were me" ("if it were me doing this, I'd do it because . . ."), and beliefs (shoulds, musts, or oughts—certain things should happen). But these are inferences. They are not pure inferences because they are not based on facts; instead they are based on guesses and hence are *impure inferences*. These inferences typically have little to do with the actual events that the person thinks is causing him or her grief.

The second step is to ask the client to overcome the impure inferences by checking out the events by describing them and asking questions about them.

Component 3: Social Skills

Poor adjustment to a drug-free life-style may be hampered by several complications in the client's social world. Eating disorders, polydrug abuse, unemployment, and family problems are among the more obvious problems. Not so typically detected are the weak (deficient) social skills and overly strong (excess) social skills that interfere with normal functioning.

Theories of psychology explain differently why deficits and excesses occur. Behaviorally, there are three main reasons for deficits and three main reasons for excesses. Deficits may occur because (1) the person never learned a skill, (2) the person learned it but the skill was inhibited (punished) under some circumstances, and (3) certain impure inferences (irrational beliefs) govern the inhibition of the skill. Excesses occur because (1) the person gets plenty of attention (reinforcement) for the wrong reasons, (2) it will delay or prevent punishment (criticism, etc.), as in the case of perfectionism or obsessive compulsion, and (3) certain impure inferences (irrational beliefs) govern the excess of the skill.

Retraining of social skills generally takes a variety of forms and is targeted to replace deficits and excesses (Lange & Jakubowski, 1976; Ruben, 1985). Basic social skills typically include:

- Basic assertiveness.
- Confrontation and assertiveness.
- Problem solving and decision making.
- Dating and initiation skills in social settings.
- Negotiation skills (for managers in industry).
- Compromise skills (for couples).
- Interview skills.

Considering the extraordinary variety of approaches to teach each skill, practitioners are advised to consult specialty manuals or to advise their clients to buy self-help books. Use of reading material, or "bibliotherapy," simplifies difficult information and personalizes the need for healthy recovery. Outside material can backfire, however, if it contradicts treatment goals or presumes a pace of progress unrealistic for clients. Books that therapists recommend should first past the test of credibility by that therapist and also be written for substance abusers (cf. Glasgow & Rosen, 1978, 1979; Rosen, 1976; Ruben, 1990c).

Component 4: Life-style Restructuring

Major changes in the day-to-day, moment-to-moment routine of the client are crucial to establish initial abstinence or reduction of drug use. Of course, abstinence is always preferred over gradual and systematic reduction, but for the continuous drinker of many years, immediate cessation of drinking is very hard and impractical, and recidivism will be high. Based on clinical decision, the goal of abstinence or drug reduction should accompany modifications of the following sorts:

Changes in work schedule. Frequently the purchase of supplies is after work or payroll checks might be cashed at the local bars (near factories, for instance). Identify and rearrange the work schedule so that the client returns home immediately after work.

Changes in transportation schedule. Frequently drug use and drinking take place while driving. If the client drives, arrange for him to drink nothing, not even soft drinks, in the car. Drinking a soft drink may seem innocuous but the behavioral pattern is identical to drinking beer or liquor; the only difference is the content, which is insufficient for lasting changes. One way to prevent unauthorized drinking is to have the client drive with his spouse, a reliable friend, or his children or to drive at hours of day or along a route not exposed to cues.

Changes in social activities. Frequently drug use and drinking accompany or follow outings, parties, dates, or other special occasions. This is particularly true for episodic drinkers. Realign the client's participation in these activities by first restricting or eliminating them, and then by minimizing participation by hours. Have the client stay 1 or 2 hours per time and then leave, monitored by a peer or spouse. Also, certain friends or certain activities other than at parties are prone (cues) to drinking. Fishing, working on the car, and business luncheons, for example, are major cues and should be dealt with.

Changes in family and spouse contact. Frequently drug use precipitates or follows contact with the immediate family. In cases of constant altercations, domestic fights, or physical abuse, drinking may be pervasive; in cases of divorce or separation, drinking may be a consequence of each visit. If drinking occurs in front of the children, this means the history and intensity of drinking are very strong. Assistance from the spouse, peers, or children (if children are adults) can limit the spouse's drinking. Another prevention is marital or couples therapy.

Changes relative to physiological problems and medication regimen. Frequently drug use or alcoholism accompanies or is the side effect of drug use, misuse, underuse, or overuse. In other words, prescribed medicines taken along with addictive drug use may cause drug interactive effects. Medications of all sorts need to be assessed to prevent fatal or contraindicated effects. The most obvious example is Antabuse, a chemical agent that blocks metabolism of alcohol. Clients prone to physical illness or suffering from diseases may exacerbate their illness or disease by drinking excessively or using drugs. Diabetes, for example, can become aggravated after drinking, accelerating visual deterioration or an imbalance in blood sugar content.

Changes in eating and mealtime schedule. Frequently drinking or drug use supersedes a regular routine of meals. When drug abuse is complicated by eating disorders (bulimia, anorexia, polydipsia, etc.), disruption of the eating routine is particularly critical. Alcohol, consumed on an empty stomach passes through the system more rapidly, increasing levels of tolerance. When drinking is to be reduced systematically, increments of food or a regularly scheduled meal is essential.

Changes in sleep schedule. Frequently drinking or drug use occurs when the client must remain awake. Those working midnight shifts who need to be awake after work may drink. While alcoholism technically is both a stimulant and depressant, depending on the person, in this case the stimulant would prevent proper rest. Adjust this schedule to encourage sleep or rearrange the family, domestic, and social commitments so that sleep is possible after work.

Changes in idle time. Frequently drinking or drug use occurs when the client has idle time. Boredom, inactivity, or inability to work due to physical disability, accidents, or other reasons may engender opportunities to drink or use drugs. This is particularly problematic for those who are handicapped. Calibrated use of time or time management helps to overcome abuse of free time.

Changes in avoidance and escape. Frequently drinking or drug use occurs due to avoidance and escape. Avoidance is the deliberate delay, postponement, or possible elimination of unpleasant circumstances anticipated by the client. A closet drinker who keeps the supplies and his habit hidden from others is avoiding confrontation. Escape is the attempt to terminate or remove unpleasant circumstances once they occur. Flight from an argument or resorting to drinking during a fight or confrontation is escape behavior. Syndromes of avoidance so widely prevail in chronic abusers that they become habitual actions, almost addictions themselves (Ruben, in press). In teaching proper social skills, it is advisable for the therapist to work directly on the client's ability to overcome avoidance and escape.

Component 5: Marital and Family Skills

Problem drinking or drug use interferes with dynamics of the family or marital relationship, and in traditional Alcoholics Anonymous literature, the problem is considered a family disease. In this component, attention is drawn to clearly defined stressors between spouses, between the addict and particular family members, or between the addict and his parents (cf. Jacobson & Margolin, 1979).

The first step is to identify spouse conflict problems. If any are found, apply problem-solving, communication, listening and expression skills, and affection-exchange skills (modality of therapy can vary).

Second, identify parent-child problems. If there are any between an addict parent and a toddler or preadolescent, apply basic methods to teach positive alternatives to discipline, plus anger control management. For those between an addict parent and an adolescent, apply communication, listening, and expression skills, and increase opportunities for positive interaction between both parties. For those between an addict teenager and parents, use parents as monitors (unless they are punitive), and change both the parents' and teenager's beliefs about the relationship. Also, identify positive peer role models in school for adolescents, encouraging nondrug activities. For those between an addict adult and his older parents, restructure the relationship to minimize dependency on the parents and maximize independence. Efforts toward independent living accompany the treatment plan. If the parent-child relationship is sexual or abusive, *do not contact proper authorities immediately.* Confidentiality of substance abuse clients is protected under federal, not state laws, and adds a needed degree of flexibility to the therapist. If one does report incidents, proper authorization of or notification to the client in writing is recommended.

Component 6: Employment Skills

Increases in drug use or drinking may be the result of poor or stressful performance at work, abrupt or anticipated unemployment, conflict relationships between worker and supervisor, or job ambiguity. Each may contribute to drug use as avoidance or escape from coping with unpleasant realities of the work force (e.g., Connellan, 1978; Halpern, 1972; Miller, 1978; Ruben, 1986). In this component, focus is on the effects of the job on the emotional stability of the addict.

High levels of stress occur because the client lacks the proper skill requirements for the job, has the skills but is absent frequently, expects personal work to be perfect, or for reasons discussed in other categories. Identify where the problem is, and teach basic steps in stress management accompanied by helping the client receive proper education for the job.

Because of politics or irrevocable performance problems, the client may expect to be fired and will deteriorate in performance while increasing or starting drug use. Vocational placement and possibly rehabilitation are needed, along with interviewing skills; encouragement is toward the reemployment process (positive and constructive) rather than on entirely dwelling on the emotional loss of the job (negative and eliminative).

Supervisor-employee problems are common in industry and employment. Generally the approach, if it is the employee who is client, is to apply basic assertiveness skills and other approaches that foster better rapport. Changes in belief systems will be needed to offset the client's self-condemnatory perceptions. It is important to delineate clearly between appropriate and inappropriate assertiveness and when to use it. A fine line exists between appropriate confrontation and insubordination. If the supervisor is the client, appropriate assertiveness and communication on the job is best taught. Should this training not be available, he can attend seminars and workshops offered by the American Management Association or local universities.

Detecting the source of supervisor-employee conflict is important. For example, is the supervisor under pressure from his boss? Is the employee overly audacious due to union or peer pressure? Are new policies in effect (realistic or unrealistic), enabling this conflict? Does the trouble stem, in other words, from a systems problem rather than a personality conflict? For example, civil service encourages in-house competition and discourages efficient work performance because of the consequences (good work earns "more work" and frequent reprimands; less work is avoidance). These are systems problems, and it is best the employee be taught how to survive within them.

Job ambiguity means the expectations or demands of a particular task or job assignment are unclear. Lack of clarity on a continuous basis forces the client to guess what is expected, and generally these guesses are inconsistent and wrong. Consequently, clients receive frequent reprimands, notices, or are confronted by supervision. Ways to reduce ambiguity include having the client request or specify a job description or task description, teaching the client to adhere to these "criteria" (description) and then solicit feedback from appropriate supervisors, and having the client ask more questions and paraphrase when any instructions are given.

Component 7: Community Resources

Part of therapy should involve the referral of the client to appropriate agencies or functions in the community that will improve attainment of emotional and behavioral goals. Another reason is to ensure a "natural" involvement in sobriety or drug-free life-style beyond the therapeutic session. Community referrals will vary. First consider the main agencies; then consider agency standards, and finally your role as monitor. Referrals typically are divided into five services: medical, social, legal, vocational, and educational.

Medical care is to assess further conditions of pathology resulting from or concurrent to drug use and abuse. Sometimes Antabuse treatment may need to be coordinated with the primary care physician unless one is on staff. Referrals can also be made to inpatient hospitalization for detoxification.

Contacts with social service agencies give access to publicly funded financial assistance programs and short-term emergency services. Specialty areas include residential, housing assistance, credit counseling, and aid to dependent mothers.

Legal aid provides counsel to persons at a minimal cost. Local attorneys specialize in cases of drunk driving, drug possession, molestation or other sexual misconduct, and wrongful firing from jobs.

Unemployed clients may lack employable occupational skills and could benefit from job training programs. Depending on many physical and psychological factors, some programs are available without cost. For example, those who are handicapped with visual loss or impairment can receive job training in the Vending Stand program at no charge. Contacts are made through the Commission for the Blind.

Two basic forms of education prevail here. First is education on alcoholism and drug or medication abuse, available from a physician or pharmacist or through highway safety and other prevention programs (e.g., Call Someone

Concerned-Albion, NCA). Second is continuing education for clients seeking a general equivalency diploma or college education toward an occupational or academic goal.

Qualified standards play a role in the evaluation of referral agencies. Most agencies to which referrals are made have a qualified referral agreement that allows the exchange of information on a confidential basis. But there are also standards that therapists should check:

1. Cost of service: Is the service affordable?
2. Eligibility requirements: Geographic (does the client live too far from the agency?); age, sex, or race (do these factors pose a problem?); and substance abuse (does the agency take only substance abusers?).
3. Range of services: Will the agency fulfill the client's needs?
4. Application procedures: Do the forms or interviews make unrealistic demands?
5. Size of program and population served: Is treatment individualized? Is it age segregated or integrated?
6. Agency requirements: Is there a minimum length of stay? What medications are involved, if any? What is the agency's detoxification philosophy?

Correctly referring a client goes beyond a telephone call to monitoring the referral. Steps in this process include the following:

1. Plan for referral needs: Involve the client in the planning process, evaluate community agencies to determine the best placement, and discuss the client's needs with selected agencies.
2. Initiate the referral process: Contact agencies, provide confidential information on the client only after he signs an authorization for disclosure, and give the client the responsibility for making subsequent contacts.
3. Monitor referrals in the treatment network.
4. Evaluate the referral process and agencies.

Component 8: Relapse Prevention

The final component in therapy is laying the groundwork more firmly for skills learned in short-term therapy to continue after therapy ends. Actually this process is ongoing in that every component is direct, based on natural changes, and involves life-style restructure. However, relapse prevention (Marlatt & Gordon, 1985) refers to some specific methods that are best introduced at the end of therapy. The exception occurs when new clients have already quit drinking or drug use for three or so months and simply want steps to maintain their abstinence. Specific intervention strategies include self-monitoring, skill training, programmed relapse, cognitive restructuring, and peer support groups.

Self-monitoring. Formal or informal methods of self-monitoring involve daily, weekly, or monthly records of the client, verifying his efforts to remain according to goals. The therapist can set up this system by using graphs, flowcharts, or in monitored relationships with the spouse. Increased awareness of what the client does builds up expectation effects, which are excellent safeguards against relapse.

Skill Training. Training in specific adjustment skills for social confrontation, supervisor-employee relations, or family and marital relations, is necessary. Training in self-control also involves stress management, anger management, sexual enhancement, and development of other skills that enable performance at work. At this point in therapy, the focus is on ensuring that these skills transfer and are maintained.

Transfer refers to learned skills in all the important places in the client's world. Assertiveness skills, for example, may be strong at home but weak at work. Therapists should identify where skills are not transferring and direct efforts to correct this (for examples of transfer problems, see Ruben & Ruben, 1987, 1989). Once transfer seems fairly consistent in all the important places, skills should be maintained. *Maintenance* refers to implanting natural (not contrived) sources of feedback for the client so that skills can continue when the primary feedback giver (the therapist) finishes treatment. Such implantation involves teaching the client how to solicit feedback, teaching the spouse or significant other how to attend to progress or positive steps in behavior, and teaching the client what positive and desirable consequences to expect for recovery steps (for instance, easier breathing or lowered blood pressure may result from sobriety or abstinence).

Programmed Relapse. Make the client aware that sobriety or abstinence is a learned process and that control over urges and cues and other emotional or behavioral factors increases the probability of but does not guarantee total prevention. As part of the aftercare plan, the therapist should specify needed steps and criteria for each step on what is necessary for achieving a high degree of sobriety or abstinence. Such a list might entail the following:

AFTERCARE PLAN

Social Activities

1. Weeknight and weekend outings; 3–5 outings weekly
   a. Day/nighttime activity with 3–5 friends
   b. Day/nighttime activity at movie or theater
   c. Day/nighttime activity involving:
      (1) child's school PTA
      (2) community services (e.g., adult education)

Rapport with Spouse

1. 1–3 weeknight or weekend activities with spouse
   a. 2 activities without friends at home
   b. 1 activity with another couple
   c. variety of sexual, personal, sports activities

Cognitive Restructuring. Reorientation to the realistic perspectives is part of Component 2: Belief Systems. Reminders of this realistic orientation implanted into prevention include frequent cognitive rehearsals of what happens (the consequences) if the client drinks or uses drugs again. Also, self-efficacy ratings are advisable here; they involve a list a specific high-risk situations for relapse and ask the client to rate the degree of temptation likely to be experienced and how confident he feels about his capacity to overcome the situation. The client then rehearses these strategies as self-instructions when experiencing urges.

Peer Support Groups. During or following treatment the client may benefit from participation in Alcoholics Anonymous (AA) or other community support groups. Certain treatment modalities necessitate immediate involvement in AA and hence adhere to the 12 steps of recovery. This is not entirely necessary, and the clients should remember that AA, Al-Anon, and other groups are not panaceas but instead are resources for stability. Use of these groups for additional strength outside the therapist's efforts is a good practice.

SUMMARY

Approaches to substance abuse based in behavioral principles have many empirical advantages over traditional approaches. Measurability, therapist accountability, generality and maintenance of results, and economy of cost rank highest among these gains. The approaches outlined here, however, may backfire without certain precautions. Addiction is a psychological, biological, and social phenomenon requiring as much physician and community input as therapist input. Treating the addiction behaviorally is incomplete unless the client's entire dependency status, from physical health and cultural contingencies to response patterns, is viewed integratively as a field of behavior. The systems approach is a first step in this direction and awaits further validity by outpatient practitioners.

REFERENCES

Arneson, A. H., Ruben, D. H. & Husain, S. (1984). Credentialing of substance abuse counselors: A field evaluation. *Journal of Drug Education, 14*, 297–306.
Bellack, A. S. & Hersen, M. (1985). *Dictionary of behavioral therapy techniques.* New York: Pergamon.
Connellan, T. K. (1978). *How to improve human performance: Behaviorism in business and industry.* New York: Harper & Row.
Delprato, D. J. (1981). The constructional approach to behavior modification. *Journal of Behavior Therapy and Experimental Psychiatry, 46*, 219–42.
Delprato, D. J. (1987). Private communication.
Dendy, R., Cooper, J. & Cantwell, T. (1977). *Assessment interviewing for treatment planning.* Arlington, Va.: National Drug Abuse Center.
Ellis, A. & Grieger, R. (1977). *Handbook of rational-emotive therapy.* New York: Springer.

Ellis, A. & Harper, R. (1975). *A new guide to rational living.* Hollywood, Ca.: Wilshire.

Glasgow, R. E. & Rosen, G. M. (1978). Behavioral bibliotherapy: A review of self-help behavior therapy manuals. *Psychological Bulletin, 85,* 1–23.

Glasgow, R. E. & Rosen, G. M. (1979). Self-help behavior therapy manuals: Recent developments and clinical usage. *Clinical Behavior Therapy Review, 1,* 1–20.

Goldberg, S. R. & Stolerman, I. P. (1985) *Behavioral analysis of drug dependence.* Orlando, Fla.: Academic Press.

Goldiamond, I. (1974). Toward a constructional approach to social problems. *Behaviorism, 2,* 1–84.

Halpern, S. (1972). *Drug abuse and your company.* New York: American Management Association.

Hayes, S. (ed.). (1989). *Rule-governed behavior.* New York: Plenum.

Hester, R. K. & Miller, W. R. (1989). *Handbook of alcoholism treatment approach.* New York: Pergamon.

Jacobson, N. S. & Margolin, G. (1979). *Marital therapy.* New York: Brunner/Mazel.

Lange, A. J. & Jakubowski, P. (1976). *Responsible assertive behavior.* Champaign, Ill.: Research Press.

Marlatt, G. A. & Gordon, J. R. (eds.). (1985). *Relapse prevention.* New York: Guilford Press.

Miller, L. (1978). *Behavior management: The new science of managing people at work.* New York: Wiley & Sons.

Monti, P. M., Abrams, D. B., Kadden, R. M. & Cooney, N. L. (1989). *Treating alcohol dependence.* New York: Guilford Press.

Rosen, G. M. (1976). The development and use of nonprescription behavior therapies. *American Psychologist, 31,* 139–41.

Ruben, D. H. (1983). Interbehavioral implications of behavior therapy: Clinical perspectives. In N. W. Smith, P. T. Mountjoy & D. H. Ruben (eds.), *Reassessment in psychology: The interbehavioral alternative* (pp. 445–69). Lanham, Md.: University Press of America.

Ruben, D. H. (1985). *Progress in assertiveness.* Metuchen, N.J.: Scarecrow Press.

Ruben, D. H. (1986). The management of role ambiguity in organizations. *Journal of Employment Counseling, 23,* 120–130.

Ruben, D. H. (1989a). Behavioral predictors of alcoholics: A "systems" alternative. *Alcoholism Treatment Quarterly, 5,* 137–162.

Ruben, D. H. (1989b). *Tips to success.* Okemos, Mich.: Best Impressions International.

Ruben, D. H. (1989c). Bibliotherapy: Practical considerations when writing for substance abuse readers. *Journal of Alcohol and Drug Education, 34,* 70–78.

Ruben, D. H. (1990a). *Aging and drug effects: A planning manual for medication and alcohol abuse treatment of the elderly,* Jefferson, N.C.: McFarland Press.

Ruben, D. H. (in press). *Avoidance syndrome.* St. Louis, Mo.: Warren Green Publishers.

Ruben, D. H. (1990b). Interbehavioral approach to treatment of substance abuse: A "new" systems model. *Alcoholism Treatment Quarterly, 7,* 47–61.

Ruben, D. H. & Ruben, M. J. (1987). Assumptions about teaching assertiveness: Training the person or behavior? In D. H. Ruben & D. J. Delprato (eds.), *New ideas in therapy* (pp. 107–18). Westport, Conn.: Greenwood Press.

Ruben. D. H. & Ruben, M. J. (1989). Why assertiveness training programs fail. *Small Group Behavior, 20,* 367–80.

Ruben, D. H. & Ruben, M. J. (in press). *60 seconds to success.* Okemos, Mich.: Best Impressions International.

Ryan, V., Arneson, A., Popour, J. L. & Ruben, D. H. (eds.) (1984). *Fundamentals of substance abuse counseling.* Lansing, Mich.: ARIS.

Schuckit, M. A. (1989). *Drug and alcohol abuse: A clinical guide to diagnosis and treatment.* New York: Plenum.

9

Multifaceted Treatment of Patients with Severe Eating Disorders

DAVID LANSKY AND JOHN L. LEVITT

This chapter outlines a treatment approach for eating disorders and a conceptualization about treatment that we have found to be useful in our work with eating-disordered patients. The unique contribution of various theoretical positions to the multifaceted approach is explored below. Detailed reviews of these approaches are also available elsewhere (Brownell & Foreyt, 1986; Blinder, Chaitin & Goldstein, 1988; Emmet, 1985; Garner & Garfinkel, 1985; Hsu, 1990). Often reviews of treatment approaches provide viewpoints that are unidimensional and do not reflect the actualities of treating patients in real-world clinical contexts. Here we present a conceptualization—a way of thinking about eating disorders and their treatment—and a way of integrating ideas from various theoretical viewpoints into a coherent, unified approach. This discussion will provide a guideline for working with these problems; it will not attempt to review inpatient treatment methods, which are well covered elsewhere (e.g., Brownell & Foreyt, 1986; Garner & Garfinkel, 1985; Blinder, Chaitin & Goldstein, 1988).

We have specialized in treating patients with eating disorders and have seen hundreds of patients with these symptoms in a variety of contexts. In a review of their work with 85 patients over a three-year period, Lansky and Levitt (1987) found that fewer than 20 percent presented with primary anorexia nervosa. The majority of patients ($N = 69$) presented with restrictive (anorectic) and/or bulimic eating patterns in conjunction with seriously dysfunctional behavioral patterns in other areas of functioning. Other symptoms presenting in this sample included affective disorders, alcohol and drug abuse, borderline personality disorder, conduct disorder, a history of physical or sexual abuse, self-injurious and self-mutilative behaviors, and dissociative disorder. The data suggest, and others have noted as well (Casper, 1983; Garfinkel, Moldofsky & Garner, 1980), that patients with primary anorexia nervosa tend to make up a relative minority of patients with eating disorders; those who are bulimic or who present with mixed eating disorder symptoms and are dysfunctional in multiple areas of functioning are encountered more frequently in clinical practice; these people are the focus of our discussion.

CONCEPTUALIZING THE PROBLEM

Patients who present with an eating disorder are different from those who do not, a fact that is often ignored by therapists who function as though identical techniques and assumptions may be applied to clients who present with varying forms of pathology. An understanding of the etiology of eating disorders and the role that symptoms play in the life of people with eating disorders must be used to inform treatment and to structure a unique treatment environment. Bruch (1973) made a similar observation when she suggested that traditional psychoanalysis created an environment that was a reexperiencing of the familial circumstances (being told what to feel and think) that precipitated anorexia nervosa in the first place. Thus, she suggested that a different approach, using similar treatment methods (individual, insight-oriented psychotherapy), was necessary with these patients.

A generalized approach to treating people with eating disorders is a helpful prerequisite for successful treatment. This approach is quite different from that used by many therapists with patients who do not manifest an eating disorder. To this end, it is important to distinguish between the structure and the content of treatment. The *structure* of treatment refers to the broad context in which treatment occurs—the positions of therapist and client in that context and permissible client and therapist behaviors within that context. For example, the therapist may need to create a context for treatment that allows for alternating between confrontation and limit setting on the one hand and nurturing and soothing support on the other (Levenkron, 1983). The *content* of treatment refers to the nature of the treatment process—the guiding theory of treatment and the targets of therapeutic interventions. Although successful therapists can operate from a variety of theoretical viewpoints, the structure of treatment for different therapists will often be similar.

STRUCTURE OF TREATMENT

Individuals who present in clinical practice with an eating disorder have often been in treatment before with varying degrees of success, experience difficulties at multiple levels of functioning over extended periods of time, and have long histories of eating and weight difficulties. Certainly personal and environmental factors influence the expression of the eating disorder among these clients, but equally important is the fact that the eating disorder, or its sequelae and correlates (e.g., depression following a binge, social isolation), tend to have a huge impact on the people and situations close to the person with the problem. In other words, not only does the environment affect the problem, but the problem affects the environment. The symptoms that the patient presents assume significance in the patient's interpersonal milieu and may represent a desire to influence or communicate to others about the patient's internal state. In fact, these individuals often interact with the world through their symptoms, which enables them to feel effective, efficient, powerful, meaningful, and so forth without directly interacting with or confronting those persons, places, and situations right in front of them. One patient, for example, while denying angry feelings or resentment toward her parents, binged and purged following each telephone conversation with them. In another case, a patient lost weight each time her marital difficulties resurfaced and gained weight with each temporary solution. In both cases, the client with the eating disorder was communicating to the world about herself and, as in the second case, may be attempting to influence others through her symptoms.

Although these observations lend themselves to the development of specific therapeutic interventions (e.g., assertiveness training, marital therapy), they are perhaps more important in terms of their implications for the structure of the treatment process. The structure of therapy must take into consideration the idea that the symptoms may constitute an attempt to influence or to communicate with the therapist or significant others in the patient's environment. In this case, symptoms, can be viewed not only as targets of change but as modes of influence and communication. Consequently, the therapist's primary goals are to alleviate the symptom and to help patients understand the significance of the symptom within their social context. Initially, the therapist must understand the symptom and its significance, be able to provide psychoeducational information about the nature of the symptom, set limits about the symptom in terms of reducing negative or dangerous consequences to the patient or therapeutic relationship, help the patient reduce intrusive feelings of anxiety and depression, facilitate the development of patient insight, and assist the patient in making major decisions about treatment that the patient either may be unable to do or may be otherwise limited in ability to perform. This must all be done without the therapist's being directly affected by the symptoms. That is, the therapist must avoid falling victim to feelings of helplessness, hopelessness, rage, and disappointment to which others, including the patient, might find themselves succumbing as a result of the symptom and, hence, reducing or limiting the effectiveness of therapy.

The therapeutic relationship thereby becomes a vehicle of change for these patients. In addition to the new learnings that take place within the relationship, the relationship becomes a situation in the patient's life where the symptom is no longer in control. This is the essential element of the treatment context with the eating-disordered patient: the symptom, which can be dangerous, frustrating, unyielding, and persistent, is no longer in control of the therapy or affecting a significant relationship.

Ideally, the therapist takes a position of neutrality relative to symptoms or a position of balanced advantages and disadvantages. It is helpful to no one for the therapist to attempt desperately to eradicate a symptom, particularly if that symptom has meaning and utility to the patient. The therapist attempts to communicate empathy, concern, warmth, and caring but does not become ensnared by the need to eliminate the symptom. Patients are encouraged to see that therapy will continue with or without symptoms (although successively more intensive interventions may be tried) and that they will not be rejected or abandoned if the eating disorder continues. The patient is encouraged to observe, recognize, and learn that open and direct communication with the therapist is possible and, in fact, preferable to indirect, symptom-based modes of communication. Consequently, the patient is often prompted to share with the therapist openly and honestly. This includes any type of feeling, even negative feelings (anger at the therapist, discomfort upon eating and/or not bingeing, fears about sexuality, etc.). There is a strong emphasis on the crucial importance of honesty and direct communication.

Patients commonly experience effective eating-disorder therapists as tough or confrontive but nevertheless appreciate the toughness and the confrontations. Patients realize that the therapist is not intimidated by their symptoms and generally find comfort in knowing that indirect communication and influence is no longer necessary in the relationship.

Once the structure of the treatment environment is well established, targets and methods of treatment can be addressed. Selection of goals and approaches may be guided by a multidimensional model of eating disorders (Garner & Garfinkel, 1982). Although this particular model itself is useful, it is not viewed as "the truth" about eating disorders. Rather, this model is more or less useful in working with patients who have eating disorders and must fit the unique needs of each patient. Too strong an allegiance to any particular model tends to obscure the view of a particular patient's situation. As Bandler and Grinder (1979) have stated, "The map is not the territory." In other words, a model or theory of treatment is a guide that may be more or less helpful but must be modified if necessary, based on succeeding learning experiences. In general, an etiological model is usually helpful only if it helps tie treatment to a particular conceptualization of the problem, if it suggests points of intervention, if it provides criteria for measuring outcomes, or if it helps to identify and localize areas where treatment might be failing.

MULTIDIMENSIONAL MODEL OF EATING DISORDERS

The model described here suggests that predisposing, precipitating, and sustaining factors interact in the development and maintenance of an eating disorder and that interventions will likely need to be aimed at these various levels.

Different treatment issues, goals, and modalities may be potentially identified by examining each of these dimensions and its constituents.

Predisposing Factors

Predisposing factors represent influences in a person's life that may contribute to development of a negative body image, low self-esteem, a sense of ineffectiveness in one's ability to manage the environment, and a view of dieting as a source—perhaps the only source—of personal strength, control, and pleasure.

Sociocultural Factors. One's culture and societal network create a social context in which weight loss, thinness, and physical beauty are inordinately esteemed as goals, superseding emotional, intellectual, or other goals. *Time* magazine (1986), for example, in a special issue on obesity and dieting, reported that nearly 90 percent of Americans feel they weigh too much; that 30 percent of adult women and 80 percent of fourth-grade girls reported dieting at least once in 1984; and that 16 percent of American women considered themselves perpetual dieters. Yet in spite of these enormous pressures, the scientific literature on weight loss indicates that significant weight loss and maintenance of weight loss remain difficult, often overwhelming, challenges indeed (e.g., Brownell & Wadden, 1986). In fact, Americans are now fatter than they have ever been; 24 percent of males and 27 percent of females are more than 20 percent above ideal body weight (*Time,* 1986). The combination of pressures to lose weight and substantial difficulties in attaining and maintaining significant weight losses creates fertile ground for people to attempt excessive, unhealthy, compulsive solutions to eating and weight problems.

While it would be helpful for advertisers to place less emphasis on thinness and for weight loss clinics to portray a more realistic image of the difficulty most people have in maintaining weight losses, these are social and political goals that cannot be effectively addressed directly in treatment. What may be addressed in the course of treatment, however, is the tendency for patients with eating disorders to seek unrealistic goals and expectations that have been foisted on them in their cultural milieu. Providing information to patients—for example, that weight loss is extremely difficult for most people and that biological factors significantly determine weight status—may be useful in helping patients to develop a realistic perspective toward the meaning of weight and weight loss.

Cultural influences are also often transmitted through families. For example, it is not unusual for patients who have received attention in their families for problems with their weight while other more serious problems were ignored or even while successful achievements in other areas of life were ignored. Eliciting feelings about these inequities and aiding patients in recognizing and understanding how their concern with weight may have in part developed from these experiences are useful in order to begin to liberate patients from unrealistic or impossible cultural expectations.

Another approach for dealing with cultural influences derives from Michael White's (1988) cybernetic systems theory of therapy. White attempts to empower his clients through a process he terms "externalization of problem influences." Externalizing problem influences for the bulimic or anorectic patient involves portraying the client as having been victimized by external (cultural) processes that have determined the problem behaviors the patient now presents in treatment. When the patient is able to view herself as a victim of these forces, she can then begin to examine the ways in which she has successfully struggled to resist the unhealthy influences. For example, she may be able to recall times she decided to resist the invitation to join another diet program, even though she was unhappy with her weight, because she knew she would not be any more successful than she was in previous efforts. Externalization is particularly important to bulimic patients who feel personally responsible for difficulties in keeping weight off, although biological processes are generally at least as important in determining weight problems as are personal psychological weaknesses (Sorensen, Price, Stunkard & Schulsinger, 1989).

Individual Psychological Factors. A person's unique psychology constitutes a second set of predisposing factors in the treatment of patients with an eating disorder. The importance of establishing a context for treatment in which honesty, direct communication, support, and confrontation may be combined to impair the personal power of symptoms has been previously discussed and described.

The psychodynamics of patients with eating disorders have already been described by Bruch (1962) and by Goodsitt (1983). Anorexia was viewed by Bruch as a symptom resulting from three interrelated primary psychological dynamics: a sense of ineffectiveness, interoceptive disturbance, and body image disturbance. Goodsitt suggests that anorectics suffer from disturbances of the self: they lack internal self-regulatory skills, which results in feeling inadequate, ineffective, and out of control; they have difficulty moderating anxiety; they become easily bored and frustrated and turn to weight loss as an activity to help them occupy time, as well as to experience themselves as successful and special; they focus on food and weight and consequently turn inwardly rather than toward other people, whom they have learned to distrust; and they fill their lives with rituals that serve to help them feel a sense of regularity, predictability, and control. Goodsitt (1985) suggests that the result of these disturbances is that anorectics "ignore, dismiss and devalue" their own inner values and feelings and set excessively high standards for themselves, while viewing their accomplishments with a critical, dissatisfied eye. Bulimic patients vacillate between success and failure, much like bingeing and purging, in maintaining restrictive eating and weight loss. Their experience of themselves is therefore more chaotic and characterized more by feelings of failure than the anorectic, who at least has been able to succeed narrowly in efforts to lose weight. Moreover, while the bulimic often appears as more accomplished, less isolated, and more mature than the anorectic, bulimic patients often feel as though they are play acting in these roles. Bulimics may have many acquaintances but few intimate relationships; they often feel like failures at work or at school, in spite of obvious accomplishments, because of their overriding focus on their failure to lose weight and to keep it off.

The therapist's task is to teach skills for coping with stress and tension, to correct faulty cognitions related to perfectionism, to help the patient stop avoiding dysphoric feelings, and to learn that these are an acceptable, normal part of being human. The therapist should be available during crises (which may occur often in early stages of therapy as the patient tests the therapist's ability to be consistent and trustworthy), speak soothingly, even hypnotically, and teach relaxation or self-hypnosis as methods of tension reduction to aid the patient's ability to acquire internal self-regulatory skills.

Cognitive therapy (e.g., Beck, 1976; Burns, 1980) offers methods to challenge irrational beliefs, such as the patient's perceived need to appear perfectly in control of all aspects of life, her tendency to "mind read" (e.g., to assume that others judge her as harshly as she judges herself), her tendency to engage in all-or-none thinking (e.g., that she is either a success or a failure rather than in between), and her high need for approval (needing to be approved of by anyone she comes into contact with and not tolerating rejection or criticism well).

Behavioral rehearsal (Goldfried & Davison, 1976) is another method for teaching self-regulatory skills. In this technique, the therapist takes an active role in helping the patient to identify difficult social situations, to discuss alternative coping methods, and then to rehearse potential solutions and outcomes.

The therapist must provide a safe, trusting environment where the patient is able to explore the hidden feelings and fears that she has long avoided. The therapist of the patient with an eating disorder must be able to assume tasks and decisions that the patient is initially unable to assume. Struggles for control of the therapy are not uncommon; often, these are viewed as tests of the therapist's patience and courage. The patient who views her therapist as inconsistent or too easily intimidated will fear abandonment and will begin to develop distrust. When a patient begins to distrust the therapist, the patient may act the "perfect patient," but symptom reduction or psychological development may be impeded. If hospitalization or another professional's consultation is necessary, the therapist must be direct and assertive. Clear limits need to be set regarding alcohol and drug abuse, use of laxatives, self-destructive behaviors, or other severely self-limiting or self-injurious behaviors. Limit setting can include hospitalization, use of medication, and use of alternative inpatient or outpatient intensive treatment programs in addition to the therapy. When the behavior in question is particularly destructive or disruptive to the therapy, a clear verbal or even written contract regarding the limits of therapy itself may need to be established. For example, an actively self-mutilating patient may not be able to be treated in outpatient therapy; if the behavior does not reduce or stop, hospitalization or appropriate referrals to other services may need to be made.

A history of often severe physical, sexual, or emotional abuse is not uncommon among patients who present in treatment with an eating disorder (Blume, 1989). In these cases, there is often a deeply held rage over not having been nurtured properly or having been abused that is suppressed because of fears that if the extent of the rage were revealed, the patient would be abandoned or possibly abused again by people close to her. This situation is frequently expressed as a conflict between desperately wanting to be rescued by others (nurtured) versus appearing, albeit superficially, to need no one. The patient may be struggling for control of the therapy by challenging, arguing with, or passively resisting the therapist. Actually the patient may be wishing secretly that the therapist is strong enough to resist her efforts to be in control. The conflict in these situations needs to observed and interpreted—telling the patient that her words say one thing ("I want to be in control") while her actions, as symptoms intensify, say another ("I cannot control myself"). Stating that the therapist will go along with the actions rather than the words places responsibility on the patient to resolve the double message either by verbalizing her fears of independence or by acting more competently and independently.

Familial Influences. The effects that the familial culture has on the patient constitutes a third set of predisposing factors that generally need to be addressed in the course of treatment. While family influences are almost always important, the age and living circumstances of the patient tend to determine how much direct therapeutic involvement with the family there should be. Younger patients who are living with their parents or have families in which the eating symptoms are central, imposing, and controlling should be actively involved in family therapy. The older the patient and the less powerful and imposing the symptom is in the family, the less family therapy involvement there need be. Occasionally, for older patients, particularly those who are living with parents, a limited number of goal-directed family sessions may be quite useful. In any case, family sessions need to be carefully thought out and planned beforehand, the purpose needs to be clearly stated to the patient, and the therapist needs to avoid being viewed as allying with parents or other family members, as this may revive fears of abandonment.

Family sessions should be undertaken cautiously when there has been a history of physical or sexual abuse in the family. It may take years before some patients are able to confront or even interact with abusive parents. Indeed, some patients may need to accept that focusing on or confronting their parents about abuse might not prove to be useful; their energy may need to be focused on separation and improvement of their own situations.

Minuchin and colleagues (Minuchin, Rosman & Baker, 1978) provide a useful structural model of families in which there is an eating disorder. They propose four general characteristics of these families' interactional patterns. First is overprotectiveness. Overprotective parents fear the world and underestimate their children's abilities to cope. In families where overprotectiveness is characteristic, the parents are misreading the child's capacity to problem solve; they are acting out their widely derived fears and anxieties in the guise of representing the child's needs.

Second is enmeshment, in which boundaries (personal space, feelings, needs, ideas, and so forth) in the family are vague and permeable. Where enmeshment patterns are excessive, children are often overinvolved with parental issues and parents are overly involved in the children's personal issues. In this case children tend to become triangulated by parental conflicts; they tend to take responsibility for or to act out parental conflict.

The third characteristic is rigidity. The family has difficulty accommodating or adapting to general changes, crises, or new situations, such as the onset of puberty in a child, loss of a job, or a move to a new home. The greater the rigidity is, the more the family struggles to maintain homeostasis in spite of change; they use old methods to cope with new problems. For example, these families may expect children to have the same relationship with the mother after she begins working outside the home and is relatively self-sufficient, or they may impose the same rules on a 10-year-old child as on a 15 year old.

Last is poor conflict resolution. Conflicts are suppressed and not acknowledged and/or efforts to resolve them within the family are routinely unsuccessful or are avoided. In this situation, even overt self-destructive problems such as alcoholism or drug dependency may be avoided, ignored, or unaddressed.

Eating disordered families often tend to communicate mixed messages to their children about the importance of growing up and becoming independent on the one hand versus remaining the loyal child in the family on the other hand. Thus, they communicate often contradictory and confusing messages regarding loyalty, independence, self-sufficiency, and responsibility to family. In these families, maturation is often equated with the ability to take care of other people; independence is mistaken for selfishness. Family conflicts regarding individuation and separation are indirectly acted out in the children's relationships with their parents. The child may often yearn for independence but fears that, if successful, the child will be abandoned. Children are faced with the reality that helplessness, while attracting care and attention, suppressing conflict, and relieving fear of abandonment, threatens independence and poses a further threat to boundaries in the family. Occasionally, the eating disorder is a direct expression of these conflicts; the patient can express her independence and personal power openly by clinging to a symptom that everyone else in the family attempts unsuccessfully to control or eradicate. In this case, the symptom may be a manifestation of a power struggle within the family—the patient struggling with other family members over who will control a basic personal function.

The therapist's tasks in relation to these family issues are to reduce overprotectiveness and enmeshment and to alleviate the threat to the family of independence, growth, and separation. For older patients, this is best done on an individual basis; this can be viewed as an example of family therapy conducted with an individual rather than with the entire family system. The patient in this situation temporarily will need to view the therapist as a safe bridge from the family; she will be terrified that her independence will be viewed negatively by the family; she will struggle with the need to confront family members when boundaries are violated or when old family patterns of judgment, criticism, or overprotectiveness interfere with her life. The patient will need to learn how to turn to other people for support and how developing intimate relationships with people outside the family can satisfy needs that have been yearned for yet have been chronically unmet within the family.

In situations where the therapist conducts family therapy with the family present, the immediate goal is to establish appropriate boundaries. This will begin to reduce the centrality of the eating disorder so that family transactions are not overly focused on the patient's helplessness, inadequacy, and sickness. Developing boundaries helps parents learn that they cannot fix the patient, that they need to detach from the symptom while ensuring that the patient's basic needs are met, and that necessary treatment is being conducted. The patient will need to learn to own the symptom without giving up personhood within the family. Minuchin, Rosman, and Baker (1978) suggest that it may be useful to frame the eating-disordered patient as "behaving irresponsibly" rather than "being sick." This sometimes helps parents distance themselves from the problem, allows them to begin treating the patient age appropriately, and enables the patient to take more personal responsibility for the problem. In some cases, therapy may also address unresolved marital conflict that causes one parent or the other to affiliate inappropriately with (usually) the sick child, thereby maintaining a special status for her.

The family therapist may need to address obsessive, unrealistic, or inappropriate weight or eating concerns in family members other than the identified patient. Several studies have shown that parents (Kalucy, Crisp & Harding, 1977) or siblings (Crisp, 1980) of eating-disordered patients may also manifest eating and weight preoccupations or disorders. It is not uncommon for patients to report that mealtimes in their families of origin were unpleasant experiences. The risks—cosmetic or physical—of excessive weight are often exaggerated in these families. Parents may need to learn to place less value on their children's appearance and to value personal accomplishments in other areas.

Because the eating disorder may constitute a struggle between family and patient over who will control the patient's eating behavior, the family therapist might frame the symptom in a positive light within the family—for example, by describing the symptoms as a reflection of the patient's strength of will or independence. In one family, the patient's bulimia was framed as unresolved grief for the loss of her sister several years earlier; the family was told that the symptoms represented the patient's only way of grieving and that therapy would focus on teaching her how to grieve. This allowed the parents to reduce their inappropriate caretaking and overinvolvement with the problem. A successful positive reframing will reduce the power struggle within the family so that the patient will be free to give up the symptom without having to experience herself as having failed in her struggle for independence.

Palazzoli (Palazzoli & Viaro, 1986; Simon, 1987) has suggested that anorectic and bulimic symptoms within the family represent the child's attempt to prove to her parents how strong she is in comparison to a domineering mother and a weak and impassive father. Palazzoli uses the "universal prescription" in therapy with these families, suggesting that the anorectic has attempted to aid the parents' failing marriage with her symptoms, thanks her, and then dismisses her from therapy. The remainder of the therapy focuses on helping the parents to arrange successively longer periods of time away from their children in unannounced and unscheduled ways. The children tend to react to the parents' leaving in many different ways but soon come to accept the new structure in the family, boundaries become less permeable, and parents and children begin to develop their own private and more independent lives.

Occasionally, family intervention is the key to recovery. This is relatively rare, however, and is true most often for primary anorectics—those who do not present multiple problems at multiple levels of functioning. For most patients, family intervention is aimed at decreasing or eliminating other people's involvement with the problem so that the patient can take appropriate personal responsibility for recovery and family therapy serves to facilitate the patient's individuation and separation from the family of origin.

Patients often experience difficulty in interpersonal relationships other than their families of origin. Difficulties with trust lead these people into heterosexual relationships that are often devoid of intimacy and may inadvertently recreate the abusive families from which they came. Occasionally, patients enter problematic relationships such as these with the intent of proving to themselves that they can successfully win the rejecting partner's love or "undo" previous family of origin experiences. Occasionally these relationships may need to be terminated by the patient in order for recovery to be realized. Marital or relationship therapy is useful to help the patient and her partner work through the conflictual issues that are not being resolved while the patient is active in her eating disorder.

Professionally led group therapy is also useful with these patients since it provides an opportunity to learn about interpersonal processes while information can be taught and shared didactically. Time-limited, structured group sessions (e.g., Johnson & Larson, 1982) can teach self-regulatory skills such as relaxation, self-monitoring, relapse prevention, and behavioral rehearsal. These groups are also useful for imparting basic information about eating and dieting and allowing participants to examine their interactions with peers. Group therapy alone, however, is usually inadequate for addressing the personal psychological issues.

Biological Factors

The final set of predisposing factors to be addressed are those related to the individual patient's biology. Recent studies (e.g., Sorenson, Price, Stunkard & Schulsinger, 1989) have suggested that much of individual variance in weight status is due to biological and genetic factors. Thus, some people may be predisposed to develop concerns about weight because their constitution has determined that they will be heavier than their peers. They need to learn that because of biological factors, they are unable to weigh a lower weight of their choice without there being significant biological or psychological costs. Eventually an acceptance of the inevitability of constitutional factors may allow the patient to focus energy on activities other than weight loss.

Biological factors may play another role in the etiology of eating disorders. Some evidence suggests that affective disorder runs in families of patients who are bulimic (Strober, Salkin, Burroughs & Morrel, 1982). For some bulimics, the eating symptom may therefore represent the presence of an underlying affective disorder. In fact, some bulimics do benefit substantially from antidepressant medication.

Precipitating Factors

Precipitating factors are influences in a person's life that cause someone who may be susceptible to an eating disorder actually to develop anorectic or bulimic symptomatology. In general, precipitating factors are events that increase stress, decrease self-confidence, increase uncertainty, or reduce the availability of support from others. Experiences of failure, threats to self-esteem, separation or loss experiences, disruptions in family functioning, or changing environmental demands (e.g., a new job) may also be related to the onset of an eating disorder. Excessive dieting or exaggerated responsiveness to pressures about physical appearance may appear to be precipitating factors for an eating disorder. These factors, however, are frequently the product of other stressful events and may therefore serve as indirect precipitants.

In the course of therapy, it is useful to explore with patients the onset of the eating disorder. This helps the patient to identify key issues, conflicts, and difficulties with which she may need to struggle in the course of her recovery. For example, one patient reported onset of her eating problems when she moved from her high school where she was voted "best-looking student" to college "where everyone was attractive" and her roommate was an accomplished model. Another patient developed bulimic symptoms when she stopped using alcohol and began to experience anxiety and depression that her abusive drinking had previously masked.

Sustaining Factors

Sustaining factors are events, situations, or processes that provide reinforcement for an eating disorder and may continue to do so even after the predisposing or precipitating factors are no longer present or functional. For example, a person's social network may encourage weight loss and dieting by praising thinness even after a person's health is endangered. Because successful dieting is highly esteemed in our culture, a person with an eating disorder who already suffers from low self-esteem and need for approval and feels out of control of her life may feel compelled to maintain an unhealthful and unrealistic weight goal in order to receive continued attention.

Physical processes are important sustaining factors as well. Lansky and Levitt (1987) described the bulimic cycle. First, they said, restrictive eating is followed by a failure in restraint, which in turn leads to an abstinence violation effect (AVE) (Marlatt & Gordon, 1985). The AVE is considered a cognitive reaction to a failure in restraint in which the individual relinquishes control ("I've blown it") of a previously controlled behavior. Then the AVE precipitates binge eating, which is functional because it helps to distract the patient from unpleasant thoughts and feelings not related to food, and it creates in some people a "hyperglycemic high." Finally, the eating binge is followed by guilt and self-deprecating thoughts, which are relieved by purging, associated with general tension reduction (Johnson & Larson, 1982). Thus, while the overall long-term consequences of this cycle are negative, there are a number of short-term positive consequences that might act to help sustain the problem behavior. The self-sustaining nature of this cycle is one reason it is so difficult to interrupt and remediate.

Lansky and Levitt (1987) suggest that a psychoeducational approach may be useful for intervening in this cycle. By learning about the self-sustaining nature of the problem, teaching alternative forms of tension regulation, and encouraging patients to refrain from purging even if binge eating has occurred, many patients are able to reduce the frequency and intensity of these bulimic symptoms significantly.

Rosen and Leitenberg (1982) suggest that purging represents a compulsive response to binge-induced anxiety, much as hand washing may become a compulsive response to anxiety about contamination. They treat bulimics using exposure and response prevention, which have been successful with other ritualized behaviors. The bulimic is encouraged to consume typical binge foods past the point when she would normally want to purge; then she is helped to cope with the anxiety while not being allowed to purge. This method does not address many areas of dysfunction for the bulimic, but it may be helpful in teaching the patient how to resist purging, which may have a secondary effect of reducing the entire bulimic pattern.

Binge eating in others' presence is usually very threatening to the bulimic; variants of exposure/response prevention can be usefully applied by the bulimic herself. For example, patients are sometimes encouraged purposely to eat foods normally associated with a binge but to do so in a planned fashion in which she is able to resist binge eating and purging.

In their discussion of relapse prevention training, Marlatt and Gordon (1985) suggest techniques for avoiding relapse that aim at helping the bulimic to anticipate problem situations before they occur and then to develop alternative coping strategies with either the therapist or in a group with other bulimic patients.

Another useful intervention is to persuade the patient that purging must stop before binge eating stops. Many patients will say that they will stop purging when they are able to resist binge eating; they believe that they purge because they binge eat. Experience with many bulimics, however, indicates that once the behavioral pattern has been well established (e.g., after a year of bulimia), the patient binge eats because she has already decided that she will purge on that day (Lansky & Levitt, 1987). Thus, the decision to binge eat follows the decision to purge, which itself may have been precipitated by an unpleasant or stressful event. The patient must commit herself to not purge and must risk relying on internal self-regulatory skills to resist binge eating. The patient may also need to accept the possibility that in doing this, she may gain some weight because binge eating will not stop immediately after the decision not to purge has been made.

The cognitive and intellectual impact of severe food restriction (Keys, Brozek, Henschel, Mickelsen & Taylor, 1950) may act as a sustaining factor for anorectics. Severe diets may result in impaired problem solving and obsessive-like concern with food. Impaired problem solving may sustain an eating disorder by interfering with the person's ability to resolve problems that predisposed or precipitated the eating disorder in the first place. This is why hospitalization and refeeding may be necessary for some anorectic patients prior to the onset of in-depth individual therapy; the emaciated anorectic may not understand the concepts and ideas articulated in the outpatient therapy alone.

Patients who abuse laxatives frequently experience rapidly developing tolerance and physical dependence. After relatively short periods of laxative use for weight loss, they may become physically dependent on laxatives in order to have bowel movements. This constitutes a sustaining factor for these patients' purging method. Laxative abusers may require close medical management in order to be able to cope with the effect of withdrawal from laxatives. Our experience is that people who habitually abuse laxatives tend to manifest a higher degree of psychopathology than nonlaxative users.

EATING DISORDERS AND ADDICTION

The fact that this chapter appears in a book on treatment of the addictions is an indication of the view held by many that bulimia and anorexia nervosa are related to other addictive disorders. Vandereycken (1990) suggested that a linkage between eating disorders and addiction is possible based on phenomenology and course of the illness (cravings, preoccupation with the substance, ambivalence toward treatment, risk of relapse, tendency to abuse other substances), family studies (a higher than expected prevalence of substance abuse among relatives of bulimics), biological studies (involvement of endogenous opiate systems in the pathogenesis of bulimia), and effects of treatment (treatments designed for other addictive behaviors appear useful for eating-disordered patients). Vandereycken (1990) argues, however, that the eating disorders differ from addictions in that the addictive substance is not clear for anorectics who refuse food or for bulimics, who may binge on many different kinds of food; there does not appear to be physical tolerance developed (requiring increasingly more of the addicting substance); and for bulimics, the ingested substance increases anxiety, while purging results in anxiety reduction. Vandereycken concludes that if there is a parallel between eating disorders and other addicitons, it is in the sense of a craving for extreme self-control that appears to drive anorectics and bulimics and often is manifest in people addicted to other substances.

There are, in fact, few data to support or to refute the idea that eating disorders are classically addictive behaviors. Ambiguity on this point, however, may not be relevant to the question of treating eating disorders as though they are addictions. In fact, the 12-step model of treatment advanced by Overeaters Anonymous (OA) (e.g., Goldner, 1984) appears to be useful for many eating-disordered patients. Adherents of more psychologically based treatments (e.g., Bemis, 1985) occasionally build strawman models of 12-step programs and do not understand what these programs can contribute to treatment. The essential element of all 12-step programs involves the "addict's" admitting that he or she is powerless to control his or her "addiction." If one agrees with Vandereycken (1990) that the essential element held in common by eating-disordered patients and by addicts is their tendency to crave extreme self-control, then the 12-step premise may be understood and appreciated. What AA and OA adherents learn is to accept the extreme difficulty of the struggle ahead of them as they attempt to escape from their abusive life-styles. Bateson (1972) pointed out the paradox of successful AA treatment wherein the addict must admit that he is out of control in order to begin to take control of his life again. The bulimic who does not recognize and accept that she is out of control may remain ambivalent about treatment. The result is that addicts never address their perfectionistic tendencies, their lack of intimate relationships outside the family, and related dysfunctions. The challenge for all 12-step treatment programs is to hold out the hope and promise of recovery through the admission of helplessness. The person who loses hope because she believes she is powerless may not be inclined to pursue recovery at all.

Patients who enter OA encounter difficulties that are not experienced in other 12-step chemical addictions programs and that need to be navigated carefully if the person is to benefit from attendance at OA meetings. First, while other "addicts" are able to relinquish their abused substance completely, OA members must continue to eat; they are therefore faced with having to make choices that other addicts do not have to make. Unlike alcohol or drug addicts who have one goal—abstinence—eating-disordered patients often pursue a relatively complex prescribed diet (no white flour, no sugar, certain number of calories per day, etc.), which often engages the obsessive perfectionism of these patients. This may result in self-punishment and feelings of failure upon non-adherence. In fact, nonadherence to prescribed diets is the rule rather than the exception even among "nonaddicts" (Dunbar & Stunkard, 1979). Second, there is a confusing mix of people at OA meetings—anorectics, bulimics, and obese compulsive overeaters. The presence of obese patients is often threatening to anorectics or bulimics, who fear that recovery might render them like the feared obese ones. Finally, it is not clear in many OA groups what "recovery" constitutes; for bulimics, recovery might involve weight gain, while for obese patients recovery might involve weight loss. Unlike AA groups in which active addictions are clear to peers, it is not always clear among OA participants who is successful and who is not and how to recognize success when it is achieved. It is not uncommon to find some people in an OA group who continue to eat sugar and white flour and who are still considered by themselves and by others to be "in recovery".

Clinicians who work with many patients who are active in OA must help these patients decide what they need from OA and how to get it and help to maximize the benefits they do obtain. Some people, particularly those who use OA prescriptions to measure their lack of success (e.g., not adhering to a diet), may need to discontinue in OA until they are able to integrate the program in meaningful and productive ways.

CONCLUSION: SURVIVAL STRATEGIES

The purpose of this chapter was to outline a context for the treatment of severely disturbed patients with eating disorders, as well as to describe specific treatment approaches for particular issues these patients bring to treatment. It is clear that the goal of treatment for the patients described here is much more than elimination of problematic eating habits; treatment must address the multiple levels of function at which disturbance is observed. Outcome must not be judged solely on the basis of change in eating habits. In some patients, the eating problems, which tend to be chronic, may remain, though at a lower intensity, while difficulties related to work, school, or family are much closer to being resolved. This is important to the clinician who may be quite invested in treating a particular patient and whose perception of outcome efficacy is based on removal of eating habits.

By the same token, it is naive to assume that changes in eating habits will follow automatically upon change in other areas of function. The eating habits themselves need to be targeted directly through nutritional education, explanation of the nature of dieting and restraint, and behavioral management techniques such as behavioral rehearsal and self-monitoring.

Treatment of the patients described here is often long term (five years is not an unrealistic time frame for changes in multiple levels of functioning) and difficult, requiring a considerable investment of time, energy, and caring.

Treatment of these patients can also be very rewarding. Given the nature of clinical work with this patient population, it is essential to emphasize the importance of maintaining a healthy context for treatment.

Lansky and Levitt (1987) have developed a number of "survival strategies" that help maintain an appropriate context.

First, if anyone is to "survive" therapy, it must be the therapist. The amount of testing that takes place, difficulties with trust, and the severity of the symptoms encountered may occasionally lead the clinician to act in exceptional ways that he or she may know are unproductive yet may may feel compelled to do so. For example, a clinician may become overly accessible to a client who claims that open access to the therapist greatly reduces the eating symptoms. If such open access or exceptions lead the therapist to feel burdened, angry, or imposed upon, the efficacy of therapy may be endangered. The clinician must be clear that too much nurturance of or availability for the client will surely be detrimental to the therapy, and the therapist must therefore be protective of his or her own survival.

Second, specialization, while recommended, is a mixed blessing. There is no substitute for good therapeutic skills in treating these patients. However, specialization contributes in that it ensures a consistent context for treatment and allows clear access to other treatment resources (e.g., medical management, hospitalization). Another benefit of specialization accrues from the fact that experience with these patients promotes at least more consistent and probably more effective treatment. The difficulty concerning specialization is the stress of having too many challenging, long-term therapy cases, which may lead to therapist exhaustion or cynicism.

Finally, to ensure therapist survival it is important to use a network of professionals for appropriate referrals; to use consultation and hospitalization as necessary for difficult cases; to avoid "getting hooked" on exciting, high-risk cases; to set limits without being intimidated by symptoms; and to pursue continuing education opportunities to refine therapeutic skills.

REFERENCES

Bandler, R. & Grinder, J. (1979). *Frogs into princes: Neurolinguistic programming.* Moab, Utah: Real People Press.

Bateson, G. (1972). *Steps to an ecology of mind.* New York: Ballantine Books.

Beck, A. T. (1976). *Cognitive therapy and the emotional disorders.* New York: International Universities Press.

Bemis, K. (1985). Abstinence and non-abstinence models for the treatment of bulimia. *International Journal of Eating Disorders, 4,* 389–406.

Blinder, B. J., Chaitin, B. F. & Goldstein, R. S. (eds.) (1988). *The eating disorders: Medical and psychological bases of diagnosis and treatment.* New York: PMA Publishing Group.

Blume, E. S. (1989). *Secret survivors: Uncovering incest and its aftereffects in women.* New York: John Wiley.

Brownell, K. D. & Foreyt, J. (eds.) (1986). *Handbook of eating disorders.* New York: Basic Books.

Brownell, K. D. & Wadden, T. A. (1986). Behavior therapy for obesity: Modern approaches and better results. In K. D. Brownell & J. Foreyt (eds.), *Handbook of eating disorders* (pp. 180–97). New York: Basic Books.

Bruch, H. (1962). Perceptual and conceptual disturbances in anorexia nervosa. *Psychosomatic Medicine, 24,* 187–94.

Bruch, H. (1973). *Eating disorders: Obesity, anorexia and the person within.* New York: Basic Books.

Burns, D. D. (1980). *Feeling good: The new mood therapy.* New York: Signet.

Casper, R. C. (1983) On the emergence of bulimia nervosa as a syndrome: A historical view. *International Journal of Eating Disorders, 2,* 3–16.

Connors, M. E., Johnson, C. & Stuckey, M. (1984). Treatment of bulimia with brief psychoeducational group therapy. *American Journal of Psychiatry, 141,* 1512–16.

Crisp, A. H. (1980). *Anorexia nervosa: Let me be.* London: Academic Press.

Dunbar, J. & Stunkard, A. (1979). Adherence to diet and drug regimen. In R. Levy, B. Rifkind, B. Dennis, & N. Ernst (eds.), *Comprehensive handbook of behavioral medicine* (pp. 55–71). New York: Raven Press.

Emmet, S. E. (ed.) (1985). *Theory and treatment of anorexia nervosa and bulimia: Biomedical, sociocultural and psychological perspectives.* New York: Brunner/ Mazel.

Garfinkel, P. E. & Garner, D. M. (1982). *Anorexia nervosa: A multidimensional perspective.* New York: Brunner/ Mazel.

Garfinkel, P. E., Moldofsky, H. & Garner, D. M. (1980). The heterogeneity of anorexia nervosa. *Archives of General Psychiatry, 37,* 1036–40.

Garner, D. M. & Garfinkel, P. E. (1985). *Handbook of psychotherapy for anorexia nervosa and bulimia.* New York: Guilford Press.

Goldfried, M. R. & Davison, G. (1976). *Clinical behavior therapy.* New York: Holt, Rinehart & Winston.

Goldner, V. (1984). Overeaters Anonymous. In A. Gartner & F. Reissman (eds.), *The self-help revolution* (pp. 65–73). New York: Human Sciences Press.

Goodsitt, A. (1983). Self regulatory disturbances in eating disorders. *International Journal of Eating Disorders, 2,* 51–60.

Goodsitt, A. (1985). Self psychology and the treatment of anorexia nervosa. In D. M. Garner & P. Garfinkel (eds.), *Handbook of psychotherapy for anorexia nervosa and bulimia* (pp. 55–82). New York: Guilford Press.

Hsu, C. K. G. (1990). *Eating disorders.* New York: Guilford Press.

Johnson, C. & Larson, R. (1982). Bulimia: An analysis of moods and behavior. *Psychosomatic Medicine, 44,* 341–53.

Kalucy, R. S., Crisp, A. H. & Harding, B. (1977). A study of 56 families with anorexia nervosa. *British Journal of Medical Psychology, 50,* 381–95.

Keys, A., Brozek, J., Henschel, A., Mickelsen, O. & Taylor, H. L. (1950). *The biology of human starvation.* Minneapolis: University of Minnesota Press.

Lansky, D. & Levitt, J. L. (1987). *Innovative methods in treating eating disorders.* Workshop presented at the 95th annual convention of the American Psychological Association, New York.

Levenkron, S. (1983). *Treating and overcoming anorexia nervosa.* New York: Warner Books.

Marlatt, A. & Gordon, J. (1985). *Relapse prevention.* New York: Guilford Press.

Minuchin, S., Rosman, B. & Baker, L. (1978). *Psychosomatic families: Anorexia nervosa in context.* Cambridge, Mass.: Harvard University Press.

Palazzoli, M. S. & Viaro, M. (1986). The anorectic process in the family: A six stage model as a guide for individual therapy. *Family Process, 27,* 129–48.

Rosen, J. & Leitenberg, H. (1982). Bulimia nervosa: Treatment with exposure and response prevention. *Behavior Therapy, 13,* 117–24.

Simon, R. (1987, September–October). An interview with Mara Selvini-Palazzoli. *Family Therapy Networker,* 17–33.

Sorensen, T., Price, R., Stunkard, A. & Schulsinger, F. (1989). Genetics of obesity in adult adoptees and their biological siblings. *British Medical Journal, 298,* 87–90.

Strober, M., Salkin, B., Burroughs, J. & Morrel, W. (1982). Validity of the bulimia-restricter distinction in anorexia nervosa: Parental personality characteristics and family psychiatric morbidity. *Journal of Nervous and Mental Disease, 170,* 345–51.

Time. 1986, January 20, 54–60.

Vandereycken, W. (1990). The addiction model in eating disorders: Some critical remarks and a selected bibliography. *International Journal of Eating Disorders, 9,* 95–101.

White, M. (1988, Winter). The process of questioning: A therapy of literary merit. *Dulwich Center Newsletter,* 8–14.

PART IV

Minorities and Special Groups

10

Native Americans and Substance Abuse

THOMAS J. YOUNG

Archeologists estimate that between 25,000 and 40,000 years ago the ancestors of native Americans migrated from northeastern Asia to North America by way of a land bridge that joined the two continents near present-day Alaska. For thousands of years, these ancestors spread throughout the Western Hemisphere, and hundreds of cultures evolved, including the complex societies of the Mayas, Incas, and Aztecs. By 1500, the aboriginal population of what is today the United States numbered perhaps 1 million, with concentrations in the South and along the coasts. By 1800 the native population declined to about 600,000, and by 1890 the effects of warfare and diseases, such as measles, smallpox, and influenza, had reduced the population to 250,000 (Price, 1976; Schaefer, 1979).

Today, native Americans represent one of the fastest-growing ethnic groups in the United States, exceeded perhaps only by Hispanics. According to the U.S. Bureau of the Census (1980), there are 1,418,195 native Americans in the United States, a 71 percent increase over the 1970 count. Many demographers and other scholars have rejected this census figure as being too low and have estimated that a truer figure may be 2 million. Regardless, most agree that this population is growing rapidly and is quite young. The median age for this ethnic group is 18 years, compared to 29 years for the rest of the population in the United States (May & Broudy, 1980; U.S. Bureau of the Census, 1980). Among the Navaho, the largest tribe in the United States, the median age is 16 years, and only 4 percent of the population is 65 years of age or older, compared to 11 percent nationally (May & Broudy, 1980; Young, 1988).

According to the U.S. Indian Health Service (IHS) statistics, native Americans are generally healthier today than in the past. For example, from the mid-1950s to the mid-1970s, the tuberculosis mortality rate decreased 75 percent, infant mortality declined 51 percent, and death due to influenza and pneumonia dropped 36 percent (American Indian Policy Review Commission, 1976; Schaefer, 1979). While the differences in health between the general population and native Americans have narrowed over the past three decades, serious problems still exist. Diseases such as otitis media, gastroenteritis, impetigo, pneumonia, influenza, and gonococcal infections continue to pose significant health problems. In many native American communities, however, the greatest health problem is the misuse of alcohol.

PREVALENCE OF NATIVE AMERICAN DRINKING

The stereotype of the drunken Indian has become an entrenched aspect of American folklore. In reality, however, there is considerable tribal variation in drinking patterns, ranging from abstinence to chronic intoxication (Westermeyer, 1974). For example, drinking and episodic drunkenness is generally accepted and highly visible among the Navaho, while the Hopi tend to condemn drinking and intoxication as an irresponsible threat to cosmic harmony (Kunitz, Levy, Odoroff & Bollinger, 1971).

Contrary to lay belief, native Americans are not a homogeneous population. Their cultural diversity is illustrated by the fact that more than 280 tribes are recognized by the U.S. Bureau of Indian Affairs (Heath, 1983) with populations ranging from fewer than 100 to more than 100,000. In Canada 575 bands are recognized by the Department of Indian Affairs and Northern Development and 2,240 reservations (Health, 1983). To appreciate the cultural diversity of native Americans is to dispel quickly the stereotype of the drunken Indian.

Researchers have reported a striking range of alcohol use from one reservation to the next. Marked variation is found even among the so-called hard-drinking tribes. Levy and Kunitz (1974) found that 30 percent of the Navaho of the Southwest use alcohol, although in some communities the adult prevalence rate was as high as 42 percent. This is in comparison to 69 percent of the Standing Rock Sioux in South Dakota (Whittacker, 1972), 80 percent of the Ute of Igacio in Colorado (Jessor, Graves, Hanson & Jessor, 1969), and 84 percent of the Ojibwa of the Brokenhead Reserve in Canada (Longclaws, Barnes, Grieve & Durnoff, 1980). The range of heavy use is also considerable. For the general U.S. population, the prevalence of heavy use has been estimated at between 9 percent (National Institute on Alcohol Abuse and Alcoholism, 1981) and 18 percent (Cahalan & Cisin, 1968). In comparison, heavy use has been reported among 9 to 24 percent of the Standing Rock Sioux (Whittacker, 1972), 26 percent of the Ute (Jessor et al., 1969), and 42 percent of the Ojibwa (Longclaws et al., 1980).

Although there is considerable variation among tribes in the use of alcohol, the U.S. Indian Health Service (1977) has cited alcoholism as the most urgent health problem facing native Americans. The U.S. Indian Health Service (1982) hospital discharge rate for alcohol-related diagnoses is about three times the U.S. national rate and double the rate for races other than non-Hispanic whites. The IHS discharge rates for nondependent abuse of alcohol and for alcohol liver disease are 3.4 times the national rates (5.8 versus 1.7 per 100,000 and 6.4 versus 1.9 per 100,000, respectively), the alcohol dependency discharge rate is nearly twice the national rate (35.8 versus 19.7 per 100,000), and the alcohol psychosis discharge rate is four times the national rate (11.8 versus 2.9 per 100,000).

Perhaps the most disturbing statistic is that 75 percent of all native American deaths can be directly or indirectly linked to alcohol. In fact, 5 of the 10 leading causes of death among native Americans are directly related to alcohol: accidents, cirrhosis of the liver, alcohol dependency, suicide, and homicide (Andre, 1979). Alcohol-related accidents are so prevalent among native Americans that this category represents the leading cause of death, with a mortality rate 3 times the national average (U.S. Indian Health Service, 1977; Young, 1988). The mortality rate for cirrhosis of the liver is 4.4 times the national rate and is 85 percent alcohol related (May, 1982). The suicide and homicide rates are 1.6 and 2.9 times that of the general population (Abbas, 1982), and alcohol is a variable in approximately 80 percent of all native American suicides and 90 percent of all homicides (French & Hornbuckle, 1982). Similar findings exist for the general population, with alcohol playing a factor in 80 percent of the suicides and 64 percent of the homicides among non-natives (Wolfgang & Ferracuti, 1982). Thus, while many of the patterns of native American drinking are culturally unique, some aspects are similar to those found in the dominant culture (Heindenreich, 1976).

PATTERNS OF NATIVE AMERICAN DRINKING

At least four types of native American drinking patterns can be described: abstinence, social, recreational, and anxiety. Abstinence is not as uncommon among some tribes as popular folklore would suggest, particularly among women and adults over 30 years old. It is quite rare and unacceptable for Navaho and Pueblo women to drink once they have passed their mid-twenties, albeit drinking at all ages is considered acceptable for women in the Plains and Basin tribes. Overall, however, abstinence is more common among native American women than their male counterparts. In addition, far more native American adults quit drinking than other adults in the United States. Among the Navaho, for instance, 37 percent of the adults over age 30 have quit drinking compared to 8 percent nationally. The problem, as May (1982) has indicated, is that too many native American youth do not live long enough to change their drinking style.

Native American social drinking is similar to social drinking within the dominant culture in that it promotes group cohesion. The social context of the drinking is often marked by a festive atmosphere, with rodeos, ceremonials, and other social events serving as popular occasions of alcohol consumption. Drinking with another is viewed as a gesture of friendship, and to decline such an offer is a faux pas. Among the Navaho, relatives commonly drink together, especially maternal uncle and nephew and brothers-in-law. It is also common for biological brothers, clan brothers, husband and wife, father and son, and father-in-law and son-in-law to drink together. Inebriety may follow social drinking, and drunkenness is generally not subject to disapproval among the Navaho except when it results in prohibited behavior, such as fighting or neglecting obligations. The composition of Navaho drinking groups, however, certainly mirrors the larger cultural emphasis placed on the maintenance of warm and stable interpersonal relationships and the preservation of the universal harmony ethic (Heath, 1964).

Recreational drinking promotes social cohesion as does social drinking, but it differs in terms of the volume, speed, and duration of the alcohol consumption. Typically, a large amount of alcohol is consumed quickly in a group situation and over an extended period of time. Drinking is sporadic, however, and marked by long periods of abstinence between each binge. Nevertheless, this style of drinking increases the probability for arrest, injury, or accidental death. Yet recreational drinking is not only tolerated but prescribed by some tribes, particularly among teenage males. Among the Santee, for example, this style of drinking is considered part of a normal rite of passage "from hell-raiser to family man" (Hill, 1974).

Cirrhosis of the liver and other alcohol-related degenerative diseases are usually seen among anxiety drinkers, who tend to drink alone and are physically and psychologically addicted to alcohol. Anxiety drinkers are usually marked by downward social mobility and are often socially ostracized. An example of this type can be found among the Hopi rural skid-row alcoholic (Young, 1988).

ALCOHOL AND CRIMINAL VIOLENCE

Alcohol-related arrests have long been recognized as a significant social problem among native Americans (Young, LaPlante & Robbins, 1987). The arrest rate for native Americans over the age of 14 is approximately 3 times that of blacks and 10 times that of whites (Harring, 1982; Reasons, 1972; Stewart, 1964). Alcohol is believed to be a factor in 70 to 80 percent of all native American arrests. With respect to violent crimes by native Americans, alcohol is involved in 90 percent of the cases (Young, 1990).

The relationship between alcohol consumption and violence has been shown in extensive longitudinal studies. One of the best-known and largest studies is that of Wolfgang (1958), who analyzed 588 homicides and reported that the offender had been drinking prior to the crime in 55 percent of the cases. In another study, Tinklenberg and associates (1974) found that 23 of 56 assailants

(41 percent) reported the use of alcohol (alone or in combination with other drugs) prior to their assaultive behavior.

Although these studies are thorough, they exemplify a fundamental problem with this type of research: they rely only on reports of alcohol use rather than on measurements of alcohol levels in the blood. In a more direct study, Shupe (1954) studied urine or blood samples obtained from suspects immediately after their arrests and detected alcohol in 144 of 163 individuals (88 percent) charged with violent crimes. This study also found that the likelihood of arrest for violent crime while under the influence of alcohol is an inverted U-shaped function of the blood alcohol concentration (BAC), increasing from 0 BAC up to 0.20 to 0.29 percent and then decreasing with increasing BAC. An exception is found in cases of pathological intoxication, which is marked by an acute disruption of behavior (including criminal violence) elicted by a small quantity of alcohol. A number of clinical studies support the notion that persons prone to temporal-lobe dysfunction may be at high risk for pathological intoxication (Marinacci & Von Hagen, 1972).

A fundamental issue is whether alcohol induces violent behavior directly or whether it acts primarily as a disinhibitor of preexisting aggressive tendencies. No available study provides proof that alcohol alone elicits violent behavior. Apparently attempts to explain the relationship between alcohol and violence must account for the expectation or even the planning of the consequences of alcohol use by the drinker (Lang, Goeckner & Adesso, 1975). Furthermore, the study of violent interactions is complicated by the fact that a proportion of victims are found to have been drinking prior to their victimization.

OTHER DRUGS

This clinical picture is complicated by the use of drugs other than alcohol. Inhalants, for example, are popular among native American youth. The voluntary use of inhalants for mind-altering purposes among native American youth is twice as high as the national rate for youth 12 to 17 years old. Nationally the prevalence rate for inhalant use among this age group is 11 percent compared to 22 percent for native American youth (Young, 1987). These drugs are popular because they are inexpensive, easy to obtain, and provide rapid onset and dissipation of intoxication (Young & Lawson, 1986).

Inhalant use increases the danger of sudden or accidental death. In most cases of acute inhalant toxicity, death is due to cardiac arrest and various cardiac arrhythmias (Bass, 1970; Taylor & Harris, 1970). Another common cause of death due to acute inhalant toxicity is suffocation, which may result from laryngospasm (Chapel & Thomas, 1970) or if the user loses consciousness while inhaling from a plastic bag (Cohen, 1977). Antisocial behavior, self-destructive acts, and excessive risk taking, which may lead to accidental death, are associated features of inhalant use (Korman, Semler & Trimbolo, 1980).

Chronic inhalant use may lead to such health problems as bone marrow depression, leukemia, anemia, encephalopathy, lead poisoning, neuropathy, and liver, kidney, cerebellar, chromosomal, and immune system damage (Young, 1987; Young & Lawson, 1986). Of course, most native American youth never use inhalants, and most users are experimenters who try inhalants as a novel experience and discontinue use after several exposures. Still, in comparison to other populations, this ethnic group is at a high risk for inhalant-related health problems.

There does not appear to be a significant difference between native Americans and non-natives in terms of the use and abuse of other drugs. Several exceptions, however, can be noted. In comparison to non-natives, native Americans have a higher prevalence rate for marijuana but a lower prevalence rate for barbiturates (Beauvais, Oetting & Edwards, 1985; May, 1982). Again, one is struck by the variation in the use of these drugs. For example, barbiturates are more likely to be used as a means of suicide among the Plains tribes than among tribes in the Southwest (May & Dizmang, 1974; May, 1982), while marijuana use among southwestern tribes is almost three times the rate found on a reservation in central Canada (Oetting, Edwards, Goldstein & Garcia-Mason, 1980; Longclaws et al., 1980).

THEORETICAL EXPLANATIONS

The most commonly found explanation for native American drinking and violence is the sociocultural theory of anomie. Essentially this theory maintains that native Americans are "mourning the loss of a historical tradition and reacting to the stresses of acculturation, including the demand to integrate and identify with mainstream society" (Lewis, 1982, p. 319). The historical events that contributed to this situation include the forced relocation of tribes, the breakup of families, constant harassment by settlers and soldiers, and the failure of the reservation system to provide a well-defined set of social roles. These historical events, it is argued, resulted in the disintegration of native American cultures and fostered a state of anomie. As a result, "contemporary warriors" assert their "Indianness" through drunkenness and "red rage."

Critics of the structural-functionalist theory of anomie contend that "it is a self-proving argument which explains all findings no matter how contradictory" (Levy & Kunitz, 1974, p. 234). Those who reject anomie theory argue that drunkenness and violence are compatible with the aboriginal goals and values of many tribes. It has been suggested, for example, that flamboyant drinking is viewed as anything but a sign of moral, social, or psychological disintegration among young Apache males. Public drinking and fighting is not seen as an anomic response to rapid social change but as a rite of passage that is compatible with such aboriginal activities as hunting, raiding, and warfare.

The theory that native Americans have an inborn weakness for alcohol has been a mainstay of popular folklore. This "firewater" theory has gained scientific credence in some circles, with supporters pointing to several decades of research that has implicated a role for genetic factors in the etiology of alcoholism. The concept of a genetic vulnerability to alcoholism has been supported by studies finding that animals can be selectively bred to show signs of alcohol-accepting characteristics (Deitrich & Spuhler, 1984), that first-degree relatives of alcoholics are more likely to be alcoholic than first-degree relatives of nonalcoholics (Cotton, 1979), that adopted-away children of alcoholic parents are more likely to develop alcoholism than adopted-away children of nonalcoholic parents (Goodwin, Schulsinger, Hermansen, Guze & Winokur, 1973), that monozygotic twins are more likely to be concordant for alcoholism than dizygotic twins (Kaij, 1960), and that children of alcoholics differ from nonalcoholics in response to alcohol (Schuckit, 1984).

A few studies have specifically examined the biological parameters of differences in alcohol tolerance among ethnic groups (Hanna, 1976). For example, Wolff (1972) reported that Japanese, Koreans, and Taiwanese all showed more facial flushing, increased pulse pressure, greater changes in optical density, and more extreme subjective reactions than Americans of European ancestry, even with half the quantity of alcohol. In a subsequent paper, Wolff (1973) reported similar findings for a study involving Cree Indians, American-born Japanese and Chinese, Eurasians, and other so-called mongoloid populations. Fenna, Mix, Schaefer, and Gilbert (1971) compared rates of alcohol metabolism and found that whites metabolized alcohol at a significantly faster rate than native Americans. Lieber (1972) and others criticized this study since blood alcohol levels were measured indirectly by the use of a Breathalyzer and because hospitalized native Americans were compared to healthy whites. In another study, Bennion and Li (1976) used more comparable subjects and a more direct analytical method and found that the mean rates of alcohol metabolism for native Americans and whites were virtually identical.

CONCLUSION

Alcohol misuse represents a serious social and clinical dilemma for many native Americans. It must be emphasized, however, that native American drinking is a highly complex, multivariate phenomenon, with many unresolved issues. In fact, there remains considerable controversy over two fundamental issues: the prevalence of native American drinking and drunkenness and why native Americans drink. There is also controversy surrounding the issue of who should be recognized as a native American (Canby, 1988). Simplistic answers must be viewed with caution because of their ethnocentric tendencies and their failure to appreciate cultural complexities.

Future research is needed on both the cultural and biological components of native American drinking. Sociological data are needed on structural variables, such as acculturation and socioeconomic status, which are assumed to be critical determinants of native American drinking. There is also a need for further research on the "firewater" theory and its claim of genetic vulnerability. At this point, however, the genetic issue has become emotionally charged and political, which has probably discouraged additional research. If a meaningful body of literature is to evolve on this topic, the dogma and polemics that have prevailed so far must be transcended. What is needed is an interdisciplinary approach that takes into consideration the cultural, psychological, and biological components of native American drinking.

Mental health policies and programs must be aware of the diverse nature of this population (Lafromboise, 1988). The approach needs to be multimodal and sensitive to the differences found among relatively affluent unacculturated native Americans; poverty-level unacculturated native Americans; relatively affluent acculturated native Americans; and poverty-level acculturated native Americans (Jessor et al., 1969). Even within these broad sociological categories, one must remain sensitive to biological, psychological, and cultural variation.

The two major components to multimodal intervention among native Americans are native approaches to health care and scientific-clinical methods. Although most native Americans do not view these two systems as antagonistic, too many clinicians have ethnocentric attitudes toward tribal health care. As Lewis (1982) has pointed out, "It appears that in some cases territorial imperative, job security, and professional concerns are reflected rather than a search for a more acceptable model which will be homogeneous to the Indian culture" (p. 323). The use of native approaches is complicated by tribal variations in health care practices and beliefs (Stone, 1962; Vogel, 1970). Nevertheless, it must be emphasized that traditional modalities based in the so-called clinical mentality may not be appropriate for all native Americans. Mental health professionals must consider how cultural factors affect basic counseling techniques such as the here-and-now focus, disclosure, feedback, meta-communication, process illumination, and the use of cognitive aids. Furthermore, clinicians trained in the scientific-clinical approach must transcend ethnocentric judgments about the practices of paraprofessionals and indigenous healers by recognizing alternative programs that respect the spiritual legacy of native Americans.

REFERENCES

Abbas, L. (1982). Alcoholism among native Americans. In W. Mitchell & M. Galletti (eds.), *Native American substance use* (pp. 44–54). Tempe: Arizona State University.

American Indian Policy Review Commission (1976). *Indian health*. Washington, D.C.: U.S. Government Printing Office.

Andre, J. M. (1979). *The epidemiology of alcoholism among American Indians and Alaska Natives*. Albuquerque, N.M.: U.S. Indian Health Services.

Bass, M. (1970). Sudden sniffing death. *Journal of the American Medical Association*, *212*, 2075–2079.

Beauvais, F., Oetting, E. R. & Edwards, R. W. (1985). Trends in the use of inhalants among American Indian adolescents. *White Cloud Journal*, *3*, 3–11.

Bennion, L. & Li, T. K. (1976). Alcohol metabolism in American Indians and whites. *New England Journal of Medicine, 294,* 9–13.

Cahalan, O. & Cisin, H. (1968). American drinking practices. *Quarterly Journal of Studies on Alcohol, 29,* 130–51.

Canby, W. C., Jr. (1988). *American Indian Law* (2d ed.). St. Paul, Minn.: West.

Chapel, J. & Thomas G. (1970). Aerosol inhalation for "kicks." *Missouri Medicine, 67,* 378–80.

Cohen, S. (1977). Inhalant abuse: An overview of the problem. In C. W. Sharp & M. L. Brehm (eds.), *Review of inhalants: euphoria to dysfunction* (pp. 2–11). Washington, D.C.: U.S. Government Printing Office. (DHEW Publication No. ADM 77-553).

Cotton, N. S. (1979). The familial incidence of alcoholism. *Journal of Studies on Alcohol, 40,* 89–116.

Deitrich, R. A. & Spuhler, K. (1984). Genetics of alcoholism and alcohol actions. In R. G. Smart, H. D. Cappell, F. B. Glaser, Y. Israel, H. Kalant, R. E. Popham, W. Schmidt & E. M. Sellers (eds.), *Research advances in alcohol and drug problems* (vol. 8, pp. 47–98). New York: Plenum.

Fenna, D., Mix, L., Schaefer, O. & Gilbert, J. A. L. (1971). Ethanol metabolism in various racial groups. *Canadian Medical Association Journal, 65,* 472–75.

French, L. & Hornbuckle, J. (1982). Indian alcoholism. In L. French (ed.), *Indians and criminal justice* (pp. 131–46). Totowa, N.J.: Allanheld, Osmun.

Goodwin, D. W., Schulsinger, F., Hermansen, L., Guze, S. G. & Winokur, G. (1973). Alcohol problems in adoptees raised apart from alcoholic biological parents. *Archives of General Psychiatry, 28,* 238–43.

Hanna, D. B. (1976). Ethnic groups, human variation, and alcohol use. In M. W. Everett, J. O. Waddell & D. B. Heath (eds.), *Cross-cultural approaches to the study of alcohol* (pp. 235–42). Paris: Mouton.

Harring, S. (1982). Native American crime in the United States. In L. French (ed.), *Indians and criminal justice* (pp. 93–108). Totowa, N.J.: Allanheld, Osmun.

Heath, D. B. (1964). Prohibition and post-repeal drinking patterns among the Navajo. *Quarterly Journal of Studies on Alcohol, 25,* 119–35.

Heath, D. B. (1983). Alcohol use among North American Indians: A cross-cultural survey of patterns and problems. In R. Smart, F. Glaser, Y. Israel, H. Kalant, R. Popham & W. Schmidt (eds.), *Research advances in alcohol and drug problems* (vol. 7, pp. 341–69). New York: Plenum.

Heidenreich, C. A. (1976). Alcohol and drug use and abuse among Indian Americans: A review of issues and sources. *Journal of Drug Issues, 6,* 256–72.

Hill, T. W. (1974). From hell-raiser to family man. In J. Spradley & D. McCurdy (eds.), *Conformity and conflict: Readings in cultural anthropology* (pp. 186–200). Boston: Little, Brown.

Jessor, R., Graves, T., Hanson, R. & Jessor, S. (1969). *Society, personality and deviant behavior: A study of a tri-ethnic community.* New York: Holt, Rinehart, & Winston.

Kaij, L. (1960). *Alcoholism in twins: Studies on the etiology and sequelae of abuse of alcohol.* Stockholm: Almquist & Wiksell.

Korman, M., Semler, I. & Trimboli, F. (1980). A psychiatric emergency room study of 162 inhalant users. *Addictive Behaviors, 5,* 143–52.

Kunitz, S. J., Levy, J. E., Odoroff, C. L. & Bollinger, J. (1971). The epidemiology of alcoholic cirrhosis in two southwestern Indian tribes. *Quarterly Journal of Studies on Alcohol, 32,* 706–20.

Lafromboise, T. D. (1988). American Indian mental health policy. *American Psychologist, 43,* 388–97.

Lang, A. R., Goeckner, D. J. & Adesso, V. J. (1975). Effects of alcohol on aggression in male social drinkers. *Journal of Abnormal Psychology, 84,* 508–18.

Levy, J. E. & Kunitz, S. J. (1974). *Indian drinking: Navajo practices and Anglo-American theories.* New York: Wiley-Interscience.

Lewis, R. G. (1982). Alcoholism and native Americans: A review of the literature. In National Institute on Alcohol Abuse and Alcoholism (ed.), *Alcohol and health: Special population issue* (pp. 315–28). Washington, D.C.: U.S. Government Printing Office. (DHHS Publication No. ADM 82-1193).

Lieber, C. S. (1972). Metabolism of ethanol and alcoholism: Racial and acquired factors. *Annals of internal Medicine, 76,* 326–27.

Longclaws, L., Barnes, G., Grieve, L. & Durnoff, R. (1980). Alcohol and drug use among the Brokenhead Ojibwa. *Journal of Studies on Alcohol, 41,* 21–26.

Marinacci, A. A. & Von Hagen, K. O. (1972). Alcohol and temporal lobe dysfunction. *Behavioral Neuropsychiatry, 3,* 2–11.

May, P. A. (1982). Substance abuse and American Indians: Prevalence and susceptibility. *International Journal of the Addictions, 17,* 1185–1209.

May, P. A. & Broudy, D. W. (1980). *Health problems of the Navajo and suggested interventions.* Window Rock, Ariz.: Navajo Health Authority.

May, P. A. & Dizmang, L. H. (1974). Suicide and the American Indian. *Psychiatric Annals, 4,* 22–28.

National Institute on Alcohol Abuse and Alcoholism (1981). *Fourth special report to the U.S. Congress on alcohol and health.* Washington, D.C.: U.S. Government Printing Office. (DHHS Publication No. ADM 81-1080).

Oetting, E. R., Edwards, R., Goldstein, G. S. & Garcia-Mason, V. (1980). Drug use among adolescents of five southwestern native American tribes. *International Journal of the Addictions, 15,* 439–45.

Price, J. A. (1976). North American Indian families. In C. H. Mindel & R. H. Habenstein (eds.), *Ethnic families in America* (pp. 248–70). New York: Elsevier.

Reasons, C. (1972). Crime and the native American. In C. Reasons & J. Kuykendall (eds.), *Race, crime and justice* (pp. 79–95). Pacific Palisades, Calif.: Goodyear.

Schaefer, R. T. (1979). *Racial and ethnic groups.* Boston: Little, Brown.

Schuckit, M. A. (1984). Subjective responses to alcohol in sons of alcoholics and control subjects. *Archives of General Psychiatry, 41,* 879–84.

Shupe, L. M. (1954). Alcohol and crime. *Journal of Criminal Law, Criminology and Police Sciences, 44,* 661–64.

Stewart, O. (1964). Questions regarding American Indian criminality. *Human Organization, 23,* 61–66.

Stone, E. (1962). *Medicine among the American Indians.* New York: Hafner.

Taylor, G. & Harris, W. (1970). Glue sniffing causes heart block in mice. *Science, 170,* 866–68.

Tinklenberg, J. R., Murphy, P. L. & Murphy, P. (1974). Drug involvement in criminal assaults by adolescents. *Archives of General Psychiatry, 30,* 685–89.

U.S. Bureau of the Census (1980). *Census of the population: subject reports, American*

Indians. Washington, D.C.: U.S. Government Printing Office (Publication No. PC 80-2-1D).

U.S. Indian Health Service (1977). *Alcoholism: A high-priority health problem.* Washington, D.C.: U.S. Government Printing Office (DHEW Publication No. HSA 77-1001).

U.S. Indian Health Service (1982). *Analysis of fiscal year 1981 IHS and U.S. hospital discharge rates by age and primacy diagnosis.* Washington, D.C.: U.S. Government Printing Office.

Vogel, V. J. (1970). *American Indian medicine.* Norman: University of Oklahoma Press.

Westermeyer, J. J. (1974). "The drunken Indian": Myths and realities. *Psychiatric Annals, 4,* 29.

Whittacker, J. O. (1972). Alcohol and the Standing Rock Sioux tribe. *Quarterly Journal of Studies on Alcohol, 23,* 468–79.

Wolff, P. H. (1972). Ethnic differences in alcohol sensitivity. *Science, 175,* 449–50.

Wolff, P. H. (1973). Vasomotor sensitivity to alcohol in diverse mongoloid populations. *American Journal of Human Genetics, 25,* 193–99.

Wolfgang, M. E. (1958). *Patterns in criminal homicide.* Philadelphia: University of Pennsylvania Press.

Wolfgang, M. E. & Ferracuti, F. (1982). *The subculture of violence.* Beverly Hills, Calif.: Sage.

Young, T. J. (1987). Inhalant use among American Indian youth. *Child Psychiatry and Human Development, 18,* 36–46.

Young, T. J. (1988). Substance use and abuse among native Americans. *Clinical Psychology Review, 8,* 125–38.

Young, T. J. (1990). Native American crime and criminal justice require criminologists' attention. *Journal of Criminal Justice Education, 1,* 111–16.

Young, T. J., LaPlante, C. & Robbins, W. (1987). Indians before the law: An assessment of contravening cultural/legal ideologies. *Quarterly Journal of Ideology, 11,* 59–70.

Young, T. J. & Lawson, G. (1986). Voluntary inhalation of volatile substances: A clinical review. *Corrective and Social Psychiatry, 32,* 49–54.

11

The Elderly and Alcohol and Medication Abuse

DOUGLAS H. RUBEN

More than ever before common signs of aging are now attributed to complications in medications or in alcohol abuse. Theories abound that alcohol use is dangerous at any age, particularly older age, and when there are drug problems, the interactive effects remain undiagnosed as the elderly person slips away into obscurity. Hospital studies show rising numbers of aged abusers whose symptoms are overlooked. In 1967, 6 percent of people over age 65 admitted to state and county mental hospitals suffered alcoholism. Of those diagnosed alcoholic, some 80% of them drank heavily longer than 10 years but never were noticed. Today about 12% of elderly seen in state and county mental hospitals are alcoholics.

Just as symptoms of elderly alcoholism are obscure, so it is that brain damage, heart disease, and gastrointestinal disorders mimic other symptoms. The symptoms disguise "medication mismanagement." In the forefront of medication abuse is the elderly's annual expenditure on preparations for personal health and hygiene. Drugs and medical sundries represent as high as $5.1 billion (per total population) and $192 (per capita) during a single year. In other words, elderly consumers who spend way beyond their affordable budgets for medication are targets for drug abuse, misuse, overuse and underuse.

This chapter overviews critical points of etiology and treatment of elderly alcoholism and medication (drug) abuse examined in that last 20 years and primarily documented in several reference manuals (e.g., Barnes, Abel & Ernst 1980; Maddox, Robins & Rosenberg, 1984; Petersen, Whittington & Payne, 1979; Ruben, 1984, 1986a, 1990). Areas covered provide both an introduction to biobehavioral issues and a referral resource base for direct care workers.

COMMON PROBLEMS AND PATTERNS OF ALCOHOL USE, MISUSE, AND ABUSE

Acute and chronic alcohol use evolves over time and is an integrative part of the person's entire life-style. Problems during childhood, adolescence, and early and late adulthood increase the person's risk of alcoholism but are not absolute causes of it. Current problems in the elderly person's life also directly bear on addiction.

Addictive Qualities

Because alcohol is an addictive drug, frequent use increases alcohol tolerance. This means that the body requires more alcohol to achieve the same effect and that the visible, behavioral effects are less obvious. Increased tolerance is an initial step toward a long-term addiction. As the addiction controls the person, the tolerance level drops and the visible effects increase. Older drinkers in particular show serious addictive effects. They likely have been drinking for 30, 40, or more years, and age-related problems consequently are more severe than in their nondrinking counterparts.

Increased Use of Medications

Older adults are more prone to chronic illness and take prescriptions and over-the-counter remedies for their illnesses. For those who drink, increased use of medication contributes to the danger of alcohol-drug interactions.

Drinking as a Moral Issue

For many older people, the teachings of religion and the influence of the prohibiton era have implanted the concept that drinking to excess is immoral. For some this is a deterrent. However, older chronic drinkers may feel guilty about this and try to deny or hide their drinking from others. Alcohol treated as a moral issue compounds the guilt the drinker already feels and usually results in continued abuse.

Lack of Knowledge about Alcohol

Physicians, service providers, family members, and older adults may not know enough about the effects of alcohol. They are unfamiliar with the symptoms of an alcohol problem, and many symptoms go unnoticed. Thus, the people close to drinkers may enable or encourage the abuse because they lack sufficient knowledge.

Confused or Overlooked Symptoms

Loss of appetite, depression, confusion, bruises, and memory loss are symptoms of an alcohol problem, but they may also be symptoms of severe depression, organic brain syndrome, or prescription drug abuse. Many people overlook alcohol as a possible source of these symptoms. Others simply attribute the symptoms to an old age or senility. Multiple chronic or acute conditions may overshadow or camouflage an alcohol problem. When the amount and frequency of alcohol is examined, older people usually drink less but more frequently than younger persons and may not exhibit obnoxious, intoxicated behaviors.

Maintaining Drinking Patterns

The older person who maintains a moderate or heavy drinking pattern from the middle years into old age may deceive those around him. Most people begin to reduce their consumption because of the increased effects of alcohol. In a sense, maintaining an earlier pattern in the later years is similar to increasing alcohol consumption. The effect is the same, and the danger of developing a drinking problem is increased.

Overprotective Care Providers

Some people in caring roles, such as family and counselors, overprotect their clients. They assume full responsibility when a client is capable of being fully or partially responsible for his actions. When family overprotect the alcoholic, they prevent crises from occurring and protect users from the consequences of drinking. Care providers mistakenly may buy the alcohol as well as prepare meals, clean up the messes, straighten out financial and legal matters, and make excuses. Overcaring basically enables continuation of the addiction. Enablers usually are unaware their actions reinforce drinking or they consider this action normal based on how their parents did the same thing.

Myths about Alcoholism

Negative attitudes about alcoholics give rise to false beliefs regarding what alcohol can do to an elderly person. Eleven of the most prevalent myths have been reviewed by Sherouse (1983, pp. 41–43):

Myth 1: *There is some other method of sobering up someone who is intoxicated besides just time.* Even the mild stimulation of giving coffee or a cold shower to somebody still does not eliminate the hangover.

Myth 2: *A person who sticks to beer will never become an alcoholic.* Beer contains as much ethyl alcohol as an ounce of liquor and act on the body in the same way.

Myth 3: *Switching drinks will make you drunk faster or, conversely, help you stay sober longer than if you stick with just one alcoholic beverage.* The amount of alcohol in a drink determines the level of intoxication, not the mixture that contains alcohol.

Myth 4: *Drinking helps overcome depression.* While sedative effects may relieve anxiety for a short time, the person is left feeling irritated, upset, paranoid, and inferior. Depression can become worse from alcohol.

Myth 5: *Every older drinker is a chronic alcoholic.* This is not true. Normal stress from adjustment can cause later life alcoholism. Moreover, symptoms of organic illness (polymorbidity) may resemble or duplicate alcoholic symptoms, supporting the myth that the person is a chronic drinker.

Myth 6: *Few women become alcoholics.* The ratio was once 10 men for every 2 women who were alcoholics. The ratio is now 3 men to every 1 woman.

Myth 7: *Certain races or religions are more prone to produce alcoholics.* Alcoholism is not indigenous to socioeconomic, racial, religious, ethnic, or cultural groups but instead is widespread among all people.

Myth 8: *People really can hold their liquor and should be envied.* Ironically, this ignores the basic toxicology of alcoholism. Increasing numbers of drinks proportionally elevates the tolerance level until a physical dependency develops.

Myth 9: *Drunkenness and alcoholism are the same thing.* Teenagers, in particular, experiment with alcohol tolerance and may get drunk after several beers or mixed drinks. Adults are no different in this respect. Incidences of inebriety, however, show only lack of control and not a physical or psychological dependency. Repeated episodes of drunkenness, with higher doses of alcohol consumed, is a better indicator of addiction.

Myth 10: *Once an alcoholic recovers, the person can drink again socially.* When Sobell and Sobell published their controversial research on controlled drinking (1973, 1976, 1978; Mills, Sobel & Schaefer, 1971), chronic drinkers, including recovered alcoholics, misinterpreted the findings to mean social drinking was again possible. The truth is that controlled drinking is still an experimental infant extremely limited to certain types of drinkers and far from being a revolutionary form of therapy.

Myth 11: *Most alcoholics are skid-row bums.* Only 3 to 5 percent of all known alcoholics in the United States are actually of the skid-row or extremely chronic variety. The remainder sample a cross-section of socioeconomic levels and are married, employed, and capable of functioning in day-to-day life.

COMMON PROBLEMS AND PATTERNS OF PRESCRIPTIVE DRUGS

In the past, substance abuse among the elderly primarily was alcoholism. Manufactured over-the-counter (OTC) drugs were fewer and tailored more for young and early-age adults. But as life-sustaining preparations advanced, so did the potential problems resulting from improper use of medications. This section covers common problems and patterns under the broad topic of drug misuse and drug mismanagement. Medication errors generally fall into six categories:

1. *Overuse:* Taking several doses of the same medication or taking medication when it is not needed.

2. *Underuse:* The failure to fill prescriptions and forgetting to take the medications. Signs are the individual's stretching out the medication to last longer or discontinuing use of it earlier than directed.

3. *Erratic use:* The failure to follow instructions. This includes missing doses, taking double doses, taking doses at the wrong time, and confusion over which drug to take at which interval.

4. *Contraindicated use:* which occurs due to incorrect storage of medications, using outdated drugs, or not monitoring side effects. A second cause is sharing or borrowing drugs, frequently termed the "gray market." Contraindicated drugs in addition can produce harmful side effects in interaction with other drugs.

5. *Abuse:* Drug misuse with intent to hurt self or toward addictive purposes.

6. *Improper prescribing practices:* Primarily a communication problem between physician and client (e.g., Ruben, 1987) but also the mistake of overprescribing or underprescribing drugs inconsistent with biological needs.

Overuse and Erratic Use

Overuse and erratic use are less prevalent than other problems but important enough to review. Prescriptions stating "prn" (take as needed) can lead the person to misuse the drug. When the choice of medications is left to the user's own judgment, medications might be taken when they are not needed. This is particularly serious when there already is dependency on substances.

Underuse

Underuse of medication is largely responsible for most medication errors. Some common reasons for underuse by the elderly include the following:

Forgetting: Not knowing what medications have been taken.

Economics: Not filling the prescription or reducing the dosage due to cost savings.

Physiological disorders: The person cannot swallow the pill or feels ill.

Physiological recovery: The person feels better and decides to stop or reduce medication.

Misplaced medication: The elderly individual cannot find the appropriate medication if needed.

Mixing up medications: Not knowing which medication is correct to take and on what schedule.

Drug-drug interactions: An adverse drug effect resulting from ingestion of two or more drugs.

Side, allergic, toxic, idiosyncratic effects: These effects can lead to severe underuse problems.

Contraindicated Use

Contraindicated use refers to several characteristics of the medications or its medical delivery systems jeopardizing proper use. Following are frequent problems cited:

Exchange of drugs: Exchanging medications with someone else who has a similar symptom or has extra (leftover) pills of a prescription also used by the borrower. Since dosage levels vary for each person despite its being the same medication, use of somebody else's medication risks harmful effects, such as a symptom aggravation or sickness.

Outdated drugs: Retaining unused pills for a later time, only to discover the pills lose their effectiveness after the expiration date.

Automatic refills: Having prescriptions refilled over the telephone or without consulting the physician or receiving a full medical examination.

Duplication: Simultaneously receiving two or more prescriptions for the same drug from different physicians or pharmacies.

Improper Prescribing Practices

Improper prescribing practices occur at a high rate. Reasons for this problem range from using many pharmacies to inadequate physician-client communication. For example, the client does not provide the physician with enough information about the health problem, other drugs being taken, or the side effects experienced; or the physician does not adjust the dosage to a level appropriate for the older client, prescribes a drug without sufficiently informing the client about possible side effects or without instructions for taking the drug accurately, or repeatedly prescribes an addictive drug without informing the client or addressing the addiction.

Other Factors

A variety of interrelated factors underlie problems of medication mismanagement beyond the six categories just covered.

Sources of misinformation. Most older people are not fully aware of the age-related changes that affect drug use. For health and drug information, they rely on their spouse and other family members, friends, physicians, and other service providers.

Self-care practices. Chronic diseases like arthritis and heart conditions now total more than 80% of all illnesses. Modern medicine has no quick cures for these chronic conditions, and health care costs have skyrocketed. One result is that the client or family is responsible for coordinating their own health care at a time when the level of medical technology is more sophisticated and complicated than ever before. Self-care is so cumbersome that typically the elderly resort to personal remedies. Self-diagnosis, self-prescribing OTC drugs, and sharing medicines become easier interventions.

High cost of medications. The high cost of medications is one of the greatest deterrents for compliance with prescribed regimens. Many people do not fill a prescription once they learn of its cost. Others have to wait until their social security check comes in, when they decide what bill will not be paid or what they cannot afford. Others purchase the medication and reduce the amount they take so the prescription lasts longer.

Brand and generic drugs. The dual system of brand and generic names is a problem. If *Haldol* and *Dilantin* sound strange, try their respective generic names: *haloperidol* and *phenytoin*. With over 7,000 commonly prescribed medications, multiplied by two, there is an overwhelming list of strange names. There is little incentive to master the art of drug information.

Mixed endorsement of generic drugs. Generic drugs get mixed reviews, with pharmacists and physicians varying in their opinions. Some generic drugs may not be suitable surrogates in special cases or may not be available. This uncertainty has been passed on to older consumers. Other reasons physicians may not endorse generic drugs is that they know the sales representatives of drug companies, they may be uncertain of the quality of a certain drug that is pharmacy selected, or they wish to support the research efforts of certain drugs.

Lack of medication monitoring. The lack of medication monitoring is another common problem. Residents of nursing homes, hospitals, and mental health facilities and recipients of home health services are the most likely victims. Medication monitoring should occur whenever the health care or distribution of medication is conducted or supervised by someone other than the medication user. Problems occur when there is no medication monitoring or when the lines of authority are unclear due to shortage of staff and lack of training in geriatric medicine.

Geriatric dosage. Most medications are tested on healthy males in their twenties. The recommended adult dosage is derived from these tests. Older people can change substantially from their young adult years and often should not be prescribed the "normal" adult dose. This is why prescribing medications for older people is a trial process. It may take awhile to find the proper dosage level.

Drug pyramiding. Drug pyramiding occurs when a drug is prescribed for a presenting problem and other drugs also are prescribed to treat the side effects caused by the first drug. The list of prescribed drugs keeps multiplying. In some cases, the drugs prescribed for side effects can block the action of the drug prescribed for the initial problem.

Prescription advice. Prescription advice and directions are frequently given at the doctor's office after diagnosis of a problem or after discharge from the hospital—not the best times for clients to comprehend the advice given. Immediately after a diagnosis, the client is likely absorbing details about illness and symptoms. Sadness and anger compound the anxiety most clients feel. The same holds true when clients leave the hospital. Older people are affected more than other age groups by relocation trauma, even if they are returning home. The client may not be ready for technical discourse on when to take medications, how often, with which foods, and what side effects may occur.

Television advertising. The problem with television advertisements as an information source is that they are made to sell a product. They do not give accurate advice on alternative therapies, and they downplay cautionary information. Advertisements also normalize self-diagnosis and OTC drugs. Manufacturers and distributors spend approximately $1.2 billion annually to advertise and promote the use of OTC medications, with many targeted to older consumers.

Style of institutional care. In most general hospitals, nursing homes, and psychiatric hospitals, the client's care is important but must fit into the framework of the institution. Because older people in hospitals frequently become disoriented, more effort goes into managing them. Faced with staff shortages, long work shifts, and client overload, short-cuts in management sacrifice quality care for the elderly client. This may involve overuse of sedatives, for example, for more rapid regiment compliance.

Myths about medication. Research demonstrates that drug effects are partly or wholly determined by what a person believes the drug will do (Einstein, 1979; Ewing & Rouse, 1978). Will it help the person sleep better? Make him feel better? Some beliefs start as true statements about drug effects but in conversation are diluted with false information. Older people who say, for instance, "drugs are different from medicine," truly are convinced of this distinction. Fictions or myths distort actual drug information and potentially misguide people on self-diagnosis and OTC medications. Following are some of the common myths and facts about generic and brand name drugs:

Myth 1: *There is a distinction between drugs and medicine.* The myth holds that drugs are used by some people and usually obtained on the street. Medicines are obtained from the doctor and used for curative purposes. *Fact:* Chemicals involved in both cases affect the body regardless of source, and the effects can be both pleasant and unpleasant.

Myth 2: *The doctor would not give me anything that would harm me.* The myth is that doctors generally do not prescribe medications that will harm a client. *Fact:* In the doctor's opinion, the benefits of a drug may outweigh the potential negative side effects. The doctor cannot control overuse or anticipate allergic or idiosyncratic effects. Thus, the client may continue to use medications that the doctor would stop or at least alter the dosage of if he or she knew problems arose.

Myth 3: *I don't like this medication's effects. [or] It isn't helping me.* This belief says clients often cease a medication regimen because they do not like the adverse drug reactions or medications do not relieve symptoms as expected. *Fact:* This attitude can be countered by a thorough explanation of drug side effects and the length of time required to produce noticeable results.

Myth 4: *I'm ill and need help, so give me something.* This is the belief that deciding to see the doctor will lead to instant recovery. *Fact:* Seeing the physician is a major psychological event for some elderly people because they "admit an illness" and expect that help will be given. Typically clients overtly and covertly pressure the doctor for medication.

Myth 5: *If it looks good, smells good, and tastes good, it can't be good for you.* Many consumers believe that medicines must look bad or taste bad as a measure of effectiveness. *Fact:* They recall the taste of medicines as a child or parent and are not aware of taste improvements made in consumer products. Corrected expectations involve an explanation from the nurse, physician, pharmacist, or other health worker.

Myth 6: *Over-the-counter drugs are not medicine.* There is a common belief that OTC drugs are not medications and therefore need not be discussed with the physician. *Fact:* OTC drugs are in fact complex preparations containing a variety of compounds that may be contraindicated, including alcohol, aspirin, belladonna alkaloids, and atropine derivatives.

Myth 7: *If this doctor is any good, he will be able to tell what's wrong with me.* Clients often assume the doctor can make definitive diagnoses with little or no help from them. *Fact:* Doctors run into many obstacles in diagnosis. When older persons forget to describe symptoms and do not identify OTC or other drugs they are taking, it complicates the diagnosis.

Myth 8: *If one pill is good, two are better.* It is common for people to increase the frequency or dosage of medication prescribed in an effort to alleviate their suffering as rapidly as possible. *Fact:* Increasing the medication at one's own discretion alters the medication regimen and is harmful to the body.

Myth 9: *I'm not ill: I'm just getting older.* Older persons may misattribute a disease state to growing older. Clients may delay seeking help until the illness requires multiple drugs or increased dosages. *Fact:* Perceptions of illness and the need for medication are subject to distortion. Invented are beliefs that growing old is automatic license to obtain pills.

Myth 10: *Generic drugs just won't work as well as brand-name drugs.* People believe that generic drugs are inferior to the standard product. *Fact:* Under the 1984 Drug Price Competition and Patent Restoration Act, generic drugs must be bioequivalent to their brand-name counterparts to gain Food and Drug Administration approval. This means that generics must contain the same active ingredients and must be identical in strength, dosage and route of administration.

Care providers must realize that myths are widespread and greatly influence decisions on drug usage. Beliefs too often multiply when accurate drug information is absent, is ambiguous, or conflicts with expectations of symptom relief. When clients are given the facts, they have a better chance of recognizing these beliefs and can be prepared to ask questions of physicians and pharmacists.

COMMON CAUSES OF ALCOHOL AND DRUG ABUSE

Ageist thinking biases many of the reasons for aged alcoholic and drug abuse. Stereotypic profiles of skid-row bums and "drunken old men" deflect attention away from truths about the etiology. This section moves beyond drug and alcoholic patterns by reviewing prevalent causes.

Bereavement

Clinical thanatology has achieved a new status for the elderly community (Sobel, 1981). Thanatologists view their objective as dismantling twentieth-century medicine, which discourages the naturalness of dying. Clinical care of bereaved friends and relatives thus is typically left to the physician and biomedical services. While survivors of friends and relatives may seek medical guidance, their biophysical changes caused by anger and confusion are best approached by counselors. Many widowed aged, for example, who pass through bereavement with rheumatoid arthritis, asthma, and other ills turn to chronic drinking.

Marriage

Many retired couples find that for the first time in their marriages, they must live 24 hours a day with each other. Previously the spouses were separated at least 8 to 10 hours a day because of work. After retirement, wives may find their husbands interfere with routine chores, or both spouses squabble over trivial differences. Fighting between spouses invokes an aversive home life from which husband and wife may seek avoidance and escape. Elderly couples who turn to drinking resist the seemingly logical solutions of divorce or marital therapy because the costs are expensive and may risk family embarrassment.

Family Relations

Families are no longer the centralized and closely allied groups they were earlier in the century. About four of every five noninstitutionalized persons over 65 may have living children, but few of those children still live in the same household. As a result, the proportion of old people living 10 minutes to 7 hours away from their children has increased, while the frequency of contacts and visits by siblings and other relatives has seriously dwindled. Widowed persons and old persons who have never married are especially at risk for loneliness (Shanas, 1982).

Retirement

The decline in income and social status after retirement leads to major social adjustments. After retirement, opportunities to generate an affordable income or to remain busy are complicated by legal and social discrimination, including ageism. Even the Age Discrimination Employment Act of 1967, which altered mandatory retirement laws, provides insufficient labor opportunities for the aged.

The authorization of the Older Americans Act of 1965 offers some opportunities but hardly compensates for the rising cost of inflation. For example, reimbursement for volunteer and foster grandparent programs is too low to meet special physical and psychosocial needs. The result of reduced funds is fewer opportunities for elderly to adopt during retirement. Unemployed elderly drinkers who neither experience nor seek such opportunities exacerbate their risk for chronic disease (Atkinson, 1981; Lutterotti, 1969).

Tax Expenditures

Fixed incomes, low educational levels, and declining physical health place the elderly in competition for existing services. The reduction in federal spending also contributes to limited availability of services, especially to services designed for welfare recipients. President George Bush's congressional budget cuts are shrinking welfare program funds and limiting tax provisions. Some major tax expenditures are the exemptions, exclusions, and credits. Such exclusions include social security benefits for retired workers, railroad retirement benefits, veterans' pensions, tax credits, and capital gains on home sales. Such exclusions presumably alter the income distribution between the aged in a manner favorable to low-income aged, but, in fact, these benefits from taxation are heavily weighted toward assisting a minority of high-income elite of elderly rather than needy individuals. Because of this inequity, the monies currently allotted under exemption provisions do not parallel direct costs for the elderly. Expenditures for one segment of the elderly population prevent expenditures for another segment, which creates higher taxes of elderly poor.

Relocation

The literature on relocation of elderly is fraught with theoretical disunity (Coffman, 1983; Horowitz & Schulz, 1983; Schulz & Brenner, 1977). Whether relocation affects the survival of institutionalized elderly or causes a transfer trauma depends on the acceptance or rejection of the relocation-mortality hypothesis, which suggests that relocation increases mortality since individuals are exposed to adverse housing effects. Coffman (1983) dismisses this hypothesis as an excuse to keep elderly clients in inferior and deteriorating facilities. Ironically, both sides of the controversy militate against deinstitutionalization. However, morality and emotionality does depend on the individual's health and the quality of the transitional living process (Ruben, 1983a). Elder cottages, for example, offer direction for reaching the underserved and benefit the infirm alcoholic unable to pay for physical therapy and other medical services.

Common Physician Mistakes

Physicians trained in geriatrics (or geropsychiatry) offer expertise in differentiating symptoms of biological aging from drug and alcohol effects; however, many physicians, including psychiatrists, lack this expertise and may unintentionally commit errors that direct care providers should be aware of. Frequent physician mistakes include the following.

Inattention to the client's medical condition. Basic medical practice requires that physicians prescribing medicine take into account the elderly's developmental status, medical conditions, and any specific physical problems. Particular attention should be paid to prior medication history to obtain clues to previously effective or ineffective treatments. When the client's condition is in doubt, the physician should consult previous doctors or appropriate medical specialists.

Failure to perform supporting laboratory tests. During the initial medical evaluation, it is usually important to perform routine blood tests and an electrocardiogram to ensure the client is not at risk. This is especially necessary if the client is to receive drug therapy. Ordered tests should be followed up by the physician or office staff.

Prescribing too low or high a dose. Perhaps the most common error made in prescribing drugs is incorrect dose. Uncertain physicians may express ambivalence by prescribing inadequate doses. Inexperienced physicians may prescribe an elderly client a regular adult dose or, in anticipation of drug side effects, may counter the side effects with other medications. Low adult doses will be too weak for relief and instead distress the client. High adult doses may cause unwanted side effects or overdose.

Inadequate drug trial. In addition to proper dosage levels, it is necessary to continue medication for a sufficient length of time to determine if the drug is effective. Treatment plans should include a dosage buildup schedule and specific time periods after which therapeutic effects will be assessed. Should the drug prove ineffective, a second drug, preferably from a different class, should be tried.

Overreacting to changes in the client's condition. Another common error occurs when physicians immediately raise or lower the dosage with every complaint from the client. Overreaction usually takes place at two stages in the client's course of treatment: during the initial phase of treatment, when physicians are building up therapeutic levels, and midway through treatment when physicians decrease or terminate medication in clients who require some stabilizing agent to prevent relapse of a recurrent disorder (physical or psychological).

Inept use of many drugs versus skillful use of few. Most seasoned physicians develop some favorite drugs or drug combinations whose activity and proper dosage indications have become familiar. Consequently they are reluctant to consider or prescribe drugs with whose actions they are unfamiliar. This conservative practice overlooks new drugs on the market that may supply benefits surpassing the action of routine drugs. Physicians who do agree to try new medications should indicate their inexperience with it, the available alternatives, and risks and benefits likely incurred from the dosage.

Failure to monitor drug use. A serious assumption is that because medication is prescribed, clients are taking it—or, for that matter, taking it correctly. When there are signs of deterioration in a client's clinical state, physicians should consider noncompliance as a leading variable. Once it is determined that this is the problem, solutions may include encouraging the family, hospital, or clinic staff to help in overseeing medications administered; using liquid medications instead of tablets or capsules that are not swallowed; and using fluphenazin decanoate or other long-acting preparations that require fewer administrations than other drugs.

Failure to reevaluate clients periodically. Once a client's condition is stabilized, physicians may discontinue drug treatment or place the client on maintenance medication. Usually precautions are taken to monitor progress and report any decay of condition. Nevertheless, it is good practice for physicians to schedule follow-up interviews at regular intervals.

Failure to counsel clients about drug effects. Confident physicians generally regard relief of client symptoms as a reliable index for regulating dosage. But what about how the elderly person feels or side effects experienced? Physicians need to spend more time telling clients about the treatment course and soliciting feedback from them over time. An unfortunate but common practice is assigning this duty to ancillary staff, such as nurses and physician assistants. Certainly these professionals may be competent, but clients' trust first and foremost is with the physician, and it is his or her obligation to reassure elderly clients of interest in their welfare.

PRIMARY PREVENTION ISSUES

Competency goes beyond the physician's territory. Direct care workers face equal challenges to competency when case finding potential alcoholic or addicted elderly in the community. Early detection is preferable but hard to accomplish, and it involves carefully crafted methods of prevention.

What Is Primary Prevention?

Primary prevention means that the potential for problems exists without problems being evident. Efforts focus on programs and strategies put in place before older adults develop alcohol or medication problems. The National Institute of Drug Abuse (NIDA) and National Institute of Alcohol Abuse and Alcoholism (NIAAA) have identified six modalities of primary drug abuse prevention (NIDA, 1981).

Information programs are designed to provide accurate and timely information about drugs and their effects on the human system. Programs are based on the human potential for self-improvement through responsible decision making.

Education programs are designed to develop critical life skills such as decision making, problem solving, and communication. These programs are premised on the theory that people are motivated to satisfy certain needs (e.g., love, security, self-identity) and that those who are deficient in critical skills may satisfy their needs through drug abuse.

Alternative programs provide positive growth experiences in which people can develop the self-discipline, confidence, and personal awareness they need to become socially mature individuals. Programs involve participation in activities that foster awareness of self and others and offer exposure to a wide range of rewarding nondrug activities.

Intervention programs provide assistance and support to people during critical periods of their lives. Programs involve person-to-person dyads, sharing of experiences, and empathic listening while aiding adjustment to personal and family problems. Techniques used are diverse but usually include counseling, hot-line assistance, topical workshops, and peer-supported activities.

Environmental change programs seek to identify and change social and physical environmental factors that directly influence behaviors and patterns of drug use and abuse. Examples include petition drives to beautify a park or evicting drug users from it.

Social policy change programs attempt to modify social policies, including laws, regulations, and enforcement procedures governing drug availability and distribution. Lobbying efforts modify advertising policies and reduce possible negative consequences through consumer product safety regulation.

Recommendations for Primary Prevention

Several national task forces assigned the duty of devising prevention strategies have disseminated their findings (e.g., Doyle, 1976; Guttman, 1972). While opinion differs to some extent, there is basic unanimity among recommendations for professionals, seniors, nonprofessionals, the pharmaceutical market, and government:

Professionals

- Communication training workshops and classes focused on communicating with elderly clients.

- Workshops and classes on the role of drugs and alcohol in health care, especially as related to dangerous combinations.

- Workshops for professionals of allied health fields, such as aging, health care, and substance abuse, on alerting senior clientele to problems associated with drugs and alcohol.

- Programs focusing on the role of doctors and pharmacists in dispensing drug information.

- Those involved with treatment programs for elderly drug users must take into account that heavy users are likely dissatisfied with their past and present life. Efforts might be directed toward helping aging individuals to cope with their lives.

Seniors

- Educational programs directed at the total elderly population. Such programs should make use of doctors and pharmacists for presenting factual drug and alcohol information. One method of presenting information is through programs on community public television.
- Programs and literature aimed at seniors focusing on the wise use of drugs, including projects to train seniors to be competent, assertive users of health care services and products.
- Programs dealing with preventative health care (exercise, nutrition, and scheduling check-ups).
- Alternative techniques for coping with life, such as relaxation, group projects, and biofeedback.
- Communications workshops to help and encourage seniors to communicate more effectively with health care professionals.
- Programs to educate seniors to make better use of public service agencies, such as aging agencies, substance abuse agencies, and mental health agencies. Skills learned are for obtaining information, educational programs, materials, and other assistance.

Nonprofessionals

- Outreach programs for network groups and substance abuse organizations coordinated with direct service treatment.
- Informational programs on self-medication and alcohol control, particularly for senior minority groups.

Market

- Clearly spelled out geriatric dosages on medicine labels.
- Precautions associated with drugs and alcohol prominently displayed in large type on both the bottle and any accompanying literature. Statements included on the bottle should say, for example, "If you have questions about this drug, consult your pharmacist."
- Literature available through pharmaceuticals or national and local clearinghouses advising on healthy drug and alcohol use.

Government

- Policymakers concerned with nonprescription and prescription drug users and alcoholics among seniors should recruit seniors in planning and implementation stages.
- Emphasis in rural areas should be put on alcoholic use, while emphasis in urban areas should be put on prescription and OTC drug use.
- Efforts should be made through government to produce creative, satisfying, and responsible methods for seniors to spend their time with a positive outlook on life.
- Emphasis should be made toward implementing local or national pharmacy hot-lines for drug information and questions.

SECONDARY PREVENTION ISSUES

Secondary prevention means identifying and reducing existing substance abuse problems at the earliest stage possible. Early symptom detection in elderly addicts is, unfortunately, difficult given their social isolation and disguise of major symptoms. Case-finding efforts may locate high-risk individuals, but the next step of treatment decision faces several confusing routes from which to choose. Treatment programs vary from individual and group counseling to self-help and bibliotherapy groups. Currently, models of counseling show renewed interest in education and aftercare programs. Two movements inspired by this trend combine pharmacology with behavioral interventions. The first deals with what is known as behavioral pharmacology and the second with behavioral psychotherapy.

Behavioral Pharmacology

Recent studies on the behavioral effects of drugs offer new hope for clinical interpretation of how environment and pharmacologic variables interact (Breuning, Davis & Poling, 1982; Breuning, Poling & Matson, 1984; Poling, 1986; Poling, Picker & Hall-Johnson, 1983). Certain principles of drug action make it clear that drugs that are self-administered (and abused) serve as positive reinforcers and reinforce drug-seeking operant responses. These operants are also influenced by the same set of variables that control nondrug responses.

There are meaningful correlations between advances in behavioral pharmacology and elderly alcohol and drug addiction. For example, considerable pharmacokinetic properties that determine drug disposition may or may not be age related. Reduced plasma, clearance rates, or decline in renal excretion, usually attributed to aging, may be instead a function of ethanol selectively influencing the person's sensitivity to one kind of stimulus (auditory, visual, olfactory) and nonselectively influencing sensitivity to other stimuli. Changes in stimulus selection ("discrimination") account for the loss or disruption of stimulus control (tendency to respond to certain stimuli, and not others) and eventual nonresponsiveness to common stimuli. Another operating influence may be levels of deprivation (hunger, time limitations, thirst) (Michael, 1982, 1983). For example, elderly with anorexia nervosa (hunger deprivation) may consume higher concentrations of ethanol, which affects their sensory orientation (Ruben, 1984).

Behavioral pharmacology holds important implications for behavioral and biomedical interventions for elders. For example, the physiological benefits of detoxification and disulfiram are limited against producing recidivism. This is because, in strictly medical treatments, there are several untreated events in the natural environment reconditioning substance abuse after the patient's discharge from the hospital. This is why treatment emphasis must always be multicausal and transactional—multicausal by considering several simultaneous reasons for addiction and transactional by the fact that addiction develops over time.

Behavioral Psychotherapy

Behavioral psychotherapies for elderly addicts usually contain two distinct parts: assessment and integration. Relatively improved systems are available to assess drinking behavior and may involve mechanical recording devices or the coordination of professionals and paraprofessionals to monitor target responses (Hersen & Barlow, 1976; Ruben, 1990). One such recording system in a nursing home also employed computers to rate validity and reliability of observational data (Schnelle & Traughber, 1983). This involves use of "simulations" or analog (Ruben, 1983b, 1989). These, in effect, attempt to structure events in the clinic so they resemble nonclinic events and thus produce "naturalistic" drinking and medication-taking behaviors. Role play, enactment, and audiovisual recording provide the usual means of measuring behavior that transfers from the person's natural environment into the clinic or hospital setting.

In treatment design, behavioral methods have assisted the movement of educational programs into alcohol prevention. Outreach projects allow counselors to visit elderly in nursing homes, community senior centers, and their own home. On-site behavioral counseling employs contingency management, homework assignments, and direct skill application (Burgio & Burgio, 1986; Carstensen & Edelstein, 1987; Patterson, Dupree, Eberly, Jackson, O'Sullivan, Penner & Dee-Kelly, 1982; Pinkston & Linsk, 1984; Ruben, in press; Skinner, 1983).

Frequently behavioral skills training involves direct modeling and imitation exercises. Instructors demonstrate, for instance, pill preparation and drug-taking steps using a step-by-step or task analysis approach. Each step in the task is brief and easy to implement and immediately is followed with skill repetition and feedback. Once steps are learned in order, they are combined into a full sequence comprising the task. For example, consider this series of steps of a task analysis for toothbrushing for elderly aphasics:

1. Pick up and hold the toothbrush.
2. Wet the toothbrush.
3. Remove the cap from the toothpaste.
4. Apply the toothpaste.
5. Replace the cap on the toothpaste.
6. Brush the biting surfaces of the teeth.
7. Brush the inside surfaces of the teeth.
8. Fill the cup with water.
9. Rinse the mouth.
10. Wipe the mouth.
11. Rinse the toothbrush.
12. Rinse the sink.
13. Put the equipment away.

Similarly, tasks that can be split up into tiny parts for keeping track of different daily medicines might involve the following list:

1. Use an egg carton and electric alarm clock.

2. Label the outside of the egg cup with numbers signifying the time of day to take the drug ("1" = "1:00 P.M.").

3. Each morning, put the day's pills in the proper egg cups. The number of pills for each drug at that hour are put in the cup. If more than one drug is taken at the hour, have separate cups for each drug and labeled with the same time (e.g., all at 1:00).

4. Set the alarm clock to go off at the first pill time (e.g., 1:00).

5. Turn the alarm off, open the egg carton, and take pills from any cup labeled that time (1:00).

6. Refasten the egg carton, and reset the alarm clock for next time interval.

Constructing a task analysis is an easy process by following basic steps:

1. Select a behavior or "response class" and watch carefully how the elderly person does it.

2. Break down the behavior or skill into tiny parts that are all observable, measurable, and easy to say the client has completed.

3. Prompt the client at each step, using imitation and modeling exercises where necessary.

4. Once the client does a step, reinforce with praise.

5. Move slowly and systematically to the next step. Each step combines each of the previous steps learned.

6. When the client fails or has trouble with a new step, return to the previous step, and redo it until he is ready to move on.

One final feature of behavioral treatment refers to integration, a linking between all relevant factors of the elderly addict's field that contribute to alcohol and drug problems. Pioneered by the work of J. R. Kantor (1959; Ruben, 1983c, 1986b; see also Chapter 1), this integrative field concept is like behavioral medicine in that it pulls together biophysiological agents into a holistic model. It is different from behavioral medicine in the same way. This holism is really a multidisciplinary approach that considers medical, behavioral, as well as historical, cultural, and physical science variables.

All in all, growing concern for the elderly drug and alcohol abuser affects a multitude of services, treatment philosophies, and scientific research. But the general picture of older abusers has been rather negative. One reason is that traditional views of elderly addiction support a unicausal, rather than multicausal, analysis of the problem. Certainly nobody disputes that elderly persons undergo transitions and face multiple health risks. The difficulty, however, lies in professional awareness of how these multiple variables interact and of the behavioral outcomes of these interactions. This chapter identified some current patterns and problems including treatment intervention. But far more energy is necessary at policymaking levels and in hospitals and outpatient clinics before a truly integrated system can expect to occur.

REFERENCES

Atkinson, J. H. (1981). Alcoholism and geriatric problems. *Advances in Alcoholism, 2,* 5–8.

Barnes, G. M., Abel, E. L. & Ernst, C. A. S. (eds.). (1980). *Alcohol and the elderly: A comprehensive bibliography.* Westport, Conn.: Greenwood Press.

Breuning, S. E., Davis, V. J. & Poling, A. D. (1982). Pharmacotherapy with the mentally retarded: Implications for clinical psychologists. *Clinical Psychology Review, 2,* 79–114.

Breuning, S. E., Poling, A. D. & Matson, J. E. (eds.). (1984). *Applied psychopharmacology: Assessment of medication effects.* New York: Grune & Stratton.

Burgio, L. D. & Burgo, K. L. (1986). Behavioral gerontology: Application of behavioral methods to problems of older adults. *Journal of Applied Behavior Analysis, 19,* 321–28.

Carstensen, L. L. & Edelstein, B. A. (1987). *Handbook of clinical gerontology.* New York: Pergamon.

Coffman, T. L. (1983). Toward an understanding of geriatric relocation. *Gerontologist, 23,* 453–59.

Doyle, J. P. (1976). *Medication use and misuse study among older persons: Final report.* Jacksonville, Fla.: Cathedral Foundation of Jacksonville.

Einstein, S. (ed.). (1979). *Drug and alcohol use: Issues and factors.* New York: Plenum.

Ewing, J. A. & Rouse, B. A. (eds.). (1978). *Drinking: Alcohol in American society— Issues and current research.* Chicago: Nelson Hall.

Guttman, D. (1972). *A study of legal drug use by older Americans.* Washington, D.C.: Department of Health, Education and Welfare. (National Institute on Drug Abuse Services Research Report).

Hersen, M. & Barlow, D. H. (1976). *Single-case experimental designs: Strategies for studying behavior change.* New York: Pergamon Press.

Horowitz, M. J. & Schulz, R. (1983). The relocation controversy: Criticism and commentary on five recent studies. *Gerontologist, 23,* 229–35.

Kantor, J. R. (1959). *Interbehavioral psychology.* Granville, Ohio: Principia Press.

Lutterotti, A. (1969). L'aspect social de l'alcoolisme dans la vieillesse. *Revue alcoolisme, 15,* 49–57.

Maddox, G., Robins, L. N. & Rosenberg, N. (eds.). (1984). *Nature and extent of alcohol problems among the elderly.* New York: Springer Publishing.

Michael, J. (1982). Distinguishing between discriminative and motivational functions of stimuli. *Journal of the Experimental Analysis of Behavior, 37,* 149–55.

Michael, J. (1983). Evocative and repertoire altering effects of an environmental event. *Verbal Behavior News, 2,* 21–23.

Mills, K. C., Sobell, M. B. & Schaefer, H. H. (1971). Training social drinking as an alternative to abstinence for alcoholics. *Behavior Therapy, 2,* 18–27.

National Institute on Drug Abuse (NIDA). (1981). *Prevention planning workbook* (vol. 1). Rockville, Md.: National Institute on Drug Abuse.

Patterson, R. L., Dupree, L. W., Eberly, D. A., Jackson, G. M., O'Sullivan, M. J.,

Penner, L. A. & Dee-Kelly, C. (1982). *Overcoming deficits of aging: A behavioral treatment.* New York: Plenum.

Petersen, D. M., Whittington, F. J. & Payne, B. P. (eds.). (1979). *Drugs and the elderly: Social and pharmacological issues.* Springfield, Ill.: Charles C. Thomas.

Pinkston, E. M. & Linsk, N. L. (1984). *Care of the elderly: A family approach.* New York: Pergamon.

Poling, A. D. (1986). *A primer of human behavioral pharmacology.* New York: Plenum.

Poling, A. D., Picker, M. & Hall-Johnson, E. (1983). Human behavioral pharmacology. *Psychological Record, 33,* 473–93.

Ruben, D. H. (1983a). Assessment and setting events and interbehavioral history for dispelling myths about aging residential elderly. *Interbehaviorist, 12,* 9–11.

Ruben, D. H. (1983b). Analogue assessments in the behavioral treatment of drug addictions. *Catalyst, 2,* 69–77.

Ruben, D. H. (1983c). Interbehavioral implications for behavior: Clinical perspectives. In N. W. Smith, P. T. Mountjoy & D. H. Ruben (eds.), *Reassessment in Psychology: The interbehavioral alternative* (pp. 445–69). Washington, D.C.: University Press of America.

Ruben, D. H. (1984). *Drug abuse and the elderly: An annotated bibliography.* Metuchen, N.J.: Scarecrow Press.

Ruben, D. H. (1986a). The elderly alcoholic: Some current dimensions. *Advances in Alcohol and Substance Abuse, 5,* 59–70.

Ruben, D. H. (1986b). What is the "interbehavioral" approach to treatment? *Journal of Contemporary Psychotherapy, 16,* 62–71.

Ruben, D. H. (1987). Improving communication between the elderly and pharmacies: A self-initiative training program. *Journal of Alcohol and Drug Education, 32,* 7–12.

Ruben, D. H. (1989). Behavioral predictors of alcoholics: A systems alternative. *Alcoholism Treatment Quarterly, 5,* 137–62.

Ruben, D. H. (1990). *The aging and drug effects: A planning manual for medication and alcohol abuse treatment of the elderly.* Jefferson, N.C.: McFarland & Company.

Ruben, D. H. (in press). Reducing interruptions in functional activity through control of self-medication and habit-reversal. *Corrective and Social Psychiatry and Journal of Behavior Technology, Methods and Therapy, 34.*

Schnelle, J. F. & Traughber, B. (1983). A behavioral assessment system applicable to geriatric nursing facility residents. *Behavioral Assessment, 5,* 231–43.

Schulz, R. & Brenner, G. (1977). Relocation of the aged: A review and theoretical analysis. *Journal of Gerontology, 32,* 323–33.

Shanas, E. (1982). The family relations of old people. *National Forum, 62,* 9–11.

Sherouse, D. L. (1983). *Professional's handbook on geriatric alcoholism.* Springfield, Ill.: Charles C. Thomas.

Skinner, B. F. (1983). Intellectual self-management in old age. *American Psychologist, 38,* 239–44.

Sobel, H. J. (ed.). (1981). *Behavior therapy in terminal care: A humanistic approach.* Cambridge, Mass.: Ballinger.

Sobell, M. B. & Sobell, L. C. (1973). Individualized behavior therapy for alcoholics. *Behavior Therapy, 4,* 49–72.

Sobell, M. B. & Sobell, L. C. (1976). Second year treatment outcome of alcoholics treated by individualized behavior therapy. *Behaviour Research and Therapy,* *14*, 195–215.

Sobell, M. B. & Sobell, L. C. (1978). *Behavioral treatment of alcohol problems: Individualized therapy and controlled drinking.* New York: Plenum Press.

12

Addiction and Traumatic Brain Injury

FRANK R. SPARADEO, JEFFREY T. BARTH, AND CHRIS E. STOUT

The occurrence of traumatic brain injury (TBI) is often referred to as the silent epidemic. Epidemiological research has indicated that the annual incidence of head injury in the general population is 2.2 to 2.4 per 1,000 (Kraus & Nourjah, 1988; Nestvold, Lundar, Blikra & Lonnum, 1988; Parkinson, Stephensen & Phillips, 1985). The most likely individual to experience a head injury is a male in the second or third decade of life (Annegers, Grabow, Kurland & Laws, 1980; Kraus & Nourjah, 1988; Nestvold et al., 1988; Parkinson, Stephensen & Phillips, 1985; Rimel, Geodani, Barth, Boll, & Jane, 1981; Rimel, Geodani, Barth & Jane, 1982). Another risk factor for traumatic brain injury is low socioeconomic status. Parkinson, Stephensen, and Phillips (1985) found that 47.5 percent of all head injuries were either welfare recipients or unemployed as compared to the general population, in which this group only represents 11 percent.

Ironically, another risk factor for traumatic brain injury is the occurrence of a previous head injury (Rimel et al., 1981, 1982). According to research by Annegers et al. (1980) the risk of head injury increases by three times if a person has already experienced previous head trauma, and after a second head injury the risk of such injury increases to eight times that found in the general population.

Substance use, particularly the use of alcohol, significantly increases the risk of head injury. Rimel et al. (1982) found that 73 percent of patients admitted to the hospital for head injury had alcohol in their bloodstreams. Sparadeo and Gill (1989) similarly discovered that of those individuals admitted to the hospital for traumatic brain injury in which blood alcohol level (BAL) was assessed, 67 percent were positive. Furthermore, over 50 percent had a blood alcohol level over the legal definition of intoxication (.100 g or 100 mg/100 ml).

The history of addiction in the head trauma population is quite high. Sparadeo and Gill (1989) found a significant and positive correlation between BAL and a history of addiction. Kreutzer et al. (1990b) note that 58 percent of all traumatic brain injury survivors sampled had a history of substance abuse. It is clear that substance abuse is related to and a major causal factor in the occurrence of head injury (Rohe & DePompolo, 1985).

MECHANISMS OF TBI INJURY

The primary mechanism of traumatic head injury is vehicular accidents (Rimel et al., 1982). Gunshots and assaults, falls, and sports injuries appear to account for the balance of head traumas (NHIF, 1988). It is well known that the occurrence of even nonvehicular traumatic brain injuries is often preceded by the use of alcohol or other drugs, which is particularly true in the case of assaults and gunshot wounds.

IMPLICATIONS OF A BLOOD ALCOHOL LEVEL

Research has indicated that the presence of a blood alcohol level at the time of a TBI has specific implications for the early recovery of the patient. Animal and human studies suggest that alcohol obscures diagnosis of medical problems and can contribute to cerebral hypoxia, edema, and hemorrhaging (Elmer, Gustafsson, Goransson & Thomson, 1983; Elmer & Lim, 1985; Flamm, Dempoulos, Seigman et al., 1977; Markwalder, 1981; Steinbok and Thomson, 1978). Kraus and Nourjah (1989) found that individuals with severe brain injuries and a BAL at the time of injury stayed in the hospital significantly longer than those with no alcohol in their systems. This finding was consistent with research by Sparadeo and Gill (1989), who also noted that amount of alcohol was not related to this outcome. In other words, just the occurrence of a positive BAL resulted in a longer length of stay than that noted in individuals who did not have a positive BAL at the time of the injury.

Edna (1982) found that patients with a positive BAL at the time of injury had a longer duration of coma and a lower level of consciousness during the acute stage of recovery (Sparadeo, Strauss & Barth, 1990). The experience of a period of agitation is common during the acute process of recovery from head trauma. Sparadeo and Gill (1989) found that although the incidence of agitation was no greater in patients with a positive BAL compared to patients with a negative BAL, the duration of the period of agitation was longer in patients with a BAL over .10 g (point of legal intoxication). Patients with a BAL at or above the level of intoxication also had a lower cognitive status at discharge from the acute care hospital (Sparadeo & Gill, 1989).

Mortality and the presence of a positive BAL at the time of injury is somewhat unclear. Ward, Flynn, Miller and Blaisdell (1982) reported that mortality was lower in patients with a positive BAL; however, they included many types of trauma. Luna, Maier, Sowder, Copasse, and Oreskovich (1984) found that mortality rates were twice as high in head-injured patients who were intoxicated as opposed to those who were not. Sparadeo and Gill (1989) were not able to make a conclusive statement about mortality; however, in six patients who died at the time of admission to the trauma center, five had positive BALs.

Long-term implications for the presence of a positive BAL at the time of injury are less clear. Recently, Brooks, Symington, Beattie, Campsie, Bryden, and McKinlay (1989) discovered that a high BAL at the time of injury was predictive of verbal memory impairments over the long term. This finding was independent of a history of addiction and age. No other neuropsychological studies have been conducted as of this writing.

CONTINUED USE OF ALCOHOL AND OTHER DRUGS

Continued use of substances following head trauma has grave implications for rehabilitation outcome and life adjustment of survivors. Sparadeo and Gill (1988) in a one-year postinjury neuropsychological study of over 60 patients determined that all patients continued to experience significant cognitive deficits, and 50 percent of this sample were using alcohol. Kreutzer at al. (1990a) found that in a sample of 74 TBI patients (mean of 6.4 years since injury) referred to a university-based supported-employment program, the use of alcohol and other substances was considerably lower than preinjury. Specifically, they noted in looking at preinjury data that one-fifth of the sample were alcohol abstainers and 66 percent were labeled as moderate or heavy drinkers. When the patients were evaluated as to current use, 57 percent of the sample were alcohol abstainers postinjury and 40 percent were moderate to heavy drinkers. Kreutzer and his colleagues also found that 36 percent of his sample had used illicit drugs preinjury as compared to only 4 percent postinjury. It must be pointed out that this sample consisted of individuals who maintained contact with the rehabilitation field and were becoming involved in treatment (employment program).

In another report, Kreutzer et al. (1990a) also discovered reduced levels of drinking in the postinjury population; however, 43.3 percent of the sample was using alcohol at either light levels or moderate to heavy levels. Although this report is optimistic in that apparently a large number of patients with a preinjury pattern of heavy drinking were either abstinent or light drinkers postinjury, the fact remains that over 40 percent of this preselected sample of brain-injured patients were drinking and therefore continued to accept the associated risks of that drinking.

The risks associated with alcohol for any person are great; for the survivor of a brain injury, they are even more serious. Such patients have altered seizure thresholds as a result of the brain injury itself, and the use of alcohol and/or other drugs is likely to alter further the seizure threshold, thus increasing the seizure likelihood. TBI survivors also must go through a period of acute, post-acute, and long-term recovery in which physical, emotional, and cognitive changes occur. The use of alcohol or other drugs during this period interferes with the natural process of recovery.

An analogy can be drawn from the literature on cognitive functioning and alcoholism. It is well known that individuals with a history of alcoholism demonstrate significant cognitive deficits (Parsons, Butters and Nathan, 1987). Parsons (1987) has found that cognitive recovery from alcoholism can be quite good if the patient ceases using alcohol and remains abstinent; however, any return to use, even at small levels, will slow, stall, or reverse the cognitive recovery curve. Many of the cognitive deficits associated with head injury are not very different from those related to long-term drinking, and until research indicates otherwise, it is safe to assume that the introduction of alcohol is likely to interfere seriously with the natural recovery of cognitive functioning.

It is not unusual for TBI survivors to be taking prescription drugs for seizure management, spasticity, anxiety, depression, pain, and/or other conditions. The use of alcohol or another nonprescribed drug presents particular risk by counteracting the medication, adding to the medication's effect, reducing the desired therapeutic outcome, or placing the patient at risk for toxic reaction.

Behavioral complications are often exacerbated by alcohol use. It is common for TBI survivors to evidence behavioral disturbance due to compromised frontal lobe functions from acceleration-deceleration motor vehicle accidents. Alcohol is a central nervous system depressant, which results in disinhibition. In other words, the combination of head trauma–related behavioral disturbance and alcohol is synergistic (Kreutzer et al., 1990a).

The use of alcohol after a TBI also increases the likelihood of another head injury (or other trauma). Because a head trauma survivor's judgment is often affected by the brain injury, he or she must develop appropriate problem-solving strategies. Strategies are dependent on a system of therapeutic interventions that eventually result in the patient's utilizing self-cuing strategies. The TBI survivor who uses alcohol will experience impaired judgment and problem solving from the pharmacologic effects of alcohol and, furthermore, will be less likely to utilize self-cuing strategies in everyday problem solving. This phenomenon puts the head-injured patient at great risk.

Finally, a TBI survivor who is involved in rehabilitation or has completed rehabilitation and uses alcohol or other drugs is likely to demonstrate inconsistent performance in rehabilitation and/or poor community reintegration (Burke, Weselowski & Guth, 1988). Inconsistent performance during the rehabilitation process can result in extended rehabilitation or incorrect clinical conclusions by the rehabilitation team.

ABSTINENCE

Drugs are not abused or desired unless their effect is to change brain functioning and state of consciousness. Clearly drugs that produce altered states of consciousness produce the desired effect by altering brain chemistry directly or indirectly. The individual who has survived a brain injury can hardly afford to ingest any substance that alters brain function further. In other words, the use of alcohol or other drugs by a brain injury survivor is contraindicated, for the many reasons cited earlier. Clinicians have an ethical responsibility to give advice to patients that is maximally healthy; either to permit alcohol or other drug use by a TBI survivor or passively permit it by not informing the individual of the dangers of its use (and the need for abstinence) is essentially harmful to the patient and violates an essential trust. Once rehabilitation clinicians adopt a policy of abstinence for their head-injured patients and patients respond with compliance, substance abuse as a problem is no longer the issue. Instead, substance use (at any level) becomes the problem to face.

The TBI rehabilitation process needs to address the issue of substance use and identify patients' needs accordingly. Many TBI survivors were light social drinkers or abstainers before the injury. In this case, the issue in treatment will be primary prevention. The rehabilitation team must provide the patient with information about the risks associated with substance use and abuse. They must also recognize the vulnerabilities, such as cognitive dysfunction and need for socialization and acceptance, that may lead the patient to alcohol and other drug experimentation, and the team must assist the patient in addressing these vulnerabilities.

Many TBI survivors have a history of substance abuse prior to the injury; however, they may not have been using alcohol or other drugs since the injury. Secondary prevention is needed in this case since the patient may have fond memories of parties and social events in which substances were used. These TBI survivors are struggling to cope with disability (cognitive and/or physical), and as the patient progresses through rehabilitation and becomes more cognizant of his or her impairments, there will be a tendency to retreat to familiar memories and behaviors associated with a previous life-style. A substance abuse history indicates an added degree of risk for returning to these old habits, and therefore the treatment team must be sure that both formal and informal relapse-prevention techniques (Marlatt & Gordon, 1985) are woven into the overall rehabilitation program. Langley (1991) points out, however, that although viewing the preinjury substance abuser as at greater risk is intuitively correct, the typical "at-risk" client is usually not the preinjury alcoholic. Langley (1991) indicates that the nonaddicted person for whom alcohol was a central life-style component before the injury and now has fewer alternative reinforcers or coping responses may represent the more typical at-risk client. His conclusions are based on the findings of Vuchinich and Tucker (1988), who indicated that the preference for alcohol use varies inversely with constraints on drinking and with the availability of alternative reinforcers and directly with constraints on access to them.

Although the majority of TBI survivors are not substance addicted, some certainly fit this category. Kreutzer et al. (1990b) found that 20 percent of TBI survivors were using alcohol at levels considered heavy. These individuals require expert substance abuse treatment as part of their head injury rehabilitation process. Despite this obvious need, a majority of head trauma programs do not offer formal substance abuse treatment. Similarly, if one of these TBI patients is admitted to a substance abuse treatment program, the availability of formal head trauma rehabilitation programming is usually absent. Hillbom and Holm (1986) indicate that approximately 40 percent of males admitted to a substance abuse program have a history of head injury. In 1987–1988 a survey was conducted by the NHIF Task Force on Substance Abuse in which 75 head injury rehabilitation facilities across the United States, representing some 1,500 TBI patients, were questioned about substance abuse. The results of the survey indicated that 40% of TBI survivors in active treatment had moderate to severe problems with substance abuse prior to the head injury. Alcohol was identified as the drug of choice by 95% of this population. Despite the number of patients with a prior history of substance abuse, as well as the presence of a number of patients with ongoing substance abuse problems, no facility indicated that it was offering specific formal substance abuse treatment, although many reported use of limited interventions such as Alcoholics Anonymous (AA) and Narcotics Anonymous (NA).

Since the time of the survey, a number of head injury programs and also a number of substance abuse centers have developed formal dual-diagnosis (head injury and substance abuse) programs. Although there is an increase in the number of services for this population, the number of programs currently available cannot meet the need.

SUBSTANCE ABUSE AND HEAD INJURY REHABILITATION

Substance Abuse Rehabilitation

A number of rehabilitation models exist in the substance abuse field. Substance abuse rehabilitation is delivered through outpatient, intensive outpatient, inpatient, and long-term inpatient formats. Within those structures, a variety of treatment approaches and theoretical models are applied, with the disease model, social learning theory, and the behavioral model the most dominant. It is not unusual to see combinations of these models applied in various treatment centers. Before discussing treatment considerations for substance abuse intervention for the TBI survivor, it is necessary to discuss certain head injury factors that have implications for substance abuse interventions.

Traumatic brain injury is likely to result in ongoing cognitive disabilities. In most vehicular head injuries, the survivor suffers from stretching of neurons in the brain stem and mid-brain, and the anterior tips of the frontal and temporal lobes may be contused. The cognitive sequelae of this type of injury include deficits in attention and concentration, learning and memory, reasoning and problem solving, impulse control, emotional regulation, and complex motor programming. In addition, many TBI survivors have difficulty with self-awareness and insight, as well as perception and certain aspects of language functioning. Substance abuse interventions must take into account these aspects of cognitive and behavioral dysfunction that are often present in TBI survivors. This includes understanding not only cognitive deficiencies but also spared cognitive functioning (strengths).

Survivors of TBI often experience significant emotional turmoil throughout their recovery and rehabilitation process. It is not unusual for families to report substantial personality changes as well. Emotional regulation is often impaired in the TBI survivor, with swift and significant mood swings prevailing. Anxiety and depression occur frequently following head injury.

Social alienation is often a by-product of TBI. Friends and relatives may perceive the survivor as different, and he may be difficult to communicate with and demonstrate behavioral difficulties or physical disabilities. All of these changes are likely to lead to a loss of social contact. Many TBI survivors complain of boredom, and drinking or other drug taking often occurs in the absence of alternate behavior.

Behavioral disorders are common in the TBI survivor. They range from severe aggression, violence, and impulsive outbursts to social introversion. The behavioral disorders associated with head injury are often secondary to frontal lobe lesions incurred in the accident and are sometimes completely out of character from the preinjury personality. Behavioral outbursts may occur in the absence of an identifiable stimulus, and it is not uncommon for behavioral disorders to increase in the presence of fatigue or stress. TBI survivors who perceive themselves as failing in the rehabilitation process will sometimes have difficulty controlling themselves in the presence of heightened frustration and anger. The use of alcohol will often result in exacerbating behavioral disorders in TBI survivors. Traditional substance abuse programs are usually not prepared to work with a TBI survivor who evidences behavioral disturbance, particularly when these problems are not linked directly or obviously with a precipitant.

Head Injury Rehabilitation

Head injury rehabilitation is characterized by many coordinated interventions. The treatment team usually consists of a physical therapist, occupational therapist, speech therapist, neuropsychologist, social worker, recreational therapist, rehabilitation counselor, rehabilitation nurse, and psychiatrist. The team often overlaps in its specific assessments and treatments. In addition to physical interventions, a major component of the rehabilitation process is cognitive rehabilitation. Head injury rehabilitation occurs in acute rehabilitation settings (inpatient), postacute (community reentry), and outpatient settings. In addition to the standard services, head injury rehabilitation often offers specialty services such as vocational rehabilitation, behavioral programs, and long-term and extended care opportunities.

Combined Rehabilitation

Combining substance abuse treatment and head injury rehabilitation is complex and difficult to manage. Before a combined intervention can result in a positive outcome, a comprehensive assessment must be completed. Kreutzer et al. (1990a) recommended specific assessment tools for understanding the degree of substance use and the detection of substance abuse. These include the General Health and History Questionnaire (Kreutzer et al., 1987), the Quantity-Frequency-Variability Index (Cahalan & Cisin, 1968a, 1968b), and the Brief Michigan Alcohol Screening Test (Zung, 1979). In addition to substance abuse assessment, full cognitive (including language and perception) evaluations, as well as a family functioning questionnaire (Bishop & Miller, 1988) and vocational assessments, are essential. These evaluations serve as pretreatment baselines, as well as guides for comprehensive treatment planning. Understanding the preinjury substance use pattern is helpful, since these patterns are often predictive of postinjury behaviors. For example, a patient who was a Saturday drinker is likely to continue to be a Saturday drinker, and before a Saturday home pass (from the rehabilitation setting) is given or an independent community reentry excursion is approved for a Saturday, relapse prevention techniques may need to be applied. Comprehensive language evaluations are important because substance abuse interventions take place through the use of language. Understanding the language strengths and weaknesses allows the treatment team to achieve maximum value regarding the transmission of important therapeutic information.

Upon completion of the formal assessment process, it is essential that the rehabilitation effort begin by integrating substance abuse and head injury interventions. Regardless of the substance abuse treatment methods (behavioral, insight, relationship, or others), the desired substance abuse outcome of long-term abstinence, independence, and overall good adjustment depends on the successful completion of a number of change factors: awareness, commitment, acceptance, achievement and growth, adjustment, and aftercare and independence. Acknowledgment of these change factors provides clinicians with a conceptual rationale for applying various models and methods of treatment. These change factors are necessary precursors for successful long-term outcome.

Awareness. In order for any treatment technique or method to have an impact, the patient must acknowledge that something needs to be changed or treated. In a sense, a lack of awareness is analogous to denial. The goal in the first part of treatment is to make it possible for the patient to be aware not only that substance use and abuse is very risky but also that there are ongoing situations that increase the probability of substance use. It is also necessary for the patient to understand the consequences of such behavior. These consequences are not always clear, and neither are the situations that stimulate substance use. Developing awareness of the triggers and consequences of substance abuse requires the patient to learn and remember this information and anticipate the occurrence of these triggers. Due to the concrete thinking often associated with head injury, the patient may not be able to develop a link between substance use and negative consequences. Utilization of group therapy for improving the patient's potential for gaining comprehensive awareness can be beneficial.

Commitment. Commitment is the process by which a patient utilizes awareness of the existence of a problem (or problems) and states the need for change. This need for change is supported by the development of goals. The TBI survivor must develop numerous goals, which are usually within the following realms: physical, cognitive, emotional, behavioral, social, and vocational. In addition, the TBI survivor who is also a substance abuser has the ongoing goal of abstinence. It is important that all rehabilitation staff and the patient's peers and family be fully aware of the patient's goals. When the patient's support system has knowledge of the patient's goals and the methods by which these goals will be achieved, they can inform the patient of any behaviors that are inconsistent with these objectives and also reinforce the consistent behaviors. The strength of the commitment to change is dependent on the patient's level of awareness of the situations that trigger drinking or other drug use and also the level of awareness of all potential consequences of alcohol use.

Acceptance. Awareness of the presence of a problem and commitment to change do not guarantee that the individual acknowledges the consequences of that change. Acceptance occurs when the patient acknowledges that the positive changes made in treatment will themselves have good consequences. In discussing substance abuse, the patients must be able to state that they realize they must be abstinent from alcohol or other drugs on a permanent basis.

Achievement and Growth. During the treatment process, it is imperative that the patient experience some success, which will validate the need to continue treatment. The stability of the treatment process and outcome is built on the patient's perception of its efficacy. Feedback from the treatment team and concrete evidence of achievement improve the probability that the patient will stay in treatment and that the treatment will be worthwhile. If those who work with the TBI survivor make frequent references to improvement in his or her cognitive functioning and other areas of rehabilitation, the chances of maintaining abstinence improve. Langley (1991) points out that the TBI survivor may have difficulty maintaining sobriety due to a sense of being overwhelmed by the consequences of TBI and impaired impulse control. These factors "may contrast sharply with the easy availability, reinforcement value and coping functions of alcohol" or other drugs (Langley, 1991, p. 2). Substance abuse treatment for the TBI survivor must focus on assisting the patient in developing behaviors and a life-style incompatible with use of substances. This development of appropriate behaviors as evidenced by treatment program accomplishments suggests that the patient is growing in the treatment process.

Adjustment. As the patient progresses through the rehabilitation process, there is a period of time in which the patient will gain momentum in a number of treatment areas. The patient is, in many cases, utilizing behaviors, coping strategies, and cognitive techniques that have seldom been used or recognized prior to the TBI. The adjustment period is a time when the patient is fully focused on the "technology" of treatment. Discharge plans begin to develop some focus, and the particulars of aftercare are investigated in relation to the patient's progress in the rehabilitation process.

Autonomy. During the change process, the patient must "try on" some of the new behaviors and strategies that have been practiced and learned during the treatment process. In residential, postacute TBI rehabilitation programs, this is the point when the patient is encouraged to plan community reentry excursions. These excursions are initially accomplished with a staff member, then with a peer, and finally alone. For the treatment team, this period of rehabilitation causes significant anxiety, and it is at this point that some patients will violate their commitment to and acceptance of abstinence. It is important to teach the patient mechanisms to respond to lapses that may occur in the community. A lapse is a drinking episode that occurs in response to some trigger, where the patient stops the drinking before becoming intoxicated and informs the treatment team or counselor of the episode. If a patient lapses during a community reentry excursion, it is important for the treatment team to reinforce the patient for stopping the lapse before intoxication and also reinforce the patient for informing a person who is in a position to help. It is also important for the treatment team to analyze the episode and determine the reason for the patient's inability to develop an alternative response to the trigger and assist the patient in developing a new approach to the situation.

Autonomy is an important change factor during the treatment process because the patient is increasing the frequency of experiences that are solely dependent on his or her ability to utilize coping skills and other TBI-related strategies to reintegrate into the community. The use of any substance severely compromises the patient's ability to reintegrate into the community, and in almost every case, when a TBI survivor fails, either at a vocational site or in the general reintegration into the community, it is often due to the use of substances (Burke et al., 1988).

Discharge and Aftercare. At the point of discharge from the combined TBI substance abuse treatment experience, planning begins for aftercare. Aftercare is essential for maintaining the momentum of treatment and securing a good long-term outcome. Utilization of the self-help system (e.g., AA or NA and also TBI support groups), as well as formal outpatient systems, is important. A significant part of aftercare is the degree to which the family or support system has been educated about their role in continuing to assist the TBI survivor in adjusting. Regarding substance abuse, the family or support system must understand the need for abstinence and what to do in the event abstinence is violated. There does appear to be a correlation between the integrity of the aftercare experience and successful long-term outcome. Many of the positive gains made during the rehabilitation process will be lost, and a significant regression will occur if the aftercare experiences are inappropriate or insufficient.

Methods of Treatment for Substance Abuse in the TBI Population

The change factors discussed are milestones that signify the effectiveness of the particular treatment methods. Referring a TBI survivor to a traditional substance abuse treatment program may prove to be ineffective because many of the head injury issues (e.g., cognitive deficits, behavior disorders, physical disabilities) are not understood or responded to by the staff. Educational methods of intervention are usually ineffective because the TBI survivor is likely to be experiencing deficits in attention and concentration, memory, and arousal that interfere with the recall of information necessary for decision making (Sanchez-Craig & Walker, 1982; Altman, Holahan, Baughman & Michels, 1989). Psychotherapeutic interventions, such as individual insight-oriented psychotherapy or group psychotherapy, are likely to fail due to deficits in areas such as concept formation.

Many traditional programs spend a great deal of time developing strategies to confront denial. It is possible that the denial witnessed may be "organic insightlessness" (Wood, 1987) or lack of awareness interfering with the recognition of the need for change. Direct confrontation of denial will typically be of little value and may be counterproductive. Langley (1991) suggests that instead of promoting decision making, direct confrontation of denial may increase anxiety and mental inflexibility. He suggests that "it is necessary to go beyond influencing the content of decisions to facilitating the process of decision making itself" (p. 8). The therapeutic focus must be to understand that the utilization of alcohol or other drugs by the patient is determined by a number of factors, including the reinforcement value of the substances used and the degree to which certain situations increase or decrease risk for use. As Langley (1991, p. 8) states, "Each high risk situation is a stimulus for decision making regarding alcohol use, and may confirm or disconfirm previous decisions." The level of awareness of situational triggers that stimulate drinking and of the consequences (cost versus benefit) of drinking are critical to good decision making.

The use of AA is frequently heavily integrated into traditional alcoholism treatment programs. Some criticism has been generated about the use of AA by TBI survivors (Langley et al., 1990) based on the cognitive demands associated with understanding and integrating the principles and concepts of this system. The use of AA can be very beneficial if it is integrated into the cognitive rehabilitation and community reintegration aspects of TBI rehabilitation. AA can be a great support network for the TBI survivor upon completion of rehabilitation. Gordon et al. (1988) have developed some cognitive rehabilitation techniques that utilize some AA slogans, quotations, and philosophy. With this system, the patient can be exposed to the psychosocial benefit of the AA experience through cognitive rehabilitation exercises. From a community reintegration point of view, it may be necessary for an individual with an understanding of cognitive functioning and TBI to accompany the patient to several AA meetings to coach the patient through the meetings, assess the specific adjunctive cognitive approaches that will be necessary for the AA experience to be beneficial, reduce anxiety, and improve the chance for success. A particular problem with introducing a TBI survivor to AA is that there is often little tolerance of some of the TBI-related behaviors by AA members, which makes it difficult for the survivor to secure a consistent and reliable sponsor. Great care must be taken in helping the TBI survivor to establish this relationship.

Unless a substance abuse treatment program can demonstrate the capability of addressing the many complex TBI rehabilitation issues and integrate them into the substance abuse treatment, it is unlikely that the treatment program will result in long-term success for this unique population.

Recently a number of TBI rehabilitation programs have developed substance abuse treatment approaches. These programs need to offer a multidisciplinary treatment approach that encompasses substance abuse counseling and a network of rehabilitation specialists. The rehabilitation specialists should develop an individualized treatment approach that constantly directs the patient toward sobriety, regardless of the discipline or type of therapy offered. In other words, all members of the treatment team (physical therapist, occupational therapist, speech therapist, recreational therapist, and others) need to understand their role in the treatment and prevention of substance abuse with all TBI patients. The speech therapist, for example, may be working on sentence sequencing as a cognitive rehabilitation intervention. It may be beneficial to utilize sentence sequencing exercises that relate specifically to the substance abuse issue rather than use exercises that are neutral.

Another example is the recreational therapist, one of the most important members of the treatment team because many TBI survivors have an altered reinforcement system. The head-injured patient often has been alienated by his or her social group, must live in a rehabilitation environment, cannot work, and faces other problems. The recreational therapist's goal is to teach the patients to recruit their own reinforcement and to develop confidence about seeking new and reinforcing experiences in life. As the frequency of reinforcers increases in a patient's life, the less likely he or she is to drink alcohol or use other drugs.

Residentially based postacute TBI rehabilitation is an excellent environment for the development of this type of integrated care. Usually these programs are community based and utilize interdisciplinary treatment teams. The rehabilitation is provided in a structured homelike environment, and treatment is functionally aimed toward the ultimate goal of community reintegration.

At the moment, only two models of combined substance abuse treatment and head injury rehabilitation have been published. These models can be classified as eclectic (Blackerby & Baumgarten, 1990) and behavioral (Langley et al., 1990; Langley, 1991). Neither model has presented significant outcome data based on a comparison of treatment approaches or models.

SUMMARY AND CONCLUSIONS

The relationship between substance use and abuse and head injury has been established. Substance abuse treatment programs, as well as head injury rehabilitation programs, have a strong need to cross-train in order to maximize the rehabilitation outcomes and increase the probability of good adjustments. Substance abuse programs must begin to understand the complexities of cognitive dysfunction and approaches to behavioral disorders. They need to develop a capability for addressing the rehabilitation needs of the TBI survivor since it is clear that a significant proportion of the patients seen are TBI survivors (Hillbom & Holm, 1986). TBI rehabilitation programs must offer substance abuse treatment. Intervention philosophies need to be developed, and the efficacy of specific models should be tested in clinical research. It is likely that such research will be forthcoming before the end of the 1990s and provide unique and efficacious approaches to this complex problem of combined substance abuse and traumatic brain injury.

REFERENCES

Altman, A. I., Holahan, J. M., Baughman, T. G. & Michels, S. (1989). Predictors of alcoholics' acquisition of treatment related knowledge. *Journal of Substance Abuse Treatment, 6,* 49–53.

Annegers, J. F., Grabow, J. D., Kurland, L. T. & Laws, Jr., E. R. (1980). The incidence, causes and secular trends of head trauma in Olmstead County, Minnesota, 1935–1974. *Neurology, 30,* 912–19.

Bishop, D. S. & Miller, I. W. (1988). Traumatic brain injury: Empirical family assessment techniques. *Journal of Head Trauma Rehabilitation, 3,* 16–30.

Blackerby, W. F. & Baumgarten, A. (1990). A model treatment program for the head-injured substance abuser: Preliminary findings. *Journal of Head Trauma Rehabilitation, 5,* 47–59.

Brooks, N., Symington, C., Beattie, A., Campsie, L., Bryden, J. & McKinlay, W. (1989). Alcohol and other predictors of cognitive recovery after severe head injury. *Brain Injury, 3,* 235–46.

Burke, W. H., Weselowski, M. D. & Guth, W. L. (1988). Comprehensive head injury rehabilitation: An outcome evaluation. *Brain Injury, 2,* 313–22.

Cahalan, D. & Cisin, I. (1968a). American drinking practices: Summary of findings from a national probability sample: I Extent of drinking by population subgroups. *Quarterly Journal of Studies on Alcohol, 29,* 130–51.

Cahalan, D. & Cisin I. (1968b). American drinking practices: Summary of findings from a national probability sample: II Measurement of massed versus spaced drinking. *Quarterly Journal of Studies on Alcohol, 29,* 130–51.

Edna, T. (1982). Alcohol influence and head injury. *Acta Chirurgica Scandinavaca 148,* 209–12.

Elmer, O., Gustafsson, L. C., Goransson, G. & Thomson, D. (1983). Acute alcohol intoxication and traumatic shock. An experimental study on circulating microaggregates and survival. *European Surgical Research, 15,* 268–75.

Elmer, O. & Lim, R. (1985). Influence of acute alcohol intoxication on the outcome of severe non-neurologic trauma. *Acta Chirurgica Scandinavica, 151,* 305–8.

Flamm, E., Dempoulos, H., Seigman, M., et al. (1977). Ethanol potentiation of central nervous system trauma. *Journal of Neurosurgery, 46,* 328–35.

Gordon, S. M., Kennedy, B. P. & McPeake, J. D. (1988). Neuropsychologically impaired alcoholics: Assessment, treatment considerations and rehabilitation. *Journal of Substance Abuse Treatment, 5,* 99–104.

Hillbom, M. & Holm, L. (1986). Contribution of traumatic head injury to neuropsychological deficits in alcoholics. *Journal of Neurology, Neurosurgery, and Psychiatry, 49,* 1348–53.

Kraus, J. F. & Nourjah, P. (1988). The epidemiology of mild, uncomplicated brain injury. *Journal of Trauma, 28,* 1637–43.

Kraus, J. F. & Nourjah, P. (1989). The epidemiology of mild head injury. In H. Levin, A. Benton & H. Eisenberg, *Mild head injury* (pp. 8–22). New York: Oxford University Press.

Kreutzer, J. S., Wehman, P., Harris, J., Burns, C. & Young, H. (1990a). *Crime and substance abuse patterns among persons with traumatic brain injury referred for supported employment.* Richmond, Va.: Rehabilitation Research and Training Center on Severe Traumatic Brain Injury, Medical College of Virginia.

Kreutzer, J. S., Doherty, K., Harris, J. & Zasler, N. (1990b). Alcohol use among persons with traumatic brain injury. *Journal of Head Trauma Rehabilitation, 5,* 9–20.

Kreutzer, J., Leininger, B., Doherty, K. & Waaland, P. (1987). *General Health and History Questionnaire.* Richmond, Va.: Rehabilitation Research and Training Center on Severe Traumatic Brain Injury, Medical College of Virginia.

Langley, M. (1991). *Preventing alcohol-related problems after traumatic brain injury: a behavioral approach.* Unpublished manuscript.

Langley, M., Lindsay, W. P., Lam, C. S. & Priddy, D. A. (1990). A comprehensive alcohol abuse treatment programme for persons with traumatic brain injury. *Brain Injury, 4,* 77–86.

Luna, M. K., Maier, R. V., Sowder, L., Copasse, M. K. & Oreskovich, M. R. (1984). The influence of ethanol intoxication on outcome of injured motorcyclists. *Journal of Trauma, 24,* 695–700.

Markwalder, T. (1981). Chronic subdural hematomas: A review. *Journal of Neurosurgery, 54,* 637–45.

Marlatt, G. & Gordon, J. (1985) *Relapse prevention: Maintenance strategies in the treatment of addictive behaviors.* New York: Guilford.

National Head Injury Foundation (1988). *Substance Abuse Task Force white paper.* Southborough, Mass.: NHIF.

Nestvold, K. Lundar, T., Blikra, G. & Lonnum, A. (1988). Head injuries during one year in a central hospital in Norway: A prospective study. Epidemiologic features. *Neuroepidemiology, 7,* 133–44.

Parkinson, D., Stephensen, S. & Phillips, S. (1985). Head injuries: A prospective, computerized study. *Canadian Journal of Surgery, 28,* 79–83.

Parsons, O. (1987). Do neuropsychological deficits predict alcoholics' treatment course and posttreatment recovery? In O. Parsons, N. Butters, & P. Nathan, (eds.), *Neuropsychology of alcoholism: Implications for diagnosis and treatment.* New York: Guilford.

Parsons, O., Butters, N. & Nathan, P. (eds.). (1987). *Neuropsychology of alcoholism: Implications for diagnosis and treatment.* New York: Guilford.

Steinbok, P. & Thompson, G. (1978). Metabolic disturbances after head injury: Abnormalities of sodium and water balance with special reference to the effects of alcohol intoxication. *Neurosurgery, 3,* 9–15.

Rimel, R. W., Geodani, B. G., Barth, J. T., Boll, T. J. & Jane, J. A. (1981). Disability caused by minor head injury. *Neurosurgery, 9,* 221–28.

Rimel, R. W., Geodani, B. G., Barth, J. T. & Jane, J. A. (1982). Moderate head injury: Completing the clinical spectrum of brain trauma. *Neurosurgery, 11,* 344–51.

Rohe, D. E. & DePompolo, R. W. (1985). Substance abuse policies in rehabilitation medicine departments. *Archives of Physical Medicine and Rehabilitation, 66,* 701–3.

Sanchez-Craig, M. & Walker, K. (1982). Teaching coping skills to alcoholics in a co-educational halfway house: 1. Assessment of programme effects. *British Journal of Addiction, 77,* 35–50.

Sparadeo, F. R. & Gill, D. (1988, August 12–16.). *Risks of alcohol use after head injury.* Presented at the American Psychological Association Symposium, Atlanta.

Sparadeo, F. R. & Gill, D. (1989). Effects of prior alcohol use on head injury recovery. *Journal of Head Trauma Rehabilitation, 4,* 75–82.

Sparadeo, F. R., Strauss, D. & Barth, J. T. (1990). The incidence, impact, and treatment of substance abuse in head trauma rehabilitation. *Journal of Head Trauma Rehabilitation, 5,* 1–8.

Vuchinich, R. E. & Tucker, J. A. (1988). Contributions from behavioral theories to choice to an analysis of alcohol abuse. *Journal of Abnormal Psychology, 97,* 181–95.

Ward, R. E., Flynn, T. C., Miller, P. W. & Blaisdell, W. F. (1982). Effects of ethanol ingestion in the severity and outcome of trauma. *American Journal of Surgery, 144,* 153–57.

Wood, R. (1987). *Brain injury rehabilitation: A neurobehavioral approach.* Rockville, Md.: Aspen Publishers.

Zung, G. (1979). Psychometric properties of the MAST and two briefer versions. *Quarterly Journal on Studies of Alcohol, 40,* 845–50.

13

Etiology and Treatment of Adult Children of Alcoholics

DOUGLAS H. RUBEN AND RHONDA SHEARED

Chemical dependency counselors and other human services workers recognize diversity in clinical groups they treat. Until recently groups such as elderly addicts and physically disabled addicts were routine client referrals receiving traditional interventions. Now these groups command specialized attention on primary and secondary intervention levels, combined with research undertakings for more individualized recovery goals. Research has shifted to another specialty group that gained high visibility in the late 1980s: adult children of alcoholics (ACOAs). ACOAs originally were not identified as a group of people having special characteristics except insofar as they might be at increased risk of developing alcoholism. Only recently, sharpened by numbers of child abuse cases and reports of family dysfunction, has there been an explosion of interest in the common risks, difficulties, needs, and problems of people reared in a family with a drinking or drug-using parent.

The nationwide conscious-raising movement among providers and ACOAs to explore and solve etiology and treatment issues rapidly abounds, generating more questions but fewer answers. As individuals begin to realize that their experiences of confusion, isolation, shame, deprivation, and danger are neither unique nor rare, they have begun to seek each other out, share experiences, attempt to heal themselves, demand recognition, and get it. The trouble, however, is the same fate affecting any other germinal consumer or professional movement propelled on emotion: frequently the emotional values interfere with empirical principles underlying the phenomenon. Principles get lost in the shuffle and must be hammered out before assessment and treatment can assume a scientific status.

That is the purpose of this chapter. Etiological factors explaining why ACOAs behave in certain ways are examined using a behavioral systems approach. Principles of conditioning and integrated field theory (Midgley & Morris, 1988) unravel confusing yet predictable patterns of personality. The second part of the chapter reviews clinically effective interventions for rapid behavioral change.

ETIOLOGY OF ACOA PATTERNS

One reason for a paucity of research on the ACOA phenomenon is disagreement among the actual behavioral parameters determining the dysfunction. Another reason is that when those afflicted enter adulthood, they assume their behaviors are relatively normal unless or until peers or members of society confront their personality defects. Once they are pointed out, similarities in emotions, behaviors, and thoughts among most ACOAs indicate there must be common denominators in childhood, particularly from effects of deprivation and punishment.

Behavioral Typology

Behavioral typology refers to specific characteristics repeatedly observed in clinical trials and from reported literature on emerging ACOA reactions. These typologies can be divided into functional characteristics, survival characteristics, superstitious characteristics, and ecological characteristics.

Functional Characteristics

Functional characteristics of behavior produced from parental punishment and deprivation start in childhood and evolve unchanged to adulthood as long as that child remains exposed to the same or similar circumstances. Alcoholic circumstances while growing up, for example, may persist while dating or married to alcoholics or engaging in alcohol oneself. In childhood, side effects of punishment include a number of predictable patterns, explained behaviorally.

First, the child learns to react to punishment for attention. Attention-seeking responses are instantly fueled by negative or aggressive parental discipline. The child learns yelling, anger, interrupting, and tantrums or noncompliance as his only response to obtain gratification, even if the consequences are aversive.

Second, the child learns to pair or associate the properties of punishment with the person administering the punishment. Repeated anger, aggression, or negativity by parents turns the parent himself into an aversive event. Properties defining the parent, such as tone of voice, physical stature, odor, and facial features, acquire threatening messages that the child avoids.

Third, the child learns to stay away from (avoid) anticipated or actual punishment. Repeated exposure to aversive situations oversensitizes a child to obvious and subtle stimuli surrounding the parent or punishing situation. Hearing a drunken parent return home late at night might cue the child to hide in his room or remain silent; hearing that parent return home at any time, drunken or not, may cue the same response.

Fourth, the child inhibits appropriate behaviors in anticipation of punishment. Anticipation of aversive situations interrupts appropriate and inappropriate behaviors. Not only does the frightened child hide underneath his bed during a loud marital argument, but the avoidance prevents him from also saying goodnight to his parents, brushing his teeth or going to the bathroom, and changing clothing. That is, appropriate behaviors that never were punished but are collateral or sequential to punished (avoidance) behaviors now undergo inhibition. Unless corrected, inhibitions develop into routines where that child simply omits normal bedtime behaviors, even into adulthood.

Fifth, the child learns inappropriate behavior in anticipation of punishment. Suppression of some inappropriate behavior from punishment does not prevent the spontaneous learning of other, more discrete inappropriate behaviors. Inappropriate behaviors ''spontaneously'' arise for two reasons: to replace necessary appropriate behaviors that are inhibited and to replace inappropriate behaviors receiving punishment. A spanked child aggressively told to stay in his bedroom at night and fears asking to use the bathroom may urinate in his bed (enuresis) out of biological necessity, sneak into the bathroom in late evening or early morning hours, forcing himself to awake at odd hours (insomnia), or void the following day on household objects or outside on the shrubbery. A second example deals with eating food. A child severely hit or verbally assaulted at mealtime (regardless of why punishment happened) may avoid meals altogether, sneak food into his bedroom and leave it under his bed or in secret places, or eat wrong or inedible substances (pica) out of biological necessity.

Sixth, the child never learns behaviors appropriate for his peer group. Social or interpersonal behaviors suppressed at home prevent learning basic peer skills. Children punished for speaking or freely playing never learn to express feelings, share objects, trust people, make mistakes, ask questions, explore their curiosity and imagination, and dismiss criticism.

Seventh, the child learns sensitivity to and generalization of avoidance and escape in punishment situations. Avoidance and escape responses learned at home instantly transfer to other situations where there is no need for avoidance and escape. Abused children refrain from talking, risking changes, and playing with friends at school. Confronted by these deficits, they may cry, act out, or aggressively attempt to escape the confrontation.

Finally, the child learns inappropriate reactions that interfere not only with normal behaviors but also the opportunities for normal learning. Afflicted children suffer two repercussions from constant suppression. One is development of spontaneous alternative behaviors, many of which are inappropriate but subtle. A second repercussion occurs when inappropriate behaviors delay, interrupt, or entirely prevent access to learning opportunities for socially appropriate behaviors. For example, aggressively acting, attention-seeking children tested for special education and who spend the majority of school in a resource or contained classroom miss precious interactions with peer groups. Mainstreaming into regular classrooms restores some opportunities, but by then prerequisites for proper peer dialogue and play are way below standards.

Adult manifestations of childhood trauma gain unfortunate momentum because of naturally developed cognitions, behavioral and emotional faculties, and the complexity of interpersonal social experience that form conceptions of oneself and the world. When early dysfunctions persist into adulthood, the enigma of suffering intensifies and causes unusual excesses and deficits.

First, personality is one of two major types: passive or aggressive. Dichotomy of behavior is predictable. ACOAs raised under a random, untrusting, and frequently punitive environment adapt by responding in one of two major ways. First, rebellion toward that environment appears in the form of challenging the abusing adults. Expressed anger is outwardly aggressive, violent, or oppositional in terms of severe tantrums, noncompliance, running away, lying, stealing, and hyperactivity. In adolescence, when verbal skills are complex, refusals and defiance intensify as the child completely distrusts his parents and assumes total control over personal goals and gratification. Into adulthood, this controlling behavior appears manipulating, domineering, and attractive to inept or deficient partners desperate for caretaking partners. Aggression subsides a bit, but the person maintains low tolerance to frustration and is easily upset by disruptions in rigidly planned schedules or decisions. Hostility shown over disruptions, however, is not to evoke conflict; conflict remains avoided at all costs.

The other extreme is more gentle, docile, and passively withdrawn from social decisions, confrontations, and ambitions. In childhood this person withdrew from familial antagonism or turned into a mediator, trying to arbitrate peace among hostile parties. Placating aggressive urges of adult parents denied the child his own personal pleasures and opportunities for peer growth and instilled fear over being autonomous outside the household. Kept within family boundaries, the frightened child developed hypersensitivity to receiving parental approval through personal sacrifice. Approval becomes identified as the only source of love, affirmation, and proof of the child's worthiness. Seeking approval by pleasing, caretaking, or assuming unwanted responsibility averted conflict.

The irony in both personality patterns is that conflict is absolutely anathema. Conflict threatens the fragile balance of confidence and self-hatred that already is shaken by frequent doubts and distrust among adults. Feared most from adults is criticism for any reason. Aggressively controlling ACOAs anticipate or dismantle conflict by injecting needles of verbal pain against their alleged predators. Rude remarks, hostile provocations, using predators as the brunt of jokes, and even egging on the predator until he or she explodes all function to delay or prevent confrontation. Passively controlling ACOAs seek the same goal exactly, and thus their behaviors operationally are identical: to defuse rising hostility. However, efforts at defusal involve satisfying the legitimate or illegitimate needs of predators in anticipation of conflict. They may surrender unwillingly to peculiar wants and needs imposed on them by predators, hoping the outcome will instantly restore peace. How long this peace lasts is irrelevant.

Second, ACOAs have trouble expressing feelings. Adults suppress their feelings internally and refuse to share anything personal. Expression would risk exposure of faults, looking incompetent, being disapproved of, or causing anger in others. Consequently speech is very selective, labored, and edited, and expressed words are replayed in thought over and over to test whether they upset the listener.

Third, ACOAs cannot seem to relax. Adults appear highly active, constantly busy, and unable to slow down their pace for fear of feeling unproductive, wasteful, and lazy. Even sitting is accompanied by fidgeting, working on projects, and racing thoughts. Slow, calming, or vegetative actions evoke sudden panic and shame. Panic is from the expectation of punishment coming from an authority or significant other (boyfriend, girlfriend, spouse), even if the person lives alone. Feelings of impending criticism overwhelm the person and mobilize him into immediate action to relieve the anxiety. Reactions of guilt or shame arise from wanting to relax but believing it is awful and immoral. Anticipatory fears evolved from never having opportunities to relax or play by oneself, if compelled to be responsible for other siblings or constantly helping other people.

Fourth, ACOAs are loyal (codependent) beyond reason. Adults become dependent personalities who are terrified of abandonment and would do anything to hold onto a relationship and not reexperience the painful separation felt from living with people who never were emotionally there for them. Loyalty also means self-appointed commitment to any cause, group, or friendships no matter how problematic or dysfunctional the situation becomes. The adult must stay aboard that *Titanic* even if every one else abandons ship. This martyrdom affirms beliefs that the adult is incomparably superior in loyalty and well deserves the praise and approval of her recipients.

Fifth ACOAs are overly responsible. A corollary to "loyal beyond reason" is taking on far more than the adult can chew. Adults have an overdeveloped sense of responsibility, focusing entirely on the welfare of another person rather than on themselves. Shifts from selfishness prevent drawing too much attention to their faults (or assets) and disapproval for being conceited. Helping others, also called caretaking or enabling, involves total consumption with organizing, solving, or directing the lives of other people to guarantee their unconditional approval and ongoing friendship. Forfeiture of personal needs varies from small sacrifices to complete self-neglect, frequently disintegrating down to living or dying depending on whether it pleases another person. Targets for enablers are generally weak people suffering some emotional or physical disability or who are underdeveloped socially. It becomes a natural challenge for enablers to commit to the rehabilitation of that person, not for the victory but for assurance of their approval.

Sixth, ACOAs fear losing control. Loss of control translates to panic over looking vulnerable. Vulnerability poses serious threats to inadequacies kept private and below the surface. Lack of leadership or denied opportunities to direct, coordinate, or organize people or things instills a fear of abandonment. That other people do not need this adult or regard his services as unimportant implies the person is incapable and incompetent and has shortcomings. Inferring this rejection, adults believe they failed certain expectations and may immediately rebound with double the amount of energy and commitment, aspiring to please the person at all costs.

Seventh, ACOAs have difficulty with relationships. Adults have two types of relationship failures: with social interactions and with interpersonal and intimate perusals. Building social peer groups is difficult because the composition of people must be passive, weak, or amenable to the adult's peculiar idiosyncrasies. For ACOAs who are shy, overprecautious, and passive, groups must already identify an assertive leader who commands authority and compliance from members. For ACOAs who are aggressive, perfectionistic, and workaholics, groups must be passively receptive to the rigid guidance and offer a surplus of laudable remarks. In intimacy, forming a cohesive relationship requires attraction to either extreme in a single person. The *failure* exists from discovering that opposite attractions turn sour very quickly or after a series of conflicts.

Eighth, ACOAs have fear of conflict. Aggressive or passive ACOAs are equally afraid of conflict. Conflict, which refers to any disagreement, criticism, or opinion lodged against the adult for inappropriate behavior, resembles situations of inescapable and unavoidable parental punishment, causing shame, self-criticism, and desperate need for approval. Hatred of conflict becomes so fierce that adults literally say or do anything to avert confrontation even if escaping it will ultimately pay the price of another confrontation.

Ninth, ACOAs are overly self-critical. Self-insultation develops from replaying what ACOA therapists call "mental tapes": essentially obsessive thoughts in the form of religious, moral, or powerfully persuasive beliefs on how behavior "should be, ought to be, and must be." Such "musterbations" (Ellis & Whiteley, 1979) take two forms. One form is constant negative assaults on imperfections or mistakes believed to be preventable or controllable, using the same words, phrases, or intonations recalled from the adult's parents when they were verbally assaultive years ago. Replays of parental verbal abuse shift from the object-mistake in question to generalized attacks regarding the adult's integrity ("You're so stupid") or unrealistic perception of life ("Who do you think you are anyway? You won't amount to anything"). A second form are internal recitations of anger toward another person for causing this grief of making mistakes or looking stupid. Projected hatred toward another person (usually an innocent bystander or good friend) disguises the adult's own unconfronted faults and protects the adult from feeling vulnerable.

Tenth, ACOAs become addicted to excitement, alcoholics, abusers, or compulsive people. ACOAs usually become alcoholic, marry an alcoholic, or both, or find another compulsive personality, such as a workaholic or overeater, to fulfill their own compulsive needs. Attraction to excitement largely occurs for the passive adult dissatisfied with the monotony of boring daily routines and desperate for escapism. But he or she is incapable of achieving this objective without coercion or caretaking for an energetic person. More aggressive ACOAs at first resist excitable, impulsive people and are more inclined to gravitate toward reserved, docile, or emotionally disabled persons who repress their abuses until the relationship (in friendship or intimacy) develops fully. ACOAs who are extroverts or introverts do, however, share a reason for addiction to excitement. Whether their parents were drug or alcoholic abusers or nonsubstance abusers, the verbal and physical abuse nonetheless stifled natural childhood impulsivity, playfulness, and creativity. Living this fun in adulthood becomes possible around profoundly impulsive adults.

Survival Characteristics

Black's theory (1984) on family survival echoes a number of works on family alcoholism (e.g., Ackerman, 1983, 1986, 1987a, 1987b; Gravitz & Bowden, 1985; Hayes, 1989; Steinglass, Bennett, Wolin & Reiss, 1987; Towers, 1989; Wegscheider, 1981). Essentially the theory holds that afflicted children must play certain roles around other family members to restore imbalance in the system. Roles usually take three or four forms, with there always being a leader, a follower, a placater, and a rebel. All family members struggle together in disharmony trying to compensate for loss of parental direction. With no direction, that is, no adult structure or control, children are helpless to develop on their own or by teachings of an elder sibling rules about right and wrong.

Survival means development. For development to occur, somebody must steer the course for the trajectory by providing opportunities. This is where the leader or responsible one fits in. He or she dictates family structure, sets the pace, and synchronizes action, allowing others a blueprint for personal growth. Applying this blueprint is the job of adjusters or followers. However, no matter how docile followers are, still there is turbulence felt among addicted, irresponsible parents and the rebel. This child essentially models the parent's detached, uncaring behavior and is unwilling to abide by the leader's orders. Rebellion frustrates the leader and threatens what little family stability exists, until the fire is put out by the placater. He or she has one function: to defuse altercations before they ruin the family and infuriate the parents. Placaters also mediate arguments between rebel and parents, aspiring to appease both parties in order to attain peace. Reaching peace, however, means the placater must sacrifice personal needs.

Support for this theory is empirical but subjective. Experience alone serves a major index proving that "these things really happen." Personal traumatic accounts of family life (Black, 1984; Brennen, 1986; Burnett, 1986; Wegscheider, 1979a, 1979b, 1980) trace step by step the foundations of each role player and reasons for retention of the role from early childhood through adolescence and into adulthood. Undisputed truths emerge from the lay understanding that parental abuse and family ambiguity breed a Darwinian impulse for survival. But this is not why the research community to date has been impotent on testing these roles. Most writers on survival theory are not scientists by training or at least lack a methodological background or instinct for designing a controlled experimental study, so very little research exists on the topic.

The results are unfortunate. Survival theory suffers from obscure definitions, subjective bias, and confusion over the developmental trajectory of each role. The "undisputed truths" are hearsay and seem replicable only because those authors recounting their roles are adults when they write the analysis. They begin with a predisposing model or orientation that may contaminate actual details of their childhood experiences. Retrospectively, they can only infer characterization of these roles, whereas prospectively, as adults reflecting on their own current behavior, the analysis is more believable. On purely scientific grounds, then, survival theory desperately needs attention.

In relation to ecobehaviorism, survival theory implies a gain-loss ratio. Risks dominate the parent-child interaction so heavily that usually one of two extremes takes place: either little expenditure of energy is put into the family or extraordinary expenditures of energy are displayed. In both cases, though, the net return is small, inconsistent, and never reciprocal. An ecobehavioral approach puts the child's cumulative losses in excellent perspective. It better explains why apathy, depression, and oppositional behavior directly worsen as the goods and services vanish and expectations for personal (the child's) gain are low to nonexistent.

Superstitious Characteristics

At times ACOAs display erratic or idiosyncratic behaviors discretely connected to ongoing situations. Sensitivity to the suppressive or potentially suppressive environment triggers them to act in stereotyped or routine ways that can be explained behaviorally as superstitious behavior. Within the tradition of experimental analysis of behavior, Skinner (1948) first showed patterns of stereotyped responding by food-deprived pigeons given grain on fixed-time schedules of reinforcement. Pigeons developed behaviors not intended for the reinforcer that accidentally recurred every time that reinforcer was available. Skinner characterized the acquisition of this responding as a "sort of superstition," because responding followed a ritual and by accident received strength from the reinforcer (Ferster & Skinner, 1957).

Superstitious behaviors have been found in humans for the same reasons (Ferster, Culberston & Boren, 1975; Hollis, 1973; Skinner, 1977). Of particular importance were pathological obsessions, compulsions, and phobias (Herrnstein, 1966; Zeiler, 1972). For adults, superstitious or ritualistic behaviors spontaneously emerged for three reasons: (1) Behaviors are accidentally paired with target behaviors for reinforcement. For instance, while waiting for a cab, if adults smoke two cigarettes, pace up and back, and sing to themselves and the cab arrives sooner than usual, the exact same sequence or ritual of behavior occurs the next time a cab is called. (2) Behaviors immediately follow reinforcement ("adjunctive behaviors"). The person waits for the cab, for example, without peculiar actions. Moments after the cab arrives early and he enters the cab, dialogue immediately starts with the cab driver where previously no dialogue occurred. (3) Avoidance and escape behavior forms the third reason. Superstitious rituals strengthen with the delay or removal of aversive events. If it is avoidance, for instance, the person stays inside a building, out of the rain, while waiting for the cab. Habits that form are always waiting inside a building and never on the curb. If it is escape, the cab driver's loud or nasty voice may scare the person back into the building or away from the cab. Escape from confrontation becomes a conditioned ritual.

Ultimately the learning of compulsive, ritualistic, or avoidance and escape behaviors arises from mistaken or adventitious conditioning occurring during childhood. Substance-abusing parents who angrily shock children into submission and develop generalized fears in them are also accidentally teaching repetitive, stereotyped actions that the children believe will avert future punishment. In this case, behaviors never occur for specific reinforcers. Behaviors are not learned for a specific reward or reinforcer because there are few or no reinforcers available; if available, they are random, arbitrary, and unpredictable; reinforcers always pair with punishers; and reinforcers never are trusted as being reinforcers. That is, after an aggressively violent mother cools down and offers her child ice cream for smiling and being happy, the ice cream is not causing smiles and happiness. A very frightened child shows smiles and happiness to avoid mother's anticipated outbursts. Nothing about the ice cream is rewarding.

Ecological Characteristics

Within the ecosystems model, certain propositions explain the extent of family adaptability and cohesion depending on the openness or closeness of boundaries (Kantor & Lehr, 1975). A boundary is defined as regions between systems and separating one system from another one in physical, material, or symbolic form. Open boundaries (systems) allow for interaction and transaction with other systems. Closed boundaries restrict or prevent interaction with other systems. Boundaries also may be random (arbitrarily closed and open). Given these variations, note the following six propositions on family ecosystems:

1. The adaptability, and hence viability, of a family system is related positively to the amount of variety in the system.

2. Undue energy demands on a family result in a lessened ability for adaptive, creative behavior and can result in stress on the family system.

3. The rigidity of the boundaries around a family system will influence their capacity to adapt to stressful situations.

4. The ambiguity of the boundaries around a family system will influence their adaptability.

5. The family members who control the information coming into the family and who
   control the family memory have greater ability to control the behavior of other family
   members.

6. Family systems that are moderately cohesive but allow for individual autonomy are
   more able to adapt to change and stress than those in which family members are
   very tightly bound to each other or those in which there is little cohesion and everyone goes his or her own way.

Propositions 2 through 5 are particularly germane for alcoholic families.
Boundary regulations limit children from autonomously expressing opinion and
from having transactions outside proximal boundaries. For instance, suspecting
parents may question children on what other adults said to them on opinions
about the parents and will presume the children are lying. Alcoholic families
limit boundaries by limiting resources. When resources communicated to children are ambiguous, the children never properly develop or satisfy basic needs
likely met in nondysfunctional families. Two types of regulated resources are
proximity (location, distance, frequency) of interaction and type or exchange
of interaction. Exchange pertains to parenting styles or discipline used on the
children.

In ecological terms, proximity affects the use of negative discipline. Proximity or the "positioning" of parents depends on household structure, access
routes (dimensions) through different rooms or hallways, and natural boundaries around certain rooms considered private or special to children, such as
their bedroom or bathroom. Proximity also includes frequency of parent-child
contact based on the children's learning or not learning to approach their parents during the day.

The second variable is method of exchange or use of discipline. Exchange
of resources usually means parents grant money, gifts, or special accolades to
children for many reasons. Noneconomic resources such as love and caring also
may be transferred. In both cases, the exchange is unconditional or noncontingent; the child owes nothing in return for the gift. In alcoholic families, the
exchange not only is contingent, but noneconomic resources such as love and
caring are a rarity. Affection and love, if given, is for a stiff price of compliance to rigid, unrealistic expectations. Such high expectations, however, are
rarely reached, and instead children receive punishment.

On a systems level, punishment disrupts this exchange system. Denial of
support, affection, and noneconomic resources distances children from parents,
siblings, and the human behavioral environment outside the family. Punishment
also closes boundaries around a child's potential, forcing fear to be unavoidable
and inescapable. While parents believe this maintains family control, in effect
the control invalidates the child's self-purpose, stifles his learning opportuni-

ties, and largely instills hostility in him toward the parents. Anger that reaches a certain peak takes the form of acting-out behavior.

Family discordance thus intensifies when proximity and noneconomic exchanges of resources are infrequent. In alcoholic families, systems theory elucidates the steps of this gradual deterioration by viewing each member in relation to each other. As barriers to adaptation rise, psychosocial development within a family crumbles and is replaced by diffused, non-goal-directed perceptions of the world. A system torn by this chaos loses its core values among the children; the parents lose interest in saving the system consumed by their own insecurities. And the inevitable decay sets the stage for children to repeat these defective patterns intergenerationally in their own family life cycles.

Several dysfunctional relationships may exist between drinking parents and the emotional or acting out behaviors of their offspring. First let us consider some initial hypotheses:

Hypothesis 1: Among alcoholic parents, there is a direct relationship between parental discipline and frequency of child acting-out behaviors.

Hypothesis 2: Among alcoholic parents, there is an inverse relationship between parental contact and child acting-out behaviors.

Hypothesis 3: Among alcoholic parents, there is a direct relationship between parents' drinking and child acting-out behaviors.

The first and third hypotheses propose similar interactions. Hypothesis 1 proposes that as parental punitive discipline intensifies, so will acting-out reactions among children. Hypothesis 3 proposes that increases (or decreases) in parental alcoholic consumption can increase (or decrease) child acting-out behaviors. Both hypotheses thus share common properties. Both statements are irreversible because acting-out behavior alone may or may not cause harsh disciplinary action or increased intake of alcohol. Both statements do have a deterministic and causal value. Punishment contingencies, shown experimentally, can induce attention-seeking or aggressive responses in children. Intoxicated parents are more prone to be punishing.

Another feature about the hypotheses is that events are sequential. Maladaptive behaviors follow from the parents' persistent discipline and drinking episodes. However, maladaptive behavior is not a linear outcome; one event does not necessarily cause the other event. The contingent relationship can be with a multilinear or infinite number of variables ranging from a disturbed, alcoholic parent to dilapidated living conditions. Finally, the relationship is positive insofar as increases (decreases) in one variable proportionally affect increases (decreases) in the other variable.

The second hypothesis is a bit different. Increases in parental contact in the form of proximity and frequency of interaction may decrease child misbehavior. But decreases in parental contact invite attention-seeking actions. Alcoholic parents are typically aloof from mainstream family needs and usually respond only when levels of misbehavior exceed a tolerance point. This tolerance point being low, negative traps catch parent and child arguing during what few contacts they have together. However, when proximity increases, as in physical or verbal affection, attention is provided for appropriate attention-seeking behaviors.

In view of this potential, the statement is different from hypotheses 1 and 3. There is a reversible relationship. Reduced acting-out tendencies can just as easily produce an increase in proximity and frequency of parental contact. Second, while still deterministic and sequential, types of interaction depend on the duration of the parents' sobriety, the child's risk-taking potentials, and the number of reinforcing family transactions without punishment.

Avoidance and Escape Patterns

Thus far, the words *avoidance* and *escape* keep recurring. Traditional learning theorists (Dollard & Miller, 1950; Mowrer, 1950; Solomon & Wynne, 1954), as well as their applied counterparts (Eysenck, 1979; Stampfl & Levis, 1967; Wolpe, 1958) have proposed that psychological symptoms can be conceptualized as avoidance behaviors designed to escape from aversive conditioned stimuli. Human laboratory experiments attesting to this phenomenon (Banks, 1965; Malloy & Levis, 1988; Maxwell, Miller & Meyer, 1971) repeatedly show that persistence of avoidance and escape patterns even in the absence of danger relates to a history of conditioning and intermittent contact with fearful stimuli. Operationally, avoidance and escape refer to response-producing changes that terminate that aversive event. Termination takes several forms. Responses may delay the impending aversive event, alter the impending aversive event before it arrives, eliminate the impending aversive event before it arrives, interrupt the aversive event while it occurs, alter the aversive event while it occurs, or eliminate the aversive event while it occurs.

Forms of defusing, diminishing, and eliminating the impact of aversive events in ACOAs vary along these six lines. This is the predictable function of behavior. Less predictable and more infinitely diverse is the response topography, that is, what the behavior actually looks like. Here we attempt to identify major avoidance and escape response patterns clinically reported in several case studies, including over 1,000 patients seen in the first author's practice. Examined closely, avoidance and escape patterns account for a large percentage of idiosyncratic or repetitive habits deeply ingrained in ACOAs.

Enabling/Caretaking

Already mentioned is the passively–seeking ambition to regulate balance in adult relationships. Adults afraid of conflict and of risking behavioral changes causing disapproval will resort to a style of accommodation. Compromising personal needs occurs so frequently and habitually that no longer is the forfeited need or object considered a loss. Sacrifices become a natural, familiar motion in daily interaction, much like breathing, eating, and sleeping. Without realizing it, enablers and caretakers operate entirely on negative reinforcement. Pleasing, satisfying, or absorbing grief for people delays, alters, and destroys impending aversive events. Consequently, enablers repeat the same behavior in the future. Reinforcement for enabling includes: amount of time elapsed before another conflict (the longer, the better), the mild or diminished intensity of arguments when they occur, the shorter duration of arguments, and the recuperative capacity of the arguer. This last one poses an interesting option. ACOAs unable to avoid or escape aversive conflict may appease the predator, hoping he will rapidly restore calmness after the argument.

Because contact with aversive events is awful, false alarms are common mistakes and acted upon in the same way. False alarms are believing there is a potential argument and intercepting it beforehand. Avoidance this far ahead creates the false inference that had steps not been taken, aversive conflict might appear. Ensuing conflicts may or may not occur, but advanced steps nonetheless speed into motion long before risk of conflict. Predators on the receiving end of this intervention are neither perplexed nor willing to reverse the caretaking tactics. A fearful husband, for example, anticipating his wife's critical words over a recent office purchase, lavished his wife with bouquets and "I love you" cards and took her out to dinner. All efforts were designed to avoid his wife's cynical remarks long before she learned of the purchases. This may be called *anticipatory caretaking*. Planning ahead seems safe, but it is no guarantee of conflict elimination. In fact, his wife may fully thrive on the voluminous reinforcers and may expect complimentary treatment repeated, regardless of her intentions of conflict.

Anticipatory caretaking usually is a methodical, systematic, and incredibly calibrated effort. ACOAs evaluate potentials for aversive contacts and immediately disinfect them in much the same way as ecologists check the atmosphere or waters for pollutants and proceed with chemical treatment. Every step built into the sequence of avoidance has a history of effectively altering one, many, or all components leading to confrontation. Synchronicity is imperative. A wife expecting her drunken husband to be physically abusive may, ahead of time, rearrange the furniture, call a friend (witness) over, evacuate the children. to their bedrooms or out of the house, and prepare a meal of his liking. These tasks all have specific *functional* reasons and must occur in this *precise* order. Calculated risks minimize mistakes in the overall scheme of avoidance.

Aggression

Anger has a twofold cause. First, anger responds to the ACOA's loss of control and resistance to vulnerability. Second, anticipating conflict, anger signals the predators to stay away (avoidance) or terminate conflict (escape). One way or another, anger rarely, if ever, is disclosure of emotional frustrations as might occur in most people claiming to be angry. Non-ACOAs accept vulnerability as the natural outgrowth of making errors or looking incompetent. ACOAs, on the other hand, carefully repress anger evoked from vulnerability and release it only as a mechanism to expedite conflict elimination. Threats of physical violence, profuse vulgarity, hostile demands, and abrasive criticism on the surface look like an aggressive assault. They lure the listener into fierce battle. But just the opposite is occurring. Insulting attacks intend to disable the listener from responding in any way.

One result is *anticipatory aggression*. Less calculated and more reflexive are aggressive assaults made in anticipation of conflict. Like *anticipatory caretaking*, inadequate proof exists that there will be a conflict. Waiting for the "alleged" conflict is intolerable. Poor control over emotions sets off a series of physiological, cognitive, and behavioral responses sequentially occurring in this order: (1) autonomic arousal (rapid heart beat, tightness of chest, perspiration, shallow breathing), (2) negative, paranoidlike statements ("Who does he think he is?" "Nobody will blame me for anything"), and (3) outward aggressive actions (yelling, hitting objects, stamping around).

Arousal is rapid and progressive and lacks the self-conscious evaluation of actions to consequences. In the end, hostile actions produce one of three outcomes upon listeners: listeners never approach the aggressor out of shock and perplexity; during the conflict, listeners stop the argument instantly, offended and perplexed by the rude interjections; or annoyed listeners who pursue the conflict in spite of obstacles accelerate aggressiveness in both parties until the ACOA resorts to physical property destruction, injury toward another, or threats of self-injury. One way or another, escape from rising confrontation will be achieved in a short time. Rarely, if ever, will the ACOA ride the storm out until the bitter end no matter who is right and who is wrong. Right and wrong are irrelevant.

Anxiety and Panic Disorder

Negative reinforcement occurs in still a third way. When conflict threatens on the horizon, panic and anxiety may set in. Relief of anxiety, by avoiding and escaping conflict, reinforces the ACOA to reexperience the anxiety or panic in future similar situations. Panic, as in *panic attacks*, builds from unregulated excitement of the sympathetic nervous system under fear situations. Rushes of dizziness, loss of breath or rapid breathing, weakness in limbs, tachycardia, and ear and eye sensitivity comprise symptomatology that triggers an urgent need for escape. Failure to leave the situation prolongs the physical misery and turns into thoughts about fainting, being disabled, and the dread of embarrassment. ACOAs expecting conflict, criticism, or rejection can react the same way. Rather than face emotional hurt, panic attacks rise moments before or just as conflict starts and shift the predator's actions from possible attack to sympathy and empathy. Panic attacks that are announced receive urgent attention from even a slightly caring spouse; sensitivity to the person's health displaces aggressive actions and restores safety to the ACOA's environment.

Variations of Patterns

Acting on avoidance and escape has more personas than simply the three types reviewed thus far. Response types also are never so uniformly black and white. Overlap among response patterns can be confusing, irritating, and misleading. Misinterpretation of these avoidance and escape patterns also accounts for incorrect diagnoses by physicians, psychologists, social workers, and other health care providers faced with strange symptoms that have ambiguous or no certain underlying pathology. Response patterns might include the following:

No communication. The person withdraws and remains mutistic under any impending threat of conflict. Attempts to penetrate this silence are met with poor eye contact, crying, or additional efforts to seek safety in a hidden spot.

Runaway. The person takes refuge by physically running away to another location—a parent's house, a friend's house, or a bar, or by driving long distances in unspecified directions.

Substance abuse. The person drinks beer or mixed drinks or smokes a joint or uses other substances in anticipation of conflict, rejection, or criticism or while it is in progress. *Contingent use of substance abuse* usually means the person engages in substances only under emotional duress or when feeling that conflict is unavoidable or inescapable.

Emotional paralysis. Studies on learned helplessness (Seligman & Johnston, 1973) and tonic immobility (Ratner, 1967; Ratner & Thompson, 1960) have application here. Panic and fright operate simultaneously upon the confronted person, who feels totally helpless under inescapable or unavoidable circumstances. Lacking adaptive alternatives, the person's only repertoire is emotional paralysis—catatonically remaining in the situation without realistic orientation or thoughts. Numbness overwhelms sensory receptors and inhibits all activating responses to combat or diminish a sense of impending doom.

Selective attention. This is the opposite of emotional paralysis. Discriminative abilities became sharper under threats of conflict, criticism, or rejection. Astute perceptions in thought, sensation, and observation alert the person to subtle behavioral changes in the predator that appear modifiable and promise avoidance and escape possibilities. Awareness—for instance, that her spouse forgot to call home ahead of his arrival—*means* he must have stopped at the bar. Inferring this, she can alter the environment ahead of his return and demobilize confrontation. Heightened sensory discriminations (visual, auditory, olfactory) further detect and clarify competing stimuli in predators such as sorting an alcohol odor from after-shave lotion. Hypersensitivity even accounts for "premonitions" of hearing noises or the spouse's saying or doing things even before his arrival.

Passivity. Passivity functions like aggression to expedite unwanted predatory attacks. Persons who electively withhold comments wait for the aggression, criticism, or rejection to finish; then they resurrect pleasant topics or move the discussion rapidly to safe territory. Shifting topics begins by asking about topics interesting or rewarding to the predator and on which he can deliver a monologue without relapsing to arguments.

Accusation. Accusing the predator ahead of conflict of inappropriate behavior either starts the conflict or defeats it. Accusations primarily arise for two reasons. First, anxious and annoyed, ACOAs may have improperly inferred information from the predator or environment. Inferences motivate the person to blame alleged predators for violations that the person finds reprehensible, although little support exists for these accusations. Second, accusations may emotionally injure or intimidate the alleged predator and thereby disable retaliation or further confrontation. Listeners stunned by this attack are equally dumbfounded when they bite the bait and politely inquire about proof for the accusation. ACOAs retort with vehemently abrasive jabs that entirely ignore peaceful problem-solving efforts and serve only to fortify resistance. Even reconciliatory efforts from listeners go unnoticed since the ACOA is engulfed in antagonism and proving his point just as he did as an aggressive child.

Feign ignorance. Passivity and emotional paralysis serve to withdraw from perceived conflict. Another avoidance tactic is pretending one simply is ignorant of facts or problems presented in the conflict. Ignorance liberates the anxious person from justifying answers, coming up with solutions, or dealing in any other way with surface anger. Usually the alternative reply from ACOAs is offering sympathy, empathy, or just listening as the predator ventilates aggravation.

Imposterism. This is a very serious type of avoidance and escape. Fear of incompetency and exposing faults and raising eyebrows to criticism and rejection may force a person into a disguise that masks or feels as if it masks his true identity. Faking knowledge or nodding in agreement on things about which the person knows very little or nothing creates the impression of strength, pride, and intelligence. However, underneath this charade is the anxious ACOA, shivering fearfully that other people will spot his stupidity and discover he is an imposter. His level of actual integrity, education, or career advancement is irrelevant in determining how sensitive a person is to imposterism. One woman, an executive director over 200 employees, a confident and outspoken lobbyist, and financially secure, struggled against the incipient fear of being discovered by her constituents as incompetent. There was nothing actually incompetent about her other than her self-imposed, persuasive belief that an approving public wanted her error free.

Shame. Avoidance and escape take the form of releasing others from their burdens. Shame does this. A person relieves the predator of anger by blaming himself for causing the conflict and now deserving the punishment. Relief occurs in three ways. First, ACOAs anticipate conflict, criticism, or rejection by volunteering their faults in hopes that these faults will match the predator's concerns. Whether it does nor does not, predators accept the confession rather than start an argument. Second, ACOAs interrupt predatory attacks with a sympathetic reinterpretation of how they caused the impropriety and inconvenienced the predator. Again, escape from conflict is nearly guaranteed as the predator accepts the testimony. Third, ACOAs blame a third person not present during the conflict or attack who can absorb full responsibility for the damage. By again absolving the predator, ACOAs regain control over the situation and eliminate their own guilt for upsetting the predator.

Depression. Kazdin's (1990) comprehensive review of childhood depression insightfully describes many convergent symptoms as *co-morbidity*. That is, many children meet criteria for more than one disorder, such as overlapping criteria for anxiety, conduct disorders, and oppositional disorders. Entering adulthood, unrelieved childhood fears, anxieties, and disorders act as weak immunity against stressors of conflict, rejection, and criticism. Predisposing emotional disabilities increase the adult's susceptibility to avoidance and escape behaviors. The problem, however, is delineating between avoidance and escape in response to ensuing conflict and avoidance and escape from endogenous or chronic depression. Most ACOAs who suffered arbitrary and critical punishment in childhood also struggle with depression. It comes on rapidly and after prolonged episodes of uncontrolled anxiety or entrapment in inescapable, unavoidable situations. Depression in ACOAs also arises for the following reasons:

- Caretaking and enabling efforts are disrupted, violated, or replaced by another caretaker or enabler.
- Caretaking and enabling efforts are refused by recipients, and misinterpreted as rejection.
- Caretaking and enabling efforts are stifled by the absence of any available recipient.
- Caretaking or aggression both fail to avoid or escape conflict, criticism, or rejection.
- Prolonged or generalized anxiety escalates to panic attacks after physical exhaustion and anxiety subsides.
- The person is forced to sit, relax, or remain immobile when alone or around the predator.
- There is removal or interruption of food, alcohol, or drugs after habitual or excessive use before, during, or after conflict, criticism, or rejection.
- The person cannot run away or hide before, during, or after conflict, criticism, or rejection.
- The person is forced to express anger, vulnerability, and/or personal feelings around the predator even if mediated by therapist.
- Prolonged guilt or shame arises from repeatedly upsetting people or inferring disapproval from other people.
- Prolonged guilt or shame arises from repeatedly asserting personal ideas, disagreements, or refusals and inferring disapproval from other people.
- Prolonged guilt or shame arises from repeatedly finding fault in self, treating self as a scapegoat for others' problems, and regarding loneliness as abandonment and rejection.

Effects of Avoidance and Escape

Predictable outcomes of avoidance and escape responses seemingly include removal of fear and restoration of control—but not always. In fact, the irony is that opposite consequences emerge that surprise ACOAs. Upon non-ACOAs, such consequences would instantly destroy all caretaking, enabling, and even aggressive reactions. ACOAs unfortunately perceive the same consequences not as lessons to stop dysfunctional behavior but as an ambitious challenge undertaken to improve their chances of approval and ultimately to fulfill an unrealistic set of expectations. They keep producing the same behavior, thinking the only reason it works or does not work lies within their control. ACOAs frequently encounter a number of consequences.

Exploitation

Generously caretaking the needs of other people builds up selfish expectations in people who demand more of the same generosity without reciprocity. At first, caretakers regard the higher demands as proof of effectively pleasing the person enough so he or she desires more of them. As demands grow, resentment slowly develops but is kept silent. ACOAs feel ashamed of their resentment and delude themselves into believing their caretaking efforts still are inadequate.

Superstitious Behavior

One peculiar consequence of *anticipatory caretaking and anticipatory aggression* is that it reinforces whatever the predator is doing before an alleged conflict. Recall that conflict may or may not be impending, and efforts to appease the predator end up accidentally shaping strange or unwanted behaviors. For example, one husband claimed his wife always greeted him with excessive affection until he finally realized that it distracted him from the mail and discovering her compulsive use of credit cards. He noticed himself more sexually aroused after work and expecting intercourse even after his wife's compulsion stopped and supposedly the need for avoidance gone. However, residual behaviors such as this manufactured from earlier avoidance behavior still continued, which caused more trouble for the wife. She hated his daily sexual demands but now faced a new obstacle of criticism, rejection, and conflict if she denied his wants. Avoidance had to continue for another reason that she never bargained for.

Rejection

Extensive caretaking efforts backfire on competent, independent recipients. Continuous appeasement finds recipients upset, angry, and rejecting the caretaker no matter how much compensatory effort goes into repairing the broken relationship. ACOAs never quite understand reasons for this rejection, attributing it largely to their own incompetency. Guilt over the rejection perpetuates more caretaking efforts that unknowingly annoy the already disturbed recipient, who resists the caretaker's efforts even more.

Inattention to Appropriate Behavior

Not all recipients take advantage of caretakers. Recipients, such as spouses, who acknowledge the caretaker's generosity may properly reciprocate with rewards. But rewards are adamantly refused by the caretaker. Resistance to reciprocity indicates inattention to and distrust of appropriate behaviors in other people, no matter how much caretakers insist on receiving reciprocity. Attention drawn to caretakers for their kindness is embarrassing, suspicious, and frequently deflected with criticism or aggression. ACOAs may tease, discount, or directly insult recipients for being kind. Punished recipients stop reciprocating immediately, and this sets the occasion for the caretaker to complain again that he receives nothing in return for doing everything. For example, a controlling wife lamented her family never helped out with house chores. On the father's initiative, the family surprised the caretaker by completing the laundry, preparing dinner, and running other odd chores. Rather than appreciate this surprise, she immediately found fault in all family participants for improperly doing the chores. Her response suppressed further initiatives by family members to help out with chores or even think of repeating similar surprises in the future.

Why do ACOAs seemingly sabotage good-natured gestures by those whom they accuse of being uncaring? The answer is threefold. First, helping out is perceived as exposing incompetency because the caretaker could not do it alone; perception of fault transforms into believing he or she is being criticized. Removal of that perception requires proving that others do inferior work. Second, helping out is distrustful; treating the caretaker nicely "must have" underlying motives believed to inauthenticate the kind gesture. Nobody ever did things in the past for this person, so why are people doing them now? Distrusted efforts receive cautious, even callous reactions that protect ACOAs from feeling vulnerable. They avoid reexperiencing the entrapment reminiscent of childhood.

Third, helping out is never as good as it should be. Expectations for reciprocity exceed realistic criteria for people returning favors or acting correctly. ACOAs invest such excessive efforts, even at perfectionistic levels, in helping others that they expect these other people to reciprocate in identical manner. However, indulgent, excessive behaviors are abnormal, highly impractical, and unlikely to be reciprocated by the average lot of responders unless they too are caretakers. Ironically, even identically repeating the same large chunks of behaviors—say, if the person is himself a caretaker—will be rejected because it still does not meet expectations. These "expectations" essentially are nonexistent, highly abstract, or unreachable objectives regarding what the caretaker believes is appropriate behavior but has never attained himself. Unrealistic adult expectations derive from never satisfying a parent's needs for approval during a dysfunctional childhood.

Provoking of Aggression

Despite pleas for others to treat caretakers with respect and reciprocity, ACOAs will desperately seek attention even if it is aggressive attention. An agreeable spouse is provoked by insults, criticisms, teasing, and repetitive threats until he or she replies angrily. The moment anger arises, ACOAs withdraw and blame the provoked person of mistreatment, negligence, or verbal abuse. Absolutely no defense offered by the provoked party is admissible; ACOAs blame the provoked spouse of being highly reactive and "grossly aggressive and self-centered."

Naturally provoked recipients are perplexed. But there is a critical reason that caretakers provoke aggression. Historically, they expect and know how to deal with aggressive attention. Enduring physically or verbally abusive attacks during childhood formed a repertoire for aggressive interactions. Habits were formed that prepared caretakers to anticipate or cope with arbitrarily arising episodes of hostility as part of survival. In adulthood, episodes that do not occur *naturally,* that is, on the recipient's own initiative, are contrived to restore familiar family situations. Once they are produced, ACOAs regain control, redeem their confidence, and feel comfortable in much the same way as couples who gain comfort in repeating certain religious or ethnic practices in the marriage that they learned in childhood.

Procrastination

Avoidance and escape nearly always produce a delay or termination of tasks the ACOAs feel are difficult to do, outside their repertoire, or prone to conflict, criticism, or rejection. Rarely, if ever, does the person admit deficiency when confronted with impossible odds regarding a task or even a small favor asked of them. Politely they accept the task rather than refuse to do it and face instant rejection. As time passes, the task remains incomplete. Reminders to complete the task or fulfill the favors are responded to with honest apologies. They may even compensate with promises to do more favors; however, these appeasements serve to extend delays even longer.

When confronted about procrastination, ACOAs react in one of four ways. First, they show fierce anger or aggression or vehemently deny accusations and their commitment to complete the task or fulfill a promise. Second, they distract the accuser by shifting to incompatible, irrelevant topics likely to upset or please the accuser. One distraction is turning the topic around to blame the accuser for not reminding them to do the task and how it is their fault for forgetting. Other shifts, also called roadblocks, are to start a new conversation, offer sex or food treats, or simply walk away. Third, they sink into spontaneous depression characterized by crying and self-criticism, promising to stop whatever they are doing that moment to fulfill the promise. Most recipients, however, refuse this spontaneous remediation because it seems preposterous, illogical, impractical, or irrelevant. In other words, for the person to stop whatever he is doing now may also interrupt the recipient who is unwilling to stop whatever he is doing. Finally, combinations of these reactions are very common. For instance, spontaneous acts of remediation ("Fine, I'll do it now") may accompany aggressive, defensive remarks.

Miscommunications

One of the severe repercussions of avoidance and escape is miscommunication. Fear of conflict, criticism, and rejection prevents inquiry into suspicious behaviors of other people, resulting in damaging inferences about why and how people do things that are not parallel to real events. Inferences distort and affirm stereotyped beliefs that never get clarified. Recently a man broke out into rage because he was given a gift he did not want. He assaulted the gift by destroying it with a hammer, conspiring the whole time in his mind that the gift was left to spite and hurt him. Never did it occur to him prior to his destructive actions to check out why the gift was left for him and whether the reason was inconsistent with his inference. Failure to investigate assumptions diminishes the risk of looking stupid or arousing unwanted conflict, whether or not these events would truly occur.

Temporary Relief

Avoidance and escape generates negative reinforcement. In principle, this means responses that remove or terminate some aversive or expected aversive event will increase in the future given similar conditions. The removal or termination produces temporary relief from either anticipatory fear of aversive events or being exposed directly to those events. Once they are gone, anxiety dissipates, and control over actions is restored. However, feeling relieved is a misleading and unproductive consequence if the aversive event was essential for healthy adjustment. For example, relief from medical illness allows for healthy adjustment. The same is not true for relief from conflict. Escaping conflict is unhealthy and denies opportunities to build proper communication and listening skills and to solve problems. Relief at the expense of developing adaptive skills is artificially satisfying but also emotionally injurious since it means avoidance and escape will be the only way to handle future conflict.

Termination of Friendships

"Cutting your nose off to spite your face" is a moral expression. It typically describes a child who aborts or destroys something that is personally gratifying at the time so that it might annoy the parent. This "annoyance" is retaliatory; the child hopes it will hurt the parent as much as it upset the child. Imagine a child thriving on a juicy hamburger. Told he must eat his vegetables or not get dessert, the stubborn child might stop eating his meal altogether and proceed to dump the entire plate of vegetables, hamburger, and french fries into the garbage can. Consequently his parents yell at him, deny offering more food, or in some other way punish these actions. Older children, however, regard the provocation of parental anger as retaliation for interrupting or denying the child his selfish needs. In adulthood, similar behavioral patterns occur in response to inferred deprivations of selfish needs. This same person who smashed a gift with a hammer, is so infuriated that he nearly terminates a relationship with the gift giver, despite a friendship for over 10 years.

Why cut his nose off to spite his face? Why, in other words, must the ACOA terminate an otherwise rewarding relationship because of one upsetting episode? How could he even believe this action truly will hurt the person just as similar actions hurt his parents during childhood? The answers lie in the incapacity to accept rejection, criticism, and hatred of conflict. As for retaliation, recipients usually never discern that termination of friendship signals vindictive motives; they simply perceive the gestalt of events as peculiar and maladaptive. Second, the ACOA would rather maintain avoidance and escape patterns than attempt solutions that would defuse false inferences and ensure the continuation of rewarding friends. Forfeiture of accumulated personal resources illustrates severely deficient coping mechanisms, and dispensing with resources so rapidly adds to the person's loneliness and isolationism.

TREATMENT CONSIDERATIONS

Structured therapy is one among many approaches guided by principles of science. In structured therapy, the therapist plans the goals and objectives, subject to client approval, and proceeds in each session to work through exercises, strategies, or emotional obstacles along the path of these goals and objectives. Diversions from the goals and objectives are normal and usually deal with personal reflections on why the goals are difficult, events happening that day or recently, or regarding new reactions of other people. Naturally attention is paid to client concerns, but the discussion should return to the goal or strategy in process, keeping the structure balanced throughout the session. Structure further establishes a milieu for teaching and learning and allows clients to predict exactly how the session will go, with minor variation. For clients with control issues, that predictability provides a strong foundation for trust. Consider the following strategies that enter into structured treatment.

Change Beliefs

Altering irrational beliefs begins with identifying inferences that govern the ACOA's behavior. Beliefs that are most dangerous are self-critical, condemnatory, or comparisons made between the ACOA and other people perceived as superior. Efforts to dispute these beliefs follow a series of three steps: (1) interrupting the beliefs, (2) asking questions of the person from whom inferences are drawn, and (3) replacing self-criticism with self-complimentary and realistic statements. Self-complimentary or realistic statements are accurate rules liberating the person from false expectations and need for perfectionism. Statements such as "It's no big deal" or "It's okay for mistakes to happen" seem superficial but combat negative tapes mentally replayed by the ACOA under stress situations.

Basic Assertion plus Self-Expression

Belief alterations provide the doorway for risking confrontations and self-expression. Basic assertions are questions asked of another person about words or actions possibly misunderstood by observation alone. "Why did you do that?" requires a brief answer that clarifies motives and reasons and obviates the ACOA's inference that offensive or uncertain action must be "due to something I did." Self-expression further includes three parts: *disagreements, opinions,* and *criticism.* Disagreements commit the ACOA to make refusals or directly dissent with opinions expressed by significant others on many different and relevant topics. They threaten an ambiance of debate and frequently discourage risky attempts resulting in conflict. But tactics shown on how to stay on the topic, resist roadblocks, and remain focused prevent digression onto irrelevant issues and personal defensiveness.

Opinions are unprompted statements regarding a spontaneous idea that contributes to the ongoing discussion or initiates discussion about some object, person, or event. Initiating opinions at first challenges the deeply rooted belief that personal ideas impose on other people who did not ask for the opinion and thus will regard it as intrusive. Opinions that decry an object, event, or person are criticisms. Unprompted or prompted statements describing why the ACOA dislikes something are appropriate around significant others.

Beyond belief interferences, *defusal tactics* aimed to calm, soften, or relieve anticipated criticism, conflict, or rejection from listeners also interfere with self-expression. Defusal tactics vary depending on individual history but generally take five forms:

1. *Apologies:* Immediately after asserting an opinion, the ACOA may sense dissent from the listener and anticipate impending conflict. Apologies accept blame for assumed discomfort imposed on the listener and relieve the listener of supposedly acting negatively in retaliation for the discomfort. Of course, many assumptions play into this ACOA response that usually are inconsistent with the listener's real events.

2. *Discrediting, disqualifying statements:* Inferences again are the misleading motivation for defusal. Perceived discomfort in the listener may trigger the ACOA to dismiss, discredit, or disqualify opinions just made by admitting they may be wrong or that little validity supports the statement. Or the ACOA may defer judgment to the listener's alleged expertise. Criticism about a modern painting received poorly by a listener might prompt the client to rescind the statement, offering instead, "Well, I don't know much about art anyway, certainly not like you do."

3. *Defensiveness:* Personal assaults signal many ACOAs to protect their vulnerability by fighting back with justifications or rationalizations. Retaliatory statements marshal

reasons, facts, and other persuasive artifacts of proof to satisfy the attacker's curiosity and support the validity of an idea. Defensiveness also rebuilds the ACOA's crumbling confidence against intrusive thoughts of "feeling like an imposter" or "looking stupid."

4. *Self-criticism:* Attack against oneself instantly is believed to relieve imminent conflict. ACOAs who expect interpersonal trouble shift to their personal faults, and away from faults of the listener, thereby cleansing the situation of anger, rejection, or conflict. Self-criticism further restores control to the listener at the expense of the ACOA's feeling inferior.

5. *Compensating:* Opinions that leave an immediate negative imprint on listeners frighten ACOAs into thinking conflict is inevitable and that they have emotionally hurt the listener. Feeling ashamed, they put into motion efforts to make up or compensate for this inconvenience by generously accommodating the listener in some capacity, either by relieving him of responsibilities or providing a service or resource guaranteed to win back his friendship.

All five defusal tactics seriously endanger the psychological profits of self-expression and invalidate assertive remarks made in hostile situations. Efforts at teaching opinions, assertiveness, and resistance to roadblocks must involve specific steps that block these tactics, despite rising anxiety levels and the ACOA's intensifying self-perception of guilt.

Reversal of Guilt

Inferred verbal statements from listeners can be easily translated into *self-shame*. Asked if she went to the grocery store, the ACOA wife might shamefully misinterpret the question to mean "How could you do such a stupid thing as forget to go to the grocery store?" Steps that prevent or interrupt guilty rules are twofold. The first step is for the client to reverse the question back to the listener, seeking more facts about the matter: "Was I supposed to go to the grocery store?" Fact finding serves the dual purpose of collecting critical objective information rather than relying on inferences, and it also puts the onus of responsibility on the listener, who must rephrase or reject the question if the topic expects to continue. The second step is literally to blame the listener for mistakes or faults related to the topic instead of the ACOA's absorbing blame. Telling the person, "You could have let me know we were out of milk," shares burdens of inadequacy and imperfection and keeps the control balanced.

Resist Rejection

Toughest of all interventions is preparing the ACOA for rejection. Rejection underlies the emotional pathology developed over years of avoidance and escape, to the point where fear of rejection is too strong to break. The following steps to guide ACOAs follow a structured but cautious series of self-restraint actions that begin once ACOAs face anger or criticism from other people:

1. Delay responding for 3 to 5 minutes. Resist engaging in defusal tactics.
2. Assertively state what the person said and your emotional disapproval of it.
3. Walk away and ignore subsequent roadblocks, attacking remarks from listeners.
4. Make self-statements that it is OK for people to be upset with you.

This last rule is crucial but contradicts the very core of caretaking behaviors. Accepting that people get angry, that rejection is normal, and it is even healthy for people to hate the ACOA challenges every rule indoctrinated in the person since childhood. Naturally, conversion to this new belief system takes time and is resisted adamantly and doubted to bring about healthy recovery. But applying the belief generates three benefits immediately visible to the risker. First, it relieves ACOAs of defusal tactics that undermine their integrity and leave them angry for being subversive; instead, confidence remains strong and gains momentum by self-restraint. Second, letting others be upset at the ACOA forces those people to adjust to new behaviors in the ACOA. Third, walking away teaches the ACOA not to depend on approval for self-esteem. Instead, confidence depends on individualized risks directly challenging the norms, morals, or values of social systems.

Building Trust

Development of trust also forces the question, *Why?* Distrust runs deeply into the chronic history of abuse suffered by most ACOAs from sexual, physical, or emotional damage. Slowly abandoning this comfort zone and sharing control or inviting others to control the ACOA faces immediate barriers of fear: the fear that trust will repeat abuse, fear that losing control will expose embarrassing imperfections and cause rejection, and fear of not knowing how to share control. Adults who were forced in childhood to care for their siblings and parents and who had accelerated responsibilities imposed on daily chores never let other people, except possibly schoolteachers, be their benefactors. They have no concept of what it means to be a beneficiary.

Taken in context, fears can impede progress toward building trust unless the fears are identified, briefly explored, and replaced by functional alternatives that allow a stepwise strategy for sharing control. Steps generally involved variations of the following:

1. Tell personal, embarrassing, or humiliating situations to a significant other. Resist using defusal tactics when telling the stories.

2. Ask significant others for favors. Ask them to do jobs you usually do or believe nobody else can do. Accept the product of their efforts regardless of errors or the inconsistency between their efforts and your own efforts.

3. Ask the significant other to interrupt your rigid schedule by that person's planning, organizing, or directing social or business events, which typically is left up to you.

4. Permit the person to make decisions or initiate efforts you typically handled yourself, without your interference even if the person recruits your assistance.

Break the Imposter Syndrome

Low self-efficacy continues as long as ACOAs perceive themselves as constantly averting exposure of faults. Fear of this exposure historically is linked to assaults of random and arbitrary punishment for unpredictable actions. Anticipating criticism at any time, ACOAs remain on guard for any chance of conflict, and they sound the alarm the moment they feel vulnerable. The imposter syndrome describes this phobia and protective habitual responding. Removing the syndrome becomes a delicate process of balancing risk with panic. Steps first prepare the person for desensitization, that is, of making verbal statements or displaying physical actions prone to errors while in a relaxed muscular state. Desensitization requires repeated use of progressive muscular relaxation using in vivo visual imagery. This is followed by the client's actually responding in the situations previously imagined. Visual imagery, for example, may picture the client telling a stupid joke and forgetting parts of it. Initial fears felt by humiliation are calmed by sensory relaxation. Once stress is lower under many images, analogues are constructed in the clinical office and then in the real world to practice this scenario. Comfort gained in the applications breaks the imposter syndrome.

Imposterism also is treated by having the person just stay in the unpleasant, aversive, or frightening situation. A less structured but equally effective desensitization is forcing the client to interact verbally or nonverbally around people, events, or objects feared as destructive to vulnerability. Around a conference table, the ACOA executive stays seated throughout the entire meeting, forces input on topics, and verbally accepts constructive criticisms given to him. While interaction flows among discussants, fears about looking stupid and feeling like an imposter vanish long enough for the person to feel confident.

Risk-taking Efforts

Following the demise of the imposter syndrome are efforts to take spontaneous risks regarded as foolish, childish, and posing further hazards to vulnerability. ACOAs first construct a list of social, sexual, or playful activities they envy in other people or wish they can do themselves. Next is to assess how many of these responses appear in the person's repertoire, despite the infrequency, inaccuracy, or overall consequences produced by them (approval, disapproval). Responses showing some strength are the first to be augmented by changing the rules governing them and, if necessary, involving the significant others they affect. For example, one woman envied people who could put on a bathing suit regardless of their weight and enjoy the swimming pool. Despite her slender fitness, this client's modesty interfered with pursuing the risk. Already in her repertoire was her ability to swim, and she was a member of a club having an indoor pool. Steps immediately began where she dressed in the bathing suit around the house for one week until feeling relaxed and unthreatened by social disapproval (desensitization process). The second step was to wear the bathing suit to the pool, swim, and gradually spend longer intervals there, around larger crowds of onlookers.

Anger Control

Control over fear involves control over anger. ACOAs must first be alert to *cues* and *urges* motivating autonomic arousal and the trajectory patterns building up to a *threshold* and *peak*. Changes in self-statements, muscular tension, and visible cues and toward altering time pressures represent steps in arresting anger.

Disabling Enabling

Like eliminating distrust, eliminating the habit of caretaking provokes severe emotional resistance. Many ACOAs expect and automatically accept this dutiful obligation without reservation and depend on doing for others as a bloodline to self-preservation. However, repercussions of enabling are devastating enough to reconsider the lifelong habit. Toward this end, disabling enabling is a three step approach.

Step 1 is to *resist rescuing*. ACOAs have a remarkable talent for being acutely aware of people in distress who must be saved. Rescue efforts launched to relieve the emotional grief, burdens, and responsibilities of the victim supposedly earn respect, gratitude, and approval from the rescuer. When told to refuse temptations to rescue, thereby allowing victims to suffer, it means the ACOA must also resist vicariously suffering the emotional grief and the guilt associated with ignoring people. Alternatively, ACOAs learn the belief that people must suffer inconvenience to make changes themselves. Steps teach the client to become distracted or refuse to help others when imposed upon.

The next step is to *resist pleasing*. Just as rescuing relieves grief observed in others, so pleasing relieves conflict, criticism, or impending rejection. ACOAs make concessions to avoid or escape arguments or interpersonal turmoil while gaining secondary benefits from the approval of seeing others happy. Giving gifts, surprises, parties, or accommodations guaranteed to maintain peace and happiness in a family or friendship all are pleasing gestures. When told to resist temptations to please, even the thought of refusing induces panic reactions because it involves enduring anger and acrimony that historically has been intolerable. Refusals instantly would upset the balance, causing distress, complaints, and abandonment of the ACOA by persons dependent on his caretaking. That is why refusals never occur until the client already demonstrates relative mastery of assertiveness, overcoming roadblocks, and expression of opinions. Second, withholding pleasing gestures occurs at the same time the client begins satisfying selfish needs. Personal gratification shifts the pendulum away from being the benefactor to becoming the beneficiary of others' efforts.

The final step is to *demand reciprocity*. Disabling enabling further requires the demand for an exchange system. Reciprocity between the client and significant others ensures that for every personal sacrifice or concession made, there is a dividend earned. Resources returned by other people can vary and need not parallel the quality, quantity, or frequency of resources supplied by the caretaker, as long as timing of the reciprocal resource is proximal. It must be given shortly after the caretaker gives a resource. Although this sounds logical, ACOAs struggle with asking for rewards from people, fearing that they will appear rude, conceited, and selfish. Rewards also seem fake. This is based on beliefs that requested or contrived rewards are inauthentic, whereas rewards or resources given on the person's own accord are genuine. However, unprompted rewards for the caretaker's efforts are infrequent and usually nonexistent. Consequently, clients fight internal messages that their actions are wrong and immoral as they modestly ask for something in return for their efforts.

Construction of Emotions

Anger, fear, anxiety, and depression comprise the emotional constellation of most ACOAs. Emotions beyond these types are unusual and command a knowledge base that is severely deficient or absent. Feelings such as love, passion, and intimacy may resemble the *compassion* ACOAs show in their caretaking gestures, but there is a difference. Love, passion, and intimacy develop from a trusting and vulnerable relationship built between two independent people whose needs are mutually satisfied and whose ambitions are largely compatible. By contrast, co-dependent, unilateral love shown by the ACOA without much gained in return is not love but rather an act of pleasing. In teasing out the difference, clients are shocked at mistaking love for pleasing and then are deeply frightened that they have no idea what love is.

Construction of emotions thus begins as a threefold process. First is trusting another person and relinquishing control. Second is learning basic touching, from simple hand holding or extended hand gestures to simple kissing (with a spouse or intimate). Affection in private is broadened to public displays of touching, embracing, and even kissing. Physical forms of exchange accompany verbal compliments and self-affirmations of looking and feeling feminine or masculine and looking attractive to a partner.

Disinhibited touching moves to the next step of sexual intimacy. Arousal first is attempted by self-stimulation and by letting a partner caress erogenous areas around the upper and lower torso. Foreplay that is excitatory continues for longer intervals instead of being a boring prelude to coitus. After foreplay is satisfactory, strategies are described for building up plateaus (for women) and stability of erection (for men) prior to and during intromission. Sustaining arousal during intercourse involves mutual selfish and benevolent efforts, shifted with balance and without one partner's feeling disgraced by the other partner. Timing and satisfaction of single and multiple climaxes involve both knowledge of the biological process (refractory period, types of excitatory stimuli, etc.) and restraint from criticisms following completion of intercourse.

Third, affection is developed and practiced around children and around persons perceived since childhood as uncaring and cold. Physical embracing, kissing, and verbal compliments toward children usually are easy, and ACOAs welcome this exercise for two reasons: it releases tenderness with special people whom they desperately want to love, and showing affection to children breaks the intergenerational lineage of repressed displays of emotion, in that the ACOA's offspring can perceive and understand touching as wonderful (not abusive, fearful, or wrong) and plan to exhibit freely for years into their own adulthood.

Overcome Avoidance and Escape

Underlying most of ACOA behavior is avoidance and escape. Actions averting criticism, conflict, and rejection constantly occupy the person's mind and keep him alert to interpersonal social situations. Because this pattern is habitual, much like caretaking, cessation of the behavior must start with awareness. Clients learn self-monitoring methods to record physically or "mentally" instances of avoidance and escape and the consequences (types of relief) generated from these patterns.

Interruption of the pattern is a twofold process. First, clients deliberately enter into apprehensive or high-anxiety-prone situations and remain stationary until the situation runs its course and naturally ends. For instance, visiting friends whom the ACOA believes hate him entails staying at the house, if invited, for a couple of hours or until there is a natural lull to leave. Confronting the awful feeling that "this person hates me" desensitizes the client's fears and allows for functional social behavior. Second, clients next do what intuitively they regard is impossible: they create conflict situations through criticism or disagreements, again feeling afraid, and midway through the argument start to problem-solve a compromise; seeking compromise of issues is diametrical to the habit of either forcing (controlling) a decision or surrendering to another's decision.

Accepting Compliments

Highly modest, shameful, and intimidated ACOAs resist drawing attention to themselves partly due to imposterism and partly due to risks of conflict, criticism, and rejection. For one reason or another, drawing compliments is especially difficult. Efforts to combat this phobia follow a structured approach consisting of three different types of compliments: conversions, directing the conversation, and solicitations.

Conversions describe the situation when the client listens to what somebody else is talking about. Then he takes the last statement or phrase and transforms it into a compliment or strength about himself. The statement describes an ability, accomplishment, or success related to the last phrase. Melanie says, "That snow outside is so ugly I just can't stand it." The client chimes in with, "I don't know; I kind of like the snow. I love skiing and getting outside with the kids." Or Bruce observes, "Can't get any secretarial help around here, and typing your own work is tedious." The client replies, "Not for everybody. I type pretty fast, thank God, and can do it myself when the clerical staff are busy."

Next is *directing the conversation*. Directing topics is control on the one hand and tooting the client's horn on the other. Moments into the dialogue or at a natural breaking point, the client shifts the conversation to something of personal interest, expanding on the interest for a couple of sentences or until the listener changes the topic. For instance, while conversing about budgetary cuts, the client waits for a pause and adds, "You know, it's a good thing we're not being laid off. I think my job is pretty secure." Two or three more sentences embellishing the client's point is enough. Nothing more is needed thereafter. By shifting gears, the client draws attention to issues or values important to himself without sounding pompous.

The third method, solicitations, is more direct. Subtlety is wonderful for beginners, but by now the client tries soliciting a compliment about some physical feature or activity she recently completed. "What do you think of this new dress?" Or, "Don't you think I got them to listen to me at that meeting!" Pointed questions regarding the client's appearance or actions waste little time getting to the issue. Egos inflate rapidly from friendly praise and approval that others typically give. Even if feedback is negative or there is none at all, just hearing himself verbalize the words puts into thought the client's pride in certain attributes.

The practice of compliments without slipping into old habits is tricky and can lead to common traps such as when the client disqualifies the compliment ("I'm good at that . . . well not really"), is self-critical after the compliment ("I'm good at that, and that's all I'm good at"), returns a compliment right away ("I'm good at that . . . but so are you"), or laughs at self ("I'm good at that. Isn't that a scream?").

New Criteria for Selecting New Relationships

Above all else, intimacy is a dark secret unless the ACOA already is married or has a significant other. Otherwise, forming new relationships or preventing repetition of bad relationships poses major obstacles because of *inexperience* and *fear of failure*. Inexperience literally means lacking the prerequisite knowledge concerning how to date, what to look for in a partner, how to engage in small talk, and remaining focused. Focus disgresses to obsessive worries of what the "date" thinks of the ACOA and whether he or she will fail this person's test. Fear of failure suggests some history of dating, forming relationships, and intimacy, but the track record is negative. Recycling one dysfunctional relationship after another leads the ACOA to conclude that all potential partners are untrustworthy. Attempts at breaking the vicious cycle are ineffective, especially during early dating or the honeymoon period, when first impressions signal a green light for the ACOA to pursue the relationship, only to discover problems later.

Repeated failures create distrust, feelings of futility, and disrespect for the opposite sex (if heterosexual). The person develops cynical and stereotyped attitudes about inherent defects of the gender—for example, "all men can't be trusted," or "all women are ditsy." Machoism, feminism, and other liberal extremes egocentrically boasting the superiority of its gender may temporarily boost confidence and disguise fears, but ultimately it disintegrates the person's capacity for a genuinely caring relationship. Disguises fade away when the ACOA realizes the world is a lonely place and needs for a companion reach desperation. At this or an earlier point, clients should construct new criteria for selecting partners who challenge their intuitive criteria and force them to learn new behaviors. Table 13.1 lists criteria for healthy relationships based on three typologies described as person A, person B, and person C. Each typology contains pervasive personality traits along the continuum of addictive, co-dependent behaviors, from person A (no addiction, well adjusted) to persons B and C (severely maladjusted, highly prone to addiction).

Therapeutic effectiveness largely depends on motivated clients who are eager to try new skills that deviate from old habits. Undertakings usually face more than normal resistance, since new skills represent behavior patterns never before performed or performed under duress. Skills that are entirely new feel mechanical and false and are treated with great skepticism. Clients reject their viability from the very beginning. Skills that are familiar but have remained repressed for many years are fearful and immediately jog memories of punitive experiences that disable motivation. That is why the therapist, the treatment, and the entire process of change is delicate no matter how rapidly learning can take place. Acquiring skills in an efficient manner is as much a function of

Table 13.1
Criteria for Healthy Relationships

PERSON A	PERSON B	PERSON C
Assertive	*Aggressive*	*Passive*
Expresses opinions	Criticizes only you	Is a "good listener"
Criticizes self and you	Boasts	Likes all that you do
Can be vulnerable	Not a listener	Discloses nothing
Admits mistakes	Makes demands	Edits remarks
Compliments self	Angry	Always apologizes
Compliments you	Very serious	Afraid to say things
Listens and talks		
Flexible	*Rigid*	*Overflexible*
Easy going	Can't break schedules	Gives in to pressure
Handles mean/nice people	Perfectionistic	Always agrees
Good with all age groups	Compulsive	Afraid of rejection
Offers to compromise	"My way or highway"	Afraid of criticism
Looks for reciprocity	Blames you	Afraid of criticism
Adjusts to new situations	Never admits fault	Eager to please
Asks for your help		
Consistent	*Impulsive*	*Inconsistent*
What he says he does	Lots of energy	Afraid to do things
Always follows through	Never follows through	Appears lazy
Admits he forgot	Blames you for forgetting	Procrastinates

methodology as it is therapist sensitivity concerning the hardships ACOAs suffer and must confront in order to gain healthy behaviors.

REFERENCES

Ackerman, R. J. (1983). *Children of alcoholics: A guidebook for educators, therapists and parents.* Holmes Beach, Fla.: Learning Publications.

Ackerman, R. J. (ed.). (1986). *Growing up in the shadow.* Hollywood, Fla.: Health Communications.

Ackerman, R. J. (1987a). *Children of alcoholics.* New York: Simon & Schuster.

Ackerman, R. J. (1987b). *Let go and grow: Recovery for adult children.* Hollywood, Fla.: Health Communications.

Banks, R. K. (1965). Effect of pairing a stimulus with presentations of the UCS on extinction of an avoidance response in humans. *Journal of Experimental Psychology, 70,* 294–99.

Bennett, R. H. & Cherek, D. R. (1990). Punished and nonpunished responding in a multiple schedule in humans: A brief report. *Psychological Record, 40,* 187–96.

Black, C. (1981). *It will never happen to me.* Denver: MAC Printing.

Black, C. (1984). Children of alcoholics. *NCA Catalyst, 1,* 15–21.

Brennen, G. P. (1986). *I know they love me anyway.* Milwaukee, Wisc.: DePaul Rehabilitation Hospital.

Burnett, C. (1986). *One more time.* New York: Random House.

Dollard, J. & Miller, N. W. (1950). *Personality and psychotherapy.* New York: McGraw-Hill.

Ellis, A. & Whiteley, J. M. (eds.). (1979). *Theoretical and empirical foundations of rational-emotive therapy.* Monterey, Cal.: Brooks Cole.

Eysenck, H. J. (1979). The conditioning model of neurosis. *Behavioral and Brain Sciences, 2,* 155–66.

Ferster, C. B. & Skinner, B. F. (1957). *Schedules of reinforcement.* Englewood Cliffs, N.J.: Prentice-Hall.

Ferster, C. B., Culberston, S. & Boren, M. C. P. (1975). *Behavior principles.* Englewood Cliffs, N.J.: Prentice-Hall.

Gravitz, H. L. & Bowden, J. D. (1985). *Guide to recovery: A book for adult children of alcoholics.* Holmes Beach, Fla.: Learning Publications.

Hayes, E. N. (1989). *Adult children of alcoholics remember.* New York: Harmony Books.

Herrnstein, R. J. (1966). Superstition: A corollary of the principles of operant conditioning. In W. K. Honig (ed.), *Operant behavior: Areas of research and application* (pp. 33–51). New York: Appleton-Century-Crofts.

Hollis, J. H. (1973). "Superstition": The effects of independent and contingent events on free operant responses in retarded children. *American Journal of Mental Deficiency, 77,* 585–96.

Kantor, D. & Lehr, W. (1975). *Inside the family.* San Francisco: Jossey-Bass.

Kazdin, A. E. (1990). Childhood depression. *Journal of Child Psychology and Psychiatry and Allied Disciplines, 31,* 121–60.

Malloy, P. & Levis, D. J. (1988). A laboratory demonstration of persistent human avoidance. *Behavior Therapy, 19,* 229–41.

Maxwell, W. A., Miller, F. D. & Meyer, P. A. (1971). The relationship between punishment and unavoidability in eliminating avoidance behavior in humans. *Psychonomic Science, 23,* 435–36.

Midgley, B. D. & Morris, E. K. (1988). The integrated field: An alternative to the behavior-analytic conceptualization of behavioral units. *Psychological Record, 38,* 483–500.

Mowrer, O. H. (1950). *Learning theory and personality dynamics.* New York: Roland Press.

Ratner, S. C. (1967). Comparative aspects of hypnosis. In J. Gordon (ed.)., *Handbook of Clinical and Experimental Hypnosis* (pp. 550–87). New York: Macmillan.

Ratner, S. C. & Thompson, R. W. (1960). Immobility reactions (fear) of domestic fowl as a function of age and prior experience. *Animal Behaviour, 8,* 186–91.

Seligman, M. E. P. & Johnston, J. C. (1973). A cognitive theory of avoidance learning. In F. J. McGuigan and D. B. Lumsden (eds.), *Contemporary approaches to learning and conditioning.* Washington, D.C.: Winston & Sons.

Skinner, B. F. (1948). Superstition in the pigeon. *Journal of Experimental Psychology, 38,* 168–72.

Skinner, B. F. (1977). The force of coincidence. In B. C. Etzel, J. M. LeBlanc & D. M. Baer (eds.), *New developments in behavioral psychology: Theory, methods and applications* (pp. 3–6). Hillsdale, N.J.: Lawrence Erlbaum.

Solomon, R. W. & Wynne, L. C. (1954). Traumatic avoidance learning: The principle of anxiety conservation and partial irreversibility. *Psychological Review, 61,* 353–85.

Stampfl, T. G. & Levis, D. J. (1967). The essentials of implosive therapy: A learning-theory-based psychodynamic behavioral therapy. *Journal of Abnormal Psychology, 72,* 496–503.

Steinglass, D., Bennett, L. A., Wolin, S. J. & Reiss, D. (eds.). (1989). *The alcoholic family.* New York: Basic Books.

Towers, R. L. (1989). *Children of alcoholics/addicts.* Washington, D.C.: National Education Association.

Wegsheider, D. (1979a). *If only my family understood me.* Minneapolis: CompCare Publications.

Wegscheider, D. (1979b). *The family trap.* Minneapolis: Nurturing Networks.

Wegscheider, D. (1980). *A second chance.* Palo Alto, Cal.: Science and Behavior Books.

Wegscheider, D. (1981). *Another chance: Hope and health for the alcoholic family.* Palo Alto, Cal.: Science and Behavior Books.

Wolpe, J. (1958). *Psychotherapy by reciprocal inhibition.* Stanford: Stanford University Press.

Zeiler, M. D. (1972). Superstitious behavior in children: An experimental analysis. In H. W. Reese (ed.), *Advances in child development and behavior* (pp. 1–29). New York: Academic Press.

14

Substance Abuse and Teenagers: A Review

CHRIS E. STOUT

The time of adolescence historically has been a period of stress and strain. We actually seem to trade stressors. From the turn of the century, we were faced with plagues, natural catastrophes, war, economic decline and depression, more war, and various cultural and political changes. Today we have parallels with AIDS, foreign conflicts, economic uncertainty, earthquakes, and so on. Recently the United States has witnessed a relatively new, but in some ways chronic, problem of substance abuse and addiction with teenagers.

ETIOLOGY

The actual causality in teenage substance addiction is unknown. Numerous researchers (Bailey, 1989; Kendel, Kessler & Margulies, 1978; Newcomb & Bentier, 1989; Morrison & Smith, 1987) note various factors: easy access and availability; peer pressures and norms that involve drug use; some are inexpensive; and stress, tension, depression, and anxiety reduction. Newcomb, Maddahian & Bentier (1986) note that it is impossible to identify accurately any specific factors, causes, or relationships for various drug types or various levels of use, misuse, or addiction. However, nine categories have been identified by Kumpfer (1987) for youth at risk for serious substance abuse: suicidal youth; disabled youth; children with mental health problems; school dropouts; pregnant teens; children from economically disadvantaged backgrounds; children who have been psychologically, sexually, or physically abused; and children whose parents abuse substances. This certainly is not a definitive group, and the average clinician may not find such information particularly helpful or predictive, since it is so inclusive of psychopathological children. It is, however, heuristic in demonstrating the lack of causation in addictive etiology.

There are also other interesting and clinically important correlates in adolescent drug addiction. Genetic research seems to hold promise. Various social correlates and antecedents have also been identified: poor parental relationships, no religious commitment, low social responsibility, depression and low self-esteem, parental/maternal/peer drug use and approval, nonconformity, rebelliousness, poor motivation and academic performance, and deviance (Bailey, 1989; Newcomb, Maddahian & Bentier, 1986; Semlitz & Gold, 1986). Psychological correlates such as personality issues (Vaillant 1980) and behavioral traits are less well understood.

EPIDEMIOLOGY

Some people show little concern regarding substance-abusing teenagers. They view the Darwinian effect of natural selection to be demonstrated on the streets, and they expect most substance abusers will either kill themselves or each other eventually. What this myopic, nonhumanitarian view fails to recognize are the societal side effects to substance abuse: increased violence, crime, gang activity, unemployment, illiteracy, teenage pregnancy, spread of disease, and a general unpreparedness to take on the responsibilities of adulthood and productive self-sufficiency.

In sum, substance addiction does nothing to benefit its addicts or society. Puberty has its onset today at a significantly earlier point than in prior generations. Girls in particular show this phenomenon. In 1840 females started to menstruate around age 16; now it has decreased to 12.5 years of age (CCAD, 1989). An unfortunate social phenomenon that parallels this biological phenomenon is the decrease in age that now occurs with the onset of drug use. Johnson, O'Malley, and Bachman (1987) note that 92 percent of the 1987 high school seniors in their sample had started drinking prior to graduating. Furthermore, 36 percent started between tenth and twelfth grades, and even more, 56 percent, had started earlier: between sixth and ninth grades. This is for graduates and does not include those users who did not graduate, which would presumably represent a higher number still. These authors also showed that 29 percent of sixth- through ninth-grade students had used illicit drugs, while a close 28 percent had done so between tenth and twelfth grades. Fifty-one percent of sixth- to ninth-grade students smoke cigarettes, followed by 16 percent of tenth to twelfth graders. In other words, alcohol use outdistances even tobacco use.

Another reason for public apathy is unawareness of the drugs being consumed. What exactly are these "drugs" or "substances"? Bailey (1989) notes five general classifications of abusable substances that are legal: inhalants, over-the-counter (OTC) medications, psychoactive medications, nicotine, and alcohol. Nicotine and alcohol could be debated as being illegal for teenagers, but for this chapter's purposes, they are viewed separately from the illegal-illicit substances of use, abuse, and addiction.

McHugh (1987) and Newcomb and Bentier (1989) indicate that inhalants are frequently the entree into further drug use. They tend to be abandoned after one to two years use in favor of more mind- or mood-altering substances (McHugh, 1987). Inhalants are actually a broad category that include glues, paints, and thinners (tolulene based); correction fluid, spot removers, air-conditioning freon, and solvents (halogenated hydrocarbons); whipping cream in cans and "laughing gas" (nitrous oxide); and "snappers"/"poppers" (amyl, n-butyl, or isobutyl nitrites).

Pentel (1984) lists various OTC drugs, including common compounds for colds, coughs, sleeping aids, weight loss aids, nasal sprays, and alertness medications. Prescription medications are often abused (Roush, Thompson & Berberian, 1980); Dilsaver (1986) notes abusive substances such as stimulants (amphetamines, dexamphetamines), sedatives (methaqualone, Valium), hypnotics, analgesics (codeine, Demerol), and antimuscarinics (trihexyphenidyl). It is important to note that Johnson, O'Malley & Bachman (1987) found (albeit preliminary) evidence that children who are prescribed psychoactive medications tend to display more illicit drug use than their peers who were not prescribed such medication.

Illegal drugs include cannabis, cocaine (and now crack), opioids (opium, heroin), phencyclidine (PCP), psilocybin (mushrooms), hallucinogens (LSD), and mescaline (peyote). This list is not static. With the advent of pharmacological advancement, new drugs are being developed to mimic other drugs' effects but with greater potency or lethality or as an effort to avoid typical illegalization standards (Petersen, 1987; Ruttenber, 1985).

Nationally there are two primary sources of data for the United States, both produced by the National Institute on Drug Abuse (NIDA). NIDA surveys hold relatively accurate validity in their representativeness of the "normal" population. For example, the National Household Survey on Drug Abuse examines U.S. households on a periodic basis, and the Monitoring the Future Survey (MFS) annually taps private and public high school seniors (Bailey, 1989).

The MFS research (Johnson et al., 1987) for 1987 noted an actual decline in marijuana, methaqualone, sedative, stimulant, and cocaine use for seniors in American high schools but an increase in inhalant use and no change in LSD, opioids, or heroin. Of curious import is alcohol's erratic pattern of use. A decline in alcohol or tobacco use since 1984 halted in 1987 (Bailey, 1989; Johnson et al., 1987). The use of tobacco is often minimized, for it has been so culturally accepted. However, smoking actually harms more teenagers in adulthood than any or all other drugs combined (Bailey, 1989; Johnson et al., 1987). Approximately one-fifth of high school seniors smoke cigarettes daily (Newcomb & Bentier, 1989).

Newcomb and Bentier (1989) report that even with the declines noted, 92 percent of U.S. seniors have used alcohol and 66 percent had used it within the last month of the survey; 5 percent are daily drinkers, and over one-third report having consumed five or more drinks consecutively.

Our society or media seem to distort or ignore the statistical findings of such epidemiological studies. In the United States, cocaine is the most fought or despised drug, but in 1985's National Household Survey, cocaine was found to be used only 5 percent of the time in comparison to inhalants at 9 percent and analgesics and stimulants at 6 percent each (NIDA, 1987).

CONSEQUENCES

Survey results of frequent drug use place teenagers at risk for school failure, impaired growth and physical maturation, lowered concentrative skills, decreased motivation, increased accident involvement, and increased risk-taking activities (CCAD, 1989). Marzuk and Mann (1988) note that "a number of studies have reported a high percentage of drug abuse among young adults who attempt or complete suicide" (p. 639). The suicide rate for 10 to 14 year olds doubled between 1980 and 1985 (Waller, Baker, & Szocka, 1989). Such an issue of co-morbidity is crucial for therapists to realize. Dusek (1987) has found that by age 15, serious delinquent, antisocial behavior has actually peaked. Thus, for 10 to 14 year olds, life events play a crucial role in their future development. The additional factor of substances complicates matters.

Numerous researchers (Donovan & Jessor, 1983; Kellen, Ensminger, & Simon, 1980; Bell & Champion, 1979; Kandel, Kessler, & Margulies, 1978; Plant, 1976; Wilcox, 1985) observe the relationship of adolescent abuse of alcohol and sociopathy, social deviancy, and poly-substance abuse. In a sophisticated statistical study by Stein, Newcomb, and Bentier (1987), path model structural equations of an eight-year study showed that "prior drug use predicted disruptive drug use and a lack of social conformity predicted problems with drug use" (p. 1094). When looking a few years forward into early adulthood, alcohol use, drug use, and associated problems manifest. Other work (Kandel & Logan, 1984) suggests that most substance-abusing adolescents might grow out of their abuse. Bailey (1989) also found that the majority of adolescents who experiment with drugs and alcohol do not experience negative consequences or chronic life problems.

The outcome of untreated substance use is an unclear and complex area. Issues of differential diagnosis among types of addictions, dual diagnosis, poly-substances, and so on add to such complexities.

Little research, for example, exists concerning public health issues of human immunodeficiency virus (HIV) and substance abuse in teenagers (Petersen, 1987). It appears that sexual orientation and HIV have little correlation. On the other hand, Drucker (1986) reports that substance abuse programs are experiencing a rise in HIV-infected patients.

A related public health concern as a consequence of perinatal substance abuse is fetal alcohol syndrome. Perinatal alcohol use is considered the primary preventable cause of mental retardation (NIDA, 1987). Fetal alcohol syndrome includes central nervous system dysfunction, craniofacial deformity (widely spaced eyes, flattened nose bridge, broad face), and growth retardation. Pletch (1988) warns, however, that adolescent perinatal substance abuse may not have the same generalized effects as with pregnant adults.

DIAGNOSTIC ISSUES

The source of diagnostic nomenclature is the *Diagnostic and Statistical Manual of Mental Disorders* (DSM-III-R) (APA, 1987). What many do not realize is that the DSM-III-R is of little aid in the clinical diagnosis of adolescent substance abuse since it does not differentiate between adults and nonadults. NIDA is developing a users' manual that will soon be published; this should markedly help the diagnostic process. Alternatively, Farrow and Deisher (1988) have developed a guide to help clinicians devise solutions.

There are various standardized tests for assessing substance abuse, but most are for adults. Winters and Henley (1988) have developed a structured interview using DSM-III-R diagnostic criteria, a self-report problem severity inventory for chemical abuse, and another self-report concerning social, family, and personal factors that go along with substance use.

Researchers (Chan, Welte & Whitney, 1987; Schuckit, 1988) have found hopeful results in using laboratory methods in diagnosing alcoholism in late adolescence. Controversy continues to plague toxicology screens for substance use indicants. Scientists (Steward, 1982) note that there are numerous problems with this method, such as drug interference, false-negatives, and false-positives.

Diagnosis of substance abuse in tandem with psychopathology is often overlooked (MacDonald, 1984). Researchers (Russell, Henderson & Blume, 1985) have identified numerous other co-morbid disorders—conduct disorders, anxiety disorders, attention deficit disorder, affective disorders, psychosis, personality disorders, and eating disorders—but such broad and encompassing categories seem to lose clinical utility.

TREATMENT

Paralleling the problems concerning etiology of substance abuse and addiction is the lack of unanimity about treatment. There is no consensus among theorists, practitioners, and researchers on the acceptance of the popular disease model or concept for alcoholism. Some of the controversy concerns its goodness of fit to other drugs or for teenage populations. It is a fairly safe generalization to say that many programs utilize a 12-step Alcoholics Anonymous (AA) orientation along with adjunctive paraprofessional or ex-addict-run support/self-help groups, but not all—and the trend away from 12-step programs adds to the confusion.

Debate as to what type of treatment works best rages on, although most types or modes of treatment fall under Bailey's (1989) four categories of outpatient, inpatient, aftercare, and residential.

Outpatient

Outpatient care can take the form of self-help groups, professionally facilitated groups, individual and family therapy, halfway houses, and crisis hot lines. Most of these services and modes of therapy are straightforward to most professional readers; however, lately there has been an area of greater evolution, with a fairly large and recent surge of publications dealing with such issues (Coombs, 1988; Szapocznik, Kurtines et al., 1989; Todd & Selekman, in press). Only time and well-designed studies will tell, but there is a strong sense of optimism about the usefulness of family systems therapies in dealing with teen drug abuse, especially regarding an increased focus on phenomena such as co-dependency, enabling, and adult children of alcoholics.

Inpatient

Inpatient treatment is often the only method by which to ensure drug-free periods, albeit only for a brief period in many cases. Most contemporary programs are 7, 14, 21, or 28 days in length; utilize certified addiction counselors in tandem with social workers, psychologists, psychiatrists, and milieu staff; and follow a medical model/disease concept along with an Alcoholics Anonymous (AA) or variant model. Detoxification procedures sometimes require other medications; however, studies have suggested that less than 5 percent of admittees actually need such intervention (CATOR, 1986).

Aftercare

Aftercare programs typically follow inpatient treatment. They take the form of day-treatment programs, aftercare groups (daily to weekly), and AA meetings and groups.

Residential

Residential treatment is typically used with adolescents who present with substance abuse in tandem with other social, familial, school, and/or criminal problems. Use of paraprofessionals is likely, and the treatment structure is quite similar to inpatient treatment, with a greater focus on the milieu of community of the residents. Length of stay tends to be considerably longer—6 to 24 months— and a focus on behavioral expectancies may be more prevalent.

The differential outcome of the various treatment setting approaches is questionable. Information on which the studies were made almost exclusively used adults in the programs.

OUTCOME EFFICACY OF TREATMENT

The issue of treatment outcome and efficacy in substance abuse is sophisticated, complicated, and convoluted. It seems that more is written about the problems of such research than the solutions (Holmberg, 1985; Kandel, Davies, Darus & Yamaguchi, 1986); Freedman & Glickman, 1987). This problem is amplified when looking at the paucity of such work in the area of adolescent addictive treatment efficacy and outcome.

The concept of relapse is "poorly understood or researched" (Bailey, 1989, p. 158) and markedly affects the empirical examination of treatment effects. Bailey states that "there is little agreement on what constitutes successful treatment outcome (e.g., abstinence vs. successful life function vs. controlled use) or how to measure it (e.g., treatment effects vs. 'maturing out' effects). There is also weak correlation between short-term and long-term treatment outcome" (p. 158).

Major studies, such as the Treatment Outcome Prospective Study (TOPS), Drug Abuse Reporting Program (DARP), and upcoming Drug Abuse Treatment Outcome Study (DATOS) (Hubbard, Marsden, Rachal, Harwood, Cavanaugh & Ginzburg, 1989), go far in the sampling techniques, rigorous methodologies, and statistical sophistication, but they too focus on adult populations.

Friedman and Glickman (1987) have identified a set of predictor factors of program structures that are statistically significant:

a) treat a large number of adolescent clients; b) have a special school for school dropouts; c) have a relatively large budget; d) employ counselors or therapists who have at least 2 years' experience in working with adolescent drug abusers; e) provide special services such as vocational counseling, recreational services, and birth control services; f) use such therapy methods as crisis intervention, gestalt therapy, music/art therapy, and group confrontation; and g) be perceived by the clients as allowing and encouraging free expression and spontaneous action by the clients. (p. 669)

Such studies are certainly an important step in improving patient care and thus outcome.

When examining patient factors associated with successful treatment, Friedman, Glickman and Morrissey (1986) found that factors such as not having marijuana as a primary addiction, being white, not having numerous treatment admissions, and having a longer length of stay correlated with good outcome. Newcomb and Bentier (1989) reported on studies that found factors related to poor outcome: being nonwhite, being a school dropout, abusing opiates, being young at abuse onset, polysubstance abuse, having less time in treatment, and having numerous pretreatment arrests.

Hoffman, Sonis and Halikas (1987) have specific suggestions concerning treatment outcome factors useful to consider. First, research should identify and examine outcome variables that make sense in a clinical or theoretical construct. Second, treatment response of adolescent patients should be adequately and accurately measured. Third, patient factors of demographics, pathology, and therapy needs should be individually tailored to a patient's treatment plan. Fourth, various treatment orientations, plans, and milieus should be identified and examined in relation to outcome effects. The same should be done with various patient factors. There also needs to be increased consistency among the various treating professionals as to classification nosologies, treatment paradigms, and various other patient-treatment factors. Additional concerns not specified by these authors include large, heterogeneous sample sizes; a national basis would be most helpful. Longitudinal studies tracking adolescents over various development phases would be telling of the interactional effects of maturation with addictive behaviors, and matched control cohorts would provide a strong comparative base for drug- versus nondrug-abusing adolescents.

This area is ripe for investigation in general and especially for adolescents and children.

PREVENTION

Issues addressed thus far would be moot if prevention strategies could be instilled that had high degrees of efficacy. As with about every other issue addressed in this chapter, there is more controversy than consensus. Peterson (1987) and DuPont (1987) report a general lack of success with prevention programs of the 1970s, such as Goodstadt's (1978) affective education or Swisher's (1979) affective-humanistic education. Going back in time the scare tactics of films such as *Reefer Madness* also show ineffectiveness. Newcomb and Bentier (1989) note that some prevention programs actually had an iatrogenic effect of increasing drug use; in fact, in 1973 the National Commission on Marijuana Abuse recommended a ban on prevention programs. More contemporary findings show that "Just Say No" is only a minimal success (Botvin, 1984). Methods of peer leadership, positive peer cultures, and the social influences approach seem to show some greater promise (Bailey, 1989).

Two recent meta-analyses of the literature on prevention program efficacy show contradictory findings. Tobler's (1986) work provided an in-depth and specific look at types of prevention programs and their efficacy. The results were optimistic. Two years later, another researcher's (Bangert-Drowns, 1988) meta-analytic study indicated that no drug prevention or education programs yielded any positive, decremental effect on teen substance abuse.

Such findings certainly call for further examination. It is important, however, to be aware that prevention programs are not simply benign at worst. Careful consideration needs to be the first step in the design of any such project so as to guard against iatrogenic risks and to diminish adolescent substance use and addiction.

CONCLUSION

Substance abuse among teenagers is a highly debated and controversial area. The tide is starting to turn from a lack of empirical investigation toward more rigorous methodologies. The field and subspecialties, however, seem no closer to any unifying, expansionistic, or reductionistic paradigm of etiology, diagnosis, treatment, evaluative methods, or prevention strategies. Without such a direction, an amorphous but growing body of literature and clinical work will continue to spin its wheels.

REFERENCES

American Psychiatric Association (1987). *Diagnostic and statistical manual of mental disorders* (3d ed. rev.). Washington, D.C.: Author.

Bailey, G. W. (1989). Current perspectives on substance abuse in youth. *Journal of the American Academy of Child and Adolescent Psychiatry, 28* (2), 151–62.

Bangert-Drowns, R. L. (1988). The effects of school-based substance abuse education: A meta-analysis. *Journal of Drug Education, 18,* 243–64.

Bell, D. S. & Champion, R. A. (1979). Deviancy, delinquency and drug use. *British Journal of Psychiatry, 134,* 269–76.

Botvin, G. (1984). *Prevention Research in Drug Abuse and Drug Abuse Research.* Rockville, Md.: National Institute on Drug Abuse.

Carnegie Council on Adolescent Development (1989). *Turning points.* Washington, D.C.: CCAD.

CATOR (1986). *Chemical abuse/Addiction treatment outcome registry.* St. Paul, Minn.: CATOR.

Chan, S. W. K., Welte, J. W. & Whitney, R. B. (1987). Identification of alcoholism in young adults by blood chemistries. *Alcohol, 4,* 175–79.

Chartbook on adolescent health (in press). Rockville, Md.: Public Health Service, Health Resources and Services Administration, Bureau of Health Care Delivery and Assistance, Division of Maternal and Child Health.

Coombs, R. H. (ed.). (1988). *The family context of adolescent drug abuse.* New York: Haworth.

Dilsaver, S. C. (1986). Antimuscarinic agents as substances of abuse. *Journal of Clinical Psychopharmacology, 8,* 14–22.

Donovan, J. E. & Jessor, R. (1983). Problem drinking and the dimension of involvement with drugs: A Guttman Scalogram Analysis of adolescent drug use. *American Journal of Public Health, 73* (5), 543–52.

Drucker, E. (1986). AIDS and addiction in New York City. *American Journal of Drug and Alcohol Abuse, 12,* 165–81.

DuPont, R. L. (1987). Prevention of adolescent chemical dependency. *Pediatric Clinics of North America, 34,* 495–505.

Dusek, J. B. (1987). *Adolescent development and behavior.* Englewood Cliffs, N.J.: Prentice-Hall.

Farrow, J. A. & Deisher, R. (1988). A practical guide to the office assessment of adolescent substance abuse. *Pediatric Annals, 15,* 675–84.

Friedman, A. S. & Glickman, N. W. (1986). Program characteristics of successful treatment of adolescent drug abuse. *Journal of Nervous and Mental Disease, 174* (11), 669–79.

Friedman, A. S. & Glickman, N. W. (1987). Effects of psychiatric symptomatology on treatment outcome for adolescent male drug abusers. *Journal of Nervous and Mental Disease, 175,* 425–30.

Friedman, A. S., Glickman, N. W. & Morrissey, M. R. (1986). Prediction of successful treatment outcome by client characteristics and retention in treatment of adolescent drug treatment programs: A large-scale cross-validation. *Journal of Drug Education, 16,* 149–65.

Goodstadt, M. S. (1978). Alcohol and drug education. *Health Education Monographs, 6,* 263–79.

Hoffman, N. G., Sonis, W. A. & Halikas, J. A. (1987). Issues in the evaluation of chemical dependency treatment programs for adolescents. *Pediatric Clinics of North America, 34,* 449–59.

Holmberg, M. B. (1985). Longitudinal studies of drug abuse in a fifteen-year-old population. *Acta Psychiatra Scandanavia, 71,* 80–91.

Hubbard, R. L., Marsden, M. E., Rachal, J. U., Harwood, H. J., Cavanaugh, E. R. & Ginzburg, H. M. (1989). *Drug abuse treatment.* Chapel Hill, N.C.: University of North Carolina Press.

Johnson, L. D., O'Malley, P. M. & Bachman, J. G. (1987). Psychotherapeutic, licit, and illicit use of drugs among adolescents. *Journal of Adolescent Health Care, 8,* 36–51.

Kandel, D. B. & Logan, J. A. (1984). Patterns of drug use from adolescence to young adulthood: I. Periods of risk for initiation, continued use, and discontinuation. *American Journal of Public Health, 74,* 660–66.

Kandel, D. B., Davies, M. A., Darus, D. & Yamaguchi, K. (1986). The consequences in young adulthood of adolescent drug involvement. *Archives of General Psychiatry, 43,* 746–54.

Kandel, D. B., Kessler, R. C. & Margulies, R. Z. (1978). Antecedents of adolescent initiation into stages of drug use: A developmental analysis. *Journal of Youth and Adolescence, 7* (11), 13–40.

Kellen, S. G., Ensminger, M. E. & Simon, M. B. (1980). Mental health in first grade and teenage drug, alcohol, and cigarette use. *Drug and Alcohol Dependence, 5,* 273–304.

Kumpfer, K. L. (1987). *Prevention of drug abuse: A critical review of risk factors and prevention strategies.* Paper prepared for the American Academy of Child and Adolescent Psychiatry's Project Prevention: An Intervention Initiative.

MacDonald, P. I. (1984). Drugs, drinking and adolescents. *American Journal of Disordered Children, 138,* 117–25.

MacDonald, P. I., MacKenzie, R. G., Cheng, M. & Haftel, A. J. (1987). The clinical utility and evaluation of drug screening techniques. *Pediatric Clinics of North America, 34,* 423–38.

McHugh, M. J. (1987). The abuse of volatile substances. *Pediatric Clinics of North America, 34,* 333–40.

Marzuk, P. M. & Mann, J. J. (1988). Suicide and substance abuse. *Psychiatric Annals, 18* (11), 639–45.

Morrison, M. M. & Smith, Q. T. (1987). Psychiatric issues of adolescent chemical dependence. *Pediatric Clinics of North America, 34,* 461–80.

National Institute on Drug Abuse. (1987). *National household survey of drug abuse: Population estimates 1985.* Rockville, Md.: Author.

Newcomb, M. D. & Bentier, P. M. (1989). Substance use and abuse among children and teenagers. *American Psychologist, 44* (2), 242–78.

Newcomb, M. D., Maddahian, E. & Bentier, P. M. (1986). Risk factors for drug use among adolescents. *American Journal of Public Health, 76,* 525–31.

Pascal, C. B. (1987). Selected legal issues about AIDS for drug abuse treatment programs. *Journal of Psychoactive Drugs, 19,* 1–12.

Pentel, P. (1984). Toxicity of over-the-counter stimulants. *Journal of American Medical Association, 252,* 1898–1903.

Petersen, R. C. (ed.). (1987). *Drug abuse and drug abuse research: The second report to Congress.* Rockville, Md.: National Institute on Drug Abuse.

Plant, M. A. (1976). Young drug and alcohol casualties compared: Review of 100 patients at a Scottish psychiatric hospital. *British Journal of Addiction, 71,* 31–43.

Pletch, P. K. (1988). Substance use and health activities of pregnant adolescents. *Journal of Adolescent Health Care, 9,* 38–45.

Roush, G. C., Thompson, W. D. & Berberian, R. M. (1980). Psychoactive medicinal and nonmedicinal drug use among high school students. *Pediatrics, 66,* 709–15.

Russell, M., Henderson, C. & Blume, S. B. (1985). *Children of alcoholics: A review of the literature.* New York: Children of Alcoholics Foundation.

Ruttenber, J. (1985). *Designer drugs; Patterns and trends of drug abuse: A national and international perspective.* Rockville, Md.: National Institute on Drug Abuse.

Schuckit, M. A. (1988). Alcoholism: Methods for better diagnosis. *Psychiatric Times, 1* (6), 15–17.

Semlitz, L. & Gold, M. S. (1986). Adolescent drug abuse. *Psychiatric Clinics of North America, 9,* 455–73.

Stein, J. A., Newcomb, M. D. & Bentier, P. M. (1987). An 8 year study of multiple influences on drug use and drug use consequences. *Journal of Personality and Social Psychology, 53* (6), 1094–1105.

Steward, D. C. (1982). The use of the clinical laboratory in the diagnosis and treatment of substance abuse. *Pediatric Annals, 11,* 669–82.

Swisher, J. D. (1979). Prevention issues. In R. I. Dupont, A. Goldstein & J. O'Donnell (eds.), *Handbook on drug abuse* (pp. 423–35). Washington, D.C.: National Institute on Drug Abuse.

Szapocznik, J. I., Kurtines, W. M. & contributors (1989). *Breakthroughs in family therapy with drug-abusing and problem youth.* New York: Springer.

Tobler, N. S. (1986). Meta-analysis of 143 adolescent drug prevention programs: Quantitative outcome results of program participants compared to a control or comparison group. *Journal of Drug Issues, 16,* 537–68.

Todd, T. C. & Selekman, M. (in press). *Family therapy approaches with adolescent substance abusers.* Boston: Allyn & Bacon.

Vaillant, G. E. (1980). Natural history of male psychological health. VIII. Antecedents of alcoholism and "orality." *American Journal of Psychiatry, 137,* 181–86.

Waller, A. E., Baker, S. P. & Szocka, A. (1989). Childhood injury deaths: National analysis and geographic variations. *American Journal of Public Health, 79* (3), 310–15.

Winters, K. & Henley, G. (1988). *The Personal Experience Inventory.* Los Angeles: Western Psychological Services.

Wilcox, J. A. (1985). Adolescent alcoholism. *Journal of Psychoactive Drugs, 12* (2), 77–85.

_____ *Part Five*

Clinical Issues

15

Countertransference in the Treatment of Addictive Disorders

ALAN M. JAFFE AND
KAREN L. JAFFE

Countertransference is a clinical phenomenon in which the therapist's ability to listen and empathize is compromised and distorted by his own unresolved psychological issues. These issues make it difficult for the therapist to differentiate himself from the patient's own cognitive and emotional experience, and thereby he feels and responds subjectively to the patient. If the therapist is unaware of his countertransference, it can result in an empathic failure with the patient. Countertransference is most likely to occur when therapists are dealing with patients whose problems evoke a personal response in the therapist, a particularly common occurrence in the treatment of the addictions, since virtually everyone's life is touched in some way by an addicted individual.

DEFINITION OF CONCEPT

Kernberg (1975) summarizes the two schools of thought regarding the phenomenon of countertransference. The classical approach, as proposed by Freud (1910), Fliess (1953), Gitelson (1952), and Reich (1960), defines countertransference as the unconscious emotional reaction of the therapist to the patient's transference. In this model, countertransference is looked upon as a disturbing factor, interfering with the objective and presumed neutral position to be taken by the therapist. It adversely colors the therapist's perception.

The totalistic definition is the alternate school, giving broader meaning to the concept. In this model, countertransference is viewed as the "total emotional reaction of the psychoanalyst to the patient in the treatment situation" (Kernberg, 1965, p. 50). Representatives of this approach view countertransference material as a valuable tool for understanding the patient. The basic assumption is that the therapist's unconscious understands the unconscious of his patient and that the emotional response of the therapist is frequently closer to the psychological state of the patient than the therapist's conscious judgment of the same.

Little (1951) highlights the importance of understanding the countertransference reaction because it can have a decisive effect on the patient's ability to reexperience childhood situations. The therapist's tendency to repeat the behavior of the patient's parents, a manifestation of countertransference, can interrupt the important opportunity to reexperience childhood emotions with a more objective and support-giving individual.

Nadelson (1977) stresses the significance of countertransference as a means of extending one's understanding of the patient that yields further information of the patient's experience of the world. This position is further discussed by Spitz (1956), who views countertransference as a "necessary prerequisite of analysis" (p. 257). Once accepting this presumption, Spitz outlines the steps involved in making the best use of countertransference material. In the first step, the therapist becomes aware in himself of the manifestations of his unconscious responses. Step 2 involves the therapist's inferring the underlying unconscious processes in himself. In step 3, the therapist possesses sufficient freedom to perform a transient trial identification with those processes in the patient that elicited his or her countertransference response. Spitz's manner of handling countertransference presupposes that the therapist is conscious of the countertransference issues involved in a given patient-therapist interaction. Marshall's (1979) configuration of possible countertransference issues suggests that what he labels "Type III countertransference" (p. 417), where the difficulties are not seen by the therapist and the patient is essentially in control of treatment, needs to become "Type IV countertransference" in which "the patient is primarily responsible for inducing thoughts and feelings (but no action) in the therapist which are fully within the therapist's awareness" (p. 417). Marshall suggests that the transition of Type III into the more usable Type IV countertransference occurs through the process of supervision and peer discussion.

Spotnitz (1979, p. 331) uses the term *subjective countertransference* to describe "atypical feeling responses which are attributable to insufficiently analyzed adjustment patterns in the therapist and are usually rooted in distortions created by memory process." Winnicot (1960) discusses a related distortion: "objective countertransference" (p. 70), which involves those therapist feelings provoked by the patient's transference feelings and attitudes. Marshall (1979) differentiates subjective and objective countertransference by stating that in the former, the countertransference feelings are "induced primarily by the internal promptings of the therapist" (p. 415), while in the latter the countertransference is generally induced by external factors, the patient.

Often in the treatment of addicted patients, anger emerges toward the therapist due to the perception that he is taking away something (the addictive symptom) that the patient perceives as critical to his existence. This is a product of the therapist-patient relationship. When experiencing anger toward the therapist, it is as if the addicted patient loses all memory of any other positive experience (Shapiro, 1978). The therapist who desires to help is frustrated not just by nonappreciation on the patient's part but is met with the patient's anger (Jaffe, 1980). Not considering the patient's behavior in a theoretical context might leave the therapist feeling worthless, restless, and bored.

OVERIDENTIFICATION

Overidentification is a countertransference problem that probably occurs with greater frequency in the treatment of addictive disorders than in any other mental health subspecialty. The reason is that there are a great number of paraprofessional counselors and therapists who are providing services to people with similar problems. For example, virtually all alcoholism and substance abuse programs have staff members who are themselves recovering alcoholics and substance abusers. Programs dealing with eating disorders, especially overeating, utilize personnel who have learned to control their eating behavior. When describing the desirability of having female therapists work with the anorexic patients, Wooley (1991) states, "The female therapist will at times experience an identification with the patient's emptiness, her dearth of energy" (p. 260). This type of treatment we refer to as *identification counseling*. This self-identification counseling approach, considered by many to be an important component of any treatment program, can be an effective therapy supplement as long as the counselor understands his ego boundaries or where his experience ends and the patient's begins.

A common countertransference pitfall for those providing help to others from the self-identifying perspective is to see the patient's experience as paralleling his own, to the point of perceiving it inaccurately (Schafer, 1959). Research has shown that recovering alcoholic counselors perceive a greater dependency on alcohol in patients than do their nonrecovering professional counterparts (Skuja, 1981). This form of overidentification causes the patient to experience the therapist as presumptuous. The therapist presumes to understand the patient better than the patient does himself because the therapist identifies with some common element. The patient also tends to perceive the therapist as being authoritarian because he, at least unconsciously, adopts the position that "my way worked for me, so it must work for you!" This approach denies the patient the uniqueness of his own phenomenology and deprives him of the accurate empathic mirroring necessary for a healthy adjustment. Problems of undifferentiation of this kind can contaminate the therapeutic process.

It is also common for overidentification countertransference to occur in a therapist for whom there is little similarity (not even a common addiction) with the patient. The prerequisite condition for overidentification, after all, is not the actual commonality between therapist and patient but the perceived commonality. A therapist who overidentifies will mistakenly respond to the properties of his own unresolved transference (Spotnitz, 1979) that appear to take form in the person of his patient. The unconscious need for the therapist to find an external object (the patient) to work through his own unresolved conflicts (Jaffe, 1977) often provokes a severe negativistic reaction in the patient, which is further misunderstood and likely to be mishandled by the therapist.

PROJECTIVE IDENTIFICATION-
COUNTERTRANSFERENCE

Projective identification describes a two-step process in which an individual projects his own conflicts, needs, anxieties, or problems onto another person (object). Second, the individual from whom the projection originates attributes with the projected material to the recipient. What differentiates projective identification from overidentification is the degree to which the therapist engages in projective countertransference with the patient. An example is the substance abuse counselor who has a tendency to overevaluate substance abuse because he is a recovering substance abuser and has an unconscious need to work through unresolved issues. We have all witnessed some overzealous recovering addiction counselors who view counseling as an obligation rather than a clinical subspecialty. These individuals exhibit a tendency to project their own addiction onto those who do not quite exhibit the symptoms; then they go about attempting to help the patient with a problem he or she does not (exactly) have.

An example of projective identification in everyday life is the stereotypic aging widow who lives in an apartment with her lap dog. She treats the dog with very special care so that its nails are always manicured, coat perfectly groomed, eats only ground beef, and never gets dirty. One might ask whether the dog requires such pampering, and of course the answer is "no"; the dog would be just as happy to roll around in dirt and eat bones off the ground. The dog does not wish to be pampered; the *woman* does. She projects her desire to be pampered onto the dog, attends to the projected need, and then identifies with the dog while it is being pampered. This represents projective identification in which an individual attempts indirectly to take care of his own needs by taking care of them in an external object.

DEALING WITH THE PATIENT'S PROJECTIVE
IDENTIFICATION

The patient also engages in projective identification, with the therapist serving as the object. "When the patient employs projective identification with the therapist, the therapist may confuse the source and feel the feelings which well up inside as her own" (Clark, 1989, p. 312). Subjecting these feelings to intrapsychic scrutiny provides a paradigm of reinternalization and "genuine psychological growth" (Ogden, 1979, p. 362).

PROJECTIVE COUNTERIDENTIFICATION

The process thus far described does not allow for the revelation of therapist's own personality and history. Of course, the individual's therapist has his own areas of strength and weakness, which can inhibit and possibly prohibit the therapist's ability to provide a corrective experience for the patient. Grinberg (1962) and Langs (1979) address the potential problems that can arise, as well as suggestions for avoiding such difficulties. Grinberg states that the patient's excessive use of projective identification "gives rise to a specific reaction in the analyst, who is unconsciously and passively 'led' to play the sort of role the patient hands over to him" (1962, p. 436). He labels this phenomenon *projective counteridentification*. This is a specific type of countertransference reaction that Grinberg differentiates from countertransference reactions resulting from the analyst's own emotional attitudes, or on his neurotic remnants, reactivated by his patient's conflicts.

In projective counteridentification, the therapist is a passive object of the patient's projections and interjections. Here the therapist's response stems from his own unresolved issues, reactivated by the patient's conflicts. However, the emotional response may be quite separate from the therapist's own emotions and appear primarily as a reaction to the patient's projections upon the therapist. Once this form of countertransference has occurred, the therapist tends to respond to the patient's projected material as if it is meant in a very real and personal way about the therapist. Occasionally the therapist becomes so personally enmeshed in this process that he may have the feeling of no longer being himself and seems to become the object the patient wanted him to be. "A feeling of bewilderment is often experienced by the therapist who may resort to rationalize the discomfort. Additional supervision and personal therapy can aid the therapist in regaining a sense of cohesive identity" (Jaffe, 1977).

REPOSITORY PROJECTION

Repository projection is a term we developed to describe countertransference phenomenon, which is similar to pure projective identification in function but not in form. The similarity lies in the unconscious projection of the therapist's issues onto the patient, the difference lies in the formal properties of the therapist's response namely, the lack of identification with the patient. So although the therapist is engaging in projection of his own material (usually negative), the patient becomes a repository for these negative issues.

A typical example is the substance abuse therapist who projects his problems with control onto the patient, seeing himself as being excessively controlling although in reality he is not. The therapist, projecting his own compensatory need for extreme control, in effect deposits this need onto the person of the patient and then responds to it as if it entirely belongs to the patient. This type of countertransference is found in therapists who tend to adopt a defensive style that involves externalization of negative aspects of the self.

The defense, which is predominant in this countertransference process, is projection, just as it is in projective identification and overidentification. Ogden (1979) considers the repository phenomenon as a type of projective identification: "as a group of fantasies and accompanying object relations having to do with the ridding of the self of unwanted aspects of the self: the depositing of those unwanted 'parts' in another person; and finally, with the 'recovery' of a modified version of what was extruded" (p. 357).

As a result, these countertransference phenomena present treatment problems and impasses, with notable boundary problems between patient and therapist. These problems with boundaries arouse additional transferences in the patient, particularly for those with dysfunctional families (as described by Schlessinger & Horberg, 1988) and especially those who were intrusive and failed to respect the patient's boundaries earlier in life. This causes a recapitulation of these earlier unresolved autonomy issues, which have a tendency to compromise the therapeutic alliance to a dysfunctional level, paralleling the early family experience. Since the therapist is himself in the dark as to the cause of this pathological interaction, he is of no help to himself or the patient to correct it without supervision. It is amazing that the therapeutic relationship does not collapse as a result.

EMPATHIC RESISTANCE

The countertransference phenomenon demonstrating the most primitive defense on the part of the therapist is what we call *emphatic resistance*. This represents a defensive posture in the therapist in which denial is prepotent. Because denial is of the lowest level of ego defense, it causes the greatest amount of distortion in the therapist's perception and therefore the treatment itself.

Empathic resistance is seen when the therapist is totally unable to understand elements of the patient's psychic functioning because he defended against seeing it internally. For some time it has been observed in medical practitioners who unknowingly work with addicted patients. Physicians unable to identify addictive problems in themselves are unable to diagnose them accurately in their patients. This has led to the gallows humor frequently told among addiction specialists, as follows: Question: "What is the definition of an alcoholic?" Answer: "A patient who drinks more than his doctor!" Anyone working in the addictions field has witnessed countless times that physicians misdiagnose patients because of their own denial defense. A great number of addictions are caused by physicians who prescribe (poorly monitored) tranquilizers to patients who are attempting to manage anxiety that the physician (due to his own defense structure) is unable to comprehend except in the most simplistic way. Blocked from understanding the true nature of their own anxiety, they unwittingly lead their patients down the road to addiction. At the very least, physicians have a tendency to diagnose or misdiagnose addictive problems according to their own internal predispositions (Horberg, Heslein & Jaffe, 1983).

Overweight therapists who are unable to see the eating addiction in their patients and cigarette-smoking clinicians who avoid dealing with this problem in the people they see are the common examples of empathic resistance.

PROBLEMS OF IDENTITY

Distortions of Diminution

This type of countertransference is similar in form to empathic resistance, but the defensive constellation that causes it is higher level. While the primary defense operating in empathic resistance is denial, problems of identification derive from the defenses of rationalization and intellectualization. Therefore, we find it necessary to develop a separate category that more accurately differentiates the defensive properties of the countertransference response. An example of a distortion of diminution is the therapist who is uncomfortable on a conscious level with the intensity of his own anger. This appears in his style of treatment by his unconscious tendency to reduce the expression of his patient's anger by the therapist's affable and somewhat jovial manner. Not only is he unconsciously manipulating the patient to limit his affective expression, but he also is unable to appreciate fully the seriousness of the patient's problem with anger when it is expressed. There is a tendency to rationalize it away or deal with the anger on a purely intellectual level. This leads the patient into believing (at an unconscious level) that his anger is unacceptable, and there ensues an unconscious collusion with the therapist to conceal or reduce the existence of any affect with which he cannot comfortably identify.

The therapist's problems identifying with certain aspects of the patient's emotional life are relayed rapidly as an unconscious communication early in the treatment and interfere with the therapy. If what occurs in the therapist is an overreliance on his cognitions, "this prevents a necessary degree of regression. Such is the case in naive, pedantic, 'psychological' explanations of patients in which generalizations substitute for concrete reference, imagery, and affective tone" (Schafer, 1959, p. 347).

Distortions of diminution are often seen in therapists (not trained in the addictions) who are uncomfortable with their own issues involving compulsivity and hence find it difficult to understand how anyone can really become addicted. They are the therapists who advise their addicted patients, "Just don't drink so much," or "Just watch how much you eat and promise yourself you won't vomit anymore." It is easy to see how this countertransference problem compromises the effectiveness of treatment because serious problems are not adequately addressed.

A study conducted at Northwestern University Medical School demonstrated that physicians are less likely to diagnose alcoholism in middle- to upper-class patients admitted for some other medical problem (Horberg, Heslein & Jaffe, 1983). It can be inferred that this statistically significant phenomenon occurs as a result of the physician's difficulty understanding that compulsive behavior can occur in the social class to which he belongs. Proof is found in the increased frequency with which alcoholism is diagnosed among low-class patients. The defense of rationalization is apparent when reading the admission notes written from members of differing social classes. The middle-to upper-class patient's note might read as follows: "A 41 y/o white, married, executive reported drinking 1 quart of vodka per day was admitted for pancreatitis," whereas a lower-class patient's note would say, "A 37 y/o white, single, unemployed alcoholic was admitted for pancreatitis." The distortion in perception is understood as a problem of physician identification with lower-class patients.

Social class appears to be an important factor in the diagnosis and management of alcoholic inpatients treated in medical and psychiatric facilities. Physicians are slower to refer and less likely to diagnose alcoholism when the patient is upper or middle class even when the alcoholic pathology is extreme, the patient openly discusses his drinking when asked, and the patient is treated for conditions resulting directly from alcoholism such as alcoholic hepatitis (Horberg, Heslein & Jaffe, 1983).

Distortions of Magnitude

Distortions of magnitude, or acting out, can be described as the countertransference response in which the therapist causes an increase in the patient's impulsivity or an increase of symptomatic behavior. The therapist's relationship to potential acting out will depend in part on the therapist's need for the patient to demonstrate (magnify) his impulse expression (the opposite of diminution). Brown (1978) suggests that the therapist's need to magnify impulsivity in the patient will certainly interfere with treatment:

Some therapists unconsciously encourage and vicariously enjoy their patients' acting out. . . . On the other hand, the therapist's being overly anxious about the patient's acting out is reacted to by the patient, who then unconsciously gratifies his sadism as well in the acting out, and gets a spurious sense of power and independence through it. (p. 466)

Part of what can make the acting-out patient annoying for the therapist, and lead to countertransference difficulties, is the implicit message in the acting out: the patient does not wish to take into account any significant etiological factors arising from within himself (Giovacchini, 1975). This can be experienced by the therapist as a negation of his value (Jaffe, 1981). The therapist's permitting of excessive abuse would be what Kernberg (1965) calls "masochistic submission" to the patient's aggression. He explains this submission as a large part of the therapist's work, which involves the experience of giving something good and receiving something bad in return. The aspect that frustrates the analyst-therapist is his inability to correct such a situation through "the usual means of dealing with reality. It is as if in his relationship with that particular patient, the analyst would have to lose confidence in the force that could neutralize aggression; this in turn reactivates the analyst's masochism" (Kernberg, 1975, p. 61). And based on Kernberg's position, a younger and less experienced therapist is particularly vulnerable to this form of submission.

One problem confronted by the young or inexperienced addiction therapists involves striking a satisfactory compromise between natural spontaneous interaction and maintaining a professional posture. It appears that professional posture is a standard that grows out of the young therapist's experience as a supervisee and out of his own fantasy about how a therapist is expected to behave. The supervisor offers his perceptions of what is taking place in the case and how it might be handled. The student can use his supervisor's perceptions as well as his own. It appears that most young therapists go through a period of discovery when they realize that their self-styled image of a professional psychotherapist has little hope of surviving against the real moment-to-moment interaction with a patient. This is particularly true when considering the intensity so characteristic of work with addicted patients.

When dealing with addicted patients, it is important for the therapist to consider the phenomenon of countertransference in the context of the family. The presence of the family, specifically the parents and other siblings, increases the number of variables that the therapist must attend to. Rather than examining one's thoughts and feelings in relation to just one individual, the therapist must examine those thoughts and feelings evoked by issues that arise from the interaction of family members. The family, with a unique set of problems, has the potential to elicit a wide range of reactions on the part of the therapist. The intense affect, which typically becomes manifest in the interactions of dysfunctional families, requires the therapist to be particularly sensitive to how he is responding to such a powerful onslaught of psychopathology. This is necessary in order to avoid acting out the conflicts of the family. It is important for the therapist to gain insight into himself and to adjust to the particular family's set of contingencies in order for the treatment to proceed. This can be applied to the expanded therapeutic encounter which includes the individuals making up the family of the addicted patient.

REFERENCES

Brown, S. (1978). Acting out in adolescence: Genesis and some treatment implications. In *Adolescent psychiatry: Developmental and clinical studies* (vol. 6). New York: Jason Aronson.

Clark, K. (1989). Countertransference to transference acting out of hopelessness. In

J. Masterson and R. Klein (eds.), *Psychotherapy of the Disorders of the Self* (pp. 308–27). New York: Brunner/Mazel.

Fliess, R. (1953). Countertransference and counteridentification. *Journal of the American Psychoanalytic Association, 1,* 268–84.

Freud, S. (1957). The future prospects of psychoanalytic therapy (1910). *Standard Edition, 11,* 139–51. London: Hogarth Press.

Giovacchini, P. L. (1975). *Psychoanalysis of character disorders.* New York: Jason Aronson.

Gitelson, M. (1952). The emotional position of analyst in psycho-analytic situation. *International Journal of Psycho-Analysis, 33,* 1010.

Grinberg, L. (1962). On a specific aspect of countertransference due to the patient's projective identification. *International Journal of Psychoanalysis, 43,* 436–40.

Horberg, L., Heslein, R. & Jaffe, A. (1983). *Reluctance to diagnose alcoholism in middle-class patients.* Paper presented at the American Psychological Association, Anaheim, Calif.

Jaffe, A. (1977). *The role of personal therapy in clinical training.* Paper presented at the Fall Conference of the Illinois Psychological Association.

Jaffe A. (1981). The negative therapeutic reaction. *Psychotherapy: Theory, Research and Practice, 3,* 313–19.

Jaffe, K. (1980). *Countertransference in the treatment of a borderline adolescent.* Ph.D. dissertation, Illinois School of Professional Psychology.

Kernberg, O. (1965). Notes on countertransference. *International Journal of Psychoanalysis, 13,* 38–55.

Kernberg, O. (1975). *Borderline conditions and pathological narcissism.* New York: Jason Aronson.

Langs, R. (1979). The international dimension of countertransference. In L. Epstein and A. Feiner (eds.), *Countertransference.* New York: Jason Aronson.

Little, M. (1951). Countertransference and the patient's response to it. *International Journal of the Psychoanalysis, 32,* 32–40.

Marshall, R. J. (1979). Countertransference with children and adolescents. In L. Epstein and A. Feiner (eds.), *Countertransference.* New York: Jason Aronson.

Nadelson, T. (1977). Borderline rage and the therapist's response. *American Journal of Psychiatry, 7,* 134.

Ogden, T. (1979). On projective identification. *Journal of Psychoanalysis, 60,* 357–73.

Reich, A. (1960). Further remarks on counter-transference. *International Journal of Psychoanalysis, 41,* 389–95.

Schafer, R. (1959). Generative empathy in the treatment situation. *Psychoanalytic Quarterly, 28,* 342–73.

Schlessinger, S. & Horberg, L. (1988). *Taking charge.* New York: Simon and Schuster.

Shapiro, E. R. (1978). The psychodynamics and developmental psychology of the borderline patient: A review of the literature. *American Journal of Psychiatry, 135,* 1305–15.

Skuja, A. (1981). Treatment attitudes of recovered alcoholic counselors and nonalcoholic counselors. *Alcohol Dependency, 8,* 61–68.

Spitz, R. (1956). Countertransference: Comments on its varying role in the analytic situation. *Journal of the American Psychoanalytic Association, 4,* 256–65.

Spotnitz, H. (1979). Narcissistic countertransference. In L. Epstein and A. Feiner (eds.), *Countertransference.* New York: Jason Aronson.

Tansey, M. J. & Burke, W. F. (1989). *Understanding countertransference.* Hillsdale, N. J.: Analytic Press.

Winnicot, D. W. (1966). Report on panel: Problems of transference in child analysis. *Journal of the American Psychoanalytic Association, 14,* 528–37.

Wooley, S. (1991). Use of countertransference in the treatment of eating disorders: A gender perspective. In C. Johnson (ed.), *Psychodynamic treatment of anorexia nervosa and bulimia* (pp. 245–94). New York: Guilford Press.

16

Supervision of Substance Abuse Counselors

*THOMAS C. TODD AND
ANTHONY W. HEATH*

Experienced substance abuse counselors have reason to be concerned. At any time, they can be drafted to provide supervision for their peers, experienced counselors who are seeking substance abuse treatment certification, or for naive students. For many, this invitation is flattering; it often promises prestige, authority, increased income, and a new challenge—or so it seems. Later it may seem that the invitation to supervise contained more malice than respect. As every manager of employees knows, personnel matters can consume every moment of time and lead otherwise reasonable people to search bookstores for advice. Supervision is hard work in every industry and even harder, we think, when the people being supervised are enthusiastically trying to help people who may very well not want any help at all. In this chapter we offer advice on how to supervise substance abuse, chemical dependency, or alcoholism counselors or therapists.

GENERAL GUIDELINES FOR SUPERVISION

There are probably as many models of counseling supervision as there are theories of counseling (Heath & Storm, 1983). Nevertheless, all the therapists who become supervisors manage to figure out some principles to guide their talks with counselors. These principles, not surprisingly, are usually similar to the ones used to steer the counseling they have done over the years. In other words, many supervisors treat counselors the way they treat their clients. This is known as isomorphism or parallel process in the supervision literature (Liddle & Saba, 1983).

The natural isomorphism between one's approach to therapy and one's approach to supervision has two noteworthy benefits for the supervisor and the counselor. First, supervisors can reference their comparably vast amount of knowledge about counseling to guide their supervision. Thus, a supervisor can employ the same methods used to address denial in a client to confront denial in the therapist. Second, counselors can observe the supervision methods used with them and use them with their clients. So, a therapist may learn from the sociable beginning of every supervision session to begin counseling sessions with a social stage (Haley, 1976).

Joining, Assessment, and Contraction

Supervisors are wise to begin supervision by joining the counselor in the learning process (Minuchin, 1974). In other words, they must talk with counselors in an effort to understand the unique background, experiences, interests, and strengths of each. This process is more than simple assessment or history taking; it is a way to become part of the counselors' lives. The supervisor learns to see as the counselor sees, to talk the counselor's talk, and to feel what the counselor feels.

In our experience, this is ideally a joint endeavor. When supervisors share themselves, they communicate trust and acceptance, two conditions that facilitate the supervision process. Thus, we often say something about our experiences in supervision, our orientations to therapy, and our history with substance abuse just as we ask our counselors to say something about each topic. This exchange also serves as a preliminary assessment of the counselor's knowledge and skill.

Once the supervisor and the counselor have reached some semblance of understanding of one another and the supervisor has a sense of the counselor's abilities, the contracting begins. The objective of contracting is to reach an overt understanding of the purpose and procedures of supervision.

Counselors have widely different expectations of the supervision process. To establish that supervision has a purpose and to ascertain the counselor's intentions, it is useful to ask a question such as, "What would you like to gain from our work together?" Some counselors submit to supervision because it is required, some use it to achieve certification, some wish to learn more about counseling, and some use it for personal growth. Many of our supervisees have wanted little from supervision except recognition, support, and encouragement. Clearly it is valuable to understand the specific purposes of every supervisee.

Similarly, counselors have divergent learning styles and prefer different supervision methods. Some want a good listener, some want precise direction, some want a free-flowing exchange of ideas, and some want career guidance. Some prefer individual supervision and others the camaraderie of groups. Some like to watch videotapes of their sessions, and others prefer not to see themselves on the television monitor. Supervisors should take the time to understand the preferences of each supervisee and to negotiate a unique contract for supervision.

The brief therapy literature (Fisch, Weakland & Segal, 1982) contains an idea that is relevant here: clients want different things from counselors; they are customers for different services. Some clients truly wish assistance in solving well-defined problems such as quitting drinking or binge eating. Other clients prefer to complain about problems. And some people are visitors at best. They are really "just looking."

Similarily, supervisors can expect their counselors to begin supervision as customers, complainers, or visitors. To maximize the value of supervision, it is essential to assess the desires and preferences of counselors and to contract for supervision based on this assessment. When one has a sense of the kind of service desired by a counselor, one can elect to provide it, negotiate a different contract, or refer the counselor to another supervisor if one is available.

Providing Ongoing Supervision

All models that describe the stages of counseling seem to have a beginning, a middle, and an end. The beginnings and endings are quite easy to describe, but the middles are notoriously difficult. How can writers ever hope to describe the complicated exchange of the counseling process? Similarly, how can we hope to represent the complexity of ongoing supervision of substance abuse counselors in a few paragraphs? Let us begin with some assumptions.

Supervision is an ongoing, collaborative dialogue between two professionals. The supervisor's primary responsibility is to create and maintain a context in which counselors can provide excellent services to clients, improve their professional skills, and function as a member of the professional community. Thus arises the temptation to become their supervisees' therapist. The counselor's primary responsibility is to provide the best possible services to clients. Secondarily, counselors have an ethical responsibility to continue the development of their professional skills in an appropriate manner. Thus, counselors focus on clients and on themselves but not on supervisors.

According to this view of the responsibilities of supervisor and counselor, supervisors should propose a structure for supervisory meetings. One supervisor we know proposed to her staff that weekly case conferences be held and suggested that counselors rotate responsibility for presenting their most difficult cases in 30 minutes each. She asked counselors to begin their presentations by drawing a diagram of the client family on the blackboard and describing how the family came in for treatment, how many sessions had been held, who had attended, and what problem had been contracted to solve. Her counselors thought that this structure would be helpful, and the group agreed to try it for two months.

Two months later several of the more experienced counselors said that they would prefer to discuss issues across cases, such as difficulties in working with cocaine addicts. Others wanted to talk about their personal reactions to their clients and their families of origin. After a long discussion with the supervisor, the group decided to allow each counselor to use the 30 minutes as he or she wished. The supervision group has maintained this structure for over a year now.

In discussing specific cases, supervisors help counselors figure out what to do next. Very few practicing counselors—with the possible exception of some beginners—appreciate constant direction, nor do they `` reciate ideas from left field or suggestions based on the supervisor's model oi counseling. Instead, they prefer assistance in implementing their own theoretical approaches, in doing what they think should be done. Thus, it is helpful to know the counselor's orientation to therapy and goals for every case discussed.

This collaborative approach to supervision seems to fall apart when the supervisor believes the counselor is jeopardizing a case and the counselor thinks everything is fine. When the perceived risk to the clients is deemed small, some supervisors allow counselors to continue their course of counseling in the belief that the supervisor could be wrong or the counselor will learn from his mistake. When the supervisor perceives a greater risk and is more confident in this assessment, the situation is more difficult. Frank and self-responsible confrontation seems the best first step in this situation, and a supervision group may assist in this process. Threats or other hierarchy-based interventions should be used as a last resort since they are likely to cause lasting harm to the relationship between supervisor and counselor. Similarly, therapeutic interpretations, especially when made in groups, usually violate the professional-to-professional relationship that has been agreed upon. It is more appropriate, we think, to suggest discreetly that counselors with apparent personal problems seek help from their Alcoholics Anonymous or Narcotics Anonymous groups and/or personal counselors.

Evaluating and Ending Supervision

Good supervisors are committed to helping their supervisees. To maximize the chance that they will be helpful, they ask questions like "How can I be helpful to you?" at the beginning of supervision sessions. To assess whether they have been helpful, supervisors ask "Has this been helpful?" at regular intervals. This constant contracting and evaluation process provides a self-correcting loop that promotes change when it is needed.

Evaluation is least threatening and most productive when it is bilateral. In other words, counselors and supervisors should evaluate each other based on stated goals and agreed-upon standards of performance. Thus, supervisors and counselors often agree on the criteria to be used in assessing the counselor's skills; similarly the criteria for evaluating the supervisor are discussed.

When supervision ends, for whatever reason, many supervisors use a ritual to mark the end of an era. The evaluation described above must be included in the ritual, but the supervisor may wish to add a more social element to it. Just as therapy ends with a shift toward a more social relationship among the individuals, so should supervision.

Supervision or Therapy

It is always difficult for supervisors and supervisees to maintain a clear distinction between supervision and therapy. Several factors make this distinction more difficult in the supervision of practitioners in the chemical dependency field. These include the importance of issues for adult children of alcoholics (ACOAs) and issues of the counselor's own recovery, as well as the lack of clear models in the training of counselors.

Many addictions counselors and therapists are ACOAs themselves and/or addicts in their own recovery programs. Given such backgrounds, it is not surprising that chemical dependency cases can stir up a variety of personal issues for counselors. Depending on whether the supervisee or the supervisor raises the issue, different problems are created for supervision.

Most supervisors prefer supervisees to raise issues themselves. It is not uncommon for supervisees to disclose to the supervisor that their own issues have been triggered by chemical dependency cases. Inevitably some of these situations begin to cross over into the domain of personal therapy for the supervisee. It is difficult to describe precisely how the supervisor can recognize when this is happening; much depends on the intuition of the supervisor. When the personal issue is clearly related to the case being supervised and when the supervisee conveys a sense of having at least a moderate grip on the issue, then it is probably safe to proceed with this topic. When the issue seems less under control and appears to spill over into many aspects of the supervisee's clinical work, the issue may need to be dealt with in personal therapy.

Supervisors often dread raising personal issues with supervisees. Supervisees often object to the conclusions of the supervisor or question whether the issue is the appropriate business of the supervisor. While conflict cannot be avoided, there are several ways to minimize difficulties: the issue must be clearly related to the case being supervised and must be creating significant impediments to the success of the case; the conclusions being drawn must be based on specific observations rather than global assertions about character pathology; and any criticisms should be positive and described in terms of the expected change in the behavior of the supervisee. The supervisor cannot insist on personal therapy for the supervisee; the supervisor can insist that the supervisee do his or her job as a therapist. Personal therapy may be one means of achieving this, but the supervisee needs to have the freedom to choose the means that works best and is most acceptable to him.

Even with sophisticated supervisees, it is likely that there will be controversies and conflicts around the contract for counselors who have not received much formal training in psychotherapy and do not draw sharp boundaries around their clinical practice. As much as possible, the supervisory contract should be as specific as possible about supervisory responsibility for the supervisee's cases, any responsibility of the supervisor to evaluate the supervisee, and the distinction between supervision and personal therapy.

SPECIAL ISSUES IN THE SUPERVISION OF CHEMICAL DEPENDENCY CASES

Some supervisory issues and dilemmas are more extreme and more prominent in working with substance-abusing clients and their families than in the general clinical population. Conversely, it is also true that the principles articulated here should be useful in supervising other difficult cases.

Negotiating a Workable Diagnosis and Contract

For a variety of reasons, chemical dependency seems to present a veritable mine field of issues when attempting to negotiate a workable treatment contract with a chemically dependent individual and his family system. Often a supervisor will observe a counselor painting himself into a corner by taking an extreme stand on the twin issues of diagnosis and treatment. Many therapists and addiction counselors seem content to "tell it like it is," at least from the individual perspective of that counselor. They then attribute the family's unwillingness or inability to hear the counselor's message and to accept the diagnosis as evidence of the power of the family's denial system rather than seeing themselves as contributing to this therapeutic impasse.

Admittedly, denial is a potent factor in family systems where chemical dependency is an issue, but a skillful supervisor can help the counselor avoid taking a position that is so extreme and so inflexible that it will alienate important family members. This seems to be an unfortunate consequence of training in the chemical dependency field, where the diagnosis of chemical dependency and addiction is often taken out of context and viewed as objective. Instead, our view is that diagnosis should be seen as a process of understanding the beliefs of the family members themselves and seeing whether these views can be brought into closer convergence with the views of the counselor.

We sometimes half-teasingly say to students that being "right" about diagnosis and treatment counts for only 10 to 20 percent; getting people to accept the wisdom of the recommendations is much more difficult and accounts for the other 80 or 90 percent. Particularly in the chemical dependency field, the task of the supervisor is often to help supervisees move beyond restating their position to the client, to the family, and even to the supervisor; instead they need to focus on the negotiating and influencing process with their clients. All too often supervisees try to use a bigger hammer to deliver the same ineffective message more frequently, louder, and more forcefully, even when it seems obvious that the message will be ignored.

This is an area where it is particularly important to get counselors to think systemically and to make diagnoses and recommendations with the knowledge and appreciation of the substance user's whole family system. It is very rare for a substance user to accept a message from a counselor, even a presumed expert, if that message is radically different from that being given by those in the family system, as well as those in the workplace or other important contexts for the abuser. Many addictions counselors have been trained predominantly in working with abusers as individuals or in groups and not working with their family systems; these counselors tend to overvalue one-on-one confrontation and do not have other techniques to fall back on when this fails. While it may be tempting to call the individual unmotivated or to believe that the abuser has not yet hit bottom, it may be more useful for the supervisor to help the counselor see the potential gain of enlarging the treatment system and helping to ascertain and ultimately shape the messages being given to the substance abuser by the family system.

No one in the substance abuse field wants to be accused of being a professional enabler, so it is important to make clear that we are not advocating having supervisees tell abusers and their families only what they want to hear, or to water down treatment recommendations so much that the abuser can feel justified in continued use. Often the best way out of this apparent dilemma is to help the individual substance abuser and, more important, those around the abuser to specify what information would be critical to determine whether substance use had reached problematic dimensions or whether the person was addicted. While the counselor and one or more family members may believe that the evidence is already overwhelming, it is often still useful for the counselor to take this extra step and wait so that subsequent events can provide convincing evidence of the severity of the problem. Often supervisees need help not only in recognizing this for themselves but also in restraining overzealous family members from taking a radical stance that would not be supported by other members of the family system.

One final recommendation on teamwork may also be helpful in this regard. Often supervisees find it difficult to make a strong statement of the need for treatment, especially inpatient or residential treatment, and still be able to help the patient and family to work through their ambivalence about the recommendations. Although the primary counselor may be competent to make a chemical dependency evaluation, it is often useful to have the evaluation made by a different member of the clinical team or by a trusted colleague. In such a position, the evaluator is often able to make recommendations and give feedback that is direct and pointed, while in ongoing sessions the counselor can work more gradually with the members of the system to digest the recommendations of the evaluator.

Confidentiality and Other Contracting Issues

The supervisor is in a position to help the supervisee to anticipate long-range consequences of particular decisions about confidentiality and other contractual issues that come up early in treatment. This may be particularly critical if the counselor being supervised works exclusively with the substance user in individual or group therapy. In such situations, it is important for the supervisor to provide perspective on the implicit contract that spouses, parents, and other family members believe to be operative, in addition to the explicit contract with the abuser. Without supervisory guidance, it is all too easy for counselors to make promises of confidentiality or to take on responsibilities without seeing the long-range consequences for the larger system. Rather than trying to undo damage that is already done, it is much more satisfactory to walk the supervisee through hypothetical situations and examine the broader implications of particular courses of therapeutic action. What will the counselor do if he learns of a relapse? of illegal activity other than drug use? How will telephone calls from family members be handled if the caller asks for the call to be kept secret from the primary patient?

TECHNICAL CONSIDERATIONS

Degree of Supervisory Control

Chemical dependency cases seem to offer particular dilemmas around the issue of responsibility. Since there is a great deal of isomorphism or parallel process between what happens in supervision and what happens in treatment (Liddle & Saba, 1983), it is not surprising that the issue of supervisory responsibility is also paramount. Often the supervisor will feel compelled to take responsibility and intervene dramatically and directly with a chemically dependency case that seems to be dangerously out of control. To a lesser extent, this could also happen when the supervisor sees little movement and believes that the supervisee is helping to enable a stuck situation. In some clinical situations, the use of live supervision makes it particularly inviting for the supervisor to intervene repeatedly or even to enter the room to offer comments to the family or couple directly. Even when live supervision is not possible, there is always the option of having the supervisor come into a session with the counselor or take over the therapy on an ongoing basis.

When this situation is viewed in the context of the discussion of responsibility, it is obvious that supervisors should be cautious in making such dramatic moves. It is tempting for the supervisor to make a dramatic one-time intervention that undercuts the treatment therapist and does little to empower the therapist. Certainly it is not the intention of the supervisor to leave the therapist and the case in worse condition than before the supervisory intervention, but this can be the unintended consequence. Supervisory interventions must therefore be considered carefully with a view toward what style of intervention and level of therapeutic sophistication will fit with the treating therapist (Todd, 1986).

The decision not to intervene as a supervisor is also difficult. While it is important to adhere to the principle of doing no harm as a supervisor, just as when acting as a therapist, sitting by passively as a supervisor and tacitly allowing a harmful course of therapy is also unethical. Probably the best way to resolve this particular dilemma is to look carefully at the parallels between what is happening in therapy and what is happening in supervision. (We will also charitably assume that the supervisor has done some careful work on his own issues around the topic of chemical dependency and the more general topic of responsibility, so that the supervisor's assessment of his reactions and motivations is comparatively accurate). Before deciding whether to intervene as a supervisor, it is often helpful to examine these parallels to see whether similar dynamics have played out between the abuser and the spouse or parents and between the family or couple and the counselor. Above all, the supervisor should try to avoid replicating patterns in other parts of the system that have proved unproductive in therapy.

Crisis Availability

The counselor must help the couple or family through drug-related crises (Stanton & Todd, 1982). Although the counselor should be available, he must also set limits and be appropriately self-protective to avoid burnout. These principles apply equally well to the supervisor and the supervisory relationship. It is extremely difficult for counselors to work with chemical dependency cases on an ongoing basis without becoming burned out unless they have strong supervisory support (Todd, Berger & Lande, 1982). This includes the possibility of quick consultations with the supervisor when a case goes into crisis. However, the supervisor must also guard against cases of their supervisees that are chronically in crisis and where the sense of crisis seems to flow rapidly up the supervisory ladder. By overreacting to such continual crises, the supervisor, like the counselor, may be contributing to a stuck situation. Instead, the supervisor needs to set appropriate limits, carefully assess whether the situation is a true emergency, take appropriate measures to avoid dealing with the same emergency over and over, and in general model for the counselor the delicate balance between being appropriately available and self-protective.

Advantages and Disadvantages of Co-Therapy

The use of co-therapy is potentially quite attractive in the chemical dependency field because of the issues of overresponsibility and burnout. Co-therapy appears to offer the advantage of keeping any single therapist from bearing exclusive responsibility for a potentially life-threatening case, especially one that erupts into crisis periodically. Co-therapy teams can offer a balance of gender, age, experience, style, and degree of responsibility. Certainly when the co-therapy relationship is one that allows the therapist to model healthy communication, problem solving, and even dealing with conflict, working with co-therapists can be a constructive experience for dysfunctional families.

Co-therapy is not without some dangers, however, even beyond the obvious danger of co-therapy relationships that do not provide healthy models of relationships. General characteristics of good co-therapy teams need not concern us here as much as the dangers and stresses of using co-therapy in a chemical dependency context. One danger concerns the multiple models of chemical dependency and chemical dependency treatment in this field. Although we welcome such diversity and believe that ultimately a comprehensive and integrative approach is ideal, this diversity can encompass considerable theoretical confusion, with team members pulling in opposite and inconsistent directions. Such theoretical conflicts, especially if they are not handled clearly and constructively, can make two co-therapists less effective as a team than either co-therapist would be acting solo.

The other danger, which is particularly acute in the chemical dependency field, is having co-therapists increasingly assume stereotyped and rigid roles, particularly on the dimension of overresponsibility and underresponsibility. Most families in which chemically dependency is a major problem can be divided into two extreme groups of overresponsible and underresponsible individuals. For such families, it is unconstructive to work with a co-therapy team that replicates these two extremes. This can become even more toxic if the responsibility issue turns into a holy war between the two therapists, with each accusing the other of a dysfunctional style of dealing with responsibility issues. Co-therapy teams need to recognize that in these families, responsibility issues will tend to polarize the team and that issues of responsibility need to be processed between team members periodically, with a particular view toward modeling flexible behavior.

Repeated crises between scheduled therapy sessions can also create havoc for co-therapy teams. It is not uncommon for one or more family members to play favorites in choosing which counselor to call between sessions to deal with an apparent crisis. Family members are certainly not unaware of differences in theapeutic style and can usually be counted on to capitalize on this by choosing the team member who will stay on the telephone longer, offer plentiful advice, and generally take considerable responsibility for solving the family's crisis. Such advice between sessions can widen the gap in styles between the more responsible and less responsible members of the team. Other family dynamics can also be replicated, such as gender stereotypes about who will be empathic, who will take strong action, and so forth. The need to handle such crises, particularly if they are frequent, can undo many of the advantages of sharing responsibility for a case through co-therapy. The co-therapy team will survive in a healthy fashion only if both members are able to continue to communicate as frequently and extensively as necessary to keep each other abreast of any new developments. When possible, the therapist who is contacted by a family member should avoid handling the crisis unilaterally and should contact the co-therapist first. Ideally a crisis session or at least a conference call involving both therapists should be scheduled. Such measures are very labor intensive and place heavy demands on the schedules of the co-therapists. When the demands on the co-therapy team are so excessive as to be unworkable in a particular clinical setting, either new limits must be set on the couple or family or the co-therapy effort must be abandoned in favor of solo therapy.

REFERENCES

Fisch, R., Weakland, J. & Segal, L. (1982). *The tactics of change: Doing therapy briefly.* San Francisco: Jossey-Bass.

Haley, J. (1976). *Problem solving therapy.* San Francisco: Jossey-Bass

Heath, A. & Storm, C. (1983). Answering the call: A manual for beginning supervisors. *Family Therapy Networker, 7* (2), 36–37, 66.

Liddle, H. & Halpin, R. (1978). Family therapy training and supervision literature: A comparative review. *Journal of Marriage and Family Counseling, 4* (4), 77–98.

Liddle, H. & Saba, G. (1983). On context replication: The isomorphic relationship of training and therapy. *Journal of Strategic and Systematic Therapies, 2,* 3–11.

Minuchin, S. (1974). *Families and family therapy.* Cambridge, Mass.: Harvard University Press.

Randolph, E. M. (1990). Supervision of adult children of alcoholics. In *Practical applications in supervision.* San Diego, Cal.: California Association of Marriage and Family Therapists.

Stanton, M. D. & Todd, T. C. (1982). The therapy model. In M. D. Stanton, et al., *The Family therapy of drug abuse and addiction.* New York: Guilford.

Todd, T. C. (1986). Consultation with mental health professionals. In L. C. Wynne, S. H. McDaniel & T. T. Weber (eds.), *Systems consultation: A new perspective for family therapy.* New York: Guilford.

Todd, T. C., Berger, H. & Lande, G. (1982). Supervisors' views on the special requirements of family therapy with drug abusers. In M. D. Stanton, et al., *The family therapy of drug abuse and addiction.* New York: Guilford.

17

Clinical Supervision of Substance Abuse Therapy

JAMES C. OVERHOLSER AND
A. MICHAEL RICCIARDI

Supervision of substance abuse therapy is important because of the high frequency of substance abuse problems today. Recent epidemiological surveys (U.S. Department of Health and Human Services, 1983; Haglund & Schuckit, 1982; Robins, Helzer & Weissman, 1984) have estimated that up to 14 percent of Americans suffer from some type of substance dependence or abuse. Furthermore, these estimates seem to be rising. Substance abusers include such diverse members of society as the stereotypic skid-row alcoholic, professionals addicted to prescription medications, assembly-line workers using cocaine daily on the job, adolescents "huffing" gasoline vapors, and college students routinely getting drunk on Saturday nights. Many people are addicted to common medications, including stimulants, sleeping pills, painkillers, diet pills, and anti-anxiety medications.

When the many direct and indirect consequences of the addictive diseases are taken into account, the impact on health care delivery systems can be massive (Secretary of Health and Human Services, 1981; West, 1984). Many people are indirectly affected by substance abuse problems—for example, when a loved one dies in an alcohol-related accident, when traumatic injuries from falls or motor vehicle accidents due to substance abuse result in long-term disabilities, or when employees miss work due to intoxication, hangover, or withdrawal symptoms. Also, substance abuse has many persistent psychological and social effects on family members (Institute of Medicine, 1980). These effects include physical, sexual, and emotional abuse of children, fetal alcohol syndrome, cocaine babies, and an increased risk for the development of substance use disorders in children of alcoholics.

Effective treatment of the substance-abusing individual is one of the most difficult problems confronting society today. Optimal treatment and supervision are necessary in order to develop any lasting change with these recalcitrant problems. This chapter focuses on dynamics of treatment supervision, examining reasons for supervision along with prescribed goals to follow in the process.

REASONS FOR SUPERVISION

Part of the problem with supervision of substance abuse therapy lies in the limited training that is provided most mental health professionals in treating substance abuse problems. Few professional training programs provide adequate instruction in substance abuse (Confusione, Leonard & Jaffe, 1988; Miller & Frances, 1986; Selin & Svanum, 1981). The mental health field has frequently minimized the importance of providing adequate training in the assessment and treatment of substance abuse problems. Substance abuse patients are often perceived as psychopathic, with little internal motivation for treatment. Because of these perceptions, many qualified professionals avoid working with substance abusers. Negative attitudes toward substance abusers (Confusione, Leonard & Jaffe, 1988) or an overemphasis on biological diseases (Kinney, Price & Bergen, 1984) can interfere with the establishment of effective training programs. At a fairly basic level, such negative attitudes need to be addressed before adequate training and supervision can be implemented. Also, substance abuse problems are so widespread that in many areas there are insufficient numbers of trained clinicians to meet the need. Because of this shortage of trained mental health professionals, many paraprofessionals serve in the role of therapist.

"Recovering" Therapists. Abstinent ("recovering") substance abusers can provide useful services under the supervision of trained professionals. They can serve as effective role models, showing clients that it is possible to get their life back together. Also, nonprofessionals can often relate to the client at a more intense level than can the professional (Blume, 1977). Typically, they are well versed in the self-help treatment model for addicts, following the 12-step program patterned after Alcoholics Anonymous (AA). Finally, nonprofessionals often can use their knowledge of street language and similar personal experiences to establish a solid therapeutic alliance with the substance-abusing client.

There are both specific and general supervision concerns when using nonprofessionals in a therapy setting. Recovering individuals can be quite dogmatic about recovery issues. They may neglect those aspects of the client that do not fit their model of addiction and recovery. Countertransference may impair the ability of a recovering alcoholic to treat substance abuse problems adequately (Krystal & Moore, 1963). The nonprofessional may overidentify with the client, making inappropriate assumptions based on personal experiences (Blume, 1977).

The recovering alcoholic's countertransference toward health professionals may affect the supervisory relationship as well. (Supervision transference issues are discussed in detail in Chapter 16.) Many recovering individuals broadly apply the concept of enabling to treatment professionals and resist recommendations and suggestions. Thus, supervisees who lack training in one of the mental health professions probably should not provide individual psychotherapy. However, nonprofessionals may be important for other forms of treatment for substance-abusing clients (Moore, 1963).

GOALS OF SUPERVISION

Clinical supervision involves a working relationship between an established therapist and a novice in order to train the novice in the many complex skills used in psychotherapy. Bradley (1989) has identified three general goals or functions of clinical supervision. First, supervision should attempt to develop in supervisees specific skills in areas directly pertaining to the services they will provide. Second, in a general way, supervision should strive to enhance the professional development of the supervisee. Third, and most important, supervision must ensure that adequate treatment is provided (Loganbill, Hardy & Delworth, 1982). Areas pertaining to each of these supervisory goals will be addressed, both in terms of the function they serve and the processes used to attain each goal.

Function 1: Promote clinical competency in the supervisee

An important function of clinical supervision involves helping supervisees develop and refine their clinical skills. A basic element of the supervision process is to ensure that supervisees possess adequate skills for the services they provide. The supervisee must possess a strong knowledge base in order to function effectively. This is the most objective and quantifiable aspect of supervision. Unfortunately, incompetent supervisees are typically described as lacking in knowledge (Peterson & Bry, 1980). Without a solid basis in the relevant theory and facts pertaining to a particular disorder, the therapist will be limited to a nonprofessional's commonsense approach. By the time a client seeks professional help, the commonsense approaches have already failed. The professional therapist must be prepared to go beyond the resources provided by a client's informal social support network.

A biopsychosocial model is helpful in addressing addiction issues (Zuker & Gomberg, 1986). Any one approach is likely to omit important issues. Multiple assessment measures are needed to capture the complexity of substance abuse problems (Wanberg & Horn, 1983). Thus, substance abuse problems necessarily involve a complex interplay of biological, psychological, and social variables. Basic areas about which the supervisee must be knowledgeable include drug assessment approaches, addictions treatment, and toxic effects of different substances. In addition to knowledge pertaining to substance use, the therapist must possess knowledge of general psychological principles. Therapists must be able to step back from the focus on substance abuse and understand the clients in relation to their psychological functioning and their social systems. Excessively focusing on the substance abuse patterns will cause a neglect of other important issues, such as other significant psychopathology, dysfunctional coping patterns, and disturbed family dynamics (Freeman, 1988).

Process 1: Education and Training

Competency can be developed in supervisees through professional education and training activities. Although this may involve didactic instruction, it should emphasize the applied aspects of the work. Education and training are most important when supervising beginning supervisees. The supervisor is serving primarily in the role of teacher (Stenack & Dye, 1982). Beginning supervisees both want and need a high degree of structure. The educational focus can provide information in a relatively efficient but structured way. As basic information and skills develop, supervisees learn to function in a more autonomous manner. Reading assignments can be useful in educating the supervisee about various aspects of assessment and treatment. The supervisee should possess basic knowledge of specific approaches pertaining to substance abuse. Because most substance-abusing clients meet criteria for one or more nonsubstance-related diagnosis, it is important for the supervisee to be familiar with the taxonomy of the *Diagnostical and Statistical Manual of Mental Disorders III* (DSM-III-R) and associated diagnostic criteria.

In contrast to the educational aspect of supervision, the training aspect involves helping the supervisee to apply knowledge to specific problem situations. Even the best books and articles leave many pragmatic questions unanswered. Many questions arise when the supervisee initially attempts to apply new techniques in clinical settings. Thus, structured clinical opportunities are often needed to allow the supervisee to develop basic clinical skills in a controlled setting. The beginning supervisee needs close monitoring in order to ensure that assessment and treatment principles are applied correctly.

One specific intervention requiring better training is group therapy skills. Group therapy may be the intervention most relevant to training in alcohol treatment (Bacorn & Connors, 1989). However, many substance abuse therapists fail to utilize in a therapeutic way the dynamic interactions within groups, instead using a didactic or confrontational approach (Powell, 1989). Group therapy requires training in and sensitivity to the many interactive dynamics that develop among group members. Insufficient attention to these factors can result in negative outcomes in therapy (Dies & Teleska, 1985). For example, younger clients often remember group therapy confrontations designed to break through the denial as being extremely negative and can become barriers to subsequent treatment.

All professionals must recognize the limitations of their own knowledge and skills, as well as the limitations of the field in general. It is inappropriate for a mental health professional to use specialized techniques of assessment or therapy without receiving adequate training or supervision. It is also inappropriate for professionals to reach beyond the limits of their field. For example, it is unethical for a psychologist to attempt to diagnose or treat the medical complications of substance abuse. Although a psychologist is not likely to attempt to prescribe medications illegally (although some do occasionally), it is more likely that someone with a background in psychology or social work may not fully appreciate the benefits of a pharmacological approach (e.g., Antabuse for prevention of relapse, Librium for detoxification). When this happens, the psychologist or social worker may discourage the client's adherence to pharmacological treatment, especially if the client expresses dissatisfaction with the medications. Because many supervisees who are recovering addicts may have been deeply inculcated in the AA tenet that "a drug is a drug is a drug," it is especially important for the supervisor to deal with a supervisee's negative attitudes toward prescribed medications when a patient is being treated pharmacologically by a physician. Thus, the effective therapist must develop a tolerance for and appreciation of different approaches to therapy.

In summary, various educational activities can ensure that a basic level of knowledge has been attained by the supervisee. Moreover, continuing education is necessary to prevent the therapist's skills from becoming outdated and obsolete (Dubin, 1972). Thus, supervisors must encourage both the learning of specific information and an interest in the process of learning.

Function 2: Enhance the Professional Development of the Supervisee

Supervision should strive to promote the professional skill and maturity of the supervisee. This can be a difficult and complex task. The supervisee often needs assistance in making the transition from trainee to independent professional. Many aspects of their clinical skills are still developing. Furthermore, anxiety over their performance, apprehension regarding being evaluated, and ambivalence over their own professional autonomy can interfere with effective supervision. All of these issues must be addressed in order to promote the supervisee's professional development.

One aspect of the supervisee's professional development involves the interpersonal aspects of all forms of treatment. Empathy, warmth, and genuineness play a critical role in the effectiveness of any form of intervention (Brady et al., 1980). Therapist empathy is closely related to the effectiveness of treatment (Millery, Taylor & West, 1980). Empathy is necessary for the therapist to understand fully the client's problems and for the client to feel understood and accepted by the therapist. This feeling of acceptance can reduce some of the client's distress and help ensure that the client remains in treatment. Thus, the quality of treatment can be important in getting the client involved in treatment and staying involved in follow-up care (Cronkite & Moos, 1978).

Relationship factors are essential for effective supervision. The best supervisors are viewed as permissive, outgoing, and self-disclosing (Nelson, 1978). In order to reduce resistance in the supervisory setting, a supportive and collaborative relationship must develop between supervisor and supervisee (Liddle, 1986). This involves the same elements of empathy, warmth, and genuineness found essential to most other treatments. The supervisee should feel understood and accepted in the supervision meetings. Furthermore, supervisees should feel that their best interests are being protected by the supervisor. However, the focus of all supervisory sessions should be on the supervisee's role as a therapist and a professional. It is inappropriate for supervision to intrude into the supervisee's personal life. Should the supervisee require personal therapy, a referral to an independent professional is necessary.

The supervisor should attempt to promote independence in the supervisee. The intermediate-level supervisee has developed many skills as a therapist, although still needing much work in order to refine the skills of case conceptualization and treatment planning. These are complex issues that often have been left to the leadership of the supervisor. In order to develop more sophisticated skills in therapy, the supervisee needs to assume responsibility for these complex tasks. It can be important to teach supervisees to develop and test hypotheses about the client's problems (Schmidt, 1979). The supervisee needs to learn what information to gather in order to develop a provisional diagnosis. Proper assessment lays the foundation for an accurate diagnosis, and the accurate diagnosis of the client's problems is essential for treatment planning. The diagnostic formulation should clearly indicate which problems need to be addressed in treatment. More specifically, a thorough assessment can suggest the proper sequence for treatment. For example, many clients simultaneously present with both depression and alcohol abuse. A thorough assessment may suggest that one client is primarily depressed and uses alcohol as a means of numbing negative emotional states. A second client may be primarily alcoholic but has become depressed due to the negative physiological and social effects of long-term alcohol abuse. Without a thorough diagnostic and historical assessment, these two clients would be treated identically.

The supervisor brings a different perspective to the client's problems, often more objective than that of the supervisee (Schlessinger, 1966). This new perspective can be essential to expanding the supervisee's views of the client; however, supervisees need to learn how to distance themselves from the therapeutic encounters and to evaluate the situation objectively. They must internalize some of the supervisor's skills and begin to use these skills independently. This level of professional development can be attained only after the supervisee has developed many of the basic therapy skills. When this stage in supervision is attained, the didactic approach should be reduced, with greater emphasis placed on the independent problem-solving ability of the supervisee.

Process 2: The Socratic Method

Overholser (in press) has applied the Socratic method to clinical supervision. The Socratic method attempts to develop self-directed problem solving in the supervisee. Supervisees should discover on their own the strengths and limitations of their therapy techniques (Ornstein, 1968). Explicit instruction can be less effective than simply providing feedback and encouraging supervisees to find the answers on their own (Claiborn & Dixon, 1982). Supervision should help the supervisee think through clinical problems and solutions (Wolberg, 1951). The Socratic method can be useful for these purposes. It incorporates three basic elements: systematic questioning, inductive reasoning, and universal definitions (Overholser, 1988).

Systematic questioning involves the use of a series of questions designed to structure the supervisee's thought processes. The questions are designed to make the supervisee think through various clinical issues. A problem-solving format (D'Zurilla & Goldfried, 1971) can be used to help the supervisee structure a client's problems (Wasik & Fishbein, 1982). Questioning can be used to ensure that the supervisee has adequately assessed all relevant aspects of the problem, has devised a reasonable treatment plan, and has anticipated realistic risks and benefits of the proposed intervention (Overholser, in press). A sequential progression of questions can be used to take a fairly crude case conceptualization and help the supervisee reason through the different issues, thus developing a more complex view of clinical problems.

Inductive reasoning is used to help the supervisee step back from specific clients with specific problems and begin to view the broader picture of problem formulation, psychotherapy process, and outcome. Supervisees can learn to identify patterns across a diverse array of situations or clients and to understand psychotherapy processes in general. As supervisees become aware of similarities across apparently different situations, knowledge can be transferred from one solution to another.

Universal definitions are used to encourage the supervisee to work from a broad conceptual base. Attempting to define issues such as success, failure, or self-control can force the supervisee to identify common elements across a variety of specific examples. The supervisee can begin looking beyond the surface to identify the underlying procedures or functions of different psychological phenomena, which can be important in helping supervisees learn to challenge their own beliefs and those of the client.

The Socratic method of supervision is most appropriate for use with intermediate-level trainees (Overholser, in press). It can help reduce problems with resistance in the supervisory sessions and can promote autonomy and self-discovery in supervisees who already possess the rudimentary skills. Finally, the approach can promote an interest in learning, emphasizing the process instead of the content of learning, which can have important ramifications for continuing education with mental health professionals.

Function 3: Ensure Adequate Treatment is Provided

An essential function of supervision is to ensure that adequate treatment is provided. Although it is probably the most important goal of supervision, it will be discussed last because it relies on the other two functions already described. Without adequate education and training, the supervisee will not have developed the skills necessary to be capable of providing effective treatment. Also, without a certain level of professional maturity, the supervisee may perform in an inappropriate manner despite possessing the prerequisite level of knowledge and skill. For example, the supervisee may use an inappropriate level of self-disclosure with the client, describing the supervisee's own history of substance use patterns. Such activities can be detrimental to the client's progress.

Therapists sometimes must decide between a therapy that is tried and tested versus using an innovative approach. There are many established psychological and pharmacological approaches to the treatment of substance abuse problems; however, it is not uncommon for a particular client to need some specialized form or adaptation of treatment. Most clients do not fit the textbook model and therefore require a completely or partially individualized approach. When this happens, it is important that the therapist remain cautious in what is done (Glenn, 1974). This basic maxim "to do no harm" is important whenever conducting new or innovative approaches to therapy. The supervisor may need to structure additional precautions to be implemented. This can involve establishing a comprehensive assessment program, using a continuous assessment format to monitor potential side effects, and explicit written consent for treatment that describes the risks and benefits of the proposed treatment and its alternatives (Sheldon-Wildgen, 1982).

The supervisor remains responsible for the treatment provided by the supervisee. Even when the supervisor makes reasonable suggestions about how to proceed in therapy, the supervisee may fail to comply with these suggestions (Slovenko, 1980). Thus, close monitoring of session activity and therapy progress is important. This should include videotape or audiotape recording of the supervisee's therapy sessions. This may need to be done on a regular basis during the early stages of training. The recording of sessions can then be reduced in frequency as the supervisee gains experience and develops competence in the specific services being provided.

Process 3: Continual Self-Monitoring and Self-Evaluation

Ethical and legal issues complicate the treatment of many psychological disorders. Legal complications become especially prominent when clients enter treatment against their will. Because many substance abusers are required to seek treatment through court orders, employer demands, or the insistence of a spouse, coercion and compliance can become important aspects of treatment.

Because of potential complications, supervisees should be monitored and evaluated for the appropriateness of services they provide. Supervisors can provide a new perspective for many difficult legal and ethical situations (Machell, 1987). Supervisees must be actively encouraged to bring forward their concerns and questions. Any areas of confusion can then be clarified in the supervisory session.

The supervisor is responsible for evaluating the performance and skills of the supervisee. This encompasses an evaluation of specific and general knowledge, generic clinical skills, technical skills specific to one theoretical orientation or to a special clinical population, and general issues related to professional demeanor. The evaluation should involve a periodic review of all aspects of the supervisee's work, examining specific skills and behaviors. However, more important than evaluating the supervisee is helping supervisees to develop their own self-evaluative abilities. Thus, the supervisee should be involved in all aspects of the evaluation process. This can be accomplished through a self-control format.

A self-control format contains elements of self-monitoring, self-evaluation, and self-reinforcement (Kanfer & Karoly, 1972). Self-monitoring involves training a person to observe and record the occurrence of specific behaviors he performs. In a supervision session, simply having the supervisee listen to an audiotape of his own performance with a client can have important beneficial effects (Beiser, 1966). This same procedure applies to having supervisees observe their own behavior in therapy. Self-observation can be effective in helping supervisees learn to reduce the frequency of inappropriate interviewing behaviors (Hosford & Johnson, 1983). Self-monitoring leads to a reduction of negative behavior by interrupting the habitual nature of certain inappropriate behaviors (Bradley, 1989). However, it can be effective only when properly structured. Subjective and global self-appraisal are of little use (Bradley, 1989).

The self-monitoring process requires the identification of specific therapeutic behaviors that should be increased or reduced. For example, the supervisee may notice that he or she asks too many questions of the client, especially closed-ended questions that can be answered with a yes or no response. This style of interviewing can be problematic because of its leading nature and interrogational style. The supervisee can learn to identify and monitor the frequency, intensity, or duration of these specific behaviors either during the actual session or by having the supervisee listen to an audiotape recording of the session later. Self-monitoring can also be useful in identifying patterns. Supervisees may learn that they ask too many questions with certain clients, about certain topics, or at certain points in the session. This additional information can be useful in helping the supervisee begin to change any maladaptive habits that were identified. A specific and concrete self-monitoring format lays the foundation for self-evaluation.

Self-evaluation is necessary for effective professional functioning. It involves having a person compare actual performance (assessed by self-monitoring) to desired performance (goals and standards). Supervisees need to develop the ability to evaluate their own work (Webb, 1983), and the supervisor's evaluation provides the foundation for the supervisee's self-monitoring and self-evaluation. The supervisor can help the overly self-critical supervisee learn to focus on his strengths as a therapist. Supportive feedback from a concerned supervisor can reduce the supervisee's apprehension about the evaluation process. The supervisor can identify areas of strengths and weaknesses and suggest ways of overcoming limitations in the supervisee's training. Over time, self-evaluation can replace evaluation from the supervisor as supervisees learn to evaluate their own performance in a critical yet constructive manner.

Self-reinforcement can be a valuable addition to the supervisory process. The extensive use of praise should be used to keep supervision a positive experience. Obviously this does not mean praising everything done by the supervisee. Instead, the selective use of verbal reinforcement can be vital to educating the supervisee in a positive manner. It can be much more tolerable and equally informative to help a supervisee identify the aspects of therapy that have been done well. Focusing on weaknesses, deficits, and mistakes can be counterproductive. Feedback from the supervisor may set the tone for one's self-feedback. A supervisor who models a verbally reinforcing style is more likely to promote self-reinforcement in supervisees. The frequent use of self-reinforcement can reduce some of the stress and burnout often found in the substance abuse field.

Self-instructional training can facilitate the evaluation process while keeping anxiety within manageable limits (Kline, 1983). Complex tasks can be broken down into their elements, and the supervisee can learn to use verbal reminders to accomplish the task. This can be useful in reducing some complex therapy skills into more manageable tasks. Using self-management procedures helps supervisees appreciate the complexities involved when attempting to change behavior (Hector, Elson & Yager, 1977).

CONCLUSIONS

The supervision of substance abuse therapy can be a difficult but rewarding process. It requires a solid knowledge base on the part of the supervisor, persistent and thorough training of the supervisee, the establishment of a collaborative working relationship between supervisor and supervisee, and the close monitoring of all services provided. These tasks are challenging for even the best supervisors.

Clinically sound and conscientious supervision of substance abuse therapy should be a high priority for the substance abuse field. Too often supervision is neglected in the mental health literature. If we are to make adequate improvements in the quality of care provided, we need to improve the selection, education, training, and monitoring of those who provide the supervision. Unfortunately, little emphasis is placed on training professionals how to serve as supervisors—a disservice to supervisor and supervisee alike. Without adequate training and preparation, even the skilled professional may have difficulties with supervision (Styczynski, 1980). Managing resistance in the supervisee is a common problem for beginning supervisors (McColley & Baker, 1982). By training mental health professionals how to supervise, it may be possible to facilitate the entire treatment process from the top down. Thus, as supervisors become more skilled in the facilitation of professional growth, even beginning-level supervisees should be capable of providing services at an acceptable level.

REFERENCES

Bacorn, C. & Connors, G. (1989). Alcohol treatment training in psychology internship programs. *Professional Psychology: Research and Practice, 20,* 51–53.

Beiser, H. (1966). Self-listening during supervision of psychotherapy. *Archives of General Psychiatry, 15,* 135–39.

Blume, S. (1977). Role of the recovered alcoholic in the treatment of alcoholism. In B. Kissin & H. Begleiter (eds.), *The biology of alcoholism: Vol 5: Treatment and rehabilitation of the chronic alcoholic* (pp. 545–65). New York: Plenum.

Bradley, L. (1989). *Counselor supervision: Principles, process, and practice* (2d ed.). Muncie, Ind.: Accelerated Development.

Brady, J. P. et al. (1980). Some views on effective principles of psychotherapy. *Cognitive Therapy and Research, 4,* 269–306.

Claiborn, C. & Dixon, D. (1982). The acquisition of conceptual skills: An exploratory study. *Counselor Education and Supervision, 21,* 274–81.

Confusione, M., Leonard, K. & Jaffe, A. (1988). Alcoholism training in a family medicine residency. *Journal of Substance Abuse Treatment, 5,* 19–22.

Cronkite, R. & Moos, R. (1978). Evaluating alcoholism treatment programs: An integrated approach. *Journal of Consulting and Clinical Psychology, 46,* 1105–19.

Dies, R. & Teleska, P. (1985). Negative outcome in group psychotherapy. In D. Mays & C. Franks (eds.), *Negative outcome in psychotherapy and what to do about it* (pp. 118–41). New York: Springer.

Dubin, S. (1972). Obsolescence or lifelong education: A choice for the professional. *American Psychologist, 27,* 486–98.

D'Zurilla, T. & Goldfried, M. (1971). Problem solving and behavior modification. *Journal of Abnormal Psychology, 78,* 107–26.

Freeman, E. (1988). Role conflicts for supervisors in alcoholism treatment programs. *Clinical Supervisor, 6,* 33–48.

Glenn, R. (1974). Standard of care in administering nontraditional psychotherapy. *University of California Davis Law Review, 7,* 56–83.

Grater, H. (1985). Stages in psychotherapy supervision: From therapy skills to skilled therapist. *Professional Psychology: Research and Practice, 16,* 605–10.

Haglund, R. M. J. & Schuckit, M. A. (1982). The epidemiology of alcoholism. In N. J. Estes & M. E. Heineman (eds.), *Alcoholism: Development, Consequences and Interventions.* St. Louis: Mosby.

Hector, M., Elson, S. & Yager, G. (1977). Teaching counseling skills through self-management procedures. *Counselor Education and Supervision, 17,* 12–22.

Hosford, R. & Johnson, M. E. (1983). A comparison of self-observation, self-modeling, and practice with video feedback for improving counselor interviewing behaviors. *Counselor Education and Supervision, 23,* 62–70.

Institute of Medicine, Division of Health Promotion and Disease Prevention. (1980). *Alcoholism, alcohol abuse, and related problems: Opportunities for research.* Washington, D.C.: National Academy of Sciences.

Kanfer, F. & Karoly, P. (1972). Self-control: A behavioristic excursion into the lion's den. *Behavior Therapy, 3,* 398–416.

Kinney, J., Price, T. & Bergen, B. (1984). Impediments to alcohol education. *Journal of Studies on Alcohol, 45,* 453–59.

Kline, W. (1983). Training counselor trainees to talk to themselves: A method of focusing attention. *Counselor Education and Supervision, 22,* 297–302.

Krystal, H. (1963). Who is qualified to treat the alcoholic? II. Advantages of the professional psychotherapist. *Quarterly Journal of Studies on Alcohol, 24,* 706–12.

Krystal, H. & Moore, R. (1963). Who is qualified to treat the alcoholic? A discussion. *Quarterly Journal of Studies on Alcohol, 24,* 705–6.

Liddle, B. (1986). Resistance in supervision: A response to perceived threat. *Counselor Education and Supervision, 26,* 117–27.

Loganbill, C., Hardy, E. & Delworth, U. (1982). Supervision: A conceptual model. *Counseling Psychologist, 10,* 3–42.

McColley, S. & Baker, E. (1982). Training activities and styles of beginning supervisors: A survey. *Professional Psychology, 13,* 283–92.

Machell, D. (1987). Obligations of a clinical supervisor. *Clinical Supervisor, 4,* 105–8.

Miller, S. I. & Frances, R. J. (1986). Psychiatrists and the treatment of addictions: Perceptions and practices. *American Journal of Drug and Alcohol Abuse, 12,* 187–89.

Miller, W. R., Taylor, C. & West, J. (1980). Focused versus broad-spectrum behavior therapy for problem drinkers. *Journal of Consulting and Clinical Psychology, 48,* 590–601.

Moore, R. (1963). Who is qualified to treat the alcoholic? III. Advantages of nonpsychotherapists. *Quarterly Journal of Studies on Alcohol, 24,* 712–18.

Nelson, G. (1978). Psychotherapy supervision from the trainee's point of view: A survey of preferences. *Professional Psychology, 9,* 539–50.

Ornstein, P. (1968). Sorcerer's apprentice: The initial phase of training and education in psychiatry. *Comprehensive Psychiatry, 9,* 293–315.

Overholser, J. C. (1988). Clinical utility of the Socratic method. In C. Stout (ed.), *Annals of clinical research* (pp. 1–7). Des Plaines, Ill.: Forest Institute.

Overholser, J. C. (in press). The Socratic method as a technique in psychotherapy supervision. *Professional Psychology: Research and Practice.*

Peterson, D. & Bry, B. (1980). Dimensions of perceived competence in professional psychology. *Professional Psychology: Research and Practice, 11,* 965–71.

Powell, D. (1989). Clinical supervision: A ten-year perspective. *Clinical Supervisor, 7,* 139–47.

Robins, L. N., Helzer, J. G., Weissman, M. M. et al. (1984). Lifetime prevalence of specific psychiatric disorders in three sites. *Archives of General Psychiatry, 41,* 949–58.

Schlessinger, N. (1966). Supervision of psychotherapy: A critical review of the literature. *Archives of General Psychiatry, 15,* 129–34.

Schmidt, J. P. (1979). Psychotherapy supervision: A cognitive-behavioral model. *Professional Psychology, 10,* 278–84.

Secretary of Health and Human Services. (1981). *Fourth special report to the U.S. Congress on alcohol and health (January).* Washington, D.C.: Department of Health and Human Services.

Selin, J. A. & Svanum, S. (1981). Alcoholism and substance abuse training: A survey of graduate programs in clinical psychology. *Professional Psychology, 12,* 717–21.

Sheldon-Wildgen, J. (1982). Avoiding legal liability: The rights and responsibilities of therapists. *Behavior Therapist, 5,* 165–69.

Slovenko, R. (1980). Legal issues in psychotherapy supervision. In A. Hess (ed.), *Psychotherapy supervision: Theory, research, and practice* (pp. 453–73). New York: Wiley.

Stenack, R. & Dye, H. (1982). Behavioral descriptions of counseling supervision roles. *Counselor Education and Supervision, 21,* 295–304.

Stoltenberg, C. & Delworth, U. (1987). *Supervising counselors and therapists: A developmental approach.* San Francisco: Jossey-Bass.

Styczynski, L. (1980). The transition from supervisee to supervisor. In A. Hess (ed.), *Psychotherapy supervision: Theory, research, and practice* (pp. 29–40). New York: Wiley.

U.S. Department of Health and Human Services. (1983). *Advances in Alcoholism Treatment Services for Women.* Washington, D.C.: U.S. Government Printing Office. (DHHS Publication No. ADM 83-1217).

Wanberg, K. W. & Horn, J. L. (1983). Assessment of alcohol use with multidimensional concepts and measures. *American Psychologist, 38,* 1055–69.

Wasik, B. & Fishbein, J. (1982). Problem solving: A model for supervision in professional psychology. *Professional Psychology, 13,* 559–64.

Webb, N. B. (1983). Developing competent clinical practitioners: A model with guidelines for supervision. *Clinical Supervisor, 1,* 41–51.

West, L. J. (1984). Alcoholism. *Annals of Internal Medicine, 100,* 405–16.

Wolberg, L. (1951). Supervision of the psychotherapeutic process. *American Journal of Psychotherapy, 5,* 147–71.

Zucker, R. & Gomberg, E. (1986). Etiology of alcoholism reconsidered: The case for a biopsychosocial process. *American Psychologist, 41,* 783–93.

Appendix A:
The Resource Guide

Individuals from all areas of life are recognizing not only when help might prove useful, but they are taking steps to obtain various services. Doctors and truck drivers, men and women, children and adolescents, movie stars and politicians are increasingly turning to self-help organizations along with professional clinicians for guidance in solving their problems. This observation may be readily supported by the rise in the number and type of treatment programs, the increased use these programs are experiencing, and the flourishing of self-help groups of all kinds.

This appendix provides a brief resource guide for beginning clients on their way toward finding sources of help in their local area. It may also be used by professionals to locate alternative or adjunctive clinical or educational services locally, within their state, and nationally. Obviously this guide cannot be comprehensive, but it does help assist in the process of searching for additional resources.

THE BEGINNING

The goal is to obtain the most useful and appropriate resource for the client and the client condition in the most efficient way. There are a few ideas that a professional referring a client to resources or a client seeking resources should keep in mind.

1. All resources should be carefully evaluated for usefulness to the client condition. It is not always the case that the more help that the client gets, the more effective or efficient will be the client's progress.

2. Timing for when to refer a client to a resource is an important consideration. Occasionally clients perceive referrals as a sign of hopelessness on the part of the professional or of dumping the client.

3. Not all resources in the community are useful for the client. Clearly, some will be more productive than others for a particular client. Some resources are rigid and absolute; a client who is unable to meet the resource's goals or perspectives may experience themselves as more of a failure or that the problem is unsolvable. Also, some community resources have avowed goals that may conflict with some therapist's orientations.

4. The client must have a sufficient amount of ability to use the resources or even to obtain them. Some clients do not know how to go about finding resources. Others may be able to locate the resources but may not be able to be able to use them due, for example, to their affective condition or limitations in their behavioral repertoire.

5. The professional should make some effort to ensure that the client actually contacts the resource and that at least making the contact may be perceived as a success. Having the client call the therapist when reaching the resource and having obtained the information is one way that will increase the likelihood of a successful outcome.

6. All resources must fit into the overall treatment strategy. It is important that additional help or support is consistent with the recovery plan and does not add to confusion or chaos.

RESOURCES

Local

There are often tremendous numbers of various resources within a community. While some communities, especially rural areas, have limited convenient access to professionals, treatment programs, or support groups, most regions have some resources available nearby. The following is a brief list of potential resources. Often the local telephone directory will provide a beginning to identify these resources. In urgent situations, the local police or fire departments may be of assistance.

- Private practitioners: Psychologists, social workers, family physicians, psychiatrists, addiction counselors.
- Hospitals: General hospitals (which often have referral services along with their own treatment programs), psychiatric hospitals, free-standing treatment programs such as drug and alcohol programs.
- Specialized treatment programs and clinics; some available through private practices or representing the entire practice.
- Local chapters of national support groups and advocacy organizations: Most national organizations have local chapters with frequent and available meeting times.
- Local community referral agencies or hot lines.
- Community services, such as the mayor's office and police and fire departments.

State

There are many state agencies, resources, and services that provide information, assessment, treatment, or referral. These may be located by looking in local, regional, or state telephone directories under the listing for that state's services. The following state resources may be used to find more local resources:

- Department of mental health
- Department of alcohol, substance abuse, or addictions
- Department of child welfare
- Department of education
- State police
- State intergroups for Alcoholics Anonymous, Al-Anon, Narcotics Anonymous, and others.

National

The federal government provides access to many services, including state and local agencies, literature, research facilities, and federally supported programs. In addition to the federal government, many national organizations can guide those making inquiries to their most accessible branches. Some of these are listed below. Federal directories are often available at a local or college library and are of assistance in finding the current name or address or may help in locating additional services.

ADULT CHILDREN OF ALCOHOLICS
Torrance, CA

ALANON & ALATEEN FAMILY GROUPS
New York, NY

ALCOHOL AND DRUG PROBLEMS
Association of North America
Washington, DC

ALCOHOL RESEARCH GROUP
Berkeley, CA

ALCOHOLICS ANONYMOUS (AA)
New York, NY

AMERICAN ANOREXIA/BULIMIA ASSOCIATION (AABA)
Teaneck, NJ

AMERICAN CANCER SOCIETY
Atlanta, GA

AMERICAN COUNCIL FOR DRUG EDUCATION (ACDE)
Rockville, MD

AMERICAN LUNG ASSOCIATION
National Headquarters
New York, NY

ANOREXIA/BULIMIA CARE (ABC)
Lincoln, MA

CHILDREN OF ALCOHOLICS FOUNDATION
New York, NY

COCAINE ANONYMOUS
Los Angeles, CA

COKENDERS
Torrance, CA

EMPLOYEE ASSISTANCE PROFESSIONAL ASSOCIATION
Arlington, VA

FAMILIES ANONYMOUS
Van Nuys, CA

INTERNATIONAL COMMISSION FOR THE PREVENTION OF
ALCOHOLISM AND DRUG DEPENDENCY
Washington, DC

MENTALLY ILL RECOVERING ALCOHOLICS (MIRA)
Rolling Meadows, IL

MOTHERS AGAINST DRUNK DRIVERS (MADD)
Hurst, TX

NAR-ANON FAMILY GROUPS
Palos Verdes, CA

NATIONAL ANOREXIC AID SOCIETY (NAAS)
Columbus, OH

NATIONAL ASSOCIATION OF ANOREXIA NERVOSA AND
ASSOCIATED DISORDERS (ANAD)
Highland Park, IL

NATIONAL ASSOCIATION FOR CHILDREN OF ALCOHOLICS
Rockville, MD

NATIONAL ASSOCIATION OF STATE ALCOHOL AND DRUG
ABUSE DIRECTORS
Washington, DC

NATIONAL CLEARINGHOUSE FOR ALCOHOL AND DRUG
INFORMATION (NCADI)
Rockville, MD

NATIONAL COCAINE HOTLINE
800-COCAINE

NATIONAL COUNCIL ON ALCOHOLISM
New York, NY

NATIONAL INSTITUTE ON ALCOHOL ABUSE AND
ALCOHOLISM
Rockville, MD

NATIONAL INSTITUTE ON DRUG ABUSE, CLEARINGHOUSE FOR
DRUG INFORMATION
Kensington, MD

NATIONAL PTA, ALCOHOL EDUCATION PUBLICATIONS
Chicago, IL

OFFICE FOR SUBSTANCE ABUSE PREVENTION,
COMMUNICATIONS DIVISION
Rockville, MD

OFFICE ON SMOKING AND HEALTH, PUBLIC
INFORMATION BRANCH
Atlanta, GA

OVEREATERS ANONYMOUS, WORLD SERVICE OFFICE
Los Angeles, CA

PARENT RESOURCE INSTITUTE FOR
DRUG EDUCATION (PRIDE)
Atlanta, GA

NICOTINE ANONYMOUS
San Francisco, CA

STUDENTS AGAINST DRUNK DRIVING (SADD)
Marlboro, MA

TOUGHLOVE
Doylestown, PA

U.S. DEPARTMENT OF HEALTH AND HUMAN SERVICES
Washington, DC

U.S. DEPARTMENT OF JUSTICE
DRUG ENFORCEMENT ADMINISTRATION
OFFICE OF PUBLIC AFFAIRS
Washington, DC

U.S. DEPARTMENT OF TRANSPORTATION, NATIONAL
HIGHWAY TRAFFIC SAFETY ADMINISTRATION
Washington, DC

WOMEN FOR SOBRIETY
Quakerstown, PA

CONCLUSION

Several guides may be helpful in locating specific resources. Although these have been distributed for use nationally, they contain the details of local and/ or state services. Some of the following guides describe only those programs or services that have paid to be included or list resources that may not be widely available or even more effective but are better known.

Ackerman, Robert, and Judith A. Michaels (1990).
Recovery Resource Guide.
Deerfield Beach, Fla. Health Communications.

Directory of Eating Disorder Programs and Therapists
Center Publishing
2514 Palm Place Drive
Palm Bay, Fla. 32905

Hart, Stan (1988).
Rehab: A Comprehensive Guide to Recommended Drug-Alcohol Treatment Centers in the U.S.
New York: Harper and Row

National Directory of Alcoholism and Addiction Treatment Programs
Quantum Press
23860 Miles Road
Cleveland, Ohio 44128

Sunshine, Linda, and John W. Wright (1988).
The 100 Best Treatment Centers for Alcohol and Drug Abuse
New York: Avon

U.S. Journal (1991).
The Treatment Directory: National Treatment Directory for Alcoholism, Drug Abuse, and Other Addiction Programs
Deerfield Beach, Fla.: Health Communications

Yoder, Barbara (1990).
The Recovery Resource Book
New York: Simon and Schuster

Appendix B:
Credentialing for Substance
Abuse Counselors by State

The following list provides state-by-state information concerning the levels of certification, requirements, and procedures for addiction counselors. Addresses and telephone numbers are provided where available. All information is correct as of September 1991. Most of the information is a quote from the state's credentialing body. Readers are encouraged to call or write to a specific agency for more information and application materials.

ALABAMA

Information: Alabama Alcohol and Drug Abuse Association
P.O. Box 1514
Birmingham, AL 35201
(205) 271-9253

Certification area(s): Associate Addictions Professional, Certified Alcohol and Drug Abuse Professional

ALASKA

Information: Division of Alcohol and Drug Abuse
3601 C, Suite 358
Anchorage, AK 99503
(907) 561-4213

Certification area(s): Levels I–III

ARIZONA

Information: Board of Behavioral Health Examiners
1624 West Adams, Room 100A
Phoenix, AZ 85007
(602) 255-1152

Certification area(s): Certified Substance Abuse Counselor

ARKANSAS

Information: The Arkansas Substance Abuse Certification Board
2213 North Reynolds Road
Union Plaza Building, Suite 25
Bryant, AR 72022
(501) 847-5249

Certification area(s): Substance Abuse Certification

CALIFORNIA

Information: California Certification Board of Alcohol and Drug Counselors
1713 J Street, Suite 207
Sacramento, CA 95814
(916) 447-9416

Certification area(s): Certified Alcohol Counselor, Certified Drug Counselor, Certified
Alcohol and Drug Counselor

COLORADO

Information: Regulations Administrator
Colorado Department of Health
Alcohol and Drug Abuse Division
4210 East 11th Avenue
Denver, CO 80220
(303) 331-8241, 331-8201

Certification area(s): Alcohol and Drug Abuse Counselor (ADAC), Levels I–III

CONNECTICUT

Information: Connecticut Alcoholism and Drug Abuse Counselor Certification Board
416 New London Turnpike
Glastonbury, CT 06033
(203) 633-6572

Certification area(s): Certified Alcoholism Counselor, Certified Drug Addictions Counselor

DELAWARE

Information: Delaware Alcohol and Drug Counselors Certification Board, Inc.
P.O. Box 154
1712 Marsh Road
Wilmington, DE 19810
(302) 421-6180

Certification area(s): Certified Alcohol Counselor, Certified Drug Counselor, Certified Alcohol and Drug Counselor, Associate Addiction Counselor

DISTRICT OF COLUMBIA

Information: Washington Area Council on Alcoholism and Drug Abuse
1232 M Street, NW
Washington, DC 20005
(202) 783-1300

Certification area(s): Certified Addiction Counselor, Clinically Certified Addictions Counselor

FLORIDA

Information: Certification Board for Addiction Professionals of Florida
835-B East Park Avenue
Tallahassee, FL 32301
(904) 222-6314

Certification area(s): Certified Associate Addiction Professional, Certified Addiction Professional

GEORGIA

Information: Georgia Addiction Counselors' Association
2300 Peachfold Road
Suite 2175
Atlanta, GA 30338
(404) 986-9510

Certification area(s): Certified Addiction Counselor (CAC), Levels I and II

HAWAII

Information: State of Hawaii
Department of Health
Alcohol and Drug Abuse Division
P.O. Box 3378
Honolulu, HI
(808) 548-4280

Certification area(s): Substance Abuse Counselor, Program Administrator

IDAHO

Information: Idaho Board of Alcoholism/Drug Counselor's Certification, Inc.
            P.O. Box 8132
            Boise, ID 83707
            (208) 343-0037

Certification area(s): Level 1 Associate Addictions Counselor, Level 2 Addictions Coun-
                        selor, Level 3 Senior Addictions Counselor

ILLINOIS

Information: Illinois Addictions Counselor Certification Board
            1305 Wabash Avenue, Suite L
            Springfield, IL
            (217) 698-8110
            (217) 698-8234 (fax)

Certification area(s): Associated Addictions Counselor, Addictions Counselor, Senior Ad-
                        dictions Counselor

INDIANA

Information: Indiana Counselors Association on Alcohol and Drug Abuse
            1800 North Meridian Street, Suite 507
            Indianapolis, IN
            (317) 923-8800

Certification area(s): Entry level: Alcoholism Counselor in Service, Drug Counselor in
                        Service
                        Certification level: Certified Alcoholism Counselor, Certified Drug
                        Counselor
                        Advanced level: Certified Alcohol and Drug Abuse Counselor

IOWA

Information: Iowa Board of Substance Abuse Certification
            P.O. Box 7284
            Grand Avenue Station
            Des Moines, IA 50309
            (515) 281-3641

Certification area(s): Certified Substance Abuse Counselor I, Certified Substance Abuse
                        Counselor II

KANSAS

Information: Kansas Alcoholism and Drug Addiction Counselors Association
            P.O. Box 1732
            Topeka, KS
            (913) 233-7145

Certification area(s): Associate Alcoholism and Drug Addiction, Certified Alcoholism and Drug Addiction Counselor, Senior Certified Alcoholism and Drug Addiction Counselor

KENTUCKY

Information: Substance Abuse Division
P.O. Box 21891
Lexington, KY 40522-1891
(606) 269-2581

Certification area(s): Certified Chemical Dependency Counselor

LOUISIANA

Information: Louisiana State Board for Certification of Substance Abuse Counselors
141 Ridegeway, Suite 205
Lafayette, LA 70503
(318) 988-4378

Certification area(s): Board Certified Substance Abuse Counselor

MAINE

Information: Maine Alcohol and Drug Abuse Clearing House
State House State #35
Augusta, ME 04333
(207) 582-7823

Certification area(s): Associate Substance Abuse Counselor, Licensed Substance Abuse Counselor

MARYLAND

Information: Maryland Addiction Counselor Certification Board
P.O. Box 3341
Frederick, MD 21701
(301) 865-3021

Certification area(s): Certified Alcohol Counselor, Certified Drug Counselor, Certified Chemical Dependency Counselor

MASSACHUSETTS

Information: Board is still in formation

MICHIGAN

Information: Michigan OSAS Certification Program c/o Michigan Institute for Human
          Resource Development
          Ellsworth Hall
          Western Michigan University
          Kalamazoo, MI 49008
          (517) 335-8809

Certification area(s): Apprentice Counselor Credential, Advanced Counselor Credential

MINNESOTA

Information: Institute for Chemical Dependency Professionals of Minnesota, Inc.
          596 South Osceola Avenue
          Saint Paul, MN 55102
          (612) 227-7584

Certification area(s): Certified Chemical Dependency Practitioner, Certified Chemical
                    Dependency Counselor, Certified Chemical Dependency Recipro-
                    cal

MISSISSIPPI

Information: MADAC
          P.O. Box 3162
          Meridian, MS 39303
          (601) 693-0126

Certification area(s): Certified Alcoholism Counselor, Certified Drug Counselor, Certi-
                    fied Alcohol and Drug Counselor

MISSOURI

Information: Missouri Substance Abuse Counselors Certification Board, Inc.
          P.O. Box 104446
          Jefferson City, MO 65110-4446
          (314) 636-8318

Certification area(s): Alcoholism Counselor, Drug Abuse Counselor, Substance Abuse
                    Counselor

MONTANA

Information: Treatment Services Division
          Chemical Dependency Bureau
          1539 11th Avenue
          Helena, MT 59620
          (406) 444-2827

Certification area(s): Chemical Dependency Counselor

NEBRASKA

Information: Counselor Certification Coordinator
State of Nebraska
Department of Public Institutions
Division on Alcoholism and Drug Abuse
P.O. Box 94728
Lincoln, NE 68509-4728
(402) 471-2851

Certification area(s): Alcohol/Drug Abuse Counselor at levels of: Associate Professional, Professional, Senior Professional

NEVADA

Information: Bureau of Alcohol and Drug Abuse
Kinkead Building, 5th Floor
505 East King Street, Room 500
State Capitol Complex
Carson City, NV 89710
(702) 885-4790

Certification area(s): Alcohol and Drug Abuse Counselor Administrator

NEW HAMPSHIRE

Information: Office of Alcohol and Drug Abuse Prevention
State Office Park South
105 Pleasant Street
Concord, NH 03301
(603) 217-6112

Certification area(s): Alcohol and Drug Abuse Counselor, Alcohol or Drug Abuse Counselor

NEW JERSEY

Information: Alcohol and Other Drugs of Abuse Counselor
Certification Board of New Jersey
90 Monmouth Street, Suite 1
Red Bank, NJ 07701
(201) 741-3835

Certification area(s): Associate Alcohol Counselor, Associate Drug Counselor, Certified Alcohol Counselor, Certified Drug Counselor, Certified Alcohol and Drug Counselor

NEW MEXICO

No certification

NEW YORK

Information: New York State Division of Alcoholism and Alcohol Abuse
194 Washington Avenue
Albany, NY 12210
(518) 474-5417

Certification area(s): Credentialed Alcoholism Counselor

NORTH CAROLINA

Information: North Carolina Substance Abuse Professional Certification Board
P.O. Box 34668
Charlotte, NC 28234
(704) 663-6967

Certification area(s): Substance Abuse Counselor Intern, Certified Substance Abuse
Counselor

NORTH DAKOTA

Information: North Dakota Board of Addiction Counseling Examiners
1406 2d Avenue, NW
Mandan, ND 58554
(701) 224-2769

Certification area(s): Addiction Counselor

OHIO

Information: Ohio Chemical Dependency Counselor's Credentialing Board
1 Marconi Place, Suite 420
Columbus, OH 43215
(614) 466-3445

Certification area(s): Certified Alcohol Counselor, Certified Drug Counselor, Certified
Chemical Dependency Counselor

OKLAHOMA

Information: Oklahoma Drug/Arc
Professional Counselor Association
9301 South I-35
Moore, OK 73160
(405) 793-1545

Certification area(s): Certified Alcoholism Counselor, Certified Alcoholism/Drug Counselor

OREGON

Information: Addiction Counselor Certification Board of Oregon
2323 5 East 55th
Portland, OR 97215
(503) 231-8164

Certification area(s): Certified Alcoholism Counselor, Certified Alcohol/Drug Counselor

PENNSYLVANIA

Information: Pennsylvania Chemical Abuse Certification Board
264 South Progress Avenue
Harrisburg, PA 17109
(717) 540-4455

Certification area(s): Associate Addiction Counselor (Levels I and II), Certified Addiction Counselor

RHODE ISLAND

Information: Certification Board, RIDCC8P
84 Broad Street
Pawtucket, RI 02860
(401) 728-6260

Certification area(s): Chemical Dependence Professional

SOUTH CAROLINA

Information: South Carolina Commission on Alcohol and Drug Abuse
3700 Forest Drive
Columbia, SC 29204
(803) 734-9520

Certification area(s): Addictions Associate, Clinical Counselor, Master Counselor, Intervention Specialist, Primary Prevention Specialist, Structured Group Leader

SOUTH DAKOTA

Information: South Dakota Chemical Dependency Counselor Certification Board
P.O. Box 1797
Sioux Falls, SD 57101-1797
(605) 773-3123

Certification area(s): Chemical Dependency Counselor (Levels I–III)

TENNESSEE

Information: Division of Alcohol and Drug Abuse Services
Department of Mental Health and Mental Retardation
Doctors' Building
706 Church Street
Nashville, TN 37219-5393
(615) 741-4242

Certification area(s): Substance Abuse Counselor

TEXAS

Information: Texas Certification Board of Alcoholism and Drug Abuse Counselors
940 East 51st Street
Austin, TX 78751-2241
(512) 459-3305

Certification area(s): Alcoholism and Drug Abuse Counselor

UTAH

Information: Graduate School of Social Work
University of Utah
Salt Lake City, UT
(801) 581-8913

Certification area(s): Certificate Training Program in Alcohol/Drug Abuse Treatment

VERMONT

Information: Office of Alcohol and Drug Abuse Programs
103 South Main Street
Waterbury, VT 05676
(802) 241-2170

Certification area(s): Alcohol and Drug Treatment Counselor (Apprentice, Approved, and Senior)

VIRGINIA

Information: Department of Health Professionals
Board of Professional Counselors
1601 Rolling Hills Drive
Richmond, VA 23229-5005
(804) 662-9912

Certification area(s): Certified Substance Abuse Counselor

WASHINGTON

Information: Department of Health
Professional Licensing Services
P.O. Box 1099
Olympia, WA 98507-1099
(206) 753-6936

Certification area(s): Registered Counselor (This is not specific to substance abuse treatment)
Northeast Indian Council on Chemical Dependency
2209 East 32d Street
Tacoma, WA 98404
(203) 593-0294

Certification area(s): Chemical Dependence Counselors (Levels I–III)

WEST VIRGINIA

Information: West Virginia Alcoholism and Drug Counselors Certification Board
P.O. Box 6761
Wheeling, WV 26003
(304) 348-2276

Certification area(s): Counselor in Service, Certified Addiction Counselor

WISCONSIN

Information: Wisconsin Alcoholism and Drug Counselor Credentialing Board
P.O. Box 768
Waukesha, WI 53187-0768
(414) 542-4144

Certification area(s): Registered Alcohol and Drug Counselor I, Certified Alcohol and Drug Counselor II, Certified Alcohol and Drug Counselor III

WYOMING

Information: Wyoming Association of Addiction Specialists
P.O. 2793
Casper, WY 82602
(307) 777-6494

Certification area(s): Certified Addiction Counselor I, Certified Addiction Counselor II, Certified Addiction Counselor III

Further Reading

In this book, both current and retrospective reviews of existing research on addiction shed light on clinical innovations since the early 1980s. Chapters covering alcohol and drug abuse and eating disorders described the most active theoretical and experimental research including methodological implications for health care network systems. Analyses sought to accomplish two main goals: to bring together in one text the eclectic advances in applied clinical technology and to recommend constructive alternatives drawn from scientific principles and seasoned practitioners that can strengthen prevention and treatment services. But *Handbook of Assessing and Treating Addictive Disorders* is only one among many reference manuals addressing these goals.

The lists that follow refer readers to other books that are conceptually and empirically relevant to each of the five sections explored in the handbook. Some are clinical guidebooks, uniquely designed for practitioners and students broadening their repertoire of applied techniques. Others either synthesize recent research findings from specialty areas within one theoretical framework (learning theory, psychoanalytic, medical, etc.) or collectively present developments across disciplines, emphasizing common themes and controversies in diagnosis, treatment, and administration of services. Readers are encouraged to consult these resources as a means of obtaining further insight on etiology or on methodology. Most of the books listed are available at college and university libraries or through interlibrary loans. Readers can also write to the authors requesting reprints of their latest articles or a bibliographic list of their publications. Personal correspondence not only is complimentary to authors but a rapid way to acquire needed facts and guidance.

PART ONE: THEORIES AND APPROACHES

Alterman, A. I. (ed.). (1985). *Substance abuse and psychopathology.* New York: Plenum.

Baker, T. B. & Cannon, D. S. (eds.). (1988). *Assessment and treatment of addictive disorders.* New York: Praeger Publishers.

Blane, H. T. & Leonard, K. E. (eds.). (1986). *Psychological theories of drinking and alcoholism.* New York: Guilford.

Brownell, K. D. & Forety, J. P. (eds.). (1986). *Handbook of eating disorders.* New York: Basic Books.

Cohen, S. & Callahan, J. F. (eds.). (1986). *The diagnosis and treatment of drug and alcohol abuse.* New York: Haworth Press.

Frances, R. J. & Miller, S. I. (1991). *Clinical textbook of addictive disorders.* New York: Guilford.

Ghodse, H. A., Kaplan, C. D. & Mann, R. D. (eds.). (1990). *Drug misuse and dependence.* Parkridge, N.J.: Parthenon Publishing Group.

Goldberg, S. R. & Stolerman, I. P. (1985). *Behavioral analysis of drug dependence.* Orlando, Fla.: Academic Press.

Hester, R. K. & Miller, W. R. (1989). *Handbook of alcoholism treatment approaches: Effective alternatives.* Elmsford, N.Y.: Pergamon Press.

Hsu, L. K. G. (1990). *Eating disorders.* New York: Guilford.

Hudson, J. L. & Pope, H. (eds.). (1987). *Psychobiology of bulimia.* Washington, D.C.: American Psychiatric Press.

Imber-Black, E. (1988). *Families and larger systems: A family therapist's guide through the labyrinth.* New York: Guilford.

Johnson, C. & Connors, M. (eds.). (1987). *The etiology and treatment of bulimia nervosa.* New York: Basic Books.

Mahan, H. C. (1968). *The interactional psychology of J. R. Kantor: An introduction.* San Marcos, Calif.: Palomar College.

Martin, P. (1990). *Handbook of behavior therapy and psychological science: An integrative approach.* Elmsford, N.Y.: Pergamon Press.

Meyer, R. D. (ed.). (1986). *Psychopathology of addictive disorders.* New York: Guilford.

Nathan, P. E., Langenbucher, J. W., McCrady, B. S. & Frankenstein, W. (eds.). (1991). *Annual review of addictions research and treatment* (vol. 1). New York: Pergamon Press.

Pronko, N. H. (1980). *Psychology from the standpoint of an interbehaviorist.* Monterey, Calif.: Brooks/Cole Publishers.

Reese, H. W. & Parrott, L. J. (eds.). (1986). *Behavior science: Philosophical, methodological, and empirical advances.* Hillsdale, N.J.: Lawrence Erlbaum Associates.

Ruben, D. H. (1992). *Family addiction: An analytical guide.* New York: Garland Press.

Ruben, D. H. & Delprato, D. J. (eds.). (1987). *New ideas in therapy: Introduction to an interdisciplinary approach.* Westport, Conn.: Greenwood Press.

Schwartzman, J. (ed.). (1984). *Families and other systems: The macrosystemic context of family therapy.* New York: Guilford.

Shiffman, S. & Wills, T. A. (eds.). (1985). *Coping and substance abuse.* Orlando, Fla.: Academic Press.

Smith, N. W., Mountjoy, P. T. & Ruben, D. H. (1983). *Reassessment in psychology:*

The interbehavioral alternative. Washington, D.C.: University Press of America.

Wolpe, J. (1990). *The practice of behavior therapy* (4th ed.). Elmsford, N.Y.: Pergamon Press.

PART TWO: ASSESSMENT OF ADDICTIVE DISORDERS

Bellack, A. S. & Hersen, M. (eds.). (1985). *Dictionary of behavior therapy techniques.* Elmsford, N.Y.: Pergamon Press.

Bellack, A. S. & Hersen, M. (eds.). (1988). *Behavioral assessment: A practical handbook* (3d ed.). Elmsford, N.Y.: Pergamon Press.

Donovan, D. M. & Marlatt, G. A. (eds.). (1988). *Assessment of addictive disorders.* New York: Guilford.

Hersen, M. & Bellack, A. S. (eds.). (1987). *Dictionary of behavioral assessment techniques.* Elmsford, N.Y.: Pergamon Press.

Khantzian, E. J., Halliday, K. S. & McAuliffe, W. E. (eds.). (1990). *Addiction and the vulnerable self.* New York: Guilford.

Mirin, S. M. (eds.). (1984). *Substance abuse and psychopathology.* Washington, D.C.: American Psychiatric Press.

Nathanson, D. L. (ed.). (1987). *The many faces of shame.* New York: Guilford.

Ruben, D. H. (in press). *Avoidance syndrome.* St. Louis, Mo.: Warren Green.

Williamson, D. A. (1990). *Assessment of eating disorders: Obesity, anorexia and bulimia nervosa.* Elmsford, N.Y.: Pergamon Press.

PART THREE: TREATMENT OF ADDICTIVE DISORDERS

Agras, W. S. (1987). *Eating disorders: Management of obesity, bulimia and anorexia nervosa.* Elmsford, N.Y.: Pergamon Press.

Ellis, A., McInerney, J. F., DiGiuseppe, R. & Yeager, R. J. (1988). *Rational-emotive therapy with alcoholics and substance abusers.* Elmsford, N.Y.: Pergamon Press.

Clarke, J. C. (1988). *Alcoholism and problem drinking: Treating addictions or modifying bad habits?* Elmsford, N.Y.: Pergamon Press.

Cox, W. M. (1986). *Treatment and prevention of alcohol problems.* Orlando, Fla.: Academic Press.

Galanter, M. & Pattison, E. M. (eds.). (1984). *Advances in the psychosocial treatment of alcoholism.* Washington, D.C.: American Psychiatric Press.

Garner, D. M. & Garfinkel, P. E. (eds.). (1984). *Handbook of psychotherapy for anorexia nervosa and bulimia.* New York: Guilford.

Hornyak, L. M. & Baker, E. K. (eds.). (1989). *Experiential therapies for eating disorders.* New York: Guilford.

Johnson, C. L. (ed.). (1990). *Psychodynamic treatment of anorexia nervosa and bulimia.* New York: Guilford.

Kaye, W. H. & Gwirtsman, H. E. (eds.). (1985). *A comprehensive approach to the treatment of normal weight bulimia.* Washington, D.C.: American Psychiatric Press.

Kirschenbaum, D. S., Johnson, W. G. & Stalonas, P. M. (eds.). (1987). *Treating childhood and adolescent obesity.* Elmsford, N.Y.: Pergamon Press.

LeBow, M. D. (1989). *Adult obesity therapy.* Elmsford, N.Y.: Pergamon Press.

Marlatt, G. A. & Gordon, J. R. (eds.). (1985). *Relapse prevention.* New York: Guilford.
Monti, P. M., Abrams, D. B., Kadden, R. M. & Cooney, N. L. (1989). *Treating alcohol dependence.* New York: Guilford.
Stanton, M. D. & Todd, T. C. (eds.). (1982). *Family therapy of drug abuse and addiction.* New York: Guilford.
Weiss, L., Katzman, M. & Wolchik, S. (eds.). (1985). *Treating bulimia: A psychoeducational approach.* Elmsford, N.Y.: Pergamon Press.

PART FOUR: MINORITIES AND SPECIAL GROUPS

Atkinson, R. M. (1984). *Alcohol and drug abuse in old age.* Washington, D.C.: American Psychiatric Press.
Brown, S. (1988). *Treating adult children of alcoholics.* New York: John Wiley & Sons.
Carstensen, L. L. & Edelstein, B. A. (1987). *Handbook of clinical gerontology.* Elmsford, New York: Pergamon Press.
Feindler, E. L. & Ecton, R. B. (1986). *Adolescent anger control: Cognitive-behavioral techniques.* Elmsford, N.Y.: Pergamon Press.
Pinkston, E. M. & Linski, N. L. (1984). *Care of the elderly: A family approach.* Elmsford, N.Y.: Pergamon Press.
Rhodes, J. E. & Jason, L. A. (1988). *Preventing substance abuse among children and adolescents.* Elmsford, N.Y.: Pergamon Press.
Ruben. D. H. (1984). *Drug abuse and the elderly: An annotated bibliography.* Metuchen, N.J.: Scarecrow Press.
Ruben, D. H. (1990). *The aging and drug effects: A planning manual for medication and alcohol abuse treatment of the elderly.* Jefferson, N.C.: McFarland & Company.
Stanley, B. (ed.). (1985). *Geriatric psychiatry: Clinical, ethical and legal issues.* Washington, D.C.: American Psychiatric Press.
Steinglass, P., Bennett, L. A., Wolin, S. J. & Reiss, D. (eds.). (1987). *The alcoholic family.* New York: Basic Books.
Vannicelli, M. (1989). *Group psychotherapy with adult children of alcoholics: Treatment techniques and countertransference considerations.* New York: Guilford.
Wadler, G. I. & Hainline, B. (1989). *Drugs and the athlete.* Philadelphia: F. A. Davis Company.
Windle, M. & Searles, J. S. (eds.). (1990). *Children of alcoholics.* New York: Guilford.

PART FIVE: CLINICAL ISSUES

APA Committee on Confidentiality. (1984). *Guidelines on confidentiality.* Washington, D.C.: American Psychiatric Press.
Jacobson, N. S. (ed.). (1984). *Psychotherapists in clinical practice: Cognitive and behavioral perspectives.* New York: Guilford.
Lakin, M. (1989). *Coping with ethical dilemmas in psychotherapy.* Elmsford, N.Y.: Pergamon Press.

Liddle, H. A., Breunlin, D. C. & Schwartz, R. C. (eds.). (1988). *Handbook of family therapy and supervision*. New York: Guilford.

Margenau, E., Ribner, N., Silver, R., Stricker, G, Ewing, C. P. & Robertiello, R. (eds.). (1989). *The encyclopedic handbook of private practice: The mental health professions*. New York: Brunner/Mazel.

Pryzwansky, W. B. & Wendt, R. N. (eds.). (1987). *Psychology as a profession: Foundations of practice*. Elmsford, N.Y.: Pergamon Press.

Stoltenberg, C. & Delworth, U. (eds.). (1987). *Supervising counselors and therapists: A developmental approach*. San Francisco: Jossey-Bass.

Index